Welcome to Panini World

Unlock EVERY Secret of Cooking Through 500 AMAZING Panini Recipes

(Unlock Cooking, Book 25)

Annie Kate

Copyright: Published in the United States by ANNIE KATE / © ANNIE KATE
Published on February 2, 2017

All rights reserved. No part of this publication may be reproduced, stored in retrieval system, copied in any form or by any means, electronic, mechanical, photocopying, recording or otherwise transmitted without written permission from the publisher. Please do not participate in or encourage piracy of this material in any way. You must not circulate this book in any format. ANNIE KATE does not control or direct users' actions and is not responsible for the information or content shared, harm and/or actions of the book readers.

In accordance with the U.S. Copyright Act of 1976, the scanning, uploading and electronic sharing of any part of this book without the permission of the publisher constitute unlawful piracy and theft of the author's intellectual property. If you would like to use material from the book (other than just simply for reviewing the book), prior permission must be obtained by contacting the author at contact@smallpassion.com

Thank you for your support of the author's rights.

Contents

Contents	3
Chapter 1: Beef	5
Chapter 2: Cheese	24
Chapter 3: Fish	77
Chapter 4: Fruits	81
Chapter 5: Pork	86
Chapter 6: Poultry	96
Chapter 7: Rice-Grains	174
Chapter 8: Vegetables	231
Chapter 9: More Panini Recipes	248
Conclusion	356
An Awesome Free Gift for You	357

Chapter 1: Beef

***

All American Roast Beef Panini

Servings: 2 | Cook: 5 mins | Prep: 30 mins | Total Time: 35 mins

Ingredients
- 3 tablespoons mayonnaise
- 1 tablespoon sour cream
- 1 tablespoon prepared horseradish
- 1 tablespoon chopped fresh marjoram
- 4 slices whole-wheat country bread (or 2 ciabatta sandwich rolls, split) or 4 slices rye bread (or 2 ciabatta sandwich rolls, split)
- 1 tablespoon unsalted butter, at room temperature
- 1/2 lb roast beef, thinly sliced
- salt
- fresh ground black pepper
- 1 ounce parmesan cheese, shaved with a vegetable peeler
- watercress, 1 small bunch, tough stems removed

Directions
1. In a small bowl, stir together the mayo, sour cream, horseradish, and marjoram; let stand for about 10 minutes at room temperature to allow the flavors to blend (alternatively, cover and refrigerate for up to 6 hours, if refrigerating, return to room temperature before using).
2. Preheat sandwich grill.
3. Place the bread slices, cut sides down, on a work surface and spread 1 side of each bread slice with the butter.
4. Turn and spread the unbuttered sides of the bread with the mayonnaise mixture.
5. On each of 2 bread slices, mayo sides up, arrange half of the roast beef.
6. Season liberally with salt and pepper.
7. Divide the cheese and watercress on top.
8. Cover with the remaining 2 bread slices, mayo sides down, and press gently to pack.
9. Place the panini in the grill, close the top plate, and cook until the bread is golden and toasted, the meat is warmed through, and the watercress is nearly wilted, 3-5 minutes.
10. Cut each sandwich in half on the diagonal and serve right away.

Beef and Shiitake Panini

Servings: 2 | *Cook:* 4 mins | *Prep:* 30 mins | *Total Time:* 34 mins

Ingredients
- 2 teaspoons olive oil
- 4 ounces shiitake mushrooms, stems removed, caps thinly sliced
- 1 tablespoon soy sauce
- 1 teaspoon Worcestershire sauce
- 4 slices sourdough bread (1/2 inch thick)
- 1 tablespoon olive oil
- 2 ounces roast beef, thinly sliced
- 2 ounces provolone cheese, thinly sliced
- 1/2 cup baby spinach leaves

Directions
1. Preheat panini grill to high.
2. In a skillet, heat oil over med-high heat; add in mushrooms and saute until they release their liquid, 3-5 minutes.
3. Decrease heat to low and add soy sauce and Worcestershire sauce; cook, stirring occasionally, until liquid is absorbed and mushrooms are tender, 7-9 minutes.
4. Remove from heat and keep warm.
5. Brush one side of each bread slice with oil.
6. Place two slices on a work surface, oiled side down, and evenly layer with beef, cheese, spinach, and mushroom mixture.
7. Cover with top halves, oiled side up, and press gently to pack.
8. Place sandwiches in grill, close the top plate and cook until golden brown, 3-4 minutes.
9. Serve immediately.

Beef Pesto Panini

Can't remember where I got this recipe, but it's good. Also great summer recipe because it keeps the house cool.
Cook: 10 mins | *Prep:* 15 mins | *Total Time:* 25 mins

Ingredients
- 8 slices Italian bread, about 1/2 in thick
- 2 tablespoons butter, softened

- 4 tablespoons prepared basil pesto
- 1/2 lb deli roast beef, cooked, thinly sliced
- 4 slices mozzarella cheese
- spaghetti sauce, if desired for dipping

Directions
1. Spread 1 side of each slice of bread with butter.
2. Place 4 slices of bread butter side down on 12-inch skillet.
3. Top bread with beef, pesto and cheese.
4. Top with remaining bread slice butter side up.
5. Cook sandwiches on skillet or grill over medium heat 4-5 minutes, turning once, until bread is crisp and cheese has melted.
6. Serve with spaghetti sauce if desired.

Bleu Roast Beef Panini

This sandwich is a perfect blend of savory, pungent, and spicy flavors. A great way to change up any lunch or dinner!
Servings: 1 | **Cook:** 4 mins | **Prep:** 10 mins | **Total Time:** 14mins

Ingredients
- 2 slices multigrain bread
- 1 tablespoon mayonnaise (chipotle)
- 1 -2 slice provolone cheese (picante)
- 1/4 cup blue cheese, crumbled
- 4 slices roast beef
- 1/8 cup red onion, diced
- nonstick cooking spray

Directions
1. Saute diced red onion until soft.
2. Set a waffle iron to high until some smoke appears.
3. While waiting for waffle iron to heat up, assemble sandwich, starting with the mayonnaise and then adding the next four ingredients.
4. Once waffle iron starts to smoke, turn heat down to medium heat and spray with non-stick spray.
5. Cook sandwich in waffle iron for 3-4 minutes.
6. Enjoy!

Corned Beef and Fontina Panini

Servings: 2 | *Cook:* 4 mins | *Prep:* 15 mins | *Total Time:* 19mins

Ingredients
- 4 slices pumpernickel bread
- 1 tablespoon butter, melted
- 2 tablespoons spicy mustard
- 4 ounces corned beef, thinly sliced
- 2 ounces Fontina cheese, thinly sliced
- 6 slices dill pickles
- 4 thin slices onions

Directions
1. Preheat panini grill to high.
2. Brush one side of each bread slice with butter.
3. Place on a work surface, buttered side down, and spread with mustard.
4. On bottom halves, evenly layer beef, cheese, pickle, and onion.
5. Cover with top halves and press gently to pack.
6. Place sandwiches in grill, close the top plate and cook until golden brown, 3-4 minutes.
7. Serve immediately.

French Dip Panini

I haven't tried this yet but it sounds really good. and easy too!
Servings: 4 | *Cook:* 10 mins | *Prep:* 15 mins | *Total Time:* 25mins

Ingredients
- 4 tablespoons butter, softened
- 1 shallot, finely chopped
- 1 tablespoon cornstarch
- 2 cups beef broth
- 1 lb sliced roast beef
- 1 baguette, split lengthwise and sliced crosswise into 4 sections
- 4 ounces sliced monterey jack pepper cheese

Directions

1. In a medium saucepan, melt 2 tablespoons butter over medium heat. Add the shallot and cook, stirring, until translucent, 1 to 2 minutes. Add the cornstarch and cook for 1 minute. Whisk in the beef broth.
2. Add the roast beef to the sauce and warm over low heat.
3. Preheat a nonstick grill pan over medium heat. Spread the remaining 2 tablespoons butter on the split sides of the baguette sections. Using tongs, top half the sections with the warm roast beef, reserving the sauce. Top with the cheese and the remaining baguette sections. Place the 4 panini on the hot pan. Weigh down with a heavy skillet and cook for 2 minutes, then flip the panini and cook for 2 minutes longer.
4. Remove the panini from the heat and divide the sauce among 4 small bowls for dipping.

Grilled Beef and Onion Panini

You can spend big bucks on a sandwich such as this in a Deli, why not make it yourself. You will need a panini maker for this (a great investment if you make a lot of sandwiches!) adjust all amounts to taste.
Prep: *20 mins* | **Total Time:** *20mins*

Ingredients

- 3 sweet onions, thinly sliced
- 2 tablespoons honey
- 1 tablespoon Dijon mustard
- 1 tablespoon apple cider vinegar
- black pepper
- softened butter
- 8 slices rye bread (or use pumpernickel bread)
- 3/4 lb thinly-sliced deli roast beef
- 8 slices American cheese

Directions

1. Place the onions, honey, Dijon and vinegar in a saucepan; cook stirring over medium heat until the onions are tender (about 8-10 minutes) then season with black pepper.
2. Butter both sides of bread.
3. Top 4 slices bread with roast beef, then 2 slices cheese and 1/4 of the onion mixture.
4. Top with remaining bread slice.
5. Heat an electric panini maker, place a sandwich in and close lid; heat until golden.

Monster Muenster Panini

Panini and grilled cheese sandwiches are nothing new but for some reason you rarely, if ever, see Muenster cheese used on them. Muenster cheese reminds me of Germany which makes me happy. Combine that with caramelized onions, roast beef, pastrami and a homemade '1000 island' style dressing instead of the sugary store bought kind on toasted buttery sourdough and you're talking about a seriously delicious sandwich
Servings: 4 | **Cook:** 20 mins | **Prep:** 15 mins | **Total Time:** 35 mins

Ingredients
Thousand Island Sandwich Dressing
- 3/4 cup mayonnaise
- 1/4 cup sour cream
- 3/4 cup ketchup
- 1 teaspoon dill relish
- 1 teaspoon sweet pickle relish
- 1 teaspoon dried onion flakes
- 1/4 teaspoon garlic powder
- 1/2 teaspoon lemon juice
- 1/2 teaspoon balsamic vinegar
- 3 -4 good shakes Tabasco sauce
- fresh ground black pepper, to taste

Panini
- 8 slices sourdough sandwich bread, good quality
- 4 ounces thousand island dressing (see recipe above)
- 4 ounces aioli or 4 ounces mayonnaise
- 8 slices muenster cheese, sliced
- 8 ounces rare roast beef, sliced thinly
- 8 ounces pastrami, sliced thinly
- dill pickle, as desired
- 4 ounces caramelized onions
- unsalted butter, melted

Directions
1. Sandwich dressing.
2. In a bowl, combine the mayonnaise, sour cream, ketchup, relishes, onion, garlic, lemon juice, balsamic vinegar, Tabasco, and black pepper to taste. Mix well! Makes about 2 cups dressing.
3. Assemble the sandwich.
4. For each Panini: on one slice of bread, spread sandwich dressing, while on the other, spread aioli or mayo. Layer Muenster cheese, roast beef, and pastrami, then top with pickles and caramelized onions. Close the sandwich. Brush outer sides of sandwich generously with melted Unsalted Tillamook Butter.

Press on Panini grill or toast in pan or on flattop grill. Serve with garlic parmesan fries, sweet potato fries or small side salad.

Panini Inglese

A grilled sandwich of rare roast beef and blue cheese with watercress.
***Servings:** 4 | **Cook:** 10 mins | **Prep:** 15 mins | **Total Time:** 25 mins*

Ingredients
- 4 soft sourdough rolls
- 10 -12 ounces blue cheese, at room temperature for easier spreading
- 8 -10 ounces rare roast beef, thinly sliced
- watercress leaf
- soft butter

Directions
1. Split each roll; spread generously with blue cheese on each side.
2. Into each roll, layer the roast beef, then the watercress leaves, and close up again, pressing well to seal.
3. Lightly butter the outside of each sandwich.
4. Heat a heavy nonstick skillet, or panini press, over med-high heat.
5. Place the sandwiches in the pan, working in 2 batches.
6. Weight down sandwiches with a heavy skillet or wide-bottomed saucepan, or close the grill; cook, turning once or twice until the bread is crisp and the cheese has melted.
7. Serve right away, cut on the diagonal.

Reuben Panini

These hot grilled sandwich offers all the traditional Reuben-on-rye flavors
***Servings:** 4 | **Cook:** 15 mins | **Prep:** 10 mins | **Total Time:** 25 mins*

Ingredients
- 8 slices rye bread or 8 slices pumpernickel bread
- 1/2 cup thousand island dressing
- 12 ounces sliced corned beef
- 2 cups sauerkraut
- 8 slices Swiss cheese
- 1/4 cup soft butter

Directions

1. Spread the dressing on one side of each bread slice.
2. Divide the corned beef among four of the dressed bread slices. Evenly distribute the sauerkraut over the meat, and top with two slices of cheese per sandwich.
3. Place the remaining dressed slices of bread dressing-side-down onto the cheese.
4. Preheat an electric Panini griddle; or heat a skillet over medium-high heat.
5. Spread the top of each sandwich with butter and place them butter-side down onto the hot surface; you'll probably need to work in batches.
6. Spread butter on the other side of each sandwich, then close the griddle, or cover the panini with a heavy lid, flipping to grill on both sides.

Roast Beef & Peppers Panini

Grilled Roast Beef on Rye Sandwich with Peppers and Swiss Cheese.
Cook: *15 mins* | **Prep:** *45 mins* | **Total Time:** *1hr*

Ingredients

- 10 slices rye bread
- 5 tablespoons mayonnaise
- 15 slices deli roast beef
- 1 green bell pepper
- 1 red bell pepper
- 1 yellow bell pepper
- 10 slices baby Swiss cheese
- 1/3 cup olive oil
- 2 tablespoons basil

Directions

1. Julienne each of the Bell Peppers into thin slices. Place into a baking pan and roast peppers under an open broiler until skin begins to brown about 5 - 10 minutes. Remove from broiler and let cool.
2. Spread a thin layer of Mayo on the inside of each slice of rye bread. Mix olive oil and basil together in a small dish. Brush the opposite side of 5 bread slices with the Basil/Olive Oil mixture.
3. Place the 5 slices of bread onto a preheated griddle with the Olive Oil side down. Layer 3 slices of roast beef on top of each slice of bread. Place Roasted Peppers over the beef. Top with 2 slices of Baby Swiss Cheese.
4. Place other other 5 slices of rye bread on top of the cheese with the mayo side down. Brush the top sides with Basil/Olive Oil mix.
5. Grill until cheese is melted and sandwich is golden brown on both sides. Cut each sandwich in half to serve.

6. Side dish suggestion (Eggplant Steak Fries with Marinara Sauce).

Roast Beef and Fontina Panini

Servings: 2 | Cook: 10 mins | Prep: 15 mins | Total Time: 25mins

Ingredients
- 2 tablespoons butter
- 1 small onion, thinly sliced
- 2 tablespoons whole grain mustard
- 1/2 loaf ciabatta, split lengthwise
- 1/3 lb thinly sliced deli roast beef
- 4 slices bacon, cooked
- 3/4 cup shredded Fontina cheese

Directions
1. Preheat panini grill.
2. In a medium skillet, melt butter over medium heat.
3. Add onion, and cook for 10-12 minutes or until very tender, stirring often.
4. Increase heat to med-high, and cook, stirring constantly, until onion is caramel colored; set aside.
5. Spread mustard over cut sides of bread.
6. Top bottom half of loaf with roast beef, bacon, caramelized onion, and shredded cheese; cover with top half of loaf.
7. Place sandwich on panini grill.
8. Close lid, and grill for 6-10 minutes or until bread is toasted and cheese is melted.
9. Cut in half and serve immediately.

Roast Beef Cheddar Panini Sandwiches

If you don't have a panini press, place sandwiches in a hot skillet, and press with a smaller heavy pan. Cook until bread is golden brown; turn and cook until other side is golden brown and cheese is melted.
Serving: 4

Ingredients
- 1 large onion, sliced
- 1 teaspoon sugar
- 1/2 teaspoon salt
- 1/2 cup prepared creamy horseradish sauce, divided

- 8 slices whole wheat bread
- 1 pound deli roast beef slices
- 4 Cheddar, Swiss, or provolone cheese slices
- 1 tablespoon melted butter

Directions
1. Sauté first 3 ingredients in a lightly greased skillet over medium-high heat 8 minutes or until onion is tender.
2. Spread 1 tablespoon horseradish sauce on each of 4 bread slices; top evenly with roast beef, cooked onion, and cheese. Top with remaining bread slices. Brush melted butter on both sides of sandwich.
3. Cook in a preheated panini press 2 to 3 minutes or until golden brown. Serve with remaining horseradish sauce.

Roast Beef Panini Sandwich With Cilantro

This is my favorite sandwich! My husband and I made this up one Sunday afternoon and it turned out so great! Hope you enjoy this sandwich as much as we do!
Cook: *5 mins |* **Prep:** *5 mins |* **Total Time:** *10mins*

Ingredients
- 10 slices sourdough bread
- 2 (4 ounce) cans whole green chilies
- 1 lb deli sliced roast beef
- 5 slices sharp cheddar cheese
- 4 ounces mozzarella cheese, grated
- 4 tablespoons fresh lime juice
- 1 garlic clove, minced
- 1/2 teaspoon hot sauce
- 1 teaspoon Dijon mustard
- 1 cup fresh cilantro leaves, chopped
- 1 cup mayonnaise
- salt and pepper

Directions
1. Mix lime juice, garlic clove, hot sauce, Dijon mustard, cilantro, mayo and salt and pepper to make the Cilantro Lime Mayo and set aside.
2. Lay out bread and top all pieces with Mayo mixture. Next on 5 slices of sour dough bread add cheese, roast beef, whole green chili and mozzarella cheese. Top with the other pieces of bread.
3. Spray with butter flavored cooking spray or butter and put in Panini press until brown and melted.

Roast Beef Panini With Chipotle Mashed P

5-Ingredient Fix Contest Entry. I like this recipe because it is quick, easy and simple to make.
Cook: 4 mins | **Prep:** 5 mins | **Total Time:** 9mins

Ingredients
- 1/2 cup Simply Potatoes Traditional Mashed Potatoes
- 1/2 cup chipotle chili mayonnaise
- 4 ciabatta rolls, split
- 8 slices smoked provolone cheese
- 1 (13 ounce) package deli roast beef or 1 lb thinly sliced deli roast beef

Directions
1. Preheat panini press according to manufacturer's instructions. In small bowl, stir together mashed potatoes and mayonnaise; mix well. Spread mixture evenly over cut sides of buns. Next, place 1 slice of cheese on each bun bottom. Divide roast beef evenly among bun bottoms, top each sandwich with remaining slices of cheese, add bun tops.
2. Grill sandwiches 3 to 4 minutes or until golden brown and cheese is melted.

Roast Beef Panini With Horseradish Mayo

This recipe can be made in a panini maker, a George Foreman type grill or a ridged grill pan on the stove. Put foil around a slightly smaller pan and use it to press the panini down. Use whatever cheese you like or happen to have at home - a creamy Havarti goes nice with it - as well as leftovers from a roast or steaks.
Cook: 10 mins | **Prep:** 15 mins | **Total Time:** 25mins

Ingredients
- 8 slices of rustic country bread
- 1/2 cup mayonnaise (or more if you like mayo)
- 1/4 cup prepared horseradish sauce
- 1/2 lb roast beef or 1/2 lb leftover steak, thinly sliced
- 1 red pepper (optional)
- 8 slices tomatoes
- 8 slices havarti cheese (or your favorite)
- 2 teaspoons olive oil (o brush the bread)
- 1 garlic clove (to rub on bread)

- herbs or salat greens (to garnish)

Directions
1. Combine mayonnaise and horseradish in a bowl, set aside.
2. Brush the bread slices on the underside with olive oil and rub a clove of garlic over them.
3. Lay them out in front of you, oil side down and spread the horseradish mayo on each slice.
4. Top with roast beef, pepper rings, tomato and cheese. Fold together.
5. Put in a grill pan and use a smaller frying pan to weigh it down.
6. Turn and brown on the other side.
7. Cut in two, garnish with salat greens and herbs
8. Enjoy!

Roast Beef Panini With the Works!

I made these for my hubby and I the other day, and they were so good, he asked if I was going to add it to zaar, LOL! (I think he was hinting so I wouldn't forget how I made it! Too funny!) Anyways, we inhaled them! Hope you like them, too! I've simplified the recipe to make just one, but you can adjust it to how ever many you need to make, of course. Have a wonderful lunch! :)
Cook: 2 mins | **Prep:** 10 mins | **Total Time:** 12mins

Ingredients
- 2 slices hearty bread, such as ciabatta
- 2 tablespoons sun-dried tomato pesto
- 4 slices deli roast beef
- 1 jarred artichoke heart, coarsely chopped
- 1 slice bacon, cooked, drained and broken in half
- 2 slices havarti cheese
- olive oil

Directions
1. *I use my cast iron grill pan for this, so if using that, turn your gas stove on to medium-low heat and get the pan heating. (Make sure it is lightly oiled first.) You can also do this in a Foreman Grill if you happen to have one, or even a pan works just fine. ;).
2. Spread 2 slices hearty bread (even regular bread works ok, too) with 2 Tbl. sun-dried tomato pesto. (1 Tbl. on each slice.) I just use my measuring spoon and then spread it on with the back of it.
3. Place a slice of havarti cheese on each slice.
4. On one slice, scrunch up each slice of roast beef and pile on. It's so much better that way than just laying them on flat.

5. On top of the roast beef, sprinkle on the chopped artichoke heart. (*My hubby hates them, so I only put them on mine when I made this for us. So this is optional.).
6. Break your piece of bacon in half, and lay the slices on top of the artichoke hearts.
7. Now just take the other slice of bread that you made with the pesto and cheese and flip it over on top. (Cheese-side down, of course! :)).
8. Brush top all over, but lightly, with a little olive oil.
9. Place, olive oil side-down onto hot grill or pan.
10. Brush top-side with more olive oil the same way.
11. Toast at least 1 minute, but check. You want it lightly toasted with nice grill marks.
12. Carefully lift up a corner with your spatula, then get under it and turn it over.
13. Toast other side.
14. Remove the same way onto a cutting board and cut in half with a sharp knife on the bias or corner-to-corner.
15. Serve immediately and enjoy!

Roast Beef Panini

Servings: 2 | Cook: 10 mins | Prep: 10 mins | Total Time: 20mins

Ingredients
- 1/4 cup mayonnaise
- 2 teaspoons sun-dried tomatoes, minced
- 1 teaspoon garlic, minced
- 1 teaspoon prepared horseradish
- 1 teaspoon ketchup
- 1 pinch cayenne pepper
- 1/3 cup red onion, slivered
- 1/3 cup pickled sweet peppers (I used a mixture of hot and sweet)
- 1 pinch red pepper flakes
- 4 slices sourdough bread, 1/2 inch thick
- butter, softened
- 1/2 cup white cheddar cheese, shredded
- 4 ounces deli roast beef, thinly sliced

Directions
1. Mix mayonnaise, tomatoes, garlic, horseradish, ketchup, and cayenne in small bowl.
2. Toss onion, peppers, pepper flakes, and some juice from the peppers in another bowl. Let it stand for at least 5 minutes for flavors to blend.

3. Spread butter on one side of each slice of bread, and spread mayo mixture on the other side. Sprinkle cheese on two slices, top with roast beef, then some of the salad mixture, then the other slice of bread, butter side up.
4. Toast sandwiches in George Foreman grill or in a skillet using another heavy skillet or foil-wrapped brick as a weight. (Cook over medium heat. When first side is browned, flip over and cook the other side, weighting again.).

Russian Panini

Had a Russian sub at a local restaurant, made several changes and turned it into a Panini.
Servings: 2 | **Cook:** 2 mins | **Prep:** 5 mins | **Total Time:** 7mins

Ingredients
- 2 (12 inch) hoagie rolls (or the bread of your choice)
- 1 tablespoon olive oil
- 3 ounces prepared Russian salad dressing
- 4 slices provolone cheese
- 6 slices deli roast beef
- 6 slices deli corned beef
- 4 slices tomatoes

Directions
1. Cut rolls open.
2. Brush outside of rolls with olive oil.
3. Brush both sides of inside of rolls with Russian dressing.
4. Cut cheese in half, add 4 halves to each roll.
5. Add 3 slices roast beef, 3 slices corned beef and 2 slices tomato to each roll.
6. Cut in half.
7. Heat in your panini press or george foreman grill.
8. Enjoy.

Smoked Brisket Panini

I made this for dinner last night-really nice flavors. Prep and cooking time does not reflect "pre cooked" brisket or marinating onions. That part is up to you.
Cook: 6 mins | **Prep:** 10 mins | **Total Time:** 16mins

Ingredients
- 4 slices onion bread

- 12 slices smoked beef brisket
- 1/4 cup barbecue sauce
- 4 tablespoons mayonnaise
- 3 tablespoons chipotle adobo seasoning
- 1/4 cup canned jalapeno slices, pickled and diced
- 1/4 red onion, sliced
- 1/4 cup red wine vinegar
- 1 teaspoon white sugar
- 8 slices monterey jack pepper cheese
- 8 slices sharp cheddar cheese
- 2 tablespoons butter

Directions
1. Slice your red onion thin.
2. In a small bowl whisk together the red wine vinegar and sugar.
3. Let marinate for 1 hour, up to 6 hours.
4. In a small bowl whisk together the mayonnaise and chipotle adobo**, set aside.
5. Slice Brisket to desired thickness.
6. Slice bread at an angle so you have "longer" slices.
7. Heat a medium skillet over medium heat.
8. Add BBQ sauce and brisket slices-heat through.
9. Lay out your slices of bread.
10. Divide the mayo mixture evenly between each slice of bread-spread.
11. On one side of two bread slices lay out the pepperjack cheese.
12. Layer brisket-6 slices each-on top of cheese.
13. Add marinated onion rings and pickled jalapeno slices.
14. Top with the the sharp cheddar slices.
15. Cover last cheese layer with bread.
16. Heat your panini maker or a heavy skillet.
17. Butter bottom side of each sandwich.
18. Place on panini maker or heated skillet.
19. Butter other side if using panini maker and close until done.
20. If using the skillet method put another heavy skillet on top of your sandwich, cooking for about 3 minutes.
21. Remove skillet, butter top of sandwich, flip and repeat.
22. Slice in half and serve.
23. **I simply take one can of Chipotles in Adobo and pour into a blender, adding 1/2 can of water. Puree and pour into a squeeze bottle. I use this for taco sauce or in recipes like the adobo mayo.

St Louis' Amighetti Sandwich Copycat

Amighetti's is a well known Italian restaurant in St. Louis, where I grew up. They have a great deli sandwich that I still crave to this day (even out here in CA). It has a really delicious spread that makes it different from other sandwiches. The true key is their famous bread, but in a pinch, you can make this sandwich at home with your own bread.
Servings: 6-8 | **Cook:** 0 mins | **Prep:** 15 mins | **Total Time:** 15mins

Ingredients
SANDWICH SPREAD
- 1/2 cup mayonnaise
- 1/4 cup sour cream
- 2 tablespoons Dijon mustard
- 2 tablespoons green onions, finely chopped
- 1 tablespoon horseradish
- 2 teaspoons fresh dill

SANDWICH
- 1 loaf French bread or 1 loaf panini bread
- 6 slices cooked ham
- 6 slices roast beef
- 6 slices genoa salami
- 6 dill pickle slices
- 6 slices tomatoes
- 6 slices Swiss cheese
- 3 pickled peppers (Pepperoncini)

Directions
1. Combine mayonnaise, sour cream, mustard, green onion, horseradish and dill. Slice baguette in half horizontally. Spread the cut surfaces with mixture.
2. On bottom half of baguette, arrange in order: ham, roast beef, salami, dill pickle slices, tomato slices, Swiss cheese and pepperoncini.
3. Place top half of baguette on filling. Cut sandwiches into pieces.

Tomato Mozzarella & Pesto Panini

Cook: 3 mins | **Prep:** 15 mins | **Total Time:** 18mins

Ingredients
- 2 large beefsteak tomatoes (or other large tomatoes)

- 1 (16 ounce) ball fresh mozzarella cheese
- 12 slices whole wheat bread, sliced 1/2-inch thick (or whole grain or white)
- 1 cup pesto sauce (homemade or storebought)
- kosher salt (optional)
- butter, unsalted, room temperature

Directions
1. Preheat a panini grill machine or a heavy skillet.
2. Core the tomatoes and slice tomatoes and mozzarella 1/4" thick.
3. Place the bread slices on a cutting board(or work surface). Spread each slice evenly with pesto. Place a layer of mozzarella(about 2 slices) on half of the bread and cover with a layer of tomato. Sprinkle the tomato with a little kosher salt.
4. Place the remaining slices of bread, pesto side down, on top. Spread the top and bottom of each sandwich with softened butter.
5. Grill the sandwiches in batches on the panini grill for 2-3 minutes, until the mozzarella starts to ooze out. If using a skillet, place a weight on top(I usually use another heavy cast iron skillet, or use a foil coverd brick, or other flat, heavy object. Cook 2-3 minutes, turn and cook other side 1-3 minutes.).
6. Cut the sandwiches in half and serve warm. Enjoy!
7. Note: This is also excellent with a slice of roasted red bell pepper in it!

Two Beef Panini

Servings: 2 | Cook: 4 mins | Prep: 15 mins | Total Time: 19mins

Ingredients
- 4 slices sourdough bread
- 1 tablespoon butter, melted
- 2 tablespoons honey mustard
- 3 ounces provolone cheese, thinly sliced
- 2 ounces corned beef, thinly sliced
- 2 ounces pastrami, thinly sliced
- 2 lettuce leaves
- 2 plum tomatoes, thinly sliced

Directions
1. Preheat panini grill to high.
2. Brush one side of each bread slice with butter.
3. Place on a work surface, buttered side down, and spread with mustard.

4. On bottom halves, evenly layer with half the cheese, then with corned beef, pastrami, the remaining cheese, lettuce and tomatoes.
5. Cover with top halves and press gently to pack.
6. Place sandwiches in grill, close the top plate and cook until golden brown, 3-4 minutes.
7. Serve immediately.

Veal and Eggplant Panini with Sun Dried Tomato Mayonnaise

Serving: 2

Ingredients
- 1/4 cup boiling water
- 6 sun-dried tomatoes, packed without oil
- 2 tablespoons skim milk
- 3 tablespoons dry breadcrumbs
- 1/4 pound lean veal scaloppine, cut into 2 equal portions
- 2 (1/4-inch-thick) eggplant slices
- Vegetable cooking spray
- 2 (3-inch) pieces Italian bread
- 1 tablespoon reduced-calorie mayonnaise

Directions
1. Combine boiling water and tomatoes in a small bowl; let stand 15 minutes or until softened. Drain tomatoes, reserving 1 teaspoon liquid. Mince tomatoes, and set aside.
2. Place milk in a bowl. Place breadcrumbs in a shallow dish. Dip veal in milk, and dredge in breadcrumbs. Repeat procedure with eggplant slices. Place veal and eggplant slices in a single layer on a jelly-roll pan coated with cooking spray. Bake at 400° for 12 minutes, turning after 6 minutes.
3. Slice each piece of bread in half horizontally. Combine minced tomatoes, reserved liquid, and mayonnaise in a small bowl; stir well. Spread mayonnaise mixture over top halves of bread. Divide veal and eggplant between bottom halves of bread; cover with top halves of bread.

Chapter 2: Cheese

***

Apple Cheddar Panini I

Servings: 4 | Cook: 10 mins | Prep: 10 mins | Total Time: 20mins

Ingredients
- 8 slices whole grain bread
- 1/4 cup honey mustard
- 2 crisp apples, thinly sliced (I like Braeburn or Fuji or Gala)
- 8 ounces mild cheddar cheese, thinly sliced
- cooking spray

Directions
1. Preheat panini press on medium heat(or use 2 heavy skillets-one to put on top of the panini while cooking to press it).
2. Lightly spread honey mustard evenly over each slice of bread.
3. Layer apple slices and cheese over 4 slices of bread, using about ½ apple and 2 ounces of cheese for each sandwich. Top each with remaining bread slices. Lightly coat panini press with cooking spray(or coat skillet.
4. Grill each sandwich for 3 to 5 minutes or until cheese has melted and bread has toasted.
5. Remove from pan and allow to cool slightly before serving. Enjoy!

Apple Chedder Panini II

Buddy Valaski is an Italian, who makes a living as a pastry chef. He has two shows on TLC called Cake Boss and Kitchen Boss. On the latter show, Buddy makes primarily Italian food, mostly from Sicily, where his family is originally from. I don't know if Paninis are Sicilian in origin, but Buddy sure knows how to make good recipes!
Servings: 4 | Cook: 20 mins | Prep: 5 mins | Total Time: 25mins

Ingredients
- 1 tablespoon butter
- 2 cups apples, thinly sliced
- 1/4 teaspoon ground cinnamon
- 8 teaspoons apple jelly
- 8 slices egg bread
- mild cheddar cheese

Directions
1. 1.Melt butter in large nonstick skillet. Add apple slices; sprinkle with cinnamon. Cook and stir over medium heat 5 minutes or until golden and tender. Remove from skillet; wipe out skillet with paper towel.
2. 2.Spread 2 teaspoons apple jelly on each of 4 bread slices; top with 1 cheese slice. Arrange one fourth of apple slices over each cheese slice. Top with remaining 4 bread slices.
3. 3.Heat same skillet over medium heat until hot. Add sandwiches; press down lightly with spatula or weigh down with small plate. Cook sandwiches 4 to 5 minutes per side or until cheese melts and sandwiches are golden brown.
4. *Use sweet apples such as Fuji or Royal Gala.

Apple Ham & Cheddar Panini With App

A caterer friend made these to test, and my goodness, wow! She did not give me exact brand of ingredients, but I'm sure as long as you use good quality ingredients, it will be just as tasty as hers. It definitely had the OMG factor to it!
Cook: 5 mins | **Prep:** 5 mins | **Total Time:** 10mins

Ingredients
- 2 slices whole grain bread
- 1 apple, sliced thin (preferably a sweet variety with soft skin)
- 1 slice thick cheddar cheese
- 2 -3 slices thin honey-roasted ham
- 1 -2 tablespoon apple butter, sweet brand
- thyme
- rosemary

Directions
1. Core and slice apple thinly, leaving the skin on.
2. Place cheese on one slice of bread.
3. Place Ham on other slice of bread.
4. Layer Apples, about 5-6 pieces, on top of cheese.
5. Spread Apple Butter on Ham.
6. Enclose the sandwich.
7. Sprinkle a pinch of thyme and rosemary on both sides of bread and press in a Panini or George Foreman grill until cheese is melting and both sides are toasted.

Apricot and White Cheddar Panini

Serving: 1

Ingredients
- 1 tablespoon apricot jam
- 2 slices bread
- 2 ounces thinly sliced white Cheddar
- 1/2 tablespoon butter

Directions
1. Spread the jam over 1 side of sliced bread. Add the Cheddar. Top with a second slice of bread. Spread 1/4 tablespoon butter on each side of the sandwich. Heat in a skillet over medium heat until the cheese melts, 2 minutes per side.

Artichoke, Fresh Mozzarella Salami Sandwiches (Panini)

Prep: 15 mins | Total Time: 15mins

Ingredients
- 2 (6 ounce) jars artichoke hearts (marinated, drained,chopped)
- 1/2 cup sun-dried tomato (oil packed, drained,chopped)
- 1/2 cup parmigiano (fresh grated)
- 1/2 cup basil (fresh,chopped)
- 2 tablespoons extra virgin olive oil
- 4 Italian rolls
- 12 ounces fresh mozzarella cheese (water packed,drained,sliced)
- 6 ounces salami (sliced thin)
- 8 tablespoons olive spread

Directions
1. Mix first 5 ingredients in a medium bowl, season with salt and fresh black pepper,divide artichoke mixture among bottom halves of rolls.
2. Top with cheese, then salami, spread top half of each roll with 2 tablespoons Olivada, place atop salami.
3. Press sandwiches lightly to compact, wrap each tightly in plastic wrap, refrigerate at least 4 hours or up to 1 day before serving.

Artichoke Tomato Panini

Servings: 1 | Cook: 5 mins | Prep: 5 mins | Total Time: 10mins

Ingredients
- 2 tablespoons artichoke dip (artichokes and and asiago or canned artichokes)
- 2 slices tomatoes
- 2 tablespoons feta cheese
- 3 slices avocados
- salt and pepper
- 1 slice of fresh focaccia bread, cut in half

Directions
1. Toast the focaccia bread (or if you have a Panini maker, save this step until later).
2. Spread the Artichoke dip on the bread. Layer on the feta cheese, tomato and avocado.
3. Add salt and pepper to taste.
4. Grill on the Panini maker if you are using one. Serve.

Bacon Caesar and Mozzarella Panini

A Pillsbury Bake-Off recipe. One with a twist on the bread.
Servings: 4 | Cook: 12 mins | Prep: 40 mins | Total Time: 52mins

Ingredients
- 1 (13 7/8 ounce) can refrigerated pizza crusts
- 4 teaspoons basil pesto
- 1/4 cup caesar salad dressing (creamy or vinaigrette style)
- 8 slices regular mozzarella cheese
- 1/4 teaspoon fresh ground pepper
- 12 slices bacon, cooked
- fresh basil leaf
- 1/4 cup butter

Directions
1. Heat oven to 375°F Spray large cookie sheet with no-ntick cooking spray. Unroll pizza crust dough on cookie sheet; press dough into 16x11-inch rectangle, pulling dough gently if necessary. Bake 9 to 16 minutes or until light brown. Cool about 15 minutes or until cool enough to handle.

2. Cut cooled pizza crust in half lengthwise and crosswise to make 4 rectangles. Remove rectangles from cookie sheet; cut each rectangle in half crosswise for a total of 8 squares.
3. On each of 4 crust slices, spread 1 teaspoon pesto; set aside. On each of remaining 4 slices, spread 1 tablespoon Caesar dressing. Place 2 cheese slices on each crust slice with Caesar dressing. Top cheese with pepper, 3 bacon slices, 2 tomato slices and 2 basil leaves. Top with remaining crust slices, pesto sides down.
4. Heat 12-inch skillet or cast-iron skillet over medium heat until hot. Melt 2 tablespoons of the butter in skillet. Place 2 sandwiches in skillet. Place smaller skillet or saucepan on sandwiches to flatten slightly; keep skillet on sandwiches while cooking. Cook 1 to 2 minutes on each side or until bread is golden brown and crisp and fillings are heated. Remove from skillet; cover with foil to keep warm. Repeat with remaining 2 tablespoons butter and sandwiches.

Bacon Cheddar & Grilled Tomato Panini

this is sooo good. I found it at paninihappy.com and just drooled. posted here for safekeeping. You can cook the tomatoes under the broiler or on the bbq as well
Servings: *4 |* **Cook:** *17 mins |* **Prep:** *15 mins |* **Total Time:** *32mins*

Ingredients
- 4 roma tomatoes, halved lengthwise, pulp and seeds removed
- olive oil
- coarse sea salt
- fresh ground black pepper
- 8 basil leaves, thinly sliced
- 2 tablespoons unsalted butter, melted
- 8 slices sourdough bread
- 8 slices bacon, fully cooked*
- 4 ounces sharp cheddar cheese, thinly sliced

Directions
1. Preheat the panini grill to high heat. Ensure the grill is on a slight tilt (not completely flat) and be sure to attach your drip tray.
2. Brush the cut side of the tomatoes with olive oil. Season with salt and pepper. Place the tomatoes, cut side down, onto the panini grill. Lower the top grate to just above the tomatoes without touching them. Grill tomatoes for 10-12 minutes until the outer skins are wrinkly and the tomatoes are soft. Check the tomatoes often, as some may cook faster than others. Remove the tomatoes from the grill and sprinkle with basil.
3. Brush melted butter onto the outer sides of each slice of bread. For each sandwich, layer two slices of bacon, two grilled tomatoes and 1/4 of the

cheese in between two slices of bread (buttered side out). Grill the panini for 5-7 minutes until the cheese is melted and the bread is toasted. Serve immediately and enjoy!

Balsamic Chicken Sandwich Or Panini

A friend of mine and I once made this from a recipe we found in a cooking magazine, but lost the recipe. I found it again, so I'm putting it here so as not to lose it again. It calls for ciabatta bread, but anything light with a good crunchy crust will be as good. It's also great grilled panini-style.
Servings: 2 | **Cook:** 15 mins | **Prep:** 5 mins | **Total Time:** 20mins

Ingredients
- 2 small boneless skinless chicken breasts
- 1 tablespoon olive oil
- salt and pepper
- 2 ciabatta rolls, sandwich size
- 2 tablespoons goat cheese
- 1 cup baby spinach leaves
- 1/2 red onion
- 1/4 cup roasted red pepper
- 1 cup white wine
- 1/2 cup balsamic vinegar
- 2 tablespoons sugar

Directions
1. Salt and pepper chicken breasts.
2. Heat olive oil in a nonstick skillet over medium high heat.
3. Cook chicken until no longer pink, about 4-5 minutes per side.
4. Remove chicken, keep warm.
5. Add wine, sugar, and vinegar to pan, increase heat to high, reduce until thick and syrupy.
6. Cut rolls in half, spread with goat cheese.
7. Add chicken, spinach, onion, peppers, and sauce.
8. You may have sauce left over. Save it. It's great on steaks, too.

Balsamic Red Onion and Gruyere Panini/Grilled Cheese

Found something great from one of my Thanksgiving leftovers (balsamic red onions).
Servings: 4 | **Cook:** 15 mins | **Prep:** 5 mins | **Total Time:** 20mins

Ingredients
- 1 red onion, thinly sliced
- 1 tablespoon balsamic vinegar (or to taste)
- 1/2 tablespoon olive oil
- 1 pinch salt
- 1 teaspoon sugar
- 8 slices sourdough bread
- 4 ounces gruyere cheese, shredded
- white truffle oil (optional)

Directions
1. Place onions, balsamic, oil, salt and sugar in sauce pan, cover and cook on medium low until very soft. The onions should still be purple in color (if they are black there is probably too much vinegar -- remember you can always add more but you can't take it out).
2. Put together cheese and onion on bread. Spray with truffle oil and grill in pan or panini press.
3. Dunk it in tomato basil soup. Yum.

Basic Grilled Cheese Sandwich

Time: about 15 minutes. This is more a method than a recipe, but you can make a fantastic sandwich with just great bread, fresh butter, and your favorite cheese. To make 2 sandwiches at once, just use a larger frying pan. If you want a thin, ultra-crisp sandwich, use a panini press set to medium (350°), or heat a cast-iron skillet on a separate burner. Set the skillet on top of your sandwich as it cooks in the frying pan, and cook about 4 minutes total.
Serving: 1

Ingredients
- 2 tablespoons butter, softened
- 2 slices of your favorite bread
- 2 slices of your favorite cheese*

Directions
1. Butter bread slices on 1 side. Turn them over.
2. Lay cheese slices on 1 bread slice. Top with the other bread slice, buttered side up. (The buttered sides face out so that they'll turn crisp and golden when they touch the hot pan.)
3. Heat a medium frying pan over medium heat. Flick a drop of water into the pan; if it sizzles and evaporates, the pan is hot enough.

4. Put sandwich, buttered side down, in pan with both hands. Let it cook 3 to 4 minutes, or until golden and crunchy underneath. Using a spatula (or one in each hand, if the bread is large), turn the sandwich over. Let it cook another 3 to 4 minutes, or until golden and crunchy on the second side.
5. *Choose a cheese that melts well. Some classics for grilled cheese: cheddar, jack and pepper jack, Colby, gruyère, Swiss, fontina, provolone. Brie works well too.

Basil and Provolone Panini

Servings: 2 | Cook: 4 mins | Prep: 10 mins | Total Time: 14mins

Ingredients
- 2 bolillo rolls, split
- 1 tablespoon olive oil
- 2 teaspoons mayonnaise
- 2 ounces provolone cheese, thinly sliced
- 1/4 cup thinly sliced fresh basil
- 1/4 cup thinly sliced red bell pepper

Directions
1. Preheat panini grill to high.
2. Place rolls, cut side down, on a work surface and brush crusts with oil.
3. Turn rolls over and spread evenly with mayonnaise.
4. On bottom halves, evenly layer provolone, basil, and red pepper.
5. Cover with top halves and press gently to pack.
6. Place sandwiches in grill; close the top plate and cook until golden brown, 3-4 minutes.
7. Serve immediately.

Bat P Bacon Arugula and Tomato Panini

Use whatever bread you choose, but I wouldn't recommend rye like I used. (Hey, I kinda rhymed!) I added some of my Immoral Mushrooms to my panini, but you can certainly do without. That's the joy of a panini... you can be creative without TOO much chance for disaster. ;o)
Servings: 1 | Cook: 5 mins | Prep: 3 mins | Total Time: 8mins

Ingredients
- 2 slices bread (ciabatta, French, Italian, wheat, sourdough, etc.)

- 1 teaspoon mayonnaise
- 2 -3 arugula leaves (a few)
- 3 slices bacon, fried crisp
- 1 small roma tomato, sliced thin
- 1 slice Swiss cheese or 1 slice provolone cheese or 1 slice mozzarella cheese
- olive oil

Directions
1. Preheat your panini press/grill.
2. Lightly baste the bread slices on the OUTSIDE with olive oil.
3. Spread the INSIDE of each slice with mayonnaise.
4. Set one slice on the press, oiled side down. On that, layer the following: arugula, bacon, tomato and cheese.
5. Top with the other bread slice, mayonnaise facing the inside of the sandwich.
6. Close the panini press and check for desired doneness in 5 minutes.

BBQ Pork Panini Sandwich

Servings: 4 | Cook: 1 hr 35 mins | Prep: 1 hr 20 mins | Total Time: 2hrs

Ingredients
- 3/4 cup white sugar
- 1 1/2 cups paprika
- 3 3/4 tablespoons onion powder
- 3 lbs roast pork loin
- 4 tablespoons butter, room temperature
- 1 garlic clove, minced
- 4 french style sandwich buns, sliced horizontally
- dill pickle slices
- 1/4 lb sliced cheddar and colby cheese
- 1/2 cup barbecue sauce

Directions
1. Mix the rub ingredients together in a bowl.
2. Place pork in a roasting dish. Pat the rub seasoning into pork to cover. (Reserve any remaining rub in a container fitted with lid for up to 6 months.) Cover with plastic wrap and refrigerate to marinate for 1 hour.
3. Preheat oven to 325 degrees F.
4. Place roast pork into oven and cook for 1 1/2 hours. When cooked, tent roast with foil so juices will settle. Slice thin.
5. Preheat your panini press.

6. In a small bowl mix the butter and the garlic. Butter the sandwich bread.
7. Divide the pork, pickles, cheese and barbecue sauce evenly between the bread.
8. Place the sandwiches in the panini press and close the lid. Grill the sandwich until the bread is toasty and the cheese is melted. Slice on a diagonal and serve warm.

BBQ Turkey Panini

If you don't have a panini grill, heat a skillet on medium heat. Cook sandwich 5 minutes on each side or until cheese is melted and sandwich is golden brown on both sides, gently press down top of sandwich with a spatula.
Servings: 1 | **Cook:** 5 mins | **Prep:** 10 mins | **Total Time:** 15mins

Ingredients
- 2 slices sourdough bread
- 2 tablespoons barbecue sauce
- 6 slices deli smoked turkey breast
- 1 slice sharp cheddar cheese
- 1 slice red onion
- 1/4 cup baby spinach leaves

Directions
1. Heat panini grill to medium heat.
2. Spread bread slices with barbecue sauce; fill with remaining ingredients.
3. Grill 5 minutes or until cheese is melted and sandwich is golden brown on both sides.
4. Enjoy!

Bellissimo Panini

You do not need a panini press to make this sandwich, just use a skillet. From the cookbook "Delizioso: Panini the Italian Way"
Servings: 4 | **Cook:** 4 mins | **Prep:** 10 mins | **Total Time:** 14mins

Ingredients
- 1 large red bell pepper, cored, seeded and thinly sliced
- 1/2 small red onion, peeled and thinly sliced
- 1 teaspoon extra virgin olive oil
- 4 ciabatta rolls, split
- 1/4 cup garlic-infused olive oil

- salt and pepper (to taste)
- 1/2 lb prosciutto, sliced thinly
- 1/4 lb provolone cheese, thinly sliced
- 1 cup arugula
- 1 tablespoon extra virgin olive oil

Directions
1. In a small saute pan over medium heat saute pepper and onion in 1 tsp olive oil until onion is translucent and pepper is softened.
2. Brush each cut side of the rolls with garlic olive oil and lightly salt and pepper.
3. Assemble sandwiches using prosciutto, cheese, arugula, and sauteed vegetables. Lightly brush outside of assembled sandwiches with remaining olive oil.
4. Cook until done, about 4-8 minutes.

Bistro Apple Panini

From Taste of Home Magazine The bacon, apple and tarragon in this recipe go together so well. If you don't have a panini maker or an indoor grill, you can easily pan-fry or broil these excellent sandwiches.

Servings: 6 | **Cook:** 5 mins | **Prep:** 20 mins | **Total Time:** 25mins

Ingredients
- 12 thick slab bacon, slices cut in half
- 1 medium apple, thinly sliced
- 1 tablespoon ginger ale
- 1 teaspoon lemon juice
- 1/4 cup apple jelly
- 4 teaspoons minced fresh tarragon
- 12 slices sourdough bread
- 6 slices reduced-fat havarti cheese
- 2 tablespoons Dijon mustard
- 3 tablespoons butter, softened

Directions
1. In a large skillet, cook bacon over medium heat until crisp. Remove to paper towels to drain. In a small bowl, toss apple with ginger ale and lemon juice; set aside.
2. Place jelly in a small microwave-safe bowl; microwave on high for 20-30 seconds or until softened. Stir in tarragon.

3. Spread jelly mixture over six bread slices. Top with cheese, apple and bacon. Spread mustard over remaining bread; place over bacon. Spread outsides of sandwiches with butter.
4. Cook on a panini maker or indoor grill for 3-4 minutes or until bread is browned and cheese is melted.

Black Friday Turkey and Stuffing Panini

It's Black Friday, the day after Thanksgiving. You've got a fridge full of leftovers, and you're famished after a morning of door-buster sales. I promise you this hot and toasty sandwich will really hit the spot!

Cook: 4 mins | Prep: 3 mins | Total Time: 7 mins

Ingredients
- 2 slices sourdough bread (or any favorite bread) or 2 slices white bread (or any favorite bread)
- 1/2 tablespoon butter, softened
- 2 ounces cooked turkey
- 1/4-1/2 cup prepared stuffing
- 2 slices cheddar cheese
- ground black pepper, to taste

Directions
1. Pre-heat panini grill to medium-high. Warm leftover turkey and stuffing in the microwave.
2. Butter 1 side of each slice of bread, lay butter-side down on your work surface.
3. On one slice of bread, layer ingredients in the following order: 1 slice cheese, turkey, stuffing, black pepper (if desired), 1 slice cheese, top piece of bread, with buttered sides facing out.
4. Place assembled sandwich on the hot grill, and close, pressing down for about a minute to consolidate ingredients. Continue cooking for a few minutes, until golden brown.

Boursin Parisian Panini

Recipe was included in a package of recently bought Boursin cheese.
Servings: 4 | Cook: 5 mins | Prep: 15 mins | Total Time: 20mins

Ingredients
- 8 slices hearty country bread

- 2 -3 tablespoons olive oil
- 1 (5 1/4 ounce) package black pepper boursin cheese
- 8 slices smoked turkey
- 8 slices smoked cooked ham
- 1 cup roasted red pepper
- 1 cup baby arugula leaf

Directions
1. Preheat panini maker or grill pan. Lightly brush one side of each slice of bread with a little olive oil. Spread the other side of each slice with Boursin Cracked Pepper cheese.
2. For each panini, layer 2 slices each of turkey and ham, then 1/4 cup each roasted red peppers and arugula leaves in between 2 slices of prepared bread with the cheese on the inside. Place panini, one at a time in panini maker or grill pan, cook 4-5 minutes or until golden brown.
3. Cut each sandwich in half and serve immediately.

Brat and Swiss Cheese Panini

Servings: 8 | Cook: 12 mins | Prep: 30 mins | Total Time: 42mins

Ingredients
- 16 slices rye bread
- 1/2 cup brown mustard
- 32 slices Swiss cheese (or 1 lb. thinly sliced Swiss cheese)
- 8 fully cooked bratwursts, sliced thinly on the diagonal
- melted butter
- nonstick cooking spray

Directions
1. Spread 8 slices of bread with 1 tablespoon of mustard.
2. Place one 1-ounce slice of Swiss cheese on eight of the slices of bread.
3. Divide the sausage into eight portions and distribute evenly on the eight cheese-topped bread slices.
4. Top the sausages with the remaining Swiss cheese.
5. Close the sandwiches with the remaining eight slices of bread.
6. Brush the outsides of each sandwich with melted butter or spray with cooking spray.
7. Cook in a panini or other sandwich press; OR cook in a nonstick saute pan set on medium heat (weight each sandwich with a cake pan holding a 28-ounce can; cook on one side until golden brown, remove the weight, turn the

sandwich, and cook on the second side until golden brown and the cheese melts).
8. Slice each sandwich in half and serve with soup or chips.

Breakfast on the Go Panini

Servings: 2 | Cook: 4 mins | Prep: 20 mins | Total Time: 24mins

Ingredients
- 4 slices Canadian bacon
- 2 teaspoons butter
- 2 eggs
- salt
- fresh ground black pepper
- 2 English muffins, split
- 1 tablespoon butter, melted
- 2 ounces cheddar cheese, sliced

Directions
1. Preheat panini grill to high.
2. Arrange bacon on bottom grill plate of panini grill, close the top plate and grill until crispy, 1-2 minutes.
3. Remove and set aside; wipe grill plates clean.
4. In a nonstick skillet, melt 2 t butter over medium heat.
5. Crack eggs into the pan and cook until whites are set but yolks are still runny.
6. Season with salt and pepper.
7. Flip eggs with a rubber spatula and cook until yolks are set; remove from heat.
8. Place muffins, cut side down on a work surface and brush crusts with melted butter.
9. Turn muffins over and, on bottom half of each muffin, evenly layer with bacon, cheese, and egg.
10. Cover with top halves and press gently to pack.
11. Place sandwiches in grill, close the top plate and cook until golden brown, 3-4 minutes.
12. Serve immediately.

Breakfast Panini

A quick and filling breakfast.
***Servings:** 2 | **Cook:** 4 mins | **Prep:** 5 mins | **Total Time:** 9mins*

Ingredients
- 1 (12 inch) hoagie rolls (or bread of your choice)
- 2 slices yellow American cheese
- 4 slices deli ham
- 4 slices sweet roasted peppers
- 2 eggs

Directions
1. Cut roll open.
2. Cut cheese in half, add the 4 halves to the bread.
3. Add the deli ham and sweet roasted peppers.
4. Fry the two eggs, break yolks and add to roll.
5. Cut roll in half.
6. Grill in your panini press or george foreman grill.
7. Enjoy.

Breakfast Scrambled Egg Panini

I thought this was a nice was to use my panini maker for breakfast, not just lunch and dinner.
***Servings:** 2 | **Cook:** 3 mins | **Prep:** 5 mins | **Total Time:** 8mins*

Ingredients
- 3 eggs
- 1/2 avocado
- 4 slices multigrain bread
- 2 slices cheddar cheese
- 2 slices ham

Directions
1. Scramble up the eggs loosely and set aside.
2. Warm panini maker.
3. Spread avocado on two pieces of bread.
4. Add one piece of cheese to each.

5. Add ham to each.
6. Add one-half of the eggs to each piece of bread.
7. Place a slice of cheddar on each.
8. Cover with second slice of bread and place them on panini maker.
9. Cook around three minutes and serve.

Brie and Apple Panini

Servings: 4 | Cook: 20 mins | Prep: 10 mins | Total Time: 30mins

Ingredients
- 12 slices bacon (preferably applewood-smoked)
- 3 tablespoons butter, divided
- 1 large golden delicious apple, unpeeled, cored, thinly sliced
- Dijon mustard
- 1 loaf focaccia bread, cut crosswise into 4 pieces, then cut horizontally in half
- 16 ounces brie cheese, rind trimmed, cheese cut into 16 slices
- 2 tablespoons olive oil

Directions
1. Cook bacon in large skillet over medium heat until crisp, about 5 minutes. Transfer bacon to paper towels to drain.
2. Melt 1 tablespoon butter in medium nonstick skillet over medium-high heat. Add apple slices; saute 4 minutes. Remove from heat.
3. Spread mustard on cut sides of bread. Place 2 cheese slices on each bottom bread piece, top with 4 to 5 apple slices, then 3 bacon slices. Top each with 2 more cheese slices, then bread pieces. Press sandwiches lightly to compact.
4. Melt 1 tablespoon butter with 1 tablespoon oil in each of 2 large nonstick skillets over medium heat. Add 2 sandwiches to each skillet. Cover skillet; cook until bottoms of sandwiches are brown, pressing with spatula to compact, about 5 minutes. Turn sandwiches over; cover and cook until brown on bottom and cheese melts, about 5 minutes.
5. Note: Use a panini press for step 4 if you have one.
6. Enjoy!

Brie Cranberry and Bacon Panini

This is based on a sandwich I often get at a local restaurant. It is absolutely delicious as a panini! In light of a review, I have adjusted the amount of cranberry sauce required from 6 tablespoons to 5. Please feel free to adjust this to taste.

Cook: 10 mins | Prep: 5 mins | Total Time: 15 mins

Ingredients
- 4 slices bread (I use 2 panini rolls but any bread will do)
- 4 slices brie cheese, 2 for each sandwich
- 5 tablespoons cranberry sauce
- 4 slices streaky bacon, cooked
- butter, if using regular bread

Directions
1. If using panini rolls, cut each roll in half. If using regular bread, spread the outside of each slice with butter.
2. Spread 2 1/2 tablespoons of cranberry sauce each on 2 slices of bread.
3. Layer the brie over the cranberry sauce.
4. Top with 2 slices of bacon and the top layer of bread, remembering to keep the buttered side facing outwards.
5. I use a George Foreman grill to cook the panini- press the lid down to heat the sandwich right through and cook for a few minutes until the cheese has melted.
6. Alternatively, cook in a skillet, pressing the sandwich firmly with a spatula while cooking.
7. Serve hot!

Buffalo Blue Cheese Chicken Panini

Taste like wings, but easier.
Servings: 4 | Cook: 25 mins | Prep: 20 mins | Total Time: 45mins

Ingredients
- 1/2 cup chunky blue cheese dressing
- 1/3 cup all-purpose flour
- 1 teaspoon paprika
- 1 teaspoon chili powder
- 1 teaspoon salt
- 1 1/2 lbs chicken, breast-thin cut about 8 slices
- 2 tablespoons olive oil, plus extra for grilling bread
- 3 tablespoons Frank's red hot sauce
- 1 tablespoon butter, melted
- 8 slices favorite bread (medium thickness)
- sliced red onion

Extras

- celery rib
- blue cheese dressing

Directions
1. In a shallow bowl combine flour, paprika, chili powder and salt. Coat chicken with flour mixture. Heat oil in a large nonstick pan over medium-high heat and cook chicken on each side until it is fully cooked, about 10 minutes. Remove from pan.
2. In a small bowl, combine hot sauce and butter. Brush each piece of chicken with hot sauce mixture. Allow chicken to cool slightly.
3. Preheat a sandwich grill or panini press. Arrange bread slices on a work surface and spread each slice with 1 tablespoon blue cheese dressing. Layer cooked chicken and onions on four slices. Cover chicken with remaining four slices of bread, dressing side down.
4. Brush top and bottom of bread with olive oil and place panini in grill or press and cover. Cook until bread is toasted, about 3 to 5 minutes. Remove from grill and cut each sandwich in half.
5. Serve sandwiches and celery sticks with extra blue cheese dressing.

Caramelized Onion Bliss

Ingredients
- Blue cheese
- Caramelized onions
- Sautéed pears
- Brioche or challah bread
- Butter, softened

Directions
1. Place blue cheese, caramelized onions, and sautéed pears on brioche or challah bread. Spread outside of sandwiches with butter. Cook in a pre-heated panini press 2 to 3 minutes or until golden.
2. Wine Suggestion: "The intense complexity of ingredients calls for a wine of equal complexity, but one that will complement, not compete. Leitz' Dragonstone Riesling ($16) would be a great choice, but any good-quality Spätlese or even Auslese-level Riesling would be wonderful as well. A village-level red Burgundy or an Oregon Pinot Noir such as Stoller ($21) would be fine choices for red." --Richard Robinson, Wine Director, The Wine Shop at Western Supermarket, Mountain Brook, Alabama

Cashew Nut Cheese

"This is a non-dairy 'cheese' recipe made from cashews (or cashew butter). It is a great cheese substitute and can be used on a roasted red pepper panini sandwich, a fancy ham and cheese sandwich, an artichoke heart wrap (that recipe is soon to come), etc."
Pre: 15 m | **Cook:** 15 m

Ingredients
- 2 cups unsalted roasted cashews
- 2 1/2 tablespoons vegetable oil
- 1 teaspoon white sugar (optional)
- 1/4 cup almond milk
- 2 tablespoons tahini
- 1/2 teaspoon onion powder
- 1/2 teaspoon salt (optional)
- 1/4 teaspoon garlic powder
- 1/4 teaspoon ground white pepper
- 1 red bell pepper, chopped
- 1 tablespoon lemon juice
- 1 1/2 cloves garlic, peeled
- Add all ingredients to list

Directions
1. Blend cashews, oil, and sugar together in a food processor or blender until smooth. Add almond milk, tahini, onion powder, salt, garlic powder, and white pepper; blend until well mixed. Add red bell pepper, lemon juice, and garlic and blend until creamy.

Cheddar BLT Panini

If you can't find French bread rolls, halve an 8-ounce baguette lengthwise, and cut into fourths. Serve with carrot sticks.
Serving: 4 | **Total Time:** 25 Minutes | **Hands-on:** 25 Minutes

Ingredients
- 3 center-cut bacon slices
- 2 (6-ounce) skinless, boneless chicken breast halves, halved lengthwise
- 4 cups baby spinach leaves
- 2 teaspoons balsamic vinegar
- 3 ounces reduced-fat white cheddar cheese, shredded (about 3/4 cup)
- 2 tablespoons 1/3-less-fat cream cheese

- 4 (2-ounce) French bread rolls, halved lengthwise
- 8 tomato slices
- Cooking spray

Directions

1. Heat a large skillet over medium heat. Add bacon; cook until crisp. Remove bacon from pan using a slotted spoon; crumble. Add chicken to drippings in pan; cook 2 minutes on each side or until done. Remove chicken from pan. Add baby spinach to pan; cook 30 seconds or until spinach begins to wilt, stirring constantly. Stir in balsamic vinegar.
2. Combine cheddar cheese and cream cheese in a small microwave-safe bowl. Microwave at HIGH 30 seconds or until melted; stir with a whisk until smooth. Stir in bacon. Spread cheese mixture evenly over cut sides of rolls. Divide tomatoes evenly over bottom halves of rolls; top with chicken and spinach mixture. Top sandwiches with top halves of rolls. Return pan to medium heat. Coat both sides of sandwiches with cooking spray. Add sandwiches to pan. Place a cast-iron skillet on top of sandwiches; press gently to flatten. Cook sandwiches 3 minutes on each side or until bread is toasted (leave skillet on sandwiches as they cook). Cut each sandwich in half diagonally.

Cheddar Cheese Panini

A beautiful and delicious sandwich. I like to sprinkle a little sugar over the cheese.
***Servings:** 2 | **Cook:** 5 mins | **Prep:** 5 mins | **Total Time:** 10 mins*

Ingredients
- 4 slices bread, county-style, each 1/2 inch thick
- unsalted butter, Melted for brushing
- 4 slices sharp cheddar cheese

Directions
1. Preheat an electric panini maker according to the manufacturer's instructions.
2. Brush one side of each bread slice with melted butter.
3. Lay the slices, buttered side down, on a clean work surface.
4. Place 2 slices of cheese on each of 2 bread slices.
5. Top each with one of the other bread slices, buttered side up.
6. Place the sandwiches on the preheated panini maker and cook according to the manufacturer's instructions until the bread is golden and the cheese is melted, 3 to 5 minutes.
7. Transfer the sandwiches to a cutting board and cut in half.
8. Serve immediately.
9. Serves 2.

Cheddar Cheese With Apple and Sage Panin

Servings: 2 | Cook: 5 mins | Prep: 15 mins | Total Time: 20mins

Ingredients
- 4 slices artisan walnut bread, sliced 1/2 inch thick (or sage focaccia, 4 pieces, each about 4 inches square, halved horizontally)
- 1 tablespoon walnut oil
- 2 tablespoons apple butter
- 3 ounces thinly sliced cheddar cheese
- 1 granny smith apple, unpeeled, cored, and cut into slices about 1/4-inch thick
- 1 tablespoon chopped fresh sage

Directions
1. Preheat the sandwich grill.
2. Place the bread slices, cut sides down, on a work surface; brush 1 side of each bread slice with the oil.
3. Turn and spread the unoiled side of 2 of the bread slices with apple butter, dividing it evenly.
4. Layer 1/4 of the cheese, half of the apple slices, and sage over the apple butter on each, then divide the remaining cheese on top.
5. Place the remaining 2 bread slices on top, oiled sides up, and press to pack gently.
6. Place the panini in the grill, close the top plate, and cook until the bread is golden and toasted, the cheese is melted, and the apple is warmed through and just beginning to soften, 3-5 minutes.
7. Cut each sandwich in half on the diagonal and serve right away.

Cheesesteak Panini

A great way to combine two of my favorite sandwiches.
Servings: 1 | Cook: 10 mins | Prep: 10 mins | Total Time: 20mins

Ingredients
- 6 ounces Steak-ums or 6 ounces shaved rib eye steaks
- 2 slices French bread (thin large oval slices)
- 2 ounces provolone cheese or 2 ounces American cheese or 2 ounces Cheese Whiz
- 1/2 cup sliced onions (or a combination) or 1/2 cup mushrooms (or a combination) or 1/2 cup green pepper (or a combination)
- 2 -3 tablespoons butter

- salt (to taste)
- pepper (to taste)
- banana peppers (optional) or pickle (optional)

Directions
1. Saute the vegetables in half the butter on a stove top griddle until soft, then top with the thinly sliced steaks, cooking until cooked through, seasoning to taste with salt and pepper.
2. Place cheese on bread with steak and veggie mix and top with peppers or pickles if you like.
3. Place bread slices together, butter each outer side and place on a panini maker, George Foreman grill, or griddle with bacon press.
4. Grill sandwich until outside is crisp and golden, turning if you make it on the stove top griddle.

Chicken Avocado & Cheese Panini

A great lunchtime recipe. Really nice to enjoy with a cool glass of white wine! I usually make this with the panini bread or a herb focaccia as it toasts really well.
Servings: 2 | **Cook:** 10 mins | **Prep:** 10 mins | **Total Time:** 20mins

Ingredients
- 2 focaccia rolls
- 2 roasted chicken breast
- brie cheese
- 1/2 cup of semi sun-dried tomato
- 1/2 ripe avocado
- mayonnaise
- salt
- pepper

Directions
1. Cut your focaccia or Turkish bread to size.
2. Slice open the middle.
3. Spread mayonnaise on the base of both slices of your bread roll.
4. Top with chicken, slices of brie cheese, semi sun-dried tomatoes and avocado, in that order.
5. Salt and pepper to taste.
6. Toast using a sandwich grill toasting machine or George Foreman grill until cooked.

Chocolate Panini

"This hot treat is quick and easy to make. Just pick up a loaf of ciabatta or French bread and some bittersweet chocolate from the grocery store."
Pre: 5 m | **Cook:** 5 m | **Ready In:** 10 m

Ingredients
- 1 (1 ounce) square bittersweet chocolate, chopped
- 2 slices ciabatta bread
- Add all ingredients to list

Directions
1. Preheat a panini press according to manufacturer's instructions.
2. Sprinkle the chopped chocolate onto one slice of the ciabatta, then place the other slice on top.
3. Cook the panini in the preheated press until the ciabatta is golden brown and the chocolate has melted, 3 to 4 minutes.

Curried Cheese and Peach Panini

Cottage cheese makes for creamy, delicious, low-fat sandwiches. Try them with slices pears or apples as well.
Prep: 30 mins | **Total Time:** 30mins

Ingredients
- 2 cups cottage cheese, low-fat
- 1 teaspoon curry powder
- 1/2 teaspoon ginger, ground
- 1/4 teaspoon lime zest, grated
- 1 stalk celery, finely diced
- 1 green onion, thinly sliced
- 10 ounces baguette, preferably sourdough, cut into 4 sandwich lengths
- 1/2 cup mango chutney (optional)
- 1 large peach, peeled and thinly sliced
- 1/2 cup sliced almonds

Directions
1. Stir together cottage cheese, curry powder, ginger, and lime zest in medium bowl. Fold in celery and green onion. Set aside.

2. Split baguette lengths, leaving one side attached. Remove some of the soft centers of bread to make room for filling. Spread 2 Tbs chutney, if using, on top and bottom of bread. Fill each sandwich with 1/2 cup cottage cheese mixture, 4 peach slices, and 2 Tbs almonds.
3. Spray panini with cooking spray. Coat skillet or grill pan with cooking spray and heat over medium heat. Place panini in pan; weight with smaller-diameter saucepan weighted with 2 cans. Cook 2 minutes. Flip, replace weight, and cook 2 minutes more.

Double Decker Bologna Cheese Panini

This is something I came up with after seeing another with minced meat and cheese. I like lots of meat, so I put meat and cheese on both sides.
Servings: 1 | **Cook:** 5 mins | **Prep:** 5 mins | **Total Time:** 10mins

Ingredients
- 2 slices bologna
- 2 slices cheese, American
- 3 slices bread
- 1 tablespoon mayonnaise
- 1/4 teaspoon sriracha sauce
- 1 tablespoon butter, softened
- lettuce (optional)

Directions
1. Combine mayo and sriracha. Spread 2 slices of bread on one side with sriracha/mayo. Lay 1 slice bologna and 1 slice of cheese on mayo side. Add lettuce, if using.
2. Butter remaining slice of bread on both sides. Stack with buttered slice in between slices with meat and cheese.
3. Place in panini maker or skillet until browned on both sides. In skillet, you will need to flip.

English Muffin Panini With Goat Cheese a

Prep: 30 mins | **Total Time:** 30mins

Ingredients
- 4 English muffins, split and toasted
- 3 tablespoons pesto sauce, prepared

- 4 ounces goat cheese
- 4 slices tomatoes, large
- 8 leaves radicchio

Directions
1. Spread toasted side of each English muffin half with pesto. Spread cheese over 4 English muffin halves; top with tomato slices, radicchio, and remaining English muffin halves.
2. Spray panini with cooking spray. Coat skillet or grill pan with cooking spray and heat over medium heat. Place panini in pan; weight with smaller-diameter saucepan weighted with 2 cans. Cook 2 minutes. Flip, replace weight, and cook 2 minutes more.

Four Cheese Panini With Basil Tomatoes

Panini with 4 Italian cheeses and tomatoes with basil....grilled cheese will never be the same again!
Servings: 4 | **Cook:** 6 mins | **Prep:** 10 mins | **Total Time:** 16mins

Ingredients
- 1/2 cup shredded fresh mozzarella cheese (3 ounces)
- 1/2 cup shredded Fontina cheese (4 ounces)
- 3 tablespoons asiago cheese (freshly grated) or 3 tablespoons parmesan cheese (freshly grated)
- 1/2 cup shredded provolone cheese (3 ounces)
- 8 slices tomatoes, thinly sliced
- 1 tablespoon fresh basil, chopped
- 4 ciabatta rolls, halved lengthwise (spread outsides with butter) or 8 slices firm white bread (spread outsides with butter)
- 8 arugula leaves (optional, but recommended)

Directions
1. In a small bowl, combine cheeses. Spread the cheese on the bottoms of the ciabatta rolls. Top with tomato slices and brush with olive oil. Sprinkle with basil and add 2 arugula leaves and close the panini.
2. Set a large cast-iron skillet or griddle over moderately high heat. Arrange the panini in skillet and weight them down with a smaller pan (can fill with water if you need more weight). Cook the panini until the outside is crisp and the cheese is melted, 3 minutes per side.
3. Cut panini in half and serve at once.

Four Cheese Panini

Servings: 2 | Cook: 4 mins | Prep: 20 mins | Total Time: 24mins

Ingredients
- 4 slices sourdough bread (1-inch thick slices)
- 1 tablespoon olive oil
- 2 ounces mozzarella cheese, thinly sliced
- 2 ounces smoked cheddar cheese, thinly sliced
- 2 ounces Fontina cheese, thinly sliced
- 2 ounces provolone cheese, thinly sliced

Directions
1. Preheat panini grill to high.
2. Brush one side of each bread slice with oil.
3. Place two slices on a work surface, oiled side down, and evenly layer with mozzarella, Cheddar, fontina, and provolone.
4. Cover with top halves, oiled side up, and press gently to pack.
5. Place sandwiches in grill, close top plate and cook until golden brown, 3-4 minutes.
6. Serve immediately.

Greek Grilled Cheese

"A Greek influenced spin on the great American classic grilled cheese. Simple, easy and soooo scrumptious. Great with pita chips and hummus. Add bell pepper, or substitute your favorite bread or cheese. These are also delicious cooked on a panini grill."
Pre: 5 m | Cook: 5 m | Ready In: 10 m

Ingredients
- 1 1/2 teaspoons butter, softened
- 2 slices whole wheat bread, or your favorite bread
- 2 tablespoons crumbled feta cheese
- 2 slices Cheddar cheese
- 1 tablespoon chopped red onion
- 1/4 tomato, thinly sliced
- Add all ingredients to list

Directions

1. Heat a skillet over medium heat. Butter one side of each slice of bread. On the non buttered side of one slice, layer the feta cheese, Cheddar cheese, red onion and tomato. Top with the other slice of bread with the butter side out.
2. Fry the sandwich until golden brown on each side, about 2 minutes per side. The second side always cooks faster.

Grilled Cheese & Honey Panini Recipe

Servings: 1 | Cook: 5 mins | Prep: 5 mins | Total Time: 10mins

Ingredients

- 1 -2 slice raclette cheese, 1/8th of an inch thick
- 1 -2 teaspoon honey (to taste)
- butter, melted
- 2 slices French bread

Directions

1. Preheat panini grill to medium-high heat (375 degrees).
2. Brush melted butter onto outer sides of each slice of bread. Spread a thin layer of honey on the inside of one slice of bread. Top with slices of raclette (enough to cover bread, about 1/8" thick). Place the other slice of bread on top, buttered side up.
3. Grill sandwich for 3 minutes until cheese is melted and golden grill marks appear. Serve immediately and enjoy!

Grilled Cheese & Tomato Panini

Love this simple panini! You don't need a panini grill to make this recipe.
Servings: 8 | Cook: 10 mins | Prep: 5 mins | Total Time: 15mins

Ingredients

- 8 slices whole-grain bread
- 8 slices cheddar cheese
- 1 medium tomatoes, sliced

Directions

1. Coat a stovetop ridged grill pan or large nonstick skillet with nonstick cooking spray; heat over medium-high.

2. Meanwhile, assemble panini; lay slices of bread on cutting board; top each with a slice of Cheddar.
3. Place a tomato slice on top of 4 slices of cheese.
4. Assemble to make 4 sandwiches.
5. Cook 3-4 minutes, turning once halfway through.
6. Press down with a spatula until cheese melts.

Grilled Cheese Panini

Servings: 1 | Cook: 15 mins | Prep: 5 mins | Total Time: 20mins

Ingredients
- 1 loaf ciabatta (Italian bread)
- 1 1/2 ounces grated grana padana parmigiano
- 1 1/2 ounces grated Cacio di Roma cheese (mild sheep's mild cheese from Rome)
- 1 1/2 ounces grated crotonese cheese (ewe's milk cheese from Calabria)
- 1 teaspoon truffle oil, drizzled

Directions
1. Grill panini press at about 250°F for about five minutes.
2. Be patient so all the cheese melts evenly.
3. Then add cracked black pepper, pinch of Kosher salt and finish with truffle oil.
4. NOTE: Don't cook with the truffle oil, it's much better to finish with it.

Grilled Cheese Skillet Panini

A gooey, golden-crisp grilled cheese sandwich is the perfect partner to our Creamy Roasted Tomato Soup. We lean on reduced-fat cheddar but add a little canola mayo to stretch the cheese and encourage extra meltiness for a mixture that has 50% less sat fat than regular cheddar and saves 190mg sodium over processed American cheese.
Serving: 4 | Total Time: 11 Minutes | Hands-on: 11 Minutes

Ingredients
- 1 tablespoon canola mayonnaise
- 1 teaspoon Dijon mustard
- 4 ounces 2% reduced-fat shredded extra-sharp cheddar cheese (about 1 cup)
- 1/8 teaspoon freshly ground black pepper
- 8 (1-ounce) slices whole-grain bread

- 2 teaspoons olive oil, divided oil, divided

Directions
1. Combine mayonnaise and mustard in a medium bowl. Add cheese and pepper, stirring well to combine (mixture will be very thick). Spread one-fourth of cheese mixture (about 2 tablespoons) over each of 4 bread slices. Top with remaining 4 bread slices.
2. Heat a large skillet over medium heat. Add 1 teaspoon oil to pan; swirl to coat. Place sandwiches in pan; cook 3 minutes or until lightly browned (do not flip). Remove sandwiches from pan. Add remaining 1 teaspoon oil to pan; swirl to coat. Turn sandwiches over, and add to pan; cook 3 minutes or until lightly browned and cheese melts. Serve immediately.

Grilled Cheese Tomato Panini With Crispy

OH BOY, OH BOY! Tried these for lunch today, they are so good! We thought we would share one of these for lunch, but had to make a second one, it was just too good! (I will try fresh tomatoes next time, although the canned were great.) from the local newspaper.

Servings: 1 | **Cook:** 5 mins | **Prep:** 10 mins | **Total Time:** 15mins

Ingredients
- 2 slices thickly cut sourdough bread or 1 submarine roll, with some of the inside removed
- 1/2 cup shredded or sliced sharp cheddar cheese
- 1/2 cup whole peeled canned tomatoes, drained and halved lengthwise or 2 large tomatoes
- 1/2 medium tart apple, such as granny smith, unpeeled and sliced thinly
- vegetable oil or olive oil, for spraying pan

Directions
1. Sprinkle half of cheese evenly over one of bread slices.
2. Arrange tomato halves over cheese, covering bread slices evenly.
3. Top with apple slices.
4. Sprinkle with remainder of cheese.
5. Top with remaining bread slice.
6. Heat a non stick sauté pan and spray lightly with veggie oil.
7. Place sandwich in pan and weigh top down by pressing a plate over sandwich,topped with a can.
8. Sauté over low heat 3 to 4 minutes.
9. Turn sandwich over and repeat process until bread is golden brown and cheese is melted.
10. Slice in two and serve immediately.

Grilled Goat Cheese and Strawberry Sandwiches

Time: 15 minutes. Sarah Van Winkle credits a sandwich from Half & Half cafe, in Portland, Oregon, with inspiring her version. She calls it "unexpectedly delicious." Van Winkle cooks them in a panini press, but we found that using a frying pan reduces the tendency of the strawberry juices to bleed.
Serving: 2

Ingredients
- 2 tablespoons softened butter
- 4 slices levain (or other hearty, rustic bread)
- 3 ounces fresh goat cheese, preferably from a local dairy
- 6 large strawberries, sliced thin
- 8 to 12 basil leaves

Directions
1. Butter 1 side of each bread slice. Generously spread goat cheese on unbuttered side of 2 slices and cook them, cheese side up, until golden underneath, about 2 minutes. Layer with strawberries and basil. Top with remaining bread slices, buttered side up; turn over and cook until golden, about 2 minutes.
2. Note: Nutritional analysis is per sandwich.

Ham and Cheese Panini

Servings: 4 | Cook: 16 mins | Prep: 30 mins | Total Time: 46mins

Ingredients
- 8 ounces loaf whole-grain Italian bread
- 2 tablespoons balsamic vinegar
- 12 radicchio, leaves
- 16 large basil leaves
- 4 ounces thinly sliced prosciutto
- 4 slices provolone cheese (1 oz. each)
- 1/4 teaspoon fresh ground black pepper
- 2 teaspoons olive oil
- cooking spray

Directions
1. Slice the bread loaf in half lengthwise; scoop out the bread to remove the soft inner portion and discard.
2. Slice the loaf crosswise into 4 equal-size pieces.
3. Drizzle the inside of each roll with 1 1/2 teaspoons balsamic vinegar.
4. Layer 3 radicchio leaves, 4 basil leaves, 1/4 of the prosciutto, and 1 slice provolone cheese in each roll.
5. Sprinkle with the pepper; close the rolls and brush each panini with 1/2 teaspoon of the olive oil.
6. Heat a heavy cast-iron skillet or other skillet over med-high heat and spray with the cooking spray.
7. Place 2 sandwiches in the skillet and weigh them down with another skillet or panini weight.
8. Toast until the cheese begins to melt and the bread is browned and toasted on the edges, 3-4 minutes.
9. Flip the sandwiches and toast for an additional 2-3 minutes.
10. Remove from pan and slice in half; repeat with the remaining 2 sandwiches.

Ham Cheese and Apple Panini

If you don't have a panini press, you can make these easy sandwiches in a nonstick skillet, much like you make grilled cheese sandwiches.
Serving: 4

Ingredients
- 1 tablespoon apple jelly
- 1/4 cup Dijon mustard
- 8 (1-ounce) slices gluten-free bread
- 8 slices lower-sodium deli ham (6 ounces) {Check for Gluten}
- 4 (0.8-ounce) cheddar cheese or cheddar-flavored nondairy slices
- 1 Granny Smith apple, cored and cut into 24 thin slices
- Butter-flavored cooking spray

Directions
1. Preheat panini press.
2. Microwave jelly at HIGH 10 seconds or until it melts. Combine jelly and mustard; spread mixture evenly over 1 side of 4 bread slices. Layer 2 ham slices, 1 cheese slice, and 6 apple slices over mustard mixture on each bread slice; top evenly with remaining bread slices.
3. Coat sandwiches with cooking spray. Add sandwiches, 2 at a time, to panini press; grill 2 minutes or until toasted.

Herbed Grilled Cheese and Pork Sandwiches

"A perfect grilled cheese with our favorite pork tenderloin added. This tasty sandwich will be sure to leave your mouth watering for more."
Pre: *10 m* | **Cook:** *35 m* | **Ready In:** *45 m*

Ingredients
- 1 Smithfield® Rosemary & Olive Oil Seasoned Pork Tenderloin
- 8 slices sandwich bread
- 2 tablespoons olive oil
- 1/4 cup mayonnaise
- 4 teaspoons capers
- 1/2 teaspoon lemon pepper
- 2 cups baby arugula
- 4 slices Havarti cheese with dill
- Add all ingredients to list

Directions
1. Roast pork according to package directions (takes approximately 30 minutes). Slice meat very thin.
2. Heat panini sandwich press, waffle iron, or skillet, depending on how you will cook your sandwiches.
3. In a small bowl, stir together mayonnaise, capers and lemon pepper.
4. Lightly brush one side of each slice of bread with olive oil. Spread the opposite side of four slices of bread with the mayonnaise mixture.
5. For each sandwich, layer arugula leaves, sliced pork and Havarti on top of mayonnaise mixture. Top with another slice of bread without mayo. (Olive oil should be facing OUT.)
6. Place each sandwich in hot sandwich press or skillet. Cook until bread is toasted and cheese is melted, flipping if necessary. Cut in half and serve immediately.

Honey Dijon Turkey and Cheese Panini

Servings: *2* | **Cook:** *4 mins* | **Prep:** *15 mins* | **Total Time:** *19mins*

Ingredients
- 4 slices sourdough bread (1/2-inch thick slices)
- 1 tablespoon olive oil
- 1 tablespoon honey dijon mustard
- 4 ounces smoked turkey breast, sliced

- 4 ounces provolone cheese, thinly sliced

Directions
1. Brush one side of each bread slice with oil.
2. Place on a work surface, oiled side down, spread with mustard.
3. On bottom halves, evenly layer with turkey and cheese, alternating layers of each.
4. Cover with top halves and press gently to pack.
5. Place sandwiches in preheated panini grill; close the top plate and cook until golden brown, 3-4 minutes.
6. Serve immediately.

Hot Buttery Brie Melts

If you don't have a panini press, place sandwiches in a hot skillet over medium heat. Press sandwiches with a cast-iron skillet or other heavy weight, and cook 3 minutes on each side or until golden brown.
Serving: 4

Ingredients
- 1 (8-oz.) Brie round or wedge
- 1 (12-oz.) French baguette
- 1/2 cup jalapeño jelly
- 1 tablespoon chopped fresh cilantro

Directions
1. Trim and discard rind from Brie. Cut Brie into 1/4-inch-thick slices, and set aside.
2. Cut baguette into 4 equal pieces; halve pieces lengthwise.
3. Heat jelly in a microwave-safe bowl at HIGH 2 minutes. Stir in cilantro. Spread mixture evenly on cut sides of each bread slice. Layer 4 bread slices, jelly sides up, evenly with Brie; top with remaining bread slices, jelly sides down.
4. Cook sandwiches, in batches, in a preheated panini press 3 minutes or until grill marks appear and cheese melts.

Italain Grilled Cheese Sandwich Panini

Mmmm... mozzarella! Try this grilled cheese sandwich with the Italian twist! If you haven't tried it before, pesto is one of the best condiments to use on a hot sandwich. Instead of cooking the sandwiches in a skillet, you can use your panini press just as easily. This recipe is from a Canadian cheese magazine. Enjoy!

Servings: 4 | Cook: 10 mins | Prep: 15 mins | Total Time: 25mins

Ingredients
- 4 panini bread
- 6 1/2 ounces mozzarella cheese, sliced
- 1/4 cup fresh parmesan cheese, grated
- 1/4 cup pesto sauce
- 2 grilled bell peppers, sliced (from the jar or homemade)

Directions
1. Slice paninis in half. Spread pesto onto each half.
2. Evenly distribute both cheeses and peppers on four bottom halves and top with four top halves.
3. Heat skillet over medium-low heat.
4. Cook sandwiches approximately 5 minutes on each side while applying pressure to flatten them.
5. Sandwich is ready when bread is browned and cheese is melted.

Melted Cheese Panini With Mustard and Honey

Source: Rick Tramonto's Osteria I haven't tried this yet but it sounds delicious! The author states that smoked mozzarella can be substituted for the Burrata or Scamorza cheese if they cannot be found.
Servings: 4 | Cook: 10 mins | Prep: 0 mins | Total Time: 10mins

Ingredients
- 4 tablespoons whole grain mustard
- 8 thick slices ciabatta
- 6 ounces scamorza cheese
- 4 ounces burrata cheese
- 4 ounces Fontina cheese
- 1 ounce parmigiano reggianno cheese, shaved
- kosher salt and black pepper, to taste
- 2 tablespoons unsalted butter, softened
- 1 teaspoon olive oil
- 2 tablespoons honey

Directions
1. Preheat a panin press to medium-high (375 degrees).
2. Spread mustard on one side of each slice of bread. Top 4 of the slices with 2 slices Scamorza, 1 slice Burrata, and 1 slice fontina. Sprinkle parmigiano

evenly between the 4 sandwiches. Sprinkle with salt and pepper and top with remaining bread slices, mustard side down.
3. Brush butter over both sides of the sandwiches. Grill on press for 5-7 minutes, until golden brown and cheese starts to melt.
4. Cut sandwiches and drizzle with honey before serving.

Mozzarella Raspberry and Brown Sugar Panini

Serving: 8

Ingredients
- 1/4 cup olive oil
- 8 (1/2-inch-thick) slices bakery-style white bread
- 1/2 cup raspberry jam
- 2 teaspoons chopped fresh rosemary
- 8 ounces fresh mozzarella cheese, drained and patted dry
- Salt (optional)
- 2 tablespoons light brown sugar

Directions
1. Preheat panini press or grill pan.
2. Using a pastry brush, brush oil on both sides of bread. Spread jam evenly over 1 side of each slice of bread; sprinkle with rosemary. Cut mozzarella into 8 slices; place 2 slices of cheese on each of 4 bread slices. Sprinkle a pinch of salt over cheese, if desired; top with remaining 4 slices of bread, jam side down. Sprinkle tops with brown sugar.
3. Grill panini in a panini press until cheese has melted and bread is golden and crispy (about 3 minutes). If you do not have a panini press or indoor grill, use a ridged grill pan: Put sandwiches in pan (in batches, if necessary); place a weight, such as a brick wrapped in aluminum foil or a heavy cast-iron skillet, on top to press them down. Brown the first side (about 2-3 minutes), flip the sandwich, replace the weight, and brown the other side (about 2-3 minutes) to finish melting the cheese. Cut paninis in half; serve.

O M G Pimento Cheese Panini

Servings: 2 | Cook: 4 mins | Prep: 15 mins | Total Time: 19mins

Ingredients
- 1 (4 ounce) jar chopped pimiento, drained
- 1 cup shredded mild cheddar cheese

- 1 cup shredded monterey jack cheese
- 1/3 cup mayonnaise
- 1/2 teaspoon fresh ground black pepper
- 1/4 teaspoon salt
- 1/4 teaspoon garlic powder
- 1/4 teaspoon paprika
- 4 slices sourdough bread (1/2-inch thick)
- 1 tablespoon butter, melted

Directions
1. Preheat panini grill to high.
2. In a bowl, combine the pimentos, Cheddar, Monterey Jack, mayonnaise, pepper, salt, garlic powder, and paprika; taste and adjust seasoning, if needed.
3. Brush one side of each bread slice with butter.
4. Place two slices on a work surface, buttered side down, and spread evenly with pimento cheese.
5. Cover with top halves, buttered side up, and press gently to pack.
6. Place sandwiches in grill, close the top plate and cook until golden brown, 3-4 minutes.
7. Serve immediately.

Panini With Chocolate and Brie

This recipe is by Giada De Laurentiis. You could also use a George foreman grill if you do not have a panini maker.
Servings: 6 | **Cook:** 15 mins | **Prep:** 25 mins | **Total Time:** 40mins

Ingredients
- 12 slices sourdough bread
- 1/3 cup extra virgin olive oil
- 12 ounces brie cheese, thinly sliced
- 12 ounces semi-sweet chocolate chips
- 1/3 cup fresh basil leaves, thinly sliced

Directions
1. Preheat the panini grill.
2. Brush both sides of the bread with olive oil. Grill the bread slices until they begin to turn golden, about 1 to 2 minutes.
3. Remove from the panini grill and place 2 ounces of cheese on 1 slice of bread (the bottom half), top the cheese with 1/3 cup chocolate chips, and a sprinkle of basil.

4. Top with another slice of bread.
5. Continue with the remaining sandwiches.
6. Return the sandwiches to the panini grill until the chocolate begins to melt, about another 2 minutes.
7. Cut the sandwiches into 2-inch wide rectangles or small triangles and transfer to a serving platter.

Panini With Sautéed Mushrooms and Gruyère

A great option for a meatless meal, this grilled panini sandwich features sautéed mushrooms, roasted red peppers, and gruyére cheese.
Serving: 4

Ingredients
- 1 tablespoon butter
- 1 (8-ounce) package mushrooms, sliced
- 4 teaspoons Dijon mustard
- 8 (1-ounce) slices whole wheat bread
- 1/2 of 1 (10-ounce) bag fresh spinach
- 1/4 cup sliced roasted red bell peppers
- 1/4 cup chopped onion
- 1 cup shredded Gruyère cheese
- 2 tablespoons butter, melted

Directions
1. Heat butter in large nonstick skillet over medium-high heat. Add mushrooms; sauté 5-6 minutes.
2. Spread mustard on 4 slices of bread; layer each with 6 spinach leaves, 1 tablespoon pepper, 1 tablespoon onion, 1/4 cup cheese, and 1/4 cup mushrooms. Top with remaining bread.
3. Brush melted butter over both sides of each sandwich. If using a skillet, heat a large nonstick skillet over medium-high heat; place sandwich- es in pan. Place another skillet on top of sandwiches; cook 2-3 minutes on each side until golden brown and cheese is melted. If using a panini maker, brush sandwiches with butter; place in machine, close, and cook 2 minutes or until done.

Peanut Butter and Chocolate Panini

"This panini can be grilled in a pan or put in a panini grill. Press the sandwiches with a heavy object of cooking in a pan. It is very versatile and great for a quick snack or a dessert that will leave everyone wanting more!"

Pre: 10 m | Cook: 15 m | Ready In: 25 m

Ingredients
- 1 teaspoon butter
- 1/2 cup crunchy peanut butter
- 8 slices firm bread
- 1/2 cup semi-sweet chocolate chips
- Add all ingredients to list

Directions
1. Preheat a panini press according to manufacturer's instructions to medium-low heat. Coat inside surfaces with butter.
2. Spread 1 to 2 tablespoons peanut butter onto half the bread slices; cover peanut butter with 1 to 2 tablespoons chocolate chips. Top each with a second slice of bread, creating 4 sandwiches.
3. Grill each sandwich in the panini press until bread is toasted and chocolate is melted, 2 to 4 minutes.

Peppery Turkey and Brie Panini

This panini has the perfect combo of sweet and spicy flavors.
Serving: 8

Ingredients
- 1 (15-oz.) Brie round
- 16 multigrain sourdough bread slices
- 2 pounds thinly sliced smoked turkey
- 1/2 cup red pepper jelly
- 2 tablespoons melted butter

Directions
1. Trim and discard rind from Brie. Cut Brie into 1/2-inch-thick slices. Layer 8 bread slices evenly with turkey and Brie.
2. Spread 1 Tbsp. pepper jelly on 1 side of each remaining 8 bread slices; place, jelly sides down, onto Brie. Brush sandwiches with melted butter.
3. Cook sandwiches, in batches, in a preheated panini press 2 to 3 minutes or until golden brown.
4. Note: For testing purposes only, we used Braswell's Red Pepper Jelly.

Pimento Cheese Panini

Cook: 0 mins | Prep: 30 mins | Total Time: 30mins

Ingredients
- 8 ounces cheddar cheese, grated (reduced fat is fine)
- 1/4 cup mayonnaise
- 1 (4 ounce) jar diced pimentos, drained
- 1 teaspoon cumin, ground
- 1/2 teaspoon chili powder
- 1/4 teaspoon cayenne pepper
- 12 slices sandwich bread, pumpernickel
- 1 zucchini, med, thinly sliced

Directions
1. Stir together cheddar, mayo, pimientos, cumin, chili powder, and cayenne in a bowl. Spread cheese mixture on six slices of bread; top with zucchini and remaining bread slices.
2. Spray panini with cooking spray. Coat skillet or grill pan with cooking spray and heat over medium heat. Place panini in pan; weight with smaller-diameter saucepan weighted with 2 cans. Cook 2 minutes. Flip, replace weight, and cook 2 minutes more.

Portabella and Asiago Cheese Panini

A hearty panini recipe for winter
Servings: 3-4 | Cook: 5 mins | Prep: 10 mins | Total Time: 15mins

Ingredients
- 1/2 lb portabella mushroom
- 1/3 cup olive oil
- 1/2 garlic clove, minced
- 2 1/2 tablespoons lime juice (lemon also works)
- 1 teaspoon fresh rosemary, chopped (or 1/2 teaspoon dried)
- 4 ciabatta, sliced in half or 8 slices of any dense bread
- 1 1/2 teaspoons salt
- 1 teaspoon pepper
- 6 teaspoons pesto sauce
- 7 ounces asiago cheese or 7 ounces cheese, of your choice
- 1 1/2 tablespoons balsamic vinegar (pomegranate infused vinegar also works, for a sweet taste)

Directions

1. Preheat oven to 400°F.
2. Combine Oil, Vinegar, Lime juice, Salt, Pepper, Garlic, and Rosemary. Mix well.
3. Gently slice washed mushrooms into 1/2 inch thick slices.
4. Pour oil and vinegar mixture over mushroom slices, and toss well. Allow to sit for 5 minutes or more. The longer you allow this to sit, the more flavorful the mushrooms will be.
5. Spread mushrooms in a single layer on a baking tray or sheet, sprinkle with more salt and pepper if desired. Roast for about 10 minutes, untill the slices are soft but still whole.
6. Toast bread lightly, this step can be omitted if using a very dense bread such as ciabatta, but I still prefer it.
7. Turn on broiler and allow to heat.
8. Spread pesto over bread, about 1 1/2 teaspoons per roll.
9. Distribute mushroom mixture evenly on to half of the sliced bread, leaving the other half aside to place on top later.
10. Cover mushroom mixture with cheese, and place under broiler until cheese is melted.
11. Cover melted cheese with the tops of the sandwiches, and serve.

Portabella Panini With Gorgonzola Cheese

Panini without bread! I recently got a panini maker and am excited to find some healthier recipes to make with it, such as this one from Ellie Krieger's Healthy Appetite T.V. show. For the Valentine's episode she cut the portobellos with heart-shaped cookie cutters. You don't need a panini maker for this recipe!
Cook: *10 mins |* **Prep:** *15 mins |* **Total Time:** *25 mins*

Ingredients

- 4 sun-dried tomatoes (not oil-packed)
- 4 portabella mushroom caps (about 2 ounces each)
- 1/4 cup crumbled gorgonzola
- 1 tablespoon olive oil
- 1 teaspoon olive oil
- salt and pepper

Directions

1. Reconstitute the sun-dried tomatoes by soaking them in boiling water for 10 minutes. Remove the tomatoes from the water and chop them.
2. Slice the stems off of the mushrooms so they can lay completely flat. Slice each cap in half so you have 8 round mushroom slices.

3. Top half of the mushrooms with 1 tablespoon of tomatoes and 1 tablespoon of cheese. Top with remaining mushroom slices. Brush the top side of each "sandwich" with olive oil.
4. Preheat a large, nonstick skillet or grill pan. Place the mushroom sandwiches in the pan carefully, oil side down, and cook for 2 minutes. Brush the top half with oil, flip, and cook for 2 minutes more. Season with salt and pepper, to taste, and serve.

Prosciutto and Fontina Panini

Serving: 2

Ingredients
- 1 (5.25-ounce) package focaccia (Italian flatbread) or 1 (8-ounce) package Italian cheese-flavored pizza crust (such as Boboli)
- 8 very thin slices prosciutto (about 2 ounces)
- 1/4 cup (1 ounce) shredded fontina cheese
- 1 cup trimmed arugula or watercress
- 2 (1/8-inch-thick) red onion slices, separated into rings
- 2 teaspoons balsamic vinegar
- 1/8 teaspoon pepper

Directions
1. Slice each bread round in half horizontally. Divide prosciutto slices between bottom halves of bread, and top each bread half with fontina cheese, arugula, and red onion slices. Drizzle balsamic vinegar over sandwiches, and sprinkle with pepper; cover with top halves of bread. Wrap sandwiches tightly in aluminum foil, and bake at 300° for 15 minutes.

Prosciutto and Smoked Gouda Panini

You'll need to cook the panini in batches; keep cooked panini warm in a 250° oven. The sandwiches make hearty lunch fare on their own, or serve them with a tossed green salad or Chicken, Chickpea, and Zucchini Stew.
Serving: 10

Ingredients
- 20 (1-ounce) slices Italian bread
- Cooking spray
- 6 ounces smoked Gouda cheese, thinly sliced

- 6 ounces thinly sliced prosciutto

Directions
1. Coat 1 side of each bread slice with cooking spray. Place 10 bread slices, coated sides down, on a work surface. Divide cheese and prosciutto evenly among 10 bread slices. Top with remaining bread slices, coated sides up.
2. Heat a large nonstick skillet over medium heat. Cook panini 5 minutes on each side or until lightly browned and cheese melts, pressing with a spatula to flatten.

Prosciutto Fontina and Fig Panini

If you don't have a panini grill, place sandwiches in a grill pan or large nonstick skillet coated with cooking spray over medium heat. Cover sandwiches with foil, and top with a heavy skillet. Cook 2 to 3 minutes on each side or until golden brown

***Serving:** 4 | **Prep:** 7 Minutes | **Cook:** 3 Minutes*

Ingredients
- 8 (0.9-ounce) slices crusty Chicago-style Italian bread
- 4 ounces very thinly sliced prosciutto
- 1 1/4 cups (4 ounces) shredded fontina cheese
- 1/2 cup baby arugula leaves
- 1/4 cup fig preserves
- Olive oil-flavored cooking spray

Directions
1. Preheat panini grill.
2. Top each of 4 bread slices evenly with prosciutto, fontina cheese, and arugula. Spread 1 tablespoon fig preserves evenly over 1 side of each of remaining 4 bread slices; top sandwiches with remaining bread slices. Coat outsides of sandwiches with cooking spray. Place sandwiches on panini grill; cook 3 to 4 minutes or until golden and cheese is melted. Cut panini in half before serving, if desired.

Provolone Panini Sandwiches

If you don't have a panini maker, warm the sandwiches in a grill pan over medium heat. Place a skillet or large saucepan as a weight over sandwiches as they cook. Cook 3 minutes on each side or until golden brown and cheese melts.
***Serving:** 2*

Ingredients
- 4 (1.1-ounce) slices firm white sandwich bread (such as Pepperidge Farm)
- 1 tablespoon light Caesar dressing
- 4 (0.5-ounce) slices light provolone cheese
- 1/2 cup bottled roasted red bell pepper strips, drained
- 8 large basil leaves

Directions
1. Lightly brush 1 side of each bread slice with dressing. Place 2 bread slices, dressing side down, on a sheet of wax paper; top each with 1 slice cheese. Arrange bell pepper strips and basil evenly over cheese slices. Top with remaining 2 slices of cheese and bread slices, placing bread with the dressing side up.
2. . Cook sandwiches in a preheated panini maker or waffle iron for 3 minutes or until golden brown and cheese melts.

Roasted Red Pepper and Cheese Sandwich

"I came up with this sandwich one afternoon when I was trying to clear out the fridge of some odds and ends. It came out so good that now I make this all the time! The cheese makes a big difference. You can leave off the lettuce and grill this for a delicious panini style hot sandwich."
Pre: 10 m | **Cook:** 10 m

Ingredients
- 2 teaspoons mayonnaise
- 1/2 teaspoon Ranch dressing
- 2 (1 inch thick) slices French bread
- 1 slice smoked fontina cheese
- 1 slice Havarti cheese
- 1/4 cup jarred roasted red pepper, drained and chopped
- 1 pepperoncini, sliced
- 3 slices dill pickle (optional)
- 1 leaf leaf lettuce
- Add all ingredients to list

Directions
1. Stir together the mayonnaise and Ranch dressing, and spread onto one slice of bread. Place the fontina and Havarti cheese slices on the bread, then top with roasted red pepper, pepperoncini, pickle and lettuce. Top with the other slice of bread.

Salty Sweet Bacon Panini

Ingredients
- Brie
- bacon
- Raisin-walnut bread
- Apple butter
- Butter, softened

Directions
1. Place Brie and bacon on raisin-walnut bread spread with apple butter. Spread outside of sandwiches with butter. Cook in a pre-heated panini press 2 to 3 minutes or until golden.
2. Wine Suggestion: "For white, try a Chenin Blanc, such as Champalou Vouvray from the Loire Valley ($17) or a California version such as Ballentine Vineyards ($17). If you just have to have red, then try Beaujolais or California Pinot Noir." --Richard Robinson, Wine Director, The Wine Shop at Western Supermarket, Mountain Brook, Alabama

Spinach Apple and Cheese Panini Sandwi

Servings: 4 | Cook: 22 mins | Total Time: 22mins

Ingredients
- 1 teaspoon extra virgin olive oil
- 1 cup sliced yellow onion (or about 1/2 a large onion)
- 1 large ambrosia apple, thinly sliced and tossed with juice of 1 lime
- 1 cup spinach leaves, stems removed
- 4 ounces low-fat Swiss cheese, thinly sliced into 4 slices
- 8 slices whole wheat sourdough bread or 4 ciabatta rolls

Directions
1. Heat a medium saucepan over medium-high heat for 1 to 2 minutes. Add oil and onions. Stir occasionally. After about 5 minutes, onions will start to caramelize, and you will need to stir constantly for about 5 more minutes. Onions should be evenly browned, not burnt. Remove from heat and set aside.
2. To assemble sandwiches, spread about 2 tablespoons of onions on each of 4 pieces of bread. Top each slice with about 4 spinach leaves, 1 slice of cheese, and 3 pieces of apple. Top with other slices of bread.
3. Heat grill. After assembling sandwiches, grill for about 2 1/2 minutes, then flip and grill for another 2 1/2 minutes. Serve with extra apple slices.

Strawberry Turkey Brie Panini

Serving: 4

Ingredients
- 1 (8-oz.) Brie round
- 8 Italian bread slices
- 8 ounces thinly sliced smoked turkey
- 8 fresh basil leaves
- 1/2 cup sliced fresh strawberries
- 2 tablespoons red pepper jelly
- 2 tablespoons butter, melted
- Garnish: strawberry halves

Directions
1. Trim and discard rind from Brie. Cut Brie into 1/2-inch-thick slices. Layer 4 bread slices evenly with turkey, basil leaves, strawberries, and Brie.
2. Spread 1 1/2 tsp. pepper jelly on 1 side of each of remaining 4 bread slices; place bread slices, jelly sides down, on top of Brie. Brush sandwiches with melted butter.
3. Cook sandwiches, in batches, in a preheated panini press 2 to 3 minutes or until golden brown. Garnish, if desired.
4. Note: For testing purposes only, we used Braswell's Red Pepper Jelly. To prepare sandwiches without a panini press, cook in a preheated grill pan over medium-high heat 2 to 3 minutes on each side or until golden.

Three Cheese Panini

Slice the cheese thinly and haphazardly, by hand.
Servings: 4 | **Cook:** 6 mins | **Prep:** 15 mins | **Total Time:** 21mins

Ingredients
- 4 ciabatta rolls
- 2 ounces grana padano (or Parmigiano-Reggiano)
- 2 ounces crotonese
- 2 ounces Cacio di Roma cheese (or Pecorino Romano)
- truffle oil

Directions
1. Preheat a panini grill.
2. Slice off the domed tops of the ciabatta rolls; rolls should now be about 1-inch thick; split rolls horizontally.
3. Spread a thin, even layer of Grana Padano, then Crotonese, and then Cacio di Roma over the bottom of each roll.
4. Generously drizzle some truffle oil over each before closing up the sandwich.
5. Grill each sandwich for about 3 minutes until the bread is golden brown and the cheese is melted.

Truffle Goat Cheese & Bell Pepper Breakfast Panini

The marriage of aromatic truffle, tangy goat cheese, roasted sweet bell pepper, and peppery arugula in these breakfast panini is blissful.
Serving: 4

Ingredients
- 5 ounces soft goat cheese with truffles
- 3 ounces shredded part-skim mozzarella cheese
- 1 tablespoon truffle oil or extra virgin olive oil
- 4 large eggs
- 1/4 teaspoon sea salt, or to taste
- 1/4 teaspoon freshly ground black pepper, or to taste
- 2 large ciabatta rolls, split
- 2 roasted orange or red bell peppers, cut into thin strips
- 1 1/2 packed cups (1 1/2 ounces) fresh baby arugula leaves

Directions
1. Preheat panini grill, or place grill pan over medium-high heat. Combine goat cheese and mozzarella in a medium bowl; set aside.
2. Heat oil in a large nonstick skillet over medium heat. Gently break eggs into hot skillet; sprinkle with salt and pepper. Cook 2 minutes on each side or until desired degree of doneness.
3. Spread reserved cheese mixture on 1 side of 2 bread slices, and top with bell pepper and eggs. (You will have 2 eggs per sandwich.) Top with arugula and remaining bread slices.
4. Place sandwiches on panini grill or grill pan; cook 3 to 4 minutes or until golden. Let stand 3 minutes. Cut each sandwich in half with a serrated knife.

Turkey 2 Cheese Panini With Sauteed Vege

This is a lunch that I came up with what was on hand. A very tasty sandwich. You can get creative with the filling. I enjoyed this with a steamy mug of chicken noodle soup. I've been seeing family in NY state, so this hit the spot on a cold day.
Cook: 20 mins | **Prep:** 15 mins | **Total Time:** 35mins

Ingredients
- 4 slices whole wheat bread (or bread of your choice)
- 6 thin turkey slices
- 1/2 cup canned mushrooms, drained or 1 cup fresh mushrooms
- 1/2 green pepper, sliced into strips
- 1 tablespoon olive oil
- 2 slices sharp cheddar cheese
- 2 slices Swiss cheese
- butter
- fresh grated pepper (optional)

Directions
1. Heat 1 Tbsp olive oil in skillet to med-hi heat.
2. Sautee mushrooms and green pepper strips until tender -- drain on paper towels. set aside.
3. Heat up panini or George Foreman grill (what I used)to high.
4. Butter the four slices of bread on one side.
5. Divide and layer turkey, cheeses, sauteed vegetables, and grated pepper between both sandwiches.
6. Put on grill so that the butter sides are out.
7. Close grill and cook until golden brown or how you like it.
8. Cut in half, and enjoy!
9. (the cooking time includes the vegetable saute and grilling time).

Turkey And Cheese Panini

I love the combination of ingredients after they come off the panini maker with the cheese melting. My 9-year-old asks for this one.
Servings: 2 | **Cook:** 3 mins | **Prep:** 3 mins | **Total Time:** 6 mins

Ingredients
- 4 slices of catherine clarke oatmeal bread
- 2 slices provolone cheese

- 3 -5 slices turkey breast (to taste)
- 1/2 avocado

Directions
1. Preheat panini-maker till ready (machines differ).
2. Lay out two slices of the bread.
3. Spread the avocado on each slice.
4. Place one slice provolone on each.
5. Place turkey slices on top.
6. Place remaining two bread pieces on top.
7. Put the two sandwiches in panini-maker, press down and cook for three minutes.
8. Remove, slice in half and serve.

Turkey Cheese and Roasted Red Pepper Pa

Yum!
***Cook:** 5 mins | **Prep:** 5 mins | **Total Time:** 10mins*

Ingredients
- 3 slices smoked turkey
- 1 tablespoon mayonnaise
- 1/4 teaspoon minced garlic
- 1 -2 ounce havarti cheese (I used dill flavored)
- 1/2 roasted red pepper
- 3 fresh basil leaves
- 1 ciabatta roll

Directions
1. preheat panini or george foreman grill.
2. spread mayo on one side of the roll and sprinkle with garlic.
3. on the other side layer cheese, roasted red pepper, basil and turkey.
4. top with the other side of the bun.
5. place on grill and grill until melted, pressing down to flatten it a little.
6. cut and serve!

Turkey Cranberry and Cheese Panini

Another idea for those holiday leftovers and very simple. Source - market flyer
Servings: 4 | **Cook:** 10 mins | **Prep:** 10 mins | **Total Time:** 20mins

Ingredients
- 1 loaf onion focaccia bread (or Italian flatbread, about 12x4 inches)
- 8 slices muenster cheese
- 4 slices cooked turkey breast
- 1/3 cup cranberry sauce
- 2 tablespoons Dijon mustard
- nonstick cooking spray

Directions
1. Cut bread into 4 pieces, each about 3 inches long. Split each slice.
2. Place 2 cheese slices on bread bottoms. Add 1 turkey slice to each.
3. Mix cranberry sauce and mustard; spread on each turkey slice.
4. Replace bread tops.
5. Spray heavy-bottomed 12-inch skillet with nonstick cooking spray and heat over medium-low heat.
6. Add panini sandwiches. Weigh down with another heavy skillet, etc and press down.
7. Cook over heat 3-4 minutes.
8. Remove the weight, turn panini over.
9. Press down again; cook 3 minutes longer or just until cheese melts.

Two Cheese Panini With Tomato Olive Pest

This is a Tom Colicchio recipe (Wichcraft) that I cut in half, but once you make the pesto, it's easy to make 1 or 20. (I still don't see how they get 20 out of it--lol)
Cook: 10 mins | **Prep:** 20 mins | **Total Time:** 30mins

Ingredients
- 1/3 cup drained sun-dried tomato packed in oil, coarsely chopped
- 3 tablespoons oil-cured black olives, pitted and coarsely chopped
- 1/2 teaspoon dried oregano
- fresh ground pepper
- 10 slices white bread
- extra virgin olive oil, for brushing
- 5 slices provolone cheese

- 1/2 lb fresh mozzarella cheese, cut into 1/4-inch slices

Directions
1. In a food processor, combine the sun-dried tomatoes with the olives and oregano. Season with pepper and process to a coarse paste.
2. Lightly brush 1 side of each slice of bread with olive oil and set on a large baking sheet, oiled side down. Top half of the bread with the provolone, spread each slice with 1 tablespoon of the tomato-olive pesto and top with the mozzarella. Close the sandwiches with the remaining bread, oiled side up.
3. Heat a griddle or a very large skillet. Arrange 3 or 4 sandwiches on the griddle and top with a cast-iron skillet: do not press the pan down. Cook the sandwiches over moderately high heat until golden on the bottom, about 2 minutes. Flip the sandwiches and cook until browned and the cheese is melted, about 2 minutes longer. Transfer to a wire rack to cool. Repeat with the remaining sandwiches.
4. Cut the crusts off the sandwiches, then cut into triangles and serve.
5. MAKE AHEAD The panini can be prepared through Step 3 and stored on a wire rack at room temperature for up to 6 hours. Reheat on a baking sheet in a 350°F oven until crisp.

Waffle Iron Grilled Cheese Sandwiches

"More method than recipe, I heated up my panini maker one night to make a grilled cheese, only to find out that I'd left the waffle plates inside. Instead of changing out the plates, I used them anyway and I loved the outcome. The sandwich gets super crispy but the cheese is still soft and gooey inside the little squares. It's my 'go to' method for grilled cheese now. Serve with spicy pickled veggies on the side!"
Pre: 10 m | Cook: 7 m | Ready In: 17 m

Ingredients
- 2 tablespoons mayonnaise
- 2 teaspoons Dijon mustard
- 4 slices whole-grain bread
- 2 ounces shredded pepperjack cheese
- Add all ingredients to list

Directions
1. Preheat a waffle iron according to manufacturer's instructions.
2. Mix mayonnaise and Dijon mustard together in a bowl; spread onto 1 side of each bread slice. Sprinkle pepperjack cheese over mayo-mustard layer of 2 bread slices. Cover cheese layer with a second bread slice, creating 2 whole sandwiches.

3. Place 1 sandwich in the waffle iron, taking care not to push down all the way. Wait until the bread begins to soften from the heat before starting to gently close the waffle iron, about 2 minutes. Apply more pressure to the top part of the iron, eventually closing it after a total of 3 to 4 minutes. Cook until browned, 2 to 3 minutes more. Repeat with the remaining sandwich.

Waffle Sandwich with Cheese Spinach and Spicy Mustard

"This sandwich is super easy to make, and children can help with the assembly or, if supervised, the waffle iron. Use multigrain or whole wheat sandwich bread for a chewy treat."

Pre: *15 m |* **Cook:** *5 m |* **Ready In:** *20 m*

Ingredients
- 1 roma (plum) tomato, thinly sliced
- salt and ground black pepper to taste
- 2 teaspoons butter, softened
- 4 thickly-sliced pieces multigrain bread
- 1 teaspoon spicy brown mustard
- 1 cup fresh spinach, or to taste
- 4 slices part-skim mozzarella cheese
- 2 teaspoons chopped sweet onion
- Add all ingredients to list

Directions
1. Preheat a waffle iron according to manufacturer's instructions.
2. Arrange tomato slices on a work surface, pouring off any excess juice. Season tomato slices with salt and pepper.
3. Spread 1/2 teaspoon butter onto 1 side of each bread slice. Lay 1 bread slice, butter-side down, in the hot waffle iron. Spread 1/2 teaspoon mustard onto bread slice in waffle iron; top with 1/4 cup spinach, 2 slices mozzarella cheese, 1 teaspoon onion, half the tomato slices, and 1/4 cup spinach, respectively. Lay 1 slice bread, butter-side up, atop the spinach layer.
4. Close waffle iron and toast sandwich until lightly browned, about 2 minutes. Repeat with remaining ingredients.

White Cheese Sauce

This white cheese sauce is the perfect accompaniment to pressed panini sandwiches.
Serving: *3*

Ingredients
- 1/4 cup butter
- 1/4 cup all-purpose flour
- 3 1/2 cups milk
- 1 cup (4 oz.) shredded Swiss cheese
- 1 cup grated Parmesan cheese
- 1/2 teaspoon salt
- 1/4 teaspoon ground red pepper

Directions
1. Melt butter in a heavy saucepan over low heat; whisk in flour until smooth. Cook 1 minute, whisking constantly. Gradually whisk in milk; cook over medium heat, whisking constantly, until mixture is thickened and bubbly. Whisk in Swiss and Parmesan cheeses, salt, and red pepper, whisking until cheeses are melted and sauce is smooth.

Chapter 3: Fish

***

Bunk's Oregon Albacore Tuna Salad

The tuna melt at Bunk Sandwiches, in Portland, scores high marks for flavor—and all the ingredients except the condiments are local. Chef and co-owner Tommy Habetz puts the salad in ciabatta rolls spread with mayo and mustard, adds medium-sharp cheddar and sliced garlic dill pickles, and then grills the works in a panini press.
Serving: *1 |* **Total Time:** *15 Minutes*

Ingredients
- 2 cans (5 oz. each) local sustainable albacore tuna
- 1/4 cup minced red onion
- 1/4 cup extra-virgin olive oil
- 1 tablespoon balsamic vinegar
- 1 tablespoon minced fresh basil leaves
- 1/2 teaspoon red chile flakes
- 1/2 teaspoon salt
- 1/2 teaspoon pepper

Directions
1. Mix all ingredients together.

Grilled Smoked Salmon Panini with Red Onion Ribbons

These grilled salmon panini sandwiches are incredibly versatile. Serve them as a hearty lunch, a light dinner, or as hors d'oeuvres. They can be assembled well ahead of time, making them perfect for entertaining.
Serving: *4*

Ingredients
- 1 tablespoon Champagne vinegar
- 3 tablespoons fresh lemon juice, divided
- 3 teaspoons Dijon mustard, divided
- 1 teaspoon minced garlic
- 3 tablespoons extra-virgin olive oil
- Salt
- Freshly ground black pepper
- 1 small red onion, halved and sliced paper-thin
- 6 ounces cream cheese, softened
- 4 ounces soft goat cheese

- 1/4 cup thinly sliced green onions
- 1 tablespoon chopped capers
- 1 teaspoon grated lemon rind
- 1/4 teaspoon freshly ground black pepper
- 1 loaf ciabatta, about 7 x 14 inches
- 8 ounces hot-smoked salmon, flaked
- 3 cups loosely packed baby spinach
- Extra-virgin olive oil

Directions
1. Whisk together vinegar, 2 tablespoons lemon juice, 2 teaspoons mustard, and garlic in a bowl. Slowly drizzle in 3 tablespoons olive oil, whisking constantly, until mixture is slightly thickened. Add salt and pepper to taste. Add red onion, tossing to coat. Let stand 30 minutes (can be made ahead and refrigerated).
2. Combine cream cheese and next 4 ingredients. Stir in 1/4 teaspoon pepper, remaining 1 tablespoon lemon juice, and remaining 1 teaspoon mustard.
3. Slice ciabatta horizontally into top and bottom halves. Spread cream cheese mixture evenly on both pieces of bread. Arrange salmon in an even layer over cheese on bottom half of bread; press salmon firmly into cheese. Top with spinach and marinated red onion. Place top half of bread on sandwich can be prepared in advance up to this point if kept tightly wrapped and refrigerated 4 to 6 hours).
4. Cut into 4 individual sandwiches. Heat panini maker or grill to medium-high heat. Brush both sides of each sandwich with olive oil. Grill about 5 minutes, or until crisp and browned. (If grilling, weigh down sandwiches with a baking sheet topped with heavy canned goods.) Cut each sandwich in half diagonally.
5. Note: To serve as hors d'oeuvres, cut each grilled sandwich into 3 or 4 rectangles or "fingers."

Tuna Panini

Serve these hearty sandwiches with fresh apple slices or a tossed green salad.
Serving: 4

Ingredients
- 3 tablespoons finely chopped red onion
- 3 tablespoons organic canola mayonnaise
- 1 teaspoon grated lemon rind
- 1/4 teaspoon fennel seeds, crushed
- 1/4 teaspoon freshly ground black pepper
- 3 slices center-cut bacon, cooked and crumbled
- 2 (5-ounce) cans albacore tuna in water, drained and flaked

- 8 slices sourdough bread
- 4 (1/2-ounce) slices provolone cheese
- Cooking spray

Directions
1. Combine first 7 ingredients in a medium bowl, stirring well to coat. Place 4 bread slices on a flat surface; top each bread slice with 1 cheese slice. Divide tuna mixture evenly among bread slices; top each serving with 1 remaining bread slice.
2. Heat a large skillet over medium heat. Lightly coat sandwiches with cooking spray. Place sandwiches in pan; top with another heavy skillet. Cook 3 minutes on each side or until lightly browned (leave skillet on sandwiches as they cook).

Chapter 4: Fruits

***

Apricot and White Cheddar Panini

Serving: 1

Ingredients
- 1 tablespoon apricot jam
- 2 slices bread
- 2 ounces thinly sliced white Cheddar
- 1/2 tablespoon butter

Directions
1. Spread the jam over 1 side of sliced bread. Add the Cheddar. Top with a second slice of bread. Spread 1/4 tablespoon butter on each side of the sandwich. Heat in a skillet over medium heat until the cheese melts, 2 minutes per side.

Cinnamon Apple Panini

With a touch of sweet spice, cream cheese richness, and tart apple crunch, these melty-sweet sandwich triangles are sure to earn grade-A ratings. Serve as an after-school snack for the kids, or treat yourself to a quick-fix dessert.

Serving: 4

Ingredients
- 2 ounces 1/3-less-fat cream cheese, softened
- 1 teaspoon honey
- 1/8 teaspoon ground cinnamon
- 4 (1-ounce) slices 100% whole-wheat cinnamon-raisin bread
- 12 thin slices Granny Smith apple
- Cooking spray
- 1/2 teaspoon water
- 2 individually wrapped caramels

Directions
1. Combine the first 3 ingredients, stirring until smooth. Spread about 1 tablespoon cream cheese mixture over 1 side of each bread slice. Top each of 2 bread slices with 6 apple slices and remaining 2 bread slices, cream cheese side down. Lightly coat sandwiches with cooking spray.
2. Heat a grill pan over medium heat; add sandwiches to pan. Cook 2 minutes on each side. Cut each into 4 triangles.

3. Combine water and unwrapped caramels in a microwave-safe bowl. Microwave at HIGH for 30 seconds or until caramels melt, stirring after 15 seconds. Drizzle sandwiches with caramel.

Country Ham and Peach Panini

It's best to use very thinly sliced ham, not thick ham steaks. Ask your deli to slice it, or look for a packet of center- and end-cut slices, which tend to be smaller.
***Serving:** 4 | **Total Time:** 20 Minutes*

Ingredients
- 8 ciabatta bread slices*
- 4 teaspoons coarse-grained Dijon mustard
- Freshly ground pepper
- 4 (1-oz.) fontina cheese slices
- 4 ounces thinly sliced country ham, prosciutto, or Serrano ham
- 2 medium peaches (about 3/4 lb.), unpeeled and sliced
- 4 teaspoons honey (optional)
- 1 tablespoon extra virgin olive oil

Directions
1. Spread each of 4 bread slices with 1 tsp. mustard, and sprinkle with desired amount of freshly ground pepper. Layer with cheese, ham, peaches, and, if desired, honey. Top with remaining bread slices, and press together gently. Brush sandwiches with olive oil.
2. Cook sandwiches, in batches, in a preheated panini press 3 to 4 minutes or until golden brown and cheese is melted. (Or use a preheated nonstick grill pan, and cook sandwiches over medium heat 3 to 4 minutes on each side.) Serve immediately.
3. *Any firm white bread may be substituted.

Grilled Goat Cheese and Strawberry Sandwiches

Time: 15 minutes. Sarah Van Winkle credits a sandwich from Half & Half cafe, in Portland, Oregon, with inspiring her version. She calls it "unexpectedly delicious." Van Winkle cooks them in a panini press, but we found that using a frying pan reduces the tendency of the strawberry juices to bleed.
***Serving:** 2*

Ingredients
- 2 tablespoons softened butter

- 4 slices levain (or other hearty, rustic bread)
- 3 ounces fresh goat cheese, preferably from a local dairy
- 6 large strawberries, sliced thin
- 8 to 12 basil leaves

Directions
1. Butter 1 side of each bread slice. Generously spread goat cheese on unbuttered side of 2 slices and cook them, cheese side up, until golden underneath, about 2 minutes. Layer with strawberries and basil. Top with remaining bread slices, buttered side up; turn over and cook until golden, about 2 minutes.
2. Note: Nutritional analysis is per sandwich.

Peach Pepper Preserves

Try It With: Coconut fried shrimp, chicken quesadillas, or ham and fontina panini.
*Serving: 3 | **Total Time:** 2 Hours, 26 Minutes*

Ingredients
- 4 1/2 cups peeled and diced peaches (about 2 1/2 lb.)
- 1 jalapeño pepper, minced
- 1/2 red bell pepper, finely chopped
- 1 1/2 cups sugar
- 3 tablespoons fresh lime juice
- 1 (1.75-oz.) package powdered fruit pectin

Directions
1. Stir together all ingredients in a 4-qt. microwave-safe glass bowl.
2. Microwave at HIGH 8 minutes (mixture will boil). Stir mixture, and microwave at HIGH 8 to 10 minutes or until thickened. (You're going for the viscosity of pancake syrup here. The mixture will thicken to soft-set preserves after it cools and chills.) Cool mixture completely (about 2 hours). Serve immediately, or cover and chill preserves in an airtight container until ready to serve. Store in refrigerator up to 3 weeks.

Pear Pecorino and Prosciutto Panini

If you prefer cooked prosciutto, sauté it until it's crisp. You'll add some crunch to this sandwich. Parmigiano-Reggiano is a good substitute for pecorino Romano cheese.
Serving: 4

Ingredients

- 1 firm, ripe pear, peeled, cored, and cut into 8 wedges
- 1/2 teaspoon sugar
- 1 (12-ounce) loaf focaccia, cut in half horizontally
- 4 teaspoons balsamic vinegar
- 1 cup trimmed arugula
- 1/2 cup (2 ounces) fresh pecorino Romano cheese, shaved
- 16 very thin slices prosciutto (about 4 ounces)

Directions

1. Heat a nonstick skillet over medium-high heat. Add pear to pan, and sprinkle with sugar. Cook 2 minutes on each side or until golden.
2. Brush cut sides of bread with vinegar. Arrange pear slices, arugula, cheese, and prosciutto evenly over bottom half of bread; cover with top half of bread.
3. Heat a large nonstick skillet over medium heat. Add stuffed loaf to pan. Place a cast-iron or heavy skillet on top of stuffed loaf; press gently to flatten. Cook 4 minutes on each side or until bread is toasted (leave cast-iron skillet on stuffed loaf while it cooks). Cut into quarters.

Prosciutto Fontina and Fig Panini

If you don't have a panini grill, place sandwiches in a grill pan or large nonstick skillet coated with cooking spray over medium heat. Cover sandwiches with foil, and top with a heavy skillet. Cook 2 to 3 minutes on each side or until golden brown.
Serving: 4 | **Prep:** 7 Minutes | **Cook:** 3 Minutes

Ingredients

- 8 (0.9-ounce) slices crusty Chicago-style Italian bread
- 4 ounces very thinly sliced prosciutto
- 1 1/4 cups (4 ounces) shredded fontina cheese
- 1/2 cup baby arugula leaves
- 1/4 cup fig preserves
- Olive oil-flavored cooking spray

Directions

1. Preheat panini grill.
2. Top each of 4 bread slices evenly with prosciutto, fontina cheese, and arugula. Spread 1 tablespoon fig preserves evenly over 1 side of each of remaining 4 bread slices; top sandwiches with remaining bread slices. Coat outsides of sandwiches with cooking spray. Place sandwiches on panini grill; cook 3 to 4 minutes or until golden and cheese is melted. Cut panini in half before serving, if desired.

Chapter 5: Pork

***

Bánh Mì

Although the bánh mì may have originated in the markets of Saigon, in bigger cities in the U.S. it is now as much of an American lunchtime staple as the burrito or panini. There are as many variations of the bánh mì as there are cooks who make it. This version combines pork, cucumber, and a pickled slaw of radish, carrot, and onion.
Serving: 4 | **Total Time:** 1 Hour, 20 Minutes | **Hands-On:** 20 Minutes

Ingredients
PICKLES:
- 1/2 cup rice vinegar
- 1/3 cup granulated sugar
- 1/3 cup water
- 2 teaspoons sambal oelek
- 1/2 cup shredded carrot
- 1/3 cup matchstick-cut radishes
- 1/3 cup thinly sliced red onion

SANDWICHES:
- 6 (2-ounce) boneless pork breakfast cutlets
- 1/4 teaspoon kosher salt
- Cooking spray
- 1 (12-ounce) French bread baguette (16 inches long)
- 1/4 cup light mayonnaise
- 1 teaspoon sambal oelek
- 1/4 cup thinly sliced peeled cucumber
- 1/2 cup cilantro leaves

Directions
1. To prepare pickles, combine first 4 ingredients (through sambal oelek) in a small saucepan. Bring to a boil, stirring until sugar dissolves. Remove from heat. Add carrot, radishes, and onion. Let stand, uncovered, at room temperature 1 hour.
2. Preheat broiler.
3. Place pork between 2 sheets of plastic wrap; pound to 1/8-inch thickness using a meat mallet or small heavy skillet. Sprinkle pork evenly with salt, and place on a broiler pan coated with cooking spray. Broil 5 minutes. Remove from pan.
4. Cut bread in half lengthwise. Hollow out bottom half of bread, leaving a 1/2-inch-thick shell; reserve torn bread for another use. Place bread halves, cut sides up, on a baking sheet. Broil 1 minute or until toasted.
5. Combine mayonnaise and 1 teaspoon sambal oelek in a small bowl. Spread mayonnaise mixture on cut side of bread top. Layer pickled vegetables, pork

slices, cucumber, and cilantro evenly on bread bottom. Cover with bread top. Cut sandwich into 4 equal portions.

Chinese Roast Pork Panini

Recently, I've began to love and discover different panini and grilled cheese in my grill panini. From Rachael Ray
Servings: 4 | **Cook:** 30 mins | **Prep:** 10 mins | **Total Time:** 40mins

Ingredients
- 1 (12 -16 ounce) pork tenderloin, trimmed and cut crosswise into 2 large pieces
- salt and pepper
- 2 tablespoons vegetable oil
- 1 onion, chopped
- 2 tablespoons hoisin sauce
- 2 tablespoons honey
- 1 tablespoon sesame oil
- 1 tablespoon soy sauce
- 4 -6 challah rolls, split (3 to 4 inches wide)

Directions
1. Preheat the oven to 450°F Season the pork with salt and pepper. Heat a heavy, medium ovenproof skillet over medium-high heat. Add 1 tablespoon oil, then the pork; cook, turning, until browned, about 2 minutes. Transfer to the oven and roast until a thermometer registers 150-, about 10 minutes. Transfer to a cutting board and let rest for 10 minutes; cut into 1/2 inch cubes.
2. In a small skillet, heat the remaining 1 tablespoon oil over medium heat. Add the onion and cook, stirring, until softened, about 8 minutes.
3. In a large bowl, whisk together the hoisin sauce, honey, sesame oil and soy sauce. Stir in the onion and the pork and its juices.
4. Preheat a panini press. Divide the pork mixture evenly among the roll bottoms, then cover with the tops. Working in batches if necessary, grill until browned and crisp.

Fig Barbecue Panini

Ingredients
- 4 bread slices
- 4 tablespoons fig preserves
- 1 pound shredded barbecued pork

- 1/4 cup thinly sliced red onion
- 8 fresh figs, sliced
- 4 provolone cheese slices
- 1 cup loosely packed baby spinach
- Melted butter

Directions
1. Spread 4 bread slices with fig preserves. Layer with barbecued pork, sliced red onion, sliced figs, cheese slices, and baby spinach. Top each with a bread slice. Brush with melted butter. Cook in a panini press 2 to 3 minutes.

Ham Cheese and Apple Panini

If you don't have a panini press, you can make these easy sandwiches in a nonstick skillet, much like you make grilled cheese sandwiches.
Serving: 4

Ingredients
- 1 tablespoon apple jelly
- 1/4 cup Dijon mustard
- 8 (1-ounce) slices gluten-free bread
- 8 slices lower-sodium deli ham (6 ounces) {Check for Gluten}
- 4 (0.8-ounce) cheddar cheese or cheddar-flavored nondairy slices
- 1 Granny Smith apple, cored and cut into 24 thin slices
- Butter-flavored cooking spray

Directions
1. Preheat panini press.
2. Microwave jelly at HIGH 10 seconds or until it melts. Combine jelly and mustard; spread mixture evenly over 1 side of 4 bread slices. Layer 2 ham slices, 1 cheese slice, and 6 apple slices over mustard mixture on each bread slice; top evenly with remaining bread slices.
3. Coat sandwiches with cooking spray. Add sandwiches, 2 at a time, to panini press; grill 2 minutes or until toasted.

Italian Style Sandwiches

For Cuban Sandwiches, layer Baked Pork Loin Roast slices with ham, Swiss, and mustard on bread and cook in a panini press until cheese melts.
Serving: 4

Ingredients
- 1 (5.3-oz.) container spreadable goat cheese
- 2 tablespoons refrigerated pesto with basil
- 1 (12-oz.) package ciabatta rolls
- 1 pound thinly sliced Baked Pork Loin Roast (about 24 slices)*
- 1 1/3 cups firmly packed arugula
- 1/2 cup jarred roasted red bell pepper strips
- 1/4 small red onion, thinly sliced

Directions
1. Stir together goat cheese and pesto. Spread goat cheese-and-pesto mixture on cut sides of rolls. Layer pork roast, arugula, and remaining ingredients on bottom halves of rolls. Cover with top halves of rolls.
2. *1 lb. thinly sliced Slow-Cooker Pork Butt Roast may be substituted.
3. Note: For testing purposes only we used Buitoni Pesto With Basil and Cobblestone Mill Ciabatta Rolls.

Mozzarella Ham and Basil Panini

Serve these simple pressed sandwiches with a pickle and some vegetable chips.
Serving: 6

Ingredients
- 1 (16-ounce) loaf ciabatta, cut in half horizontally
- 4 teaspoons Dijon mustard
- 4 teaspoons balsamic vinegar
- 1 1/3 cups (8 ounces) thinly sliced fresh mozzarella cheese
- 12 basil leaves
- 8 ounces sliced 33%-less-sodium cooked deli ham (such as Healthy Choice)
- 2 sweetened hot cherry peppers, sliced
- 1 large plum tomato, thinly sliced
- Cooking spray

Directions
1. Brush cut side of the bottom bread half with mustard; brush cut side of top half with vinegar. Top bottom half with mozzarella, basil, ham, peppers, and tomato. Top with remaining bread half.
2. Heat a large nonstick skillet over medium heat. Coat pan with cooking spray. Add sandwich to pan; top with another heavy skillet. Cook 3 minutes on each side or until golden. Cut sandwich into 6 wedges.

Pear Pecorino and Prosciutto Panini

If you prefer cooked prosciutto, sauté it until it's crisp. You'll add some crunch to this sandwich. Parmigiano-Reggiano is a good substitute for pecorino Romano cheese.
***Serving:** 4*

Ingredients
- 1 firm, ripe pear, peeled, cored, and cut into 8 wedges
- 1/2 teaspoon sugar
- 1 (12-ounce) loaf focaccia, cut in half horizontally
- 4 teaspoons balsamic vinegar
- 1 cup trimmed arugula
- 1/2 cup (2 ounces) fresh pecorino Romano cheese, shaved
- 16 very thin slices prosciutto (about 4 ounces)

Directions
1. Heat a nonstick skillet over medium-high heat. Add pear to pan, and sprinkle with sugar. Cook 2 minutes on each side or until golden.
2. Brush cut sides of bread with vinegar. Arrange pear slices, arugula, cheese, and prosciutto evenly over bottom half of bread; cover with top half of bread.
3. Heat a large nonstick skillet over medium heat. Add stuffed loaf to pan. Place a cast-iron or heavy skillet on top of stuffed loaf; press gently to flatten. Cook 4 minutes on each side or until bread is toasted (leave cast-iron skillet on stuffed loaf while it cooks). Cut into quarters.

Pork Pesto Panini

With the addition of a few high-flavored ingredients, leftover pork tenderloins are turned into a quick-fix supper of tasty Pesto Panini.
***Serving:** 6*

Ingredients
- Pork Tenderloins with Balsamic Strawberries
- 1 (7-oz.) jar roasted red bell peppers
- 12 teaspoons pesto
- 12 artisan bread slices
- 6 (1-oz.) Havarti cheese slices

Directions
1. Cut reserved pork from Pork Tenderloins with Balsamic Strawberries into 18 thin slices. Drain roasted red bell peppers; cut peppers into 6 pieces. Spread 2 tsp. pesto on each of 6 artisan bread slices. Top each with 3 pork slices, 1 red pepper piece, 1 Havarti cheese slice, and 1 bread slice. Cook in a preheated panini press 2 to 3 minutes or until golden.

Pressed Cuban Sandwiches

We made these sandwiches in a skillet, but feel free to use a hot panini press instead. You'll still get the same tasty results.
Serving: 4

Ingredients
- 1 (12-oz.) Cuban bread loaf, cut in half crosswise
- 6 to 8 Tbsp. yellow mustard
- 1/3 pound thinly sliced Baked Pork Loin Roast (about 8 to 10 slices)*
- 1/3 pound thinly sliced baked ham
- 1/3 pound thinly sliced provolone cheese
- 1/4 to 1/3 cup dill pickle chips
- 2 tablespoons butter, softened

Directions
1. Cut bread halves lengthwise, cutting to but not through opposite side. Spread mustard on cut sides of bread. Layer with Baked Pork Loin Roast and next 3 ingredients. Close sandwiches, and spread outsides with butter.
2. Place 1 sandwich in a hot, large skillet over medium heat. Place a heavy skillet on top of sandwich. Cook 2 to 3 minutes on each side or until cheese is melted and sandwich is flat. Repeat with remaining sandwich. Cut each sandwich in half, and serve immediately.
3. *1/3 lb. thinly sliced Slow-Cooker Pork Butt Roast may be substituted.

Prosciutto and Fontina Panini

Serving: 2

Ingredients
- 1 (5.25-ounce) package focaccia (Italian flatbread) or 1 (8-ounce) package Italian cheese-flavored pizza crust (such as Boboli)
- 8 very thin slices prosciutto (about 2 ounces)
- 1/4 cup (1 ounce) shredded fontina cheese

- 1 cup trimmed arugula or watercress
- 2 (1/8-inch-thick) red onion slices, separated into rings
- 2 teaspoons balsamic vinegar
- 1/8 teaspoon pepper

Directions
1. Slice each bread round in half horizontally. Divide prosciutto slices between bottom halves of bread, and top each bread half with fontina cheese, arugula, and red onion slices. Drizzle balsamic vinegar over sandwiches, and sprinkle with pepper; cover with top halves of bread. Wrap sandwiches tightly in aluminum foil, and bake at 300° for 15 minutes.

Prosciutto and Smoked Gouda Panini

You'll need to cook the panini in batches; keep cooked panini warm in a 250° oven. The sandwiches make hearty lunch fare on their own, or serve them with a tossed green salad or Chicken, Chickpea, and Zucchini Stew.
Serving: 10

Ingredients
- 20 (1-ounce) slices Italian bread
- Cooking spray
- 6 ounces smoked Gouda cheese, thinly sliced
- 6 ounces thinly sliced prosciutto

Directions
1. Coat 1 side of each bread slice with cooking spray. Place 10 bread slices, coated sides down, on a work surface. Divide cheese and prosciutto evenly among 10 bread slices. Top with remaining bread slices, coated sides up.
2. Heat a large nonstick skillet over medium heat. Cook panini 5 minutes on each side or until lightly browned and cheese melts, pressing with a spatula to flatten.

Prosciutto Fontina and Fig Panini

If you don't have a panini grill, place sandwiches in a grill pan or large nonstick skillet coated with cooking spray over medium heat. Cover sandwiches with foil, and top with a heavy skillet. Cook 2 to 3 minutes on each side or until golden brown.
Serving: 4 | Prep: 7 Minutes | Cook: 3 Minutes

Ingredients
- 8 (0.9-ounce) slices crusty Chicago-style Italian bread
- 4 ounces very thinly sliced prosciutto
- 1 1/4 cups (4 ounces) shredded fontina cheese
- 1/2 cup baby arugula leaves
- 1/4 cup fig preserves
- Olive oil-flavored cooking spray

Directions
1. Preheat panini grill.
2. Top each of 4 bread slices evenly with prosciutto, fontina cheese, and arugula. Spread 1 tablespoon fig preserves evenly over 1 side of each of remaining 4 bread slices; top sandwiches with remaining bread slices. Coat outsides of sandwiches with cooking spray. Place sandwiches on panini grill; cook 3 to 4 minutes or until golden and cheese is melted. Cut panini in half before serving, if desired.

Prosciutto Mozzarella and Arugula Panini

The key to a good panino (singular) is high-quality bread, usually ciabatta, and fresh ingredients. Look for long, flat, rectangular-shaped loaves of ciabatta in your favorite deli or bakery.
Serving: 4

Ingredients
- 4 teaspoons balsamic vinegar
- 2 teaspoons extravirgin olive oil
- 1/4 teaspoon black pepper
- 1 garlic clove, minced
- 1 (9-ounce) loaf ciabatta, cut in half horizontally
- 16 very thin slices prosciutto (about 4 ounces)
- 4 (1-ounce) slices part-skim mozzarella cheese
- 8 (1/4-inch-thick) slices tomato (1 medium tomato)
- 1 cup lightly packed trimmed arugula or spinach
- Olive oil-flavored cooking spray

Directions
1. Combine first 4 ingredients in a small bowl; stir well with a whisk.
2. Brush cut sides of bread with vinaigrette. Arrange prosciutto and next 3 ingredients over bottom half of bread; replace top half of bread. Cut loaf in half crosswise, and coat with cooking spray.

3. Heat a large grill pan or nonstick skillet over medium heat. Add sandwich halves to pan. Place a heavy skillet on top of sandwiches to weigh them down. Cook 3 minutes on each side or until bread is toasted and cheese melts. Cut each sandwich half in half again to form 4 equal portions. Serve immediately.
4. Note: Focaccia may be substituted for ciabatta.
5. Panini (pah-NEE-nee) translates as "rolls" or "little bread," but in Italy, the name is synonymous with sandwiches.

Prosciutto Panini

Ingredients
- 1 6-inch length sweet baguette (2 in. wide)
- 2 teaspoons extra-virgin olive oil
- 1 1/2 ounces (1/4 cup) chèvre (goat) cheese
- 1/2 cup arugula leaves
- 2 to 3 ounces thin-sliced prosciutto
- Lemon juice (optional)
- Fresh-ground pepper (optional)

Directions
1. Split baguette in half horizontally. Drizzle cut surfaces with oil. On cut side of baguette bottom, spread goat cheese. Top with arugula leaves and prosciutto. If desired, add a squeeze of lemon juice and a sprinkle pepper. Set baguette top, cut side down, on filling.
2. Nutritional analysis per sandwich.

Chapter 6: Poultry

***

Basil Lemon Chicken Panini

This takes some of my favorite flavors, basil and lemon, marries them with grilled chicken and melting cheese on a hot grilled bun. yum. I will post the chicken recipe on its own as well (you can use scaloppine too, I prefer the thicker cut) What I do is cook the chicken for dinner making extras and use the leftovers for the panini :)
Servings: 4 | **Cook:** 15 mins | **Prep:** 30 mins | **Total Time:** 45mins

Ingredients
- 4 boneless skinless chicken breasts
- 2 large lemons
- 2 garlic cloves, coarsely chopped
- 1 tablespoon olive oil
- salt & pepper
- 2 teaspoons fresh basil
- 1 loaf ciabatta or 1 loaf other rustic bread
- 1/4 cup basil pesto or 2 tablespoons fresh basil
- 1 large tomatoes, beefsteak, sliced
- 6 ounces Italian fontina, sliced
- 2 ounces fresh bagged Baby Spinach

Directions
1. *For the chicken*.
2. Zest the lemon and squeeze the juice, combine zest and juice with oil and garlic in a small bowl.
3. Put chicken breasts between wax paper and pound to an even thickness.
4. Place in glad bag or bowl with marinade and leave for 30 minutes to 20 hours.
5. Grill chicken on bbq or broil it or even cook it in a hot skillet, 6-8 minutes approximately.
6. Cut ciabatta into 4 sandwich size pieces or use whatever bread you prefer. put 1 tbs of pesto on both sides of bread. (or fresh basil).
7. Add chicken, fontina cheese, tomatoes and spinach to each.
8. Grill in panini press or in a cast iron pan with another heated cast iron pan on top of it to press it down until cheese is melted.

Bird's Nest Breakfast Cups

"I got the basics of this recipe from a friend of mine and thought it was a great idea since these little nests can be made ahead, which I love. They are delicious, easy to make, and can be customized to your own tastes. I not only use the recipe as a delicious

grab-and-go breakfast, but serve it to guests nestled into some lovely cheese grits, alongside fresh fruits and French toast made on a panini press. Oh, and don't forget the mimosas!"
Pre: 20 m | Cook: 30 m | Ready In: 50 m

Ingredients
- 1 (30 ounce) package frozen shredded hash brown potatoes, thawed
- 2 1/2 teaspoons salt
- 1 teaspoon ground black pepper
- 2 1/2 tablespoons olive oil
- 2/3 cup shredded Cheddar cheese
- 12 eggs
- 2 tablespoons water
- 8 slices cooked bacon, crumbled - divided
- 1/4 cup shredded Cheddar cheese, divided
- Add all ingredients to list

Directions
1. Preheat oven to 425 degrees F (220 degrees C). Grease 24 muffin cups.
2. Mix hash brown potatoes, salt, black pepper, olive oil, and 2/3 cup shredded Cheddar cheese in a bowl. Divide mixture between prepared muffin cups and use your fingers to shape potato mixture into nests with hollows in the middle.
3. Bake in the preheated oven until hash browns are browned on the edges and cheese has melted, 15 to 18 minutes. Remove hash brown nests.
4. Reduce oven temperature to 350 degrees F (175 degrees C).
5. Whisk eggs and water in a bowl until thoroughly combined; season with salt and black pepper. Pour equal amount of egg mixture into each nest; sprinkle with bacon crumbles and 1 teaspoon Cheddar cheese.
6. Bake in the oven until eggs are set, 13 to 16 minutes. Let cool in pans and remove by sliding a knife between potato crust and muffin cup.

Buffalo Chicken Panini

Gooey goodness. The perfect combination of buffalo chicken flavors on a sandwich.
Cook: 5 mins | Prep: 5 mins | Total Time: 10mins

Ingredients
- 6 ounces cooked chicken (I use buffalo deli chicken)
- 2 teaspoons diced green onions
- 1/4 cup blue cheese
- 1/2 cup Baby Spinach

- 2 teaspoons mayonnaise
- 2 -3 teaspoons buffalo wing sauce (bottle variety)
- 4 slices bread, your choice (I use either flat bread or Italian)

Directions
1. Combine mayo and wing sauce.
2. Spread top and bottom of inside of sandwich with this mayo mixture.
3. Assemble sandwich layering chicken, onion, spinach, and cheese.
4. Grill on panini press, George Forman, or skillet until heated through and cheese has melted.
5. Serve with plenty of napkins.

California Club Chicken Wraps

"I work in a corporate office, and our cafe has a 'wrap station' every Friday and these are a huge hit with everyone. I got hooked so I watched closely and finally made my own version at home; they are so delicious! If desired, place wrap in a panini maker for 1 to 2 minutes, or until wrap has grill marks and cheese is slightly melted."
***Pre:** 15 m | **Cook:** 1 m | **Ready In:** 16 m*

Ingredients
CHIPOTLE MAYONNAISE
- 1/2 cup mayonnaise
- 1/2 cup plain yogurt
- 2 chipotle chiles in adobo sauce, finely chopped

WRAPS
- 2 large spinach tortillas
- 1/2 cup shredded lettuce, or to taste
- 1 1/2 cups shredded Monterey Jack cheese
- 1 Haas avocado - peeled, pitted, and diced
- 4 slices cooked bacon, chopped
- 1 red onion, finely chopped
- 1 tomato, chopped
- 2 cooked chicken breasts, cut into chunks
- Add all ingredients to list

Directions
1. Whisk mayonnaise, yogurt, and chipotle chiles together in a bowl.
2. Cook tortillas in the microwave until warm and pliable, about 30 seconds.
3. Spread 1 tablespoon chipotle mayonnaise down the center of each tortilla. Spread 1/2 the lettuce, 1/2 the Monterey Jack cheese, 1/2 the avocado, 1/2

the bacon, 1/2 the red onion, 1/2 the tomato, and 1/2 the chicken, respectively, in the center of each tortilla. Fold opposing edges of the tortilla to overlap the filling. Roll 1 of the opposing edges around the filling into a wrap.

Cheddar and Turkey Panini

For a tasty treat this weekend, treat family or friends and serve them paninis of toasted whole grains, melted aged cheddar, lean turkey and a burst of flavour from a Mcintosh apple - so good! I found the recipe in our local newspaper, and it is really good for the leftover turkey at holiday time, it makes something just a little different to use up the leftovers -
Cook: *0 mins |* **Prep:** *10 mins |* **Total Time:** *10mins*

Ingredients
- 4 slices aged cheddar cheese
- 4 slices whole grain bread
- 1 mcintosh apple, peeled, cored and thinly sliced
- 4 slices smoked turkey breast or 4 slices leftover turkey breast, will do
- 2 teaspoons honey mustard
- 1/2 cup Baby Spinach

Directions
1. Heat a panini press or a cast iron pan over medium-high heat. Divide cheddar evenly between two slices of whole grain bread, followed by 2 slices apple and 2 slices of smoked turkey.
2. Spread remaining two slices of bread with honey mustard and place on top of the turkey (mustard side down).
3. Place sandwiches in heated panini press or cast iron pan and grill for 4-5 minutes, turning as necessary to evenly brown the bread on both sides of the sandwich.
4. Once cheese is melted and bread is golden brown, remove sandwiches from the heat. Remove tops of sandwiches, add spinach. replace tops and serve immediately.

Chicken and Apple Panini

Bought some "Oroweat Sandwich Thins" and saw this recipe on their website. Looks delicious!
Servings: *1 |* **Cook:** *5 mins |* **Prep:** *5 mins |* **Total Time:** *10mins*

Ingredients
- 1 whole grain buns
- 4 ounces chicken breasts, skinless and boneless
- 2 slices reduced-fat Swiss cheese
- 4 slices apples, thinly sliced (any variety)
- 1 teaspoon reduced-fat mayonnaise
- 1/2 cup baby spinach leaves

Directions
1. Preheat a nonstick griddle or skillet to medium.
2. Grill each side of the chicken breast for 5 to 7 minutes, making sure chicken is thoroughly cooked.
3. Spread one side of the Sandwich Thins® roll with reduced-fat mayonnaise.
4. Assemble the sandwich by layering a slice of cheese, apples, chicken, baby spinach and the remaining slice of cheese.
5. Grill the sandwich about 90 seconds on each side, weighing the sandwich down with a small skillet as it cooks.

Chicken and Avocado Panini Sandwiches

The tastes of summer are terrific in this quick fix meal. You do NOT need a panini press for this sandwich.
Servings: 2 | **Cook:** 10 mins | **Prep:** 10 mins | **Total Time:** 20mins

Ingredients
- 1 avocado
- 1 teaspoon fresh lemon juice
- 1/4 cup red onion, diced
- 1/4 cup cilantro, chopped
- 1/3 cup grape tomatoes, quartered
- 2 teaspoons jalapenos, chopped (jarred variety)
- salt and pepper
- 2 pieces naan bread (or can use tortillas or any other bread)
- 4 pieces bacon, cooked crisp
- 1 cooked chicken breast half, sliced thin (I usually used left over grilled or smoked)
- 3 ounces monterey jack pepper cheese, sliced (I use half-light by Cabot)
- 1 -2 teaspoon fat-free mayonnaise
- 1/4 cup fat-free cheddar cheese, grated

Directions

1. Heat panini press to medium. (Or can grill on skillet or George Foreman).
2. Peel and remove pit of avocado. Coarsely mash avocado in bowl using fork (leave some chunks). Add lemon juice and stir. Stir in onion, cilantro, chopped jalapeños, and tomatoes. Salt and pepper to taste.
3. Spread thin layer of mayo on bread slices.
4. Assemble sandwich by layering onto bread sliced jack cheese, chicken, bacon, avocado mixture, and grated cheddar. Top with remaining slice of bread.
5. Grill until heated through and crispy on the outside. If using Naan bread, slice into six triangles. (If using other bread/tortilla, cut according to size of sandwich).

Chicken and Bacon Panini With Spicy Chip

Eat Drink Love's inspiration on Brio Tuscan Grill's panini. The tomatoes can be substituted with avocado slices.
Servings: 2 | **Cook:** 6 mins | **Prep:** 20 mins | **Total Time:** 26mins

Ingredients
For the Spicy Chipotle Mayo
- 1 chipotle chile in adobo
- 1/2 cup mayonnaise
- 1 lime, juice of
- 1/2 teaspoon adobo seasoning

For the Panini
- 1 1/2 cups cooked chicken breasts
- 4 slices cooked bacon
- 1/2 cup shredded cheddar cheese (or more to taste)
- 1/2 tomatoes, sliced into 4 slices (can sub fresh avocado slices)
- 2 teaspoons olive oil
- salt
- 4 slices bread (something hearty like Italian)
- butter

Directions

1. For the Spicy Chipotle Mayo: Add all ingredients into a food processor and puree until smooth. Add salt and pepper to taste, if needed.
2. For the Panini: Turn the oven to broil. Place the tomato slices on a lined baking sheet. Drizzle with a little olive oil and sprinkle with salt. Place into the oven and roast the tomatoes until the top is slightly charred. Remove from the oven and set aside. (Note: This step may be skipped and replaced with slices of avocado.).

3. Heat a panini grill or grill pan on medium heat. Spread a little bit of butter on one side of each piece of the bread.
4. Evenly distribute the chicken, cheese, bacon and tomatoes (or avocado slices) on top of two slices, butter side down.
5. On the other pieces of bread, spread some of the chipotle mayonnaise on the side that is not buttered. Place on top of the sandwich. Place the sandwiches on the grill. If you are using a grill pan, place a heavy pan on top of each sandwich.
6. Cook for about 2-3 minutes until the bread is golden brown. Gently flip the sandwich over and cook for another 2-3 minutes until the other side is golden brown.

Chicken and Fontina Panini

Crusty on the outside, gooey on the inside, this sandwich requires little effort and makes a satisfying lunch or light dinner.
Serving: 2 | **Total Time:** 10 Minutes

Ingredients
- 1 (8-oz.) loaf ciabatta bread, cut in half horizontally
- 3 tablespoons pesto sauce
- 2 plum tomatoes, sliced
- 1 cup shredded rotisserie chicken
- 2 slices fontina cheese

Directions
1. Preheat panini press.
2. Spread bottom half of bread with pesto. Top with tomato slices, chicken, and cheese. Top with bread.
3. Place sandwich in panini press; cook 3 to 4 minutes or until cheese melts and bread is toasted. Cut into quarters, and serve hot.

Chicken and Grape Panini

Servings: 4 | **Cook:** 10 mins | **Prep:** 5 mins | **Total Time:** 15mins

Ingredients
- 1 cup coarsely chopped seedless grapes
- 1 cup frozen corn kernels or 1 cup canned corn kernel
- 1/4 cup chopped onion

- 1 garlic clove, minced
- 2 tablespoons chopped cilantro
- 1/3 cup bottled low-fat Italian salad dressing
- 1 cup shredded lowfat mozzarella cheese
- 1 loaf focaccia bread, sliced in half horizontally
- 1 lb cooked chicken breast

Directions
1. Combine grapes, corn, onion, garlic, cilantro and dressing;refrigerate.
2. Sprinkle 1/2 cup cheese on bottom half of focaccia bread, arrange chicken on cheese, top with 1 cup grape relish and sprinkle remaining cheese over relish.
3. Wrap in heavy-duty foil and grill over medium heat 5 minutes, turn and grill 5 minutes longer.
4. Carefully unwrap sandwich, cut into 4 wedge-shaped portions and serve hot with remaining relish.

Chicken and Ham Panini

I made this recipe up when i was trying to use up some leftovers. I tried to dress the flavors up as much as i could by marinading the chicken, peppering the bacon before warming it up, and adding the banana peppers. Hope you enjoy!
Cook: *5 mins |* **Prep:** *30 mins |* **Total Time:** *35mins*

Ingredients
- olive oil
- 2 hamburger buns (or your preference of bread)
- 1 cup Italian dressing
- 2 chicken breasts
- 2 slices colby-monterey jack cheese
- 2 slices monterey jack pepper cheese
- 4 slices bacon (precooked, 2 per sandwich)
- 2 slices ham
- ranch dressing or spicy brown mustard
- banana pepper

Directions
1. Marinade the chicken breasts in Italian dressing for 30 min to an hour.
2. Grill the chicken breasts.
3. To assemble the panini: Brush olive oil onto your bun, stack the chicken breast, sliced ham, bacon, and cheeses. (If you wish to add the peppers put them on under the cheese). Top with Ranch dressing or spicy brown mustard if you choose.

4. Put on your panini press or forman grill and give them about 4-5 minute or until your cheese is melted.

Chicken and Mushroom Panini

Cook: 8 mins | Prep: 12 mins | Total Time: 20mins

Ingredients
- cooking spray
- 2 cups pre-sliced cremini mushrooms or 2 cups pre-sliced button mushrooms
- 1 teaspoon minced garlic
- 1/4 cup canola mayonnaise (to which you add crushed red pepper flakes)
- 2 tablespoons chopped sun-dried tomatoes, packed without oil
- 1 tablespoon capers
- 8 slices ciabatta (1 1/2 oz) or 8 slices sourdough bread (1 1/2 oz)
- 8 ounces chopped skinless boneless rotisserie chicken breasts
- 4 slices reduced-fat provolone cheese

Directions
1. Heat a large nonstick skillet over medium-high heat; coat pan with cooking spray.
2. Add mushrooms and garlic to pan, sauté 3 minutes or until mushrooms are tender; remove from heat and set aside.
3. Combine mayonnaise (with crushed red pepper flakes), tomatoes, and capers in a mini food processor; pulse until well combined.
4. Spread 1 T mayonnaise mixture over each of 4 bread slices; top each with 1/4 cup mushroom mixture, 2 oz chicken, 1 cheese slice and 1 bread slice.
5. Heat a large grill pan over medium heat.
6. Coat pan with cooking spray.
7. Add sandwiches to pan; place a cast-iron skillet or other heavy skillet on top of sandwiches, press gently to flatten sandwiches.
8. Cook 2 minutes on each side or until bread is toasted (leave cast-iron skillet on top of sandwiches while they cook.).

Chicken and Roasted Pepper Panini

Layer wine-marinated chicken, creamy chevre cheese, roasted sweet peppers, and fresh basil for a simple sandwich supper they'll love. From BHG website. I will be trying this one soon..
Cook: 10 mins | Prep: 30 mins | Total Time: 40mins

Ingredients

- 1/4 cup olive oil
- 4 teaspoons red wine vinegar
- 1 tablespoon fresh thyme
- 1/2 teaspoon salt
- 1/4 teaspoon crushed red pepper flakes
- 4 boneless skinless chicken breast halves
- 4 slices Italian bread, 1-inch bias-cut slices
- 1/4 cup semi- soft cheese, with herbs or 1/4 cup semisoft chevre cheese
- 1 cup roasted red pepper, cut into strips (about one 7-ounce jar)
- 1/2 cup fresh basil or 1/2 cup watercress or 1/2 cup baby spinach leaves

Directions

1. For marinade, in a small bowl whisk together oil, vinegar, thyme, salt, and crushed red pepper. Reserve 2 tablespoons of mixture; set aside.
2. Place chicken between two sheets of plastic wrap; pound lightly with the flat side of a meat mallet to about 1/2-inch thickness.
3. Place in a resealable plastic bag set in a shallow dish. Add remaining marinade; seal bag. Marinate at room temperature about 15 minutes or in the refrigerator for up to 1 hour.
4. Lightly grease the rack of an indoor electric grill or lightly coat with nonstick cooking spray. Preheat grill. Drain chicken, discarding marinade. Place chicken on the grill rack. If using a covered grill, close the lid. Grill until chicken is no longer pink (170°F).
5. Brush cut sides of bread with reserved marinade. Place bread, cut sides down, on grill rack. If using a covered grill, close the lid. Grill until lightly toasted.
6. To serve, place a chicken breast on each grilled bread slice. Spread with cheese. Top each sandwich with sweet pepper and basil. Makes 4 sandwiches.

Chicken and Roasted Red Pepper Panini St

I love chicken and roasted red peppers, so I put this sandwich together--it was so yummy! My family loves them. The chicken can also be left out and the sandwich is still delicious. Add a bowl of soup or a salad and you have a perfect lunch or dinner!
Cook: *10 mins |* **Prep:** *10 mins |* **Total Time:** *20mins*

Ingredients

- 1 cooked chicken breast, sliced (or you can use the ready-made chicken slices in the grocery store)
- 1 (12 ounce) jar roasted red peppers
- 8 slices mozzarella cheese
- 4 tablespoons mayonnaise
- 2 tablespoons ranch dressing

- 1 loaf focaccia bread
- olive oil flavored cooking spray

Directions
1. Cut 8 thick slice of Foccacia bread.
2. Mix mayonnaise and Ranch dressing in small bowl.
3. Spread mayo mixture on 4 slices of Foccacia.
4. On top of mayo mixture, layer each slice with equal amounts of chicken and place one slice of mozzarella cheese.
5. Next, add the roasted red peppers and another slice of mozzarella on top of the peppers (this helps hold the sandwich together).
6. Top each sandwich with remaining slices bread.
7. Spray frying pan with Olive Oil spray (or other cooking spray).
8. Fry each sandwich on medium until they are golden brown.
9. Pop the sandwiches in the microwave for about 20-25 seconds to melt the cheese.
10. Enjoy! These are so yummy!

Chicken Asparagus Panini

This is a delicious sandwich, great for summertime.
Cook: *15 mins |* **Prep:** *5 mins |* **Total Time:** *20mins*

Ingredients
- 2 slices white bread
- 4 ounces grilled boneless skinless chicken breasts
- 4 asparagus spears, cooked
- 1 slice Swiss cheese

Directions
1. Grill chicken breast.
2. grill or steam four spears of asparagus with heads cut off.
3. Place chicken on slice of white bread , lay the 4 spears of asparagus on top of chicken, and place Swiss cheese over asparagus.
4. After placing final piece of bread over the cheese, grill panini using panini press or pan.

Chicken Bacon Ranch Panini

For all its simplicity, this panini is really something yummy... and a little spicy! And if you don't have a panini maker, don't fret! Just grill the sandwich in the skillet with a second (heavy) skillet on top of it to press it together. It'll make you feel inventive and nifty.

Servings: 4 | **Cook:** 15 mins | **Prep:** 5 mins | **Total Time:** 20mins

Ingredients
Panini
- 8 slices crusty French bread
- 4 tablespoons softened butter
- 2 whole chicken breasts, Cut In Half From Top To Bottom
- garlic powder
- salt
- pepper
- chili powder
- blackening seasoning
- red pepper
- spicy mustard
- peppercorn ranch dressing
- 4 slices thick monterey jack cheese
- 8 slices pepper bacon, Cooked Until Chewy And Cut In Half
- diced tomato
- diced onion
- diced green pepper

Blackening Seasoning
- 1 teaspoon ground basil
- 1 teaspoon ground thyme
- 1 teaspoon garlic
- 1 teaspoon white pepper
- 1 teaspoon black pepper
- 1 teaspoon salt (sea salt is better)
- 1 teaspoon onion powder
- 1 teaspoon cayenne pepper
- 1 teaspoon paprika
- 1 teaspoon cumin

Directions
1. Season the chicken breasts with salt, pepper, garlic powder, chili powder, red pepper, and the blackening seasoning.

2. Add 1-2 tablespoons of olive oil to a pan and cook the chicken breasts until cooked through, about 10-12 minutes. Slice into strips or shred, and set aside.
3. Cook the bacon.
4. To assemble the sandwiches, spread a generous amount of mustard on one half of the bread. Spread a generous amount of ranch dressing on the other half. (Definitely be generous; when the sandwich cooks, these will turn into more of a "sauce.").
5. Arrange chicken, bacon slices, and cheese slices on the bottom half. Top with the top slice. Butter both sides of the bread generously, then grill in the panini maker. (If you do not have a panini maker, you can grill the sandwiches in a skillet, laying a heavy skillet on top of the sandwich to press it together. Turn to grill the other side in the same way.).
6. Slice in half and gobble it down immediately.

Chicken Basil Roasted Red Pepper Panin

I made this "panini" style sandwich up one night at the supermarket while searching for something new to make for dinner. I make it in the broiler and then put a heavy frying pan on top of it for the panini effect-but if you have an panini maker or Foreman grill that's even better!
Servings: 4 | **Cook:** 15 mins | **Prep:** 5 mins | **Total Time:** 20mins

Ingredients
- 1 loaf panini bread
- 2 -3 thin sliced boneless chicken breasts
- 1 roasted red pepper (jar or fresh)
- 5 -6 large fresh basil leaves
- 2 -3 slices cheddar cheese
- 1 tablespoon crumbled goat cheese

Directions
1. Season chicken breasts with salt and pepper and cook in broiler or grill 3-4 minutes per side until cooked through. Set aside and cover with foil to keep warm.
2. Slice panini and place in heated broiler with outsides up. Broil 1-2 minutes until outside is warm and firm.
3. Flip panini over. Place slices of red pepper and goat cheese on top slice. Place cheddar cheese on bottom slice. Return to broiler for 1-2 minutes until cheese is melted and bread is crusty.
4. Take out of broiler. Place basil on top of cheddar cheese and chicken on top of basil. Put the top slice of bread on top of chicken.
5. Place sandwich on cutting board. Put clean dishtowel on top of sandwich and a heavy fry pan on top of that to "squish" the sandwich. Let sit for 2 minutes.

6. Slice the sandwich. Serve with a salad or a vegetable side (pan seared asparagus would be good).

Chicken Chipotle Panini Sandwich

I enjoy a panini grilled sandwich with a kick of heat, and this one satisfies that need.
***Cook:** 5 mins | **Prep:** 5 mins | **Total Time:** 10mins*

Ingredients
- 4 slices French bread (1/2-inch thick)
- 6 slices cooked bacon (I use the ready to eat one)
- 4 slices havarti cheese
- 8 -10 ounces sliced roasted chicken breast
- 4 -6 tablespoons chipotle hummus (or more if needed)

Directions
1. Heat the panini press on high.
2. Spread one side of each slice of bread with the chipotle hummus to cover completely.
3. Place the sliced chicken on top of the hummus on two of the bread slices.
4. Microwave the bacon for 10 seconds. Place the bacon on top of the chicken, then the cheese.
5. Finish the sandwich by adding the remaining bread slices, hummus side in, on top of the cheese.
6. Place the two sandwiches on the press and cook for several minutes, or until the bread is crisp and the cheese has melted.
7. Remove the sandwiches and cut in half before serving.

Chicken Cordon Bleu Panini I

Breaded chicken breast, cheese and ham transform easily into a sandwich, along with a sweet kick of honey mustard.
***Servings:** 4 | **Cook:** 25 mins | **Prep:** 15 mins | **Total Time:** 40mins*

Ingredients
For the chicken
- 2 boneless skinless chicken breasts, halved horizontally to make 4 cutlets
- 1/2 teaspoon coarse salt
- 1/8 teaspoon fresh ground black pepper
- 1/2 cup all-purpose flour

- 1 large egg, beaten
- 1/2 cup plain breadcrumbs
- 2 tablespoons extra virgin olive oil

For the sandwich
- 1/4 cup honey
- 1/4 cup Dijon mustard
- 1/4 cup butter, at room temperature
- 8 slices rustic white bread, sliced from a dense bakery loaf
- 4 ounces sliced ham
- 4 ounces Swiss cheese, sliced

Directions

1. Season the chicken with salt and pepper on both sides. Set up a dredging station with the flour, beaten egg and bread crumbs each in its own separate shallow bowl.
2. In a large skillet, heat the olive oil over medium-high heat. Dredge each piece of chicken in the flour, then the egg, then the bread crumbs and place it carefully in the skillet.
3. Cook the chicken for 3 to 4 minutes on each side. Transfer the chicken to a wire rack or a paper towel-lined plate to drain.
4. For the panini: Heat the panini press to medium-high heat.
5. Whisk together the honey and Dijon mustard in a small bowl; set aside.
6. For each sandwich: Spread butter on two slices of bread to flavor the outside of the sandwich. Flip over both slices and spread 1 tablespoon honey mustard on the other side of each slice. Top one slice with a breaded chicken breast, followed by ham and cheese slices.
7. Close the sandwich with the other slice of bread, buttered side up.
8. Grill two panini at a time, with the lid closed, until the cheese is melted and the bread is toasted, 4 to 5 minutes.

Chicken Cordon Blue Panini II

*Cook: 2 mins | **Prep:** 10 mins | **Total Time:** 12mins*

Ingredients
- 2 slices hearty bread
- 2 tablespoons mayonnaise
- 1 teaspoon spicy brown mustard or 1 teaspoon mustard, of your choice
- 1/2 cup cooked chicken, see note at bottom
- 2 slices prosciutto
- 2 slices Swiss cheese, more if needed

- olive oil

Directions
1. Preheat whatever pan, griddle, etc., that you are using.
2. In very small bowl, mix mayo and mustard, set aside.
3. Spread evenly on 2 slices bread.
4. Top each slice of bread with the Swiss cheese.
5. On one slice, top with chicken.
6. Scrunch up proscuitto, and place on top of chicken.
7. Top with other slice of bread.
8. Brush top with a little olive oil, evenly and thinly.
9. Place sandwich, olive oiled side-down onto hot pan.
10. Brush top lightly with more olive oil.
11. Press lightly once with spatula.
12. Grill/cook about 30 seconds to 1 minute, depending on how hot your pan is. Check to see for yourself. You want it lightly toasted with nice grill marks.
13. With your spatula, lift up a corner and hold it up with your fingers. Then slip the spatula underneath, and turn over carefully.
14. Brown other side the same way, and remove to cutting surface.
15. Cut in half diagonally and enjoy!
16. *Note: Any kind of chicken that you happen to have on hand works fine for this, such as leftover roasted, rotisserie, grilled, baked or stewed. Nice way to use up some leftovers and not feel like they're "leftover". Leftover turkey can be subbed as well.
17. *Also, the amount of chicken is just approximate. Make your sandwich how YOU like it using as much or little as you want.
18. Don't have proscuitto? That's ok, subbing a thin slice or 2 of any kind of ham is just fine. ;).

Chicken Florentine Panini I

Great tasting sandwich. I try to cook the chicken on a night I'm already making chicken to shorten the cook time.
Servings: *2-4 |* **Cook:** *45 mins |* **Prep:** *15 mins |* **Total Time:** *1hr*

Ingredients
- 1 (10 ounce) can prepared pizza crust
- 1 (9 ounce) package frozen spinach
- 1/4 cup light mayonnaise
- 1 clove garlic, minced
- 1 tablespoon olive oil
- 1 cup chopped red onion

- 1 tablespoon sugar
- 1 tablespoon cider vinegar or 1 tablespoon red wine vinegar or 1 tablespoon balsamic vinegar
- 2 boneless skinless chicken breast halves
- 1/2 teaspoon dried Italian seasoning
- 1 clove garlic, minced
- 4 slices provolone cheese

Directions
1. Heat oven to 375°F.
2. Unroll dough; place in ungreased 15x10x1-inch baking pan.
3. Starting at center, press out dough to edges of pan.
4. Bake at 375°F for 10 minutes.
5. Cool 15 minutes or until completely cooled.
6. Meanwhile, cook spinach as directed on package.
7. Drain well; squeeze dry with paper towels.
8. In small bowl, combine mayonnaise and 1 of the garlic cloves; mix well.
9. Refrigerate.
10. Heat oil in small saucepan over medium-high heat until hot.
11. Add onion;cook and stir 2 to 3 minutes or until crisp-tender.
12. Add sugar and vinegar.
13. Reduce heat to low; simmer 3 to 5 minutes or until most of liquid has evaporated, stirring occasionally.
14. To flatten each chicken breast half, place, boned side up, between 2 pieces of plastic wrap or waxed paper.
15. Working from center, gently pound chicken with flat side of meat mallet or rolling pin until about 1/4 inch thick; remove wrap.
16. Sprinkle chicken with Italian seasoning and minced garlic.
17. Spray large skillet with nonstick cooking spray.
18. Heat over medium-high heat until hot.
19. Add chicken; cook 8 minutes or until browned, fork-tender and juices run clear, turning once.
20. Cut cooled pizza crust into 4 rectangles.
21. Remove rectangles from pan; spread each with 1 tablespoon mayonnaise mixture.
22. Top 2 rectangles with chicken, spinach, onion mixture, cheese and remaining crust rectangles, mayonnaise side down.
23. Heat large skillet or cast iron skillet over medium heat until hot.
24. Place sandwiches in skillet.
25. Place smaller skillet on sandwiches to flatten slightly.
26. Cook about 1 to 2 minutes or until crisp and heated, turning once.
27. Cut each warm sandwich into quarters.

Chicken Florentine Panini II

Servings: 4 | Cook: 3 mins | Prep: 25 mins | Total Time: 28mins

Ingredients
- 1 (6 ounce) packaged fresh Baby Spinach
- 2 teaspoons olive oil
- 1/4 cup butter, softened
- 8 slices sourdough bread
- 1/4 cup Italian salad dressing
- 8 slices provolone cheese
- 1/2 lb shaved deli chicken
- 2 slices red onions, separated into rings

Directions
1. In a large skillet, saute spinach in oil for 2 minutes or until wilted. Butter one side of each slice of bread. Spread the unbuttered side of four slices with salad dressing; layer with a cheese slice, chicken, spinach, onion and another cheese slice. Top with remaining bread, buttered side up, Cook in a panini maker or on a griddle until golden brown on both sides.

Chicken Mozzarella and Basil Panini

Servings: 4 | Cook: 5 mins | Prep: 10 mins | Total Time: 15mins

Ingredients
- 8 slices rustic bread
- 1 cup cooked chicken, shredded
- 4 ounces fresh mozzarella cheese, thinly sliced
- 1 tomatoes, sliced
- 8 -12 fresh basil leaves
- kosher salt
- 2 tablespoons olive oil

Directions
1. On 1 slice of the bread layer 1/4 of the chicken, 1 or 2 slices of cheese and 2 or 3 basil leaves.
2. Sprinkle with salt, place other piece of bread on top.
3. Repeat step one and two, 3 more times.
4. Put oil in a pan large enough to hold all 4 sandwiches.

5. Place another large heavy pan on top of sandwiches.
6. When bread is crisp and cheese starts to melt, about 3-4 mins, flip them over.
7. Repeat for the other side, this takes about 2-3 minutes.

Chicken Mozzarella Panini With Red Peppe

I got a Cuisinart Panini Grill and just put together my favorite chicken fajita ingredients, instead of rolled in a tortilla shell it is placed layer by layer onto fresh Ciabatta bread and topped with oregano and pesto. An Italian touch to fajitas. I recommend getting the Ciabatta rolls at Costco- they are fresh and delicious! My family LOVED them. Each panini is a very large and filling sandwich. Might want to split in half and share one!
Cook: *5 mins |* **Prep:** *10 mins |* **Total Time:** *15mins*

Ingredients
- 4 boneless chicken breasts
- 1 red pepper
- 1 red onion
- olive oil
- 4 slices mozzarella cheese
- Morton nature seasons seasoning blend
- oregano
- butoni basil pesto
- 4 ciabatta rolls

Directions
1. Flatten chicken breasts and season them with Natures Seasoning and Olive oil. Let marinate while doing the next steps.
2. Cut the red peppers into 5 wedges per pepper so they can lay flat on grill or you can substitute sliced sun dried tomatoes right out of the jar instead of peppers. These are ready to put right on the sandwich without grilling if you prefer.
3. Slice the red onion into rings.
4. Coat the onions and peppers with olive oil.
5. Heat up your grill for panini on high. I use the Cuisinart Griddler I just got and it is excellent because it adjusts evenly to the thickness of whatever you are cooking.
6. Season chicken with Morton Natures Seasoning and oregano. Grill the chicken breasts first- 2 at a time with top of grill down which will leave perfect grill lines. Take off when done and put on plate.
7. Grill red peppers (flat) and next grill the red onion rings. Place on plate.
8. Clean off grill. I add a little olive oil or Pam to grill with a piece of paper towel before grilling sandwiches.

9. Spread a good amount of the Pesto on the top half of each sandwich.
10. Layer the panini. Chicken breast, Red pepper or sun dried tomatoes, Red onion slices, 1 slice of mozzarella cheese - Make sure everything fits perfectly within the size of the bread you are using.
11. Top each panini with the top half you have already spread the Pesto on.
12. Carefully place the sandwiches on grill (I can fit 2 at a time) and smoosh down if needed. Bread will have lines, cheese will be melted, and the sandwich will be nice and hot and perfect when ready!
13. There are other variations to this. My son is not crazy about Pesto -- so he just used Chicken, Mozzarella cheese and Paul Newman's jarred Marinara sauce and sprinkled Parmesan cheese on top of the sauce on his instead and Loved It!
14. A Chicken Parmesan Panini!
15. Hope you like it!

Chicken Panini With Fig Jam

From Cooking Light magazine. I did not add the arugula or lemon juice to my sandwich.
Servings: *4 |* ***Cook:*** *10 mins |* ***Prep:*** *10 mins |* ***Total Time:*** *20mins*

Ingredients
- 1/4 cup fig preserves
- 1 (8 ounce) ciabatta, cut lengthwise
- 1/4 cup crumbled blue cheese
- 2 tablespoons butter, softened
- 8 ounces sliced cooked chicken breasts
- 1/8 teaspoon fresh ground black pepper
- 2 cups arugula leaves
- 1 teaspoon fresh lemon juice

Directions
1. Spread jam over cut side of top half of bread.
2. Combine cheese and butter in a bowl, stirring until smooth.
3. Spread cheese mixture over cut side of bottom half of bread.
4. Arrange chicken evenly over cheese mixture; sprinkle with pepper.
5. Place top half of bread, jam side down, over chicken.
6. Heat a large nonstick skillet over medium heat, and add sandwich to pan.
7. Place a heavy cast-iron skillet on sandwich; cook 5 minutes or until both sides are browned, turning once.
8. (Or use a panini maker as you usually would. I don't have one. I have no idea how long it would take to make the sandwich that way.).

9. Place arugula in a bowl.
10. Drizzle lemon juice over arugula; toss gently.
11. Remove top bread half from sandwich. Arrange arugula mixture over chicken. Replace top bread half.
12. Cut sandwich into 4 equal portions.

Chicken Panini With Gouda Red Onion and

Servings: 2 | Cook: 3 mins | Prep: 20 mins | Total Time: 23mins

Ingredients
- 2 ciabatta rolls
- 2 tablespoons honey mustard dressing
- 1 cooked chicken breast
- 8 thinly sliced red onion rings
- arugula (2 handfuls)
- 3 ounces gouda cheese, sliced
- vegetable oil, for sauteing and brushing

Directions
1. Preheat a Panini grill.
2. Trim the top and bottom off the ciabatta rolls so that they are about 1 inch thick.
3. Slice open lengthwise.
4. Spread the honey-mustard over the inside of each sandwich.
5. Slice the chicken into four pieces lengthwise.
6. On roll bottoms, layer with cheese, follow with onion and arugula, finishing with cheese; cover with roll tops.
7. Brush both sides of the Panini with oil and grill in the preheated Panini press for 3 minutes, or according to the manufacturer's instructions.
8. The bread should be golden brown and the filling warmed through.
9. Serve with extra honey-mustard dressing on the side for dipping.

Chicken Parmesan Panini

"Crispy pan-fried chicken cutlets are sandwiched between thick slices of crusty bread with mozzarella cheese and traditional tomato sauce, then toasted in a panini press."
Pre: 10 m | Cook: 15 m | Ready In: 25 m

Ingredients

- 1/4 cup flour
- 1 teaspoon garlic powder
- 1/2 teaspoon salt
- 1/4 teaspoon black pepper
- 1 egg, beaten
- 1 cup panko bread crumbs
- 1/4 cup Parmesan cheese
- 4 small chicken cutlets*
- 2 tablespoons olive oil
- 4 slices fresh mozzarella cheese
- 1/4 cup Parmesan cheese
- 8 thick slices artisanal-style bread
- 1 (24 ounce) jar Ragu® Old World Style® Traditional Sauce
- Add all ingredients to list

Directions

1. Mix together the flour, garlic powder, salt and pepper in a shallow bowl. Place beaten egg in another bowl. Mix together panko bread crumbs and Parmesan cheese in a third shallow bowl.
2. Dredge each piece of chicken in the flour, coating both sides; shake off the extra. Dip chicken in beaten egg, and then press into the breadcrumbs, making sure to coat well on both sides. Set on a plate.
3. Heat olive oil in large skillet over medium-high heat. Pan fry chicken until no longer pink in the center and the juices run clear, about 4 minutes per side.
4. Place chicken on slices of bread. Spread about 1/4 cup of Ragu(R) Old World Style(R) Traditional Sauce over each piece of chicken. Top with a slice of cheese and a tablespoon of Parmesan cheese. Top with the remaining slices of bread. Heat in a panini press or in a large skillet until the cheese is melted. Heat remaining sauce for dipping.

Chicken Pesto and Olive Panini

Excellent blend of flavors. You don't need a panini press or Foreman Grill to make these delicious sandwiches.
Cook: *5 mins |* **Prep:** *5 mins |* **Total Time:** *10mins*

Ingredients

- 2 pieces flat bread (I use Toufayan brand)
- 1/2 teaspoon olive oil
- 2 tablespoons pesto sauce (I used Pesto or can use store bought pesto)
- 1/2 cup kalamata olive, pitted and coarsely chopped

- 1/2 tomatoes, seeded and coarsely chopped
- 10 leaves Baby Spinach
- 6 ounces fresh mozzarella cheese, sliced
- 1/2 cooked chicken breast, sliced (I used leftover grilled chicken)
- salt

Directions
1. On bottom of both bread pieces brush on olive oil.
2. Spread one tablespoon of pesto (or more if you like) on each piece of bread on the top side. So the bottom will have olive oil and the top will have pesto.
3. On the the pesto side on ONE HALF of bread place spinach leaves. Repeat with other bread.
4. On top of spinach place 1/4 of mozzarella. Repeat with other bread.
5. Layer on chicken, olives, tomatoes and 1/4 of mozzarella. Repeat on other bread to make two complete sandwiches. Fold in half with the olive oil side on the outside.
6. Grill on panini press or Foreman Grill.
7. If you don't have these (as I don't) heat grill pan to medium heat. Wash two bricks and cover with foil. Place sandwiches side by side on grill pan. Place foil covered bricks on top. Cook on medium for 4-6 minutes. Turn over and replace bricks. Cook an additional 4-6 minutes until cheese is melted and bread is toasted brown.

Chicken Pesto Paninis

"A delicious mix of chicken, pesto, veggies, and cheese all melted together on flavorful focaccia bread. Simple, fast, and very tasty - a nice change from normal sandwiches."
Pre: 15 m | Cook: 5 m | Ready In: 20 m

Ingredients
- 1 focaccia bread, quartered
- 1/2 cup prepared basil pesto
- 1 cup diced cooked chicken
- 1/2 cup diced green bell pepper
- 1/4 cup diced red onion
- 1 cup shredded Monterey Jack cheese
- Add all ingredients to list

Directions
1. Preheat a panini grill.

2. Slice each quarter of focaccia bread in half horizontally. Spread each half with pesto. Layer bottom halves with equal amounts chicken, bell pepper, onion, and cheese. Top with remaining focaccia halves, forming 4 sandwiches.
3. Grill paninis 5 minutes in the preheated grill, or until focaccia bread is golden brown and cheese is melted.

Chicken Pizziola Panini With Green Tea S

Cook: 15 mins | Prep: 0 mins | Total Time: 15mins

Ingredients
Chicken Pizziola Panini
- 1 teaspoon bread-dip seasoning (Parmesan blend)
- 4 boneless chicken cutlets (about 1 lb)
- cooking spray
- 8 teaspoons sun-dried tomatoes, spread
- 4 deli flavored folding flat bread
- 8 slices deli sandwich-style pepperoni
- provolone cheese

Green Tea Spiced Pears
- 6 bartlett pears
- 1/3 cup sugar
- 1/2 cup golden raisin
- 1/2 cup deli green tea with ginger and honey
- 1 teaspoon ginger, spice paste
- 1/4 teaspoon cinnamon
- 1 tablespoon cornstarch

Directions
1. Chicken Pizziola Panini:.
2. Preheat two-sided tabletop grill. Sprinkle seasoning over chicken, then coat with spray. Place chicken on grill and close lid; grill 2–3 minutes or until chicken is 165°F.
3. Spread 2 teaspoons tomato spread over the inside of each flatbread; top with chicken, 2 slices pepperoni, and 1 slice cheese. Close flatbreads.
4. Coat sandwiches with spray and place on grill, pressing lid down gently; grill 2–3 minutes or until crisp and golden. Serve.
5. Green Tea Spiced Pears:.
6. Peel pears and remove core; cut pears into small cubes.
7. Combine remaining ingredients in medium saucepan on medium heat and bring to a simmer; cook 5–6 minutes or until sugar dissolves and mixture thickens slightly.

8. Stir in pears and cornstarch; cook and stir 4–5 more minutes or until tender and sauce has thickened. Serve warm.

Chicken Salad and Roasted Veggie Panini

This is a delicious panini. Chicken salad, leftover roasted veggies (Roasted Vegetables), and Provolone cheese. Put this on homemade bread (Anadama Bread) and you have one yummy lunch.
Cook: 0 mins | **Prep:** 10 mins | **Total Time:** 10mins

Ingredients
- 2 slices of homemade bread
- 1/2 cup chicken salad (your choice)
- 1/2 cup roasted vegetables
- 1 sliced provolone cheese
- mayonnaise (as desired)

Directions
1. Spread bread with mayonnaise on the inside and a little butter on the outside.
2. Put one slice on the panini griddle.
3. Add the cheese, chicken salad, and veggies.
4. Put top slice of bread on and grill.

Chicken Salad Panini

Have any left over chicken that you don't know what to do with? How about trying this sandwich? The honey mustard dressing gives the chicken plenty of pizzazz, and the apples and pecans lend a lively crunch!
Servings: 2 | **Cook:** 5 mins | **Prep:** 20 mins | **Total Time:** 25mins

Ingredients
- 1/4 cup mayonnaise
- 1 1/2 teaspoons honey
- 3/4 teaspoon snipped fresh dill
- 3/4 teaspoon Dijon mustard
- 1 dash salt
- 1 dash pepper
- 1 cup cubed cooked chicken breast
- 3/4 cup shredded cheddar cheese
- 1/2 cup chopped peeled apple

- 1/4 cup chopped pecans, toasted
- 6 slices white bread
- 4 teaspoons butter, softened

Directions
1. In a small bowl, combine the first six ingredients.
2. In another bowl, combine the chicken, cheese, apple and pecans; add dressing and toss to coat.
3. Spread half of the chicken salad on two slices of bread.
4. Top each with another slice of bread, remaining chicken salad and remaining bread. Spread butter on both sides of sandwiches. Cook on a panini maker or indoor grill until bread is toasted and cheese is melted.

Chipotle Turkey Panini

Servings: 4 | Cook: 10 mins | Prep: 15 mins | Total Time: 25mins

Ingredients
- 8 slices sourdough bread
- 1/4-1/2 cup mayonnaise
- 1 -2 tablespoon chipotle chile in adobo, pureed
- 8 slices cooked bacon
- 1/2 onion, thinly sliced
- 1 tomatoes, thinly sliced
- 1 lb sliced deli turkey or 1 lb chopped cooked turkey
- 4 slices monterey jack cheese
- 1/4 cup olive oil (or less)

Directions
1. Preheat a panini grill (If you co not have a panini grill this can be done in a skillet or on your outdoor grill).
2. Stir together mayonnaise and chipotle chile sauce in a small bowl.
3. Stir half of the chipotle sauce in with the turkey.
4. Spread one side of each slice of sourdough with remaining chipotle sauce. Layer bottom halves with equal amounts turkey, onion, bacon, tomato and cheese. Top with remaining bread slices, forming 4 sandwiches.
5. Gently press sandwiches together with your hand. Brush both outer sides of sandwiches with olive oil; you will probably not use an entire 1/4 cup of olive oil.
6. Grill paninis about 5 minutes in the preheated grill, or until bread is golden brown and cheese is melted. Or heat them over medium-low heat, covered, in

a large skillet for about 4 minutes on each side, until bread is toasted on both sides and sandwich is heated throughout.

Creamy Wild Rice Soup with Smoked Turkey

This top-rated smoked turkey soup recipe is perfect paired with a hot grilled cheese sandwich or hearty panini.
Serving: 8

Ingredients
- 2 teaspoons butter or stick margarine
- 1 cup chopped carrot
- 1 cup chopped onion
- 1 cup chopped green onions
- 1 teaspoon chopped fresh or 1/4 teaspoon dried rosemary
- 1/4 teaspoon black pepper
- 3 garlic cloves, minced
- 2 (16-ounce) cans fat-free, less-sodium chicken broth
- 1 1/2 cups chopped smoked turkey breast (1/2 pound)
- 1 cup uncooked wild rice
- 1/3 cup all-purpose flour
- 2 3/4 cups 2% reduced-fat milk
- 2 tablespoons dry sherry
- 1/2 teaspoon salt

Directions
1. Melt the butter in a Dutch oven over medium-high heat. Add carrot and next 5 ingredients (carrot through garlic). Sauté 8 minutes or until browned. Stir in broth, scraping pan to loosen browned bits. Stir in turkey and rice; bring to a boil. Cover, reduce heat, and simmer 1 hour and 15 minutes or until rice is tender.
2. Lightly spoon flour into a dry measuring cup; level with a knife. Combine flour and milk in a small bowl, stirring with a whisk. Add to pan. Cook over medium heat until thick (about 8 minutes), stirring frequently. Stir in sherry and salt.

Darthlaurie's Turkey Avocado Panini Mash

I wanted a decadent turkey avocado sandwich. I wanted to make it on our old waffle iron--it has a flat side that we use for tuna melts. This sandwich is absolutely decadent when you use sharp provolone and the best sourdough bread you can find (I like thick slices). Enjoy!

Servings: 1 | Cook: 5 mins | Prep: 10 mins | Total Time: 15mins

Ingredients

- 2 tablespoons olive oil
- 1 tablespoon Italian seasoning
- 1 teaspoon garlic powder or 1 teaspoon roasted garlic powder
- 2 slices sourdough bread
- 2 slices provolone cheese (preferably sharp)
- 6 slices mesquite smoked turkey, sliced wafer thin
- 1/2 avocado, sliced

Directions

1. Heat panini press, waffle iron, or pan.
2. Combine olive oil and seasonings.
3. On one slice of bread stack one slice of cheese, all the turkey and avocado and then the last slice of cheese. Top with second slice of bread.
4. Brush half of the olive oil mixture on the top piece of bread. Flip over and brush remaining olive oil mixture on the other piece of bread.
5. Cook in the panini press or waffle iron until golden brown or cook in pan until one side is golden brown and then flip over and cook until the other side is golden brown.
6. Enjoy!

Day After Turkey Day Panini

The last thing you want the day after Thanksgiving is another turkey dinner! Reinvent those leftovers into a yummy panini sandwich and have all the flavors you love in a new inventive way! This is also great any day you are craving Thanksgiving! Amounts are approximate. Use the amount you want for each sandwich!
Servings: 1 | Cook: 5 mins | Prep: 2 mins | Total Time: 7mins

Ingredients

- 2 slices bread, thick sliced, preferably day old
- 1/2 cup turkey gravy, leftover
- 2 ounces cooked turkey
- 1/4 cup turkey stuffing, leftover (aka dressing)
- 1/4 cup cranberry sauce
- salt & freshly ground black pepper, to taste
- 1/8 teaspoon ground sage
- 1 ounce monterey jack pepper cheese, sliced (any type of cheese is good)

Directions
1. Spread some cold gravy over one side of each slice of bread. Heat the rest of the gravy and use for dipping! On one piece of bread layer turkey and dressing/stuffing and cheese if desired. Top with some cranberry sauce and season with sage, salt and pepper if desired. Place other bread slice of top, gravy side down.
2. Butter the outside of the sandwich on the each side. I butter the top of the sandwich and then lay the sandwich in the preheated pan with that buttered side now on the bottom. Now butter the new 'top' of the sandwich, close or cover and weigh down and toast til done.
3. Toast to golden brown in a panini press or in a cast iron skillet with another pot or pan on top of sandwich with a heavy can weighing it down to 'press' the sandwich.

Fig Glazed Chicken Panini with Brie

For sandwiches with great crunch, look for a rustic whole-grain bread boule. If you have trouble cutting 1-ounce slices across the width of the boule, cut it in half first.
Serving: *4 |* ***Total Time:*** *24 Minutes |* ***Hands-on:*** *24 Minutes*

Ingredients
- 2 teaspoons canola oil
- 3 (4-ounce) skinless, boneless chicken thighs
- 2 tablespoons fig jam
- 3/8 teaspoon kosher salt, divided
- 3/8 teaspoon freshly ground black pepper, divided
- 1 cup chopped Lacinato kale
- 1 teaspoon sherry vinegar
- 8 (1-ounce) slices whole-grain bread
- 1 small ripe pear, cut into 12 thin slices
- 3 ounces Brie cheese, chopped
- Cooking spray

Directions
1. Heat a large skillet over medium-high heat. Add oil; swirl to coat. Add chicken to pan; cook 4 minutes or until browned. Turn chicken over; cook 2 minutes or until done. Remove chicken from pan; let stand 5 minutes. Cut chicken into thin slices. Combine chicken, jam, 1/4 teaspoon salt, and 1/4 teaspoon pepper; toss to coat.
2. Combine kale and vinegar in a medium bowl; toss to coat. Divide chicken mixture evenly among 4 bread slices. Top each with 3 pear slices and 3/4 ounce cheese; sprinkle remaining 1/8 teaspoon salt and remaining 1/8 teaspoon pepper over sandwiches. Divide kale mixture evenly among

sandwiches; top with remaining bread slices. Lightly coat sandwiches with cooking spray.
3. Return pan to medium heat. Add sandwiches to pan. Place a cast-iron or heavy skillet on top of sandwiches, pressing gently to flatten; cook 2 minutes on each side or until browned and cheese begins to melt.

Greek Marinated Chicken Panini With Pest

Excellent tasting panini. I recommend using a panini press but if you don't have one then you can use two cast iron skillets. This is a recipe i came up with on a whim and it tasted great.
Servings: 4 | **Cook:** 6 mins | **Prep:** 0 mins | **Total Time:** 6mins

Ingredients
- 8 slices whole grain bread
- 2 boneless chicken breasts
- 1 (8 ounce) bottle marinated artichoke hearts
- 4 slices Swiss cheese
- 8 teaspoons of bail pesto sauce
- 1/2 cup extra virgin olive oil
- 1 tablespoon dried oregano
- 1 teaspoon sugar
- 1 teaspoon lemon pepper seasoning
- 1 teaspoon fresh ground pepper
- 1/2 teaspoon kosher salt
- 3 garlic cloves, minced
- 1 lemon, juice and zest of

Directions
1. Add marinade ingredients to large ziplock bag (oil,oregano, sugar, lemon pepper seasoning, salt, pepper, garlic, and both the zest and juice from 1 lemon).
2. With a fork punch several holes in chicken breast so marinade can penetrate. Add chicken to bag and marinade for 4 hours.
3. Remove chicken from marinade and grill on charcoal/gas grill with a hunk of smoking wood until juices run clear. Remove and let chicken cool slightly to handle.
4. Put your palm flat on each chicken breast and slice each chicken breast in 1/2 so that each piece is 1/2 as thick as original chicken breast. Spread about 2 teaspoons of pesto over 4 slices of the bread. Add cheese and then 1/2 of each breast of chicken that you cut above. Add 3 artichoke per sandwich, broken up. Put other 4 slices of bread on top.

5. Grill in panini press until bread is nicely toasted and cheese is melted (about 4 minutes).

Grilled Chicken and Swiss Panini

Smoked turkey and ham make tasty substitutes for the smoked chicken in these pressed Italian sandwiches.
Serving: 2 | **Prep:** 2 Minutes | **Cook:** 5 Minutes

Ingredients
- 1/4 pound thinly sliced smoked chicken breast
- 2 (3/4-ounce) slices reduced-fat, reduced-sodium Swiss cheese (such as Alpine Lace)
- 4 (0.5-ounce) slices very thin white bread
- Butter-flavored cooking spray

Directions
1. Divide chicken and cheese evenly between 2 bread slices. Top with remaining bread slices.
2. Coat tops of sandwiches with cooking spray. Place sandwiches, coated sides down, in a grill pan or large nonstick skillet over medium heat. Coat tops of sandwiches with cooking spray. Place a piece of foil over sandwiches in pan; place a heavy skillet on top of foil to press sandwiches. Cook 3 minutes or until lightly browned. Turn sandwiches over; replace foil and heavy skillet. Cook 2 minutes or until lightly browned. Cut sandwiches in half, and serve immediately.
3. Note: We used a smaller skillet weighted with 2 canned goods to press the sandwiches, but a cast-iron skillet would also do the trick.

Grilled Chicken Pesto Panini

If you have an electric panini maker then use it for this, if not you need two skillets, one heavy cast iron skillet or similar for the top to weigh down the panini. This makes a perfect lunch or light dinner. Plan ahead the chicken needs to marinade for 1 hour before cooking....this works with a George Foreman grill, just make certain to hold down on the top lid firmly while cooking to ensure toasting the bread, or maybe you are lucky enough to own a panini maker, then you will not need the heavy skillet for the top. Double the recipe if desired. You will love this!
Servings: 4 | **Cook:** 0 mins | **Prep:** 1 hr 30 mins | **Total Time:** 1hr

Ingredients
- 4 boneless skinless chicken breasts, and pounded thin

- 3 tablespoons olive oil
- 1 tablespoon fresh minced garlic
- 1 tablespoon dried Italian seasoning
- salt and pepper
- 1 1/2 cups roasted red peppers (bottled or canned)
- 4 slices provolone cheese (sliced thick)
- 1/2-3/4 cup pesto sauce (bottled or homemade)
- 8 slices Italian bread (sliced 1/2-inch thick, can use about 4 x 4-inch ciabatta rolls in place of the Italian bread)
- olive oil, for brushing on bread

Directions
1. Pound the chicken fillets until thin between two pieces of waxed paper, then marinate in oil, garlic, pepper and Italian seasoning for about 1-1/2 hours.
2. Heat a grill pan or sauté pan (the breasts can also be grilled on the BBQ).
3. Season the breasts with salt and pepper.
4. Cook the chicken on medium heat for about 5 minutes per side, or until golden and cooked through.
5. Remove from pan and place on a plate or board.
6. Top each fillet with some of the roasted peppers and a slice of cheese.
7. Spread BOTH sides of the bread with pesto sauce.
8. Place chicken inside the bread and form to a sandwich.
9. Brush both sides of the outside of bread with olive oil.
10. Heat a grill pan or a 10-inch skillet on medium high heat. Place the panini in the pan (only 2 at a time).
11. Weigh the panini down with another heavy skillet and then top with a heavy can (a very large can of tomato juice works great for this!) cook for about 3 minutes, or until bread is toasted.
12. Turn the panini, and weigh it down again with a heavy skillet and a can on top, and toast for another 3 minutes.
13. Remove from pan and cut in half.

Grilled Turkey and Swiss Panini Sandwich

After serving this to hubby for lunch today, he said "I HAVE to have that again!" Based on Lainey's Turkey Panini and made with ingredients you'll already have on hand.
*Cook: 3 mins | **Prep:** 5 mins | **Total Time:** 8mins*

Ingredients
- 2 slices sourdough bread
- 1 -2 tablespoon apricot jam
- 4 ounces sliced turkey breast

- 1 slice sweet onion
- 1/2 tablespoon chopped roasted red pepper (from a jar)
- 2 slices Swiss cheese
- nonstick cooking spray (olive oil or butter flavored)

Directions
1. Preheat skillet or griddle to medium high and spray with nonstick spray.
2. Spread jam on one piece of bread.
3. On other piece of bread, place turkey, onion slice, roasted red peppers and Swiss cheese.
4. Place bread spread with jam on top of other side of sandwich and put on griddle.
5. Cover with a deep pot lid and cook a minute or so (until lightly browned).
6. Remove lid, flip sandwich carefully and cook other side about a minute of so (until lightly browned).
7. If sandwich browns before cheese melts, put it in the microwave for 15 seconds or so.

Grilled Turkey Asparagus Pesto Paninis

"These are fast, yet tasty sandwiches and are best on the grill! The oatmeal bread really gives these paninis great flavor, but you could use another type of hearty bread as well. My husband and I love them in the summer when the asparagus and basil are in season. Serve with a side of coleslaw for a satisfying crunchy side dish."
Pre: *20 m |* **Cook:** *20 m |* **Ready In:** *40 m*

Ingredients
PESTO
- 2 cups chopped fresh basil
- 1/2 cup grated Parmesan cheese
- 1/4 cup extra-virgin olive oil
- 2 garlic cloves
- coarse salt and freshly ground black pepper to taste
- 1/4 cup pine nuts

PANINI
- 8 fresh asparagus spears, trimmed, or more to taste
- 2 tablespoons butter, softened
- 4 slices soft oatmeal bread (such as Pepperidge Farm®)
- 4 slices provolone cheese
- 1/4 pound sliced deli turkey meat
- Add all ingredients to list

Directions
1. Blend basil, Parmesan cheese, olive oil, garlic, salt, and pepper in a food processor or blender until smooth, scraping down sides as needed. Add pine nuts and pulse just until pine nuts are chopped, but still visible.
2. Preheat grill for medium-low heat and lightly oil the grate.
3. Cook asparagus on the preheated grill directly on the grate or on a grill pan until tender, 5 to 10 minutes.
4. Spread 1 1/2 teaspoons butter onto 1 side of each bread slice. Spread desired amount of pesto onto the opposite side of each bread slice. Layer provolone cheese and turkey on the pesto-side of 2 bread slices; top with a second bread slice, pesto-side down.
5. Place sandwiches directly on the grill and cook until golden brown and cheese is melted, about 6 minutes per side. Remove from grill and cut each sandwich in half.

Grilled Turkey Cuban Sandwiches

"Grilled turkey breast, ham, cheese and pickles in a panini-style sandwich."
***Pre:** 15 m | **Cook:** 2 h | **Ready In:** 2 h 15 m*

Ingredients
- Non-stick cooking spray
- 1 (3 pound) Butterball® Boneless Breast of Turkey Roast, thawed
- 2 cloves garlic, peeled, sliced
- 1 tablespoon canola oil
- 1 tablespoon ground cumin
- 2 teaspoons salt
- 1 teaspoon coarsely ground black pepper
- 2 loaves Cuban, French or Italian bread (15 inches long)
- 1/4 cup honey mustard
- 1/2 pound smoked ham
- 1/2 pound sliced Swiss cheese
- 12 sandwich-style dill pickle slices
- Add all ingredients to list

Directions
1. Spray cold grate of outdoor gas grill with cooking spray. Prepare grill for medium indirect heat.
2. Remove turkey from package. Dry with paper towels. Discard gravy packet or refrigerate for another use (within 2 - 3 days). Lift string netting and shift position on roast for easier removal after cooking. Cut small slits, at least 1 inch apart, over entire surface of turkey. Insert 1 garlic slice into each slit. Brush turkey with oil.

3. Combine cumin, salt and pepper. Sprinkle over turkey.
4. Place turkey on grill grate over drip pan. Cover grill with lid. Grill 1 1/4 to 1-3/4 hours, or until meat thermometer reaches 170 degrees F when inserted into center of roast. Remove from grill. Let stand 10 minutes.
5. Remove string netting. Cut half of the turkey into six 1/8-inch-thick slices. Set aside. Refrigerate unsliced turkey for another use.
6. Cut each bread loaf lengthwise in half. Then, cut each into 3 pieces (for 6 sandwiches). Spread the bottom half of each section with 2 teaspoons mustard. Top with the sliced turkey, ham, cheese and pickles. Cover with tops of bread loaves. Press sandwiches with hands to flatten. Tightly wrap individually in aluminum foil.
7. Place wrapped sandwiches on grill grate. Top each with heavy iron skillet or brick. Grill 3 to 5 minutes on each side, or until heated through.
8. Serve sandwiches warm, wrapped in aluminum foil.

Grilled Turkey Panini Sandwiches

I first had one of these in the brewery in Grand Marais, Michigan in the Upper Peninsula of Michigan. I love these leftover turkey sandwiches, may also use chicken. I will also roast turkey breast when I get a craving for these sandwiches. May add more or take away the amounts of ingredients in the sandwich spread, they are guestimates, as I just dump and add to taste.
Servings: 2 | **Cook:** 15 mins | **Prep:** 15 mins | **Total Time:** 30mins

Ingredients
- 2 slices turkey breast
- 4 leaves red leaf lettuce
- 1 slice red onion
- 2 -4 slices tomatoes
- 2 -4 slices Swiss cheese
- Sandwich spread
- 1 cup mayonnaise
- 1 tablespoon mustard
- 1 teaspoon garlic powder
- 1 teaspoon onion powder
- 1 dash cayenne pepper
- 1/2 teaspoon basil
- 1/2 teaspoon parsley
- 6 drops hot sauce
- salt and pepper
- 1/2 teaspoon lemon juice, fresh squeezed

Directions

1. Mix up the sandwich spread and let marinate a minimum of 4 hours.
2. Slice up all the vegetables and get them ready.
3. Grill the bread slices, add the turkey and Swiss cheese til warm.
4. Place on a plate, add the vegetables, add sandwich spread, cut in half and enjoy!

Grilled Turkey Panini

A delicious panini sandwich with mushrooms, apples, cheese, and turkey. Just concocted the recipe with the new panini press we got and it was GOOD
***Cook:** 4 mins | **Prep:** 5 mins | **Total Time:** 9mins*

Ingredients

- 2 slices portabello grilling mushrooms
- 2 -3 thin slices granny smith apples
- 2 slices of deli sliced Swiss cheese
- 5 slices of oven baked turkey
- 1 teaspoon spicy brown mustard
- 1 teaspoon Miracle Whip
- 2 slices of your favorite panini bread (I use Texas Toast or Portaguese rolls)

Directions

1. Mix the miracle whip and spicy mustard in a bowl.
2. Then, butter the OUTSIDE of the roll/bread for toasting use. Then spread your sauce mixture on both insides.
3. Start with 2 slices of Turkey.
4. Place your 2 slices of mushroom.
5. 2 more slices of turkey.
6. Put your slices of apple.
7. Then top with the last slice of turkey and your 2 slices of Swiss cheese.
8. Put on the grill or wherever you make your sandwich. Grill for about 4 minutes. Voila.

Grilled Tuscan Chicken Panini

***Servings:** 4-6 | **Cook:** 10 mins | **Prep:** 2 hrs | **Total Time:** 2hrs*

Ingredients

- 1 cup mayonnaise
- 1/4 cup chopped fresh basil
- 4 tablespoons fresh lemon juice, divided
- 4 teaspoons minced garlic, divided
- 1/4 cup olive oil
- 1/2 teaspoon Italian seasoning
- 1 teaspoon kosher salt
- 1/2 teaspoon ground black pepper
- 1 lb chicken tenderloins
- 1 lb loaf ciabatta, halved lengthwise
- 1 tomatoes, thinly sliced
- 2 avocados, pitted, peeled and sliced
- 4 -6 slices provolone cheese

Directions

1. In a small bowl, combine mayonnaise, basil, 1 tablespoon lemon juice, and 1 teaspoon garlic. Cover and refrigerate at least 2 hours.
2. In a large resealable plastic bag, combine olive oil, remaining 3 tablespoons lemon juice, remaining 3 teaspoons garlic, Italian seasoning, salt, and pepper. Add chicken; seal bag and toss gently to combine. Refrigerate for 1 hour.
3. Heat a medium skillet over medium-high heat. Remove chicken from bag, discarding marinade. Cook chicken until browned on both sides and cooked through, about 5 minutes per side.
4. Preheat panini press to medium-high heat. Spread mayonnaise mixture on cut sides of bread. On bottom half of bread, layer chicken, tomato, avocado, cheese, and top half of bread. Cut sandwich into fourths or sixths. Cook on panini press according to manufacturer's instructions. Serve immediately.

Hot Brown Panini

This richly delicious sandwich was inspired by reader Julie Morgan's recipe for a Kentucky classic.
Serving: 8

Ingredients

- 2 tablespoons melted butter
- 16 (1/2-inch-thick) Italian bread slices
- 1 cup (4 oz.) shredded Swiss cheese, divided
- 3 cups chopped cooked chicken or turkey
- 4 plum tomatoes, sliced
- 3 cups warm White Cheese Sauce, divided

- 13 cooked bacon slices, crumbled

Directions
1. Brush melted butter evenly on 1 side of 16 bread slices. Place, butter sides down, on wax paper.
2. Sprinkle 1 Tbsp. Swiss cheese on top of each of 8 bread slices; top evenly with chicken, tomato slices, and 1 cup warm White Cheese Sauce. Sprinkle with bacon and remaining cheese, and top with remaining bread slices, butter sides up.
3. Cook sandwiches, in batches, in a preheated panini press 2 to 3 minutes or until golden brown. Serve with remaining 2 cups warm White Cheese Sauce for dipping.

Jerk Turkey Panini

From Betty Crocker. This is really just a grilled sandwich; not cooked on a panini press.
Servings: *4 |* **Cook:** *5 mins |* **Prep:** *10 mins |* **Total Time:** *15mins*

Ingredients
- 8 slices crusty bread (1/2-inch thick slices)
- 2 tablespoons margarine or 2 tablespoons butter, softened
- 1/2 lb thinly sliced cooked deli turkey
- 1 medium papaya, peeled, pitted, and sliced
- 4 slices monterey jack pepper cheese
- 1/4 cup caribbean jerk seasoning, sauce or 1/4 cup fruit chutney

Directions
1. Spread 1 side of each bread slices with margarine.
2. Place 4 bread slices margarine side down; top with turkey, papaya, and cheese.
3. Top with remaining bread slices, margarine sides up.
4. Place sandwiches in a large nonstick skillet over medium heat (do in batches if necessary).
5. Cover and cook 4-5 minutes, turning once, until bread is crisp and cheese is melted.
6. Serve with sauce.

Marinated Chicken Panini

Based on a recipe I found in "Classic Home Cooking". I usually skip the honey. Use whatever herbs you like. I usually use parsley, cilantro, and thyme.

***Servings:** 6 | **Cook:** 8 mins | **Prep:** 30 mins | **Total Time:** 38mins*

Ingredients
- 3 1/2 lbs chicken, roasted
- 1 large red pepper
- 1 large yellow pepper
- 1 cup pitted black olives
- 1 cup arugula leaf
- 6 hoagie rolls
- 1 tablespoon olive oil

MARINADE
- 4 tablespoons olive oil
- 2 tablespoons honey
- 1/2 lemon, juice of
- 1 tablespoon chopped herbs
- salt and pepper

Directions
1. Strip chicken meat from bones and cut into bite-sized strips.
2. Combine marinade ingredients and toss with chicken, cover and let the flavors develop.
3. Preheat grill and roast peppers until mostly blackened.
4. Place in a paper bag until cool, remove skins and discard.
5. Cut peppers into strips.
6. Make the panini: Brush the (outside) top and bottom of the rolls with olive oil.
7. Cover the bottom of the rolls with the peppers, then the chicken, then the olives and top with the arugula leaves.
8. Brush the inside of the top half with the leftover marinade, if you have any.
9. Cover the rolls with their tops and grill in a panini press until done.
10. NOTE: Mozzarella cheese and onion slices are also nice additions to this sandwich.

Mediterranean Chicken Panini

This was a bit of a strange combination that turned out just amazing!! The flavors are strong and vibrant, complimenting the chicken nicely. You could probably use left over or rotisserie chicken to speed things up, although I cooked up some breasts for this sandwich. For the chorizo, you want to use the kind that you get at the deli and has already been cooked and cured, not the raw stuff. The amounts are really just estimates, since it'll vary depending on the size of your bread. For grilling the bread, use a panini press, a Foreman grill, or even just a pan to toast the bread. I recommend the bread have a strong enough texture, like a ciabatta, saloio, or my favorite is the

Cook: 15 mins | Prep: 5 mins | Total Time: 20mins

Ingredients
- 1 lb boneless skinless chicken, cooked and heated
- 6 tablespoons olive tapenade
- 1/4 lb chorizo sausage, sliced thin
- 1/4 lb sharp provolone cheese
- 1 tomatoes, sliced
- 8 slices bread (thin slices)
- olive oil

Directions
1. Heat your panini press or pan to med. high - high. Brush one side of each piece of bread with olive oil. Cut the chicken into thin strips.
2. Place bread, olive oil side down. Place a layer of provolone, then spread a thin layer of olive tapenade. Add a layer of chicken, a layer of tomato slices and then a layer of the chorizo. Top with another piece of bread, olive oil side out. Repeat for additional sandwiches.
3. Place sandwich on pan or press, cooking till both sides are golden brown (with a pan, you'll need to flip the sandwich). Cut in half and serve immediately.

Next Day Turkey Panini

Servings: 4 | Cook: 6 mins | Prep: 20 mins | Total Time: 26mins

Ingredients
- 4 soft French rolls or 4 sourdough rolls
- olive oil
- 1/4-1/2 cup cranberry sauce or 1/4-1/2 cup chutney
- fresh baby spinach leaves or flat leaf parsley or fresh sage leaf
- 8 ounces sliced cooked turkey (leftover)
- 2 ounces thinly sliced country ham or 2 ounces prosciutto
- 8 ounces sliced smoked mozzarella cheese or 8 ounces provolone cheese or 8 ounces cheddar cheese

Directions
1. Split rolls horizontally. Lightly brush cut sides of rolls with olive oil. Spread 1 to 2 tablespoons cranberry relish on bottom halves of rolls. Layer the greens, turkey, ham, and cheese on rolls. Place tops of rolls on filling.
2. Preheat covered indoor grill. Place sandwiches in grill. Cover and cook for 6 minutes or until cheese is melted and rolls are crisp.

Orange Chicken Panini

Just got a new panini maker and I tried this recipe from the Sandwich Maker Cookbook to make an interesting sandwich.
Servings: 1 | **Cook:** 10 mins | **Prep:** 10 mins | **Total Time:** 20mins

Ingredients
- 2 slices whole wheat bread or 2 slices rye bread or 2 slices white bread or 2 slices sourdough bread or 2 slices raisin bread or 2 slices nut bread
- 1 teaspoon mayonnaise
- 2 slices cooked turkey or 2 slices cooked chicken
- 2 slices mozzarella cheese
- 1 orange, 3 segments used
- cilantro
- salt

Directions
1. Spread inside of bread slices with mayonnaise, Layer chicken, cheese, and orange segments on bread.
2. Sprinkle with cilantro and salt.
3. Make in sandwich maker or panini maker, follow machines directions.

Panera Bread's Turkey Artichoke Panini

This is my favorite sandwich at Panera so I was happy to find the recipe and share! It's a terrific way to use up leftover spinach artichoke dip, or an excuse to make some up...try Low Fat Spinach and Artichoke Dip or Skinny Spinach Artichoke Dip to cut out some of the fat.
Cook: 5 mins | **Prep:** 15 mins | **Total Time:** 20mins

Ingredients
- 1 loaf pesto focaccia bread
- 8 ounces freshly sliced turkey
- 4 ounces spinach artichoke spread (Available at your local grocer)
- 2 ounces asiago cheese (asiago parmesan blend)
- 1 small red onion, diced
- 1 tablespoon olive oil
- 1 tablespoon balsamic vinegar
- 1 -2 tomatoes, sliced (6-8 slices)

- 1 pinch salt and pepper

Directions
1. Preheat panini grill to medium temperature. In a medium sauce pan, sauté diced red onion in olive oil until transparent. Add balsamic vinegar and salt and pepper to taste.
2. Slice the loaf of pesto focaccia into two semi-circles, and halve each semi-circle. Layer the turkey onto the bottom halves of the focaccia bread, and spread spinach artichoke mix over turkey. Layer sautéed onions, asiago/parmesan blend and tomato slices. Close face of panini with the top halves of focaccia bread.
3. Add panini to preheated grill and press lightly. Grill 5 minutes on medium or until the cheese begins to melt and there are grill marks on the focaccia bread.
4. Serve hot with chips or your favorite soup!

Peppery Turkey and Brie Panini

This panini has the perfect combo of sweet and spicy flavors.
Serving: 8

Ingredients
- 1 (15-oz.) Brie round
- 16 multigrain sourdough bread slices
- 2 pounds thinly sliced smoked turkey
- 1/2 cup red pepper jelly
- 2 tablespoons melted butter

Directions
1. Trim and discard rind from Brie. Cut Brie into 1/2-inch-thick slices. Layer 8 bread slices evenly with turkey and Brie.
2. Spread 1 Tbsp. pepper jelly on 1 side of each remaining 8 bread slices; place, jelly sides down, onto Brie. Brush sandwiches with melted butter.
3. Cook sandwiches, in batches, in a preheated panini press 2 to 3 minutes or until golden brown.
4. Note: For testing purposes only, we used Braswell's Red Pepper Jelly.

Pesto Chicken and Arugula Panini

***Servings:** 2 | **Cook:** 5 mins | **Prep:** 5 mins | **Total Time:** 10mins*

Ingredients
- 2 French rolls
- 2 tablespoons basil pesto
- 6 ounces grilled chicken, thinly sliced
- 2 ounces gruyere cheese, sliced
- 1 cup arugula leaf

Directions
1. Preheat panini press or stovetop griddle pan.
2. Slice buns in half. Pick out some of the bread from the top and bottom halves to create a slight depression.
3. Brush outsides of buns lightly with oil.
4. Spread cut sides of buns with pesto.
5. Top one side of each bun with chicken, cheese and arugula. Close buns.
6. Place on panini press or griddle. Cover with grill top or grill press.
7. Grill 2-3 minutes on each side or until golden and cheese starts to melt.

Philly Turkey Panini

Servings: 4 | Cook: 5 mins | Prep: 6 mins | Total Time: 11mins

Ingredients
- 8 slices rye bread, 1/2 inch thick
- 2 tablespoons margarine (softened)
- 1/2 lb turkey, thinly sliced cooked deli
- 4 slices mozzarella cheese

Directions
1. Spread one side of each bread slice with margarine. Place 4 bread slices margarine sides down in a 12-inch skillet;top with turkey and cheese. Top with remaining bread slices, margarine sides up.
2. Cover and cook sandwiches over medium heat 4 to 5 minutes, turning once, until bread is crisp and cheese is melted.

Pomegranate & Turkey Panini With Hor

I just came up with this and it turned out really yummy. I little sweet, a little hot, and quick and easy to make. The ingredients listed are for a typical sandwich size so you may need to adjust the amounts if you're making a larger size sandwich.

Servings: 1 | Cook: 4 mins | Prep: 2 mins | Total Time: 6mins

Ingredients

- 2 slices bread (foccacia or a bagel would work well also)
- 1 slice monterey jack cheese (from the deli)
- 3 slices smoked turkey
- 1 tablespoon horseradish mayonnaise
- 1 1/2 tablespoons pomegranate jelly
- Optional toppings
- lettuce
- tomatoes

Directions

1. Layer on a piece of bread the cheese and turkey and then place on a panini maker or G.F. grill.
2. Toast till bread has browned and cheese has melted.
3. Open sandwich and spread the mayo and jelly onto the sandwich and add any additional toppings.
4. Put back together and enjoy.

Rejuvenated Rustic Turkey – Artichoke Pa

Similar to one of my favorite selections at Panera Bread restaurant--this one will work for lunch as is with a few carrot-sticks on the side OR add a cup of soup or small salad for delicious dinner-time fare. I don't have a panini-maker--so my two large cast-iron frying pans get called into action.
Cook: 10 mins | Prep: 15 mins | Total Time: 25mins

Ingredients

- 1/4 cup pine nuts
- 2 tablespoons butter
- 1/2 cup shallot, sliced
- 1 (8 ounce) jar artichokes, quartered, drained
- 1 loaf focaccia bread
- 8 tablespoons mayonnaise, divided
- 1 bunch spinach, fresh, divided
- 1 cup asiago cheese, grated
- 1 lb turkey breast, sliced, divided
- salt & pepper, taste
- 1 dash cayenne chili pepper flakes (optional)

- 8 slices sun-dried tomatoes, packed in oil, drained

Directions
1. Lightly toast pine nuts in cast-iron frying pan or oven; pour nuts into small bowl; set aside to cool.
2. Melt butter in empty pan, sauté shallots, stirring lightly; set aside.
3. Coarsely chop artichokes, then add to shallots in warm pan; set aside.
4. Cut focaccia bread into four equal sandwich portions, then slice horizontally; spread each slice with one tablespoon of mayonnaise.
5. Layer spinach and tomato slices equally on four of the bread slices.
6. Add the grated cheese and toasted pine-nuts to the artichokes-shallot mixture in the pan; quickly divide into four portions and spoon over the spinach and tomatoes.
7. Add one fourth of the turkey breast meat to each of the sandwiches, lightly add salt & pepper and cayenne pepper flakes to taste; put the lid on the sandwich and press lightly.
8. Place sandwiches into panini-maker and heat per manufacturer's suggestions….OR….place sandwiches into large buttered medium-hot frying pan, place another heavy frying pan on top; then press down firmly to heat sandwich like this for 1-2 minutes.

Roasted Turkey Panini With Cranberry Com

Great for holiday leftovers or when you wish it was Thanksgiving, but it's July. If you can't get fresh cranberries, I have taken whole cranberry sauce and mix sauteed red onions with it.
Cook: 3 mins | **Prep:** 10 mins | **Total Time:** 13mins

Ingredients
- 2 loaves onion focaccia bread
- 1 lb roasted turkey breast
- 6 ounces dried cranberries
- 4 slices cheese
- 1 small diced red onion
- 1/2 tablespoon olive oil
- salt & pepper

Directions
1. Saute the dried cranberries and red onion in the olive oil for two minutes.
2. Add salt and pepper to taste.
3. Add one teaspoon of water to keep ingredients moist.
4. Set cranberry compote aside.

5. Slice the foccacia in half, then horizontally to create a top and bottom for the sandwich.
6. Cover the bottom half of the foccacia with cranberry compote and top with 4 ounces of turkey and one slice of cheese.
7. Place top of foccacia over sandwich.
8. Grill over medium-high heat on both sides or use an authentic panini grill.

Roasted Turkey Panini

great for leftovers, but chicken is fine too.
Servings: 4 | **Cook:** 5 mins | **Prep:** 5 mins | **Total Time:** 10mins

Ingredients
- 1 rosemary and onion focaccia bread
- 1 lb roasted turkey breast
- 6 ounces dried cranberries
- 4 slices sharp cheddar cheese (1 oz ea)
- 1 small red onion, diced
- 1/2 tablespoon olive oil
- salt
- fresh ground black pepper

Directions
1. Saute the dried cranberries and red onion in olive oil for two minutes. Add salt and pepper to taste. Add one tablespoon of water to keep ingredients moist. Set cranberry compote aside.
2. Slice the rosemary & onion focaccias in half, then slice horizontally to create the top and bottom sandwich portions.
3. Cover the bottom half of the focaccia with cranberry compote and top with 4 ounces of roasted turkey breast and one slice of sharp cheddar cheese.
4. Place top of focaccia over sandwich. Grill over medium-high heat on both sides.

Roasted Turkey Pesto Panini

healthy and delicious
Servings: 1 | **Cook:** 0 mins | **Prep:** 4 mins | **Total Time:** 4mins

Ingredients
- 4 ounces turkey meat

- 2 ounces roasted pepper
- 1 ounce lettuce greens
- 1/2 ounce pesto sauce
- 2 ounces goat cheese
- 1 loaf ciabatta

Directions
1. Place ingredients on bread and heat on grill.

Rosemary Chicken Panini with Spinach and Sun Dried Tomatoes

Grilled Rosemary-Chicken Panini with Spinach and Sun-Dried Tomatoes is a delicious solution to the busy weeknight dinner dilemma. This excellent sandwich is loaded with fresh flavor and is guaranteed to satisfy any appetite.
Serving: 4 | Total Time: *1 Hour, 10 Minutes |* **Hands-on:** *40 Minutes*

Ingredients
- 2 tablespoons extra-virgin olive oil, divided
- 1 teaspoon chopped fresh rosemary
- 4 (4-ounce) chicken cutlets
- 1/4 cup chopped drained oil-packed sun-dried tomato
- 1/8 teaspoon crushed red pepper
- 8 garlic cloves, thinly sliced
- 1 (6-ounce) package fresh baby spinach
- 3/8 teaspoon salt, divided
- Cooking spray
- 1/8 teaspoon freshly ground black pepper
- 8 (1-ounce) slices country-style Italian bread
- 1/2 cup (2 ounces) shredded fresh mozzarella cheese

Directions
1. Combine 2 teaspoons olive oil, rosemary, and chicken in a large zip-top plastic bag. Seal and marinate in refrigerator 30 minutes.
2. Heat a large nonstick skillet over medium-high heat. Add remaining 4 teaspoons oil to pan. Add sun-dried tomato, red pepper, and garlic; sauté 1 minute or until garlic begins to brown. Add spinach; cook 1 minute or until spinach barely wilts. Stir in 1/8 teaspoon salt; set aside.
3. Heat a grill pan over medium-high heat; coat with cooking spray. Sprinkle chicken with remaining 1/4 teaspoon salt and black pepper. Cook chicken 3 minutes on each side or until done. Remove chicken from pan; keep pan on medium-high heat.

4. Top each of 4 bread slices with 1 tablespoon cheese, 1 chicken cutlet, one quarter of spinach mixture, 1 additional tablespoon cheese, and remaining 4 bread slices.
5. Recoat grill pan with cooking spray. Arrange 2 sandwiches in pan. Place a cast-iron or heavy skillet on top of sandwiches; press gently to flatten. Cook 4 minutes on each side (leave skillet on sandwiches while they cook). Repeat procedure with remaining 2 sandwiches. Cut each sandwich in half; serve immediately.

Rosemary Smoked Chicken Panini

I like to experiment with my table top grill on panini like sandwiches. This one is easy and tasted awesome! From a TV show special on warm comfort food type meals. Feel free to use what ever method you have available if you dont own a panini press. These are just as good done as a traditionally made grilled cheese in a skillet or griddle but if using this method it helps to weigh the sandwich down with something heavy such as an iron skillet or a brick covered in heavy duty foil.
Servings: 1 | **Cook:** 5 mins | **Prep:** 5 mins | **Total Time:** 10mins

Ingredients
- 2 slices crusty artisan bread, sliced about 1/2 inch thick
- 1/2 tablespoon extra virgin olive oil
- 2 ounces smoked gouda cheese, sliced
- 4 ounces smoked chicken breasts, sliced
- 1 tomatoes, sliced thin into 2-3 slices
- 1/2 teaspoon fresh rosemary, finely minced
- salt and pepper, to taste

Directions
1. Preheat your panini press to high or use a foreman type grill or do on stovetop in skillet.
2. Lightly brush one side of bread slices with EVOO.
3. Place oiled side down on a work surface and place equal amounts of cheese on each slice.
4. Arrange chicken slices on one slice and tomato slices on the other.
5. Sprinkle chicken with rosemary, salt and pepper.
6. Put two slices together.
7. Place panini in your press and press lightly for about 30 seconds.
8. Continue to bake for 3 minutes until bread is grilled and crispy and cheese is melted.
9. Remove from grill, slice and serve hot.

Rustic Turkey With Brie and Apples Panin

Servings: 2 | Cook: 5 mins | Prep: 20 mins | Total Time: 25mins

Ingredients
- 2 tablespoons walnut oil
- 2 teaspoons chopped fresh thyme
- 4 slices whole wheat country bread, 1/2 inch thick slices
- 2 ounces thinly sliced brie cheese
- 2 ounces thinly sliced smoked turkey
- 6 thin slices granny smith apples, unpeeled
- 1 small bunch watercress, tough stems removed
- 1/2 teaspoon fresh lemon juice
- fresh ground black pepper

Directions
1. Preheat the sandwich grill.
2. In a small bowl, stir together the oil and chopped thyme.
3. Place the bread slices on a work surface and brush 1 side of each with 1 tablespoon thyme oil, dividing evenly.
4. Turn 2 of the slices oiled side down and layer 1/4 of the brie, half of the turkey, 3 slices of apple, and a few sprigs of watercress on the unoiled side of each.
5. Drizzle with the lemon juice and the remaining 1 tablespoon thyme oil, dividing evenly, and sprinkle with pepper to taste.
6. Divide the remaining brie on top.
7. Place the remaining 2 bread slices on top, oiled sides up, and press to pack gently.
8. Place the panini in the grill, close the top plate, and cook until the bread is golden and toasted, the apple and turkey are heated through, and the cheese is melted, 3-5 minutes.
9. Cut each sandwich in half and serve right away.
10. *Can substitute pear for the apple.

Sausage and Spinach Panini

Serving: 2

Ingredients
- Vegetable cooking spray

- 1 (4-ounce) Italian-flavored turkey sausage link, cut in half crosswise
- 4 cups torn spinach
- 2 (1 1/2-ounce) French bread rolls
- 1 garlic clove, halved
- 1 teaspoon olive oil
- 1/8 teaspoon ground red pepper
- Dash of salt

Directions
1. Coat a large nonstick skillet with cooking spray, and place over medium heat until hot. Add sausage, and cook 10 minutes, turning occasionally.
2. Remove sausage from skillet; carefully slice each piece in half lengthwise, cutting to, but not through, other side. Open the halves, laying sausage flat. Return sausage to skillet, placing cut sides down; cook 2 minutes or until sausage is done. Remove sausage from skillet; set aside, and keep warm. Add spinach to skillet; cover and cook 2 minutes or until wilted. Remove spinach from skillet; set aside, and keep warm.
3. Slice each French bread roll in half horizontally. Rub cut sides of bread with garlic halves, and brush with olive oil. Coat skillet with cooking spray, and place skillet over medium-high heat until hot. Arrange bread, cut sides down, in skillet, and cook for 1 minute or until toasted.
4. Divide spinach between bottom halves of bread, and sprinkle with pepper and salt. Top each sandwich with sausage, and cover with top halves of bread.

Sautéed Greens Smoked Turkey and Provolone Panini

What Makes It Great: The crusty grilled exterior gives way to a cheesy, savory interior loaded with earthy kale. Even finicky eaters will find this a delicious way to get their greens.
Serving: 4 | Total Time: 15 Minutes | **Hands-on:** 15 Minutes

Ingredients
- 1 tablespoon olive oil
- 1/4 teaspoon crushed red pepper
- 2 large garlic cloves, minced
- 5 ounces chopped kale
- 2 tablespoons water
- 4 ounces thinly sliced reduced-fat provolone cheese
- 8 (3/4-ounce) slices ciabatta bread
- 4 ounces thinly sliced smoked turkey breast (such as Applegate Farms)
- Cooking spray

Directions

1. Heat a large cast-iron skillet over medium heat. Add oil to pan; swirl to coat. Add red pepper and garlic, and cook 1 minute, stirring frequently. Add kale and 2 tablespoons water; cook 4 minutes or until kale wilts, stirring occasionally.
2. Divide half of cheese evenly among 4 bread slices. Top evenly with smoked turkey and kale mixture. Top evenly with remaining half of cheese and remaining bread slices.
3. Heat a grill pan over medium-high heat. Lightly coat both sides of sandwiches with cooking spray. Arrange sandwiches in pan. Place cast-iron skillet on top of sandwiches; press gently to flatten. Cook sandwiches 2 minutes on each side or until cheese melts and bread is toasted (leave skillet on sandwiches while they cook). Cut each sandwich in half.

Slow Cooker Tuscan Chicken Panini

This recipe features slow-cooked chicken which is then used to make a panini sandwich. I clipped this recipe from Redbook magazine and hope to try it soon. This recipe uses chicken thighs, bone-in, but skinless. You can slow cook the chicken up to one day ahead and refrigerated. To grill the sandwich, a panini press, sandwich grill or a stovetop grill pan with a heavy skillet on top can be used.
Servings: *4 |* **Cook:** *4 hrs |* **Prep:** *20 mins |* **Total Time:** *4hrs*

Ingredients
Slow-Cooked Chicken
- 1 1/2 teaspoons Italian herb seasoning
- 1 teaspoon smoked paprika
- 1/2 teaspoon kosher salt
- 1/2 teaspoon fresh ground black pepper
- 6 skinless chicken thighs, trimmed of visible fat (2 1/2 pounds)
- 1 tablespoon extra virgin olive oil
- 1/2 cup dry white wine
- 4 garlic cloves, flattened with side of knife

Panini
- 4 pieces focaccia bread, halved horizontally (4 4-inch squares, about 1-inch thick, or 8 thick slices white bread)
- 1 (15 ounce) jar roasted peppers, preferably red and yellow, drained
- 4 ounces provolone cheese, sliced
- olive oil flavored cooking spray

Directions
1. For slow-cooked chicken, mix Italian seasoning, paprika, salt and pepper in a small cup.

2. Brush chicken with olive oil; rub seasoning mixture all over chicken.
3. Put wine and garlic in a 4 1/2 to 6 quart slow cooker; add chicken thighs in a single layer, bone side down.
4. Cover; cook on low-heat setting for 4 hours, or until fork tender.
5. Remove from cooker; let stand until cool enough to handle (chicken can be cooked up to 1 day ahead and refrigerated).
6. Remove bones; tear chicken into large pieces.
7. For the panini: Assemble sandwiches on focaccia with chicken, roasted peppers and provolone.
8. Spray sandwiches with olive oil cooking spray.
9. Grill sandwiches in a panini press or sandwich grill, or on a stovetop grill pan with a heavy skillet on top.
10. Grill sandwiches until bread is lightly toasted and cheese is melted, about 5 minutes.

Smoked Turkey Pine Nut Pesto and Sharp

Cook: 5 mins | Prep: 10 mins | Total Time: 15mins

Ingredients
- 2 tablespoons pine nuts
- 3 tablespoons extra virgin olive oil
- 8 slices sargento deli style sliced provolone cheese, divided
- salt and pepper
- 4 -6 turkey slices (thin)
- 4 slices ciabatta
- 1 bunch baby arugula

Directions
1. Pulse pine nuts in blender to chop. Add oil, 3 slices cheese torn in small pieces and salt and pepper. Blend to form pesto.
2. Place turkey on bread.
3. Add 7-8 pieces arugula and another slice of cheese.
4. Spread 3 tablespoons pesto on top.
5. Close sandwiches and grill for 3-5 minutes or until golden brown.

Smoked Turkey Tomato & Gouda Panini

Make as is or you can add cooked bacon slices.
Servings: 4 | **Cook:** 6 mins | **Prep:** 10 mins | **Total Time:** 16mins

Ingredients
- 8 slices crusty country bread (like ciabatta)
- 4 teaspoons extra virgin olive oil
- 2 teaspoons dijon-style mustard
- 4 ounces gouda cheese (shredded or very thinly sliced)
- 8 ounces smoked turkey breast, thinly sliced
- 12 thin slices tomatoes or 16 thin slices roma tomatoes
- 2 ounces red onions, very thinly sliced

Directions
1. Preheat a grill pan.
2. Lightly brush one side of each slice of bread with the olive oil. Lay 4 slices of bread on the work surface oiled side down. Spread lightly with mustard.
3. Build the sandwiches by placing cheese, smoked turkey and tomato, using equal amounts of each item on each sandwich. Top with the remaining sliced bread, oiled side up.
4. Lay two sandwiches on the grill plate. Close the grill cover or place on top the grill cover and apply light pressure to handle for about 30 seconds.
5. Grill the panini for 3 to 3-1/2 minutes. Remove to a rack and keep warm (an oven preheated to 175°F). Grill remaining 2 sandwiches in the same way. Cut in half on the diagonal to serve.

Smoky Chicken Panini with Basil Mayo

Smoky Gouda cheese, sun-dried tomatoes, and baby spinach join grilled chicken breasts in this panini that's slathered with fresh Basil Mayo.
Serving: 4 | **Total Time:** 45 Minutes

Ingredients
- 4 skinned and boned chicken breasts (about 1 lb.)
- 1/2 teaspoon salt
- 1/8 teaspoon freshly ground pepper
- 1/2 cup mayonnaise
- 2 tablespoons chopped fresh basil
- 1/2 teaspoon lemon zest
- 8 sourdough bread slices

- 1/2 pound smoked Gouda cheese, sliced
- 1 cup loosely packed baby spinach
- 1/4 cup thinly sliced sun-dried tomatoes
- 3 tablespoons butter, melted

Directions
1. Preheat grill to 350° to 400° (medium-high) heat. Sprinkle chicken with salt and pepper. Grill chicken, covered with grill lid, 7 to 10 minutes on each side or until done. Let stand 10 minutes, and cut into slices.
2. Stir together mayonnaise and next 2 ingredients. Spread mixture on 1 side of each bread slice. Top 4 bread slices with chicken, Gouda, and next 2 ingredients. Top with remaining bread slices, mayonnaise mixture sides down. Brush sandwiches with melted butter.
3. Cook sandwiches, in batches, in a preheated panini press 2 to 3 minutes or until golden brown.

Smoky Turkey Roasted BLT Panini

This is a great sandwich with huge flavor. The smoky cheese and flavor of the roasted tomato, smoky bacon with spicy arugula and fresh avocado just make this perfect. It has so many great flavors that make this sandwich perfect.
Cook: *10 mins |* **Prep:** *30 mins |* **Total Time:** *40mins*

Ingredients
- 8 slices bread (I like Cibatta or a good Italian bread)
- 16 slices smoked turkey, sliced (deli is fine, but not shaved or chipped)
- 4 plum tomatoes, lightly seeded and roasted
- 4 tablespoons mayonnaise
- 1 teaspoon olive oil
- 1 teaspoon salt
- 1/2 teaspoon ground black pepper
- 4 ounces gouda cheese, smoked (approximately 1 cup)
- 8 slices bacon (smoked or hickory)
- 2 cups arugula
- 1 avocado, thin sliced

Directions
1. Tomatoes -- Roasting the tomatoes. Just cut in quarters (de-seed, just lightly squeeze to get rid of most of the seeds), drizzle with olive oil, salt and pepper and roast at 400 for approximately 15 minutes until somewhat soft but not over done. Remove and let cool. Once cool dice fine and mix with the mayonaise, some salt and pepper. Cover and chill.

2. Bacon -- Honestly, just cook in the microwave. Put on a paper plate topped with a paper towel topped with the bacon and then top with another paper towel and cook 3-4 minutes until crisp. Remove and let cool as you build your sandwich.
3. Sandwich -- Spread the tomato mayonaise on the bread, top with cheese, 2 slices of bacon, arugula, avocado and turkey, more cheese and top with another slice of bread spread with the tomato mayo. Put either on a lightly oiled grill pan, panini press or just a regular non stick pan. If you don't have a panini press, just weight down sandwich with a heavy pan or a brick wrapped in foil. Anything heavy will work. Sometimes I will just add a couple of heavy cans to a small pan and it works just fine. Just something to weight them down a bit. Cook until golden brown. Let cool a few minutes and slice.
4. The ultimate turkey BLT!

Sourdough Chicken Pesto Panini

I got a new grill pan for the stove and was just trying some things out and this turned out great. I actually grilled the chicken up the night before and then stored it in the fridge until the next afternoon. That way too, it gave me time to let the grill pan cool so I could clean it for the pressing of the sandwich. If you are using a grill pan you will need something heavy to place on top to press it, I used a pot that I just placed a heavy bottle of water into for the weight(Okay it looked a bit strange.. so if you have a panini press go right ahead and use it!, if not this does work!)Also this recipe is for one sandwich, but of course you can double or triple it to meet your needs. You can make your own pesto, but to save time I used store bought.
Servings: 1 | Cook: 15 mins | Prep: 5 mins | Total Time: 20mins

Ingredients
- 1 boneless skinless chicken breast
- 1/2 teaspoon grill mates Montreal chicken seasoning
- 2 slices sourdough bread (1 inch thick)
- 2 slices fresh mozzarella cheese (1/2 inch thick)
- 1 tablespoon pesto sauce
- 1 tablespoon butter (to spread on sourdough for grilling)
- cooking spray

Directions
1. Pound the chicken breast to a uniform thickness.
2. Sprinkle both sides with the grill seasoning.
3. Grease pan with cooking spray.
4. Grill up the chicken till cooked through.
5. Slice Chicken into 1 inch strips.

6. Next get your bread ready, you will need 2 slices (if using uncut loaf cut 2 one-inch slices), Butter both slices on one side. And spread Pesto on one side of one Slice(opposite of the butter of course).
7. Cut 2 1/2 inch thick slices off of Fresh Mozzarella ball.
8. Now we are ready to layer.
9. Start with one slice bread then add chicken strips, mozzarella and the top slice of bread with the pesto on it.
10. Press and enjoy!

Sourdough Chipotle Chicken Panini

"Sourdough bread, melted cheese, Caesar dressing, bacon and chipotle spice come together to make an unforgettable taste. It's a delicious and easy-to-make chicken panini and is both tangy and spicy."
***Pre:** 10 m | **Cook:** 5 m | **Ready In:** 15 m*

Ingredients
- 2 slices sourdough bread
- 1/4 cup Caesar salad dressing
- 1 cooked chicken breast, diced
- 1/2 cup shredded Cheddar cheese
- 1 tablespoon bacon bits
- 1 1/2 teaspoons chipotle chile powder, or to taste
- 2 tablespoons softened butter
- Add all ingredients to list

Directions
1. Preheat a panini press for medium-high heat.
2. Spread one side of each piece of bread with the Caesar dressing. Place the chicken on top of the bottom slice, sprinkle with Cheddar cheese, bacon bits, and chipotle chile powder. Place the top piece of bread onto the sandwich, and butter the outsides with the softened butter.
3. Cook on the preheated grill until the bread is crispy and golden brown, and the inside of the sandwich is hot, about 5 minutes.

Southwest Chicken Panini

***Cook:** 3 mins | **Prep:** 5 mins | **Total Time:** 8mins*

Ingredients
- 1 (6 inch) flour tortillas
- 1 tablespoon chipotle mayonnaise (suggested, Kraft reduced-fat)
- 4 slices lunch meat (suggested, Oscar Mayer Deli Fresh Rotisserie Seasoned Chicken Breast)
- 1 slice colby-monterey jack cheese (suggested, Kraft Big Slice)
- 1/4 cup red pepper, cut into strips
- 2 tablespoons chopped fresh cilantro

Directions
1. Heat panini grill sprayed with cooking spray.
2. Spread tortilla with mayonnaise.
3. Layer remaining ingredients on half of tortilla; fold tortilla in half.
4. Grill 2 to 3 minutes or until golden brown.
5. Variations: No Panini Grill? Use a skillet. Heat skillet on medium heat. Cook sandwich 3 minutes on each side or until cheese is melted and sandwich is golden brown on both sides, gently pressing down top of sandwich with spatula to flatten slightly as it cooks.

Southwest Chicken Salad Panini

I received a booklet from Kraft Foods today which is called "food & family" and this is one of the recipes in it that I am posting here to try at a later date.
Cook: 3 mins | **Prep:** 10 mins | **Total Time:** 13mins

Ingredients
- 2 cups chicken breasts, finely chopped, cooked
- 1 1/2 teaspoons chili powder
- 2 tablespoons Miracle Whip light
- 2 tablespoons kraft reduced-fat ranch dressing
- 8 slices Italian bread
- 1 large tomatoes, cut into 8 thin slices
- 4 slices kraft 2% American cheese singles

Directions
1. Heat panini grill to medium-high heat. Mix chicken, chili powder and dressings.
2. Make sandwich with bread slices, chicken mixture, tomatoes and cheese singles.
3. Grill 3 to 5 minutes or until cheese is melted and sandwiches are golden brown on both sides.

4. If you don't have a panini grill: cook in large skilled on medium heat 3 to 5 minutes on each side or until sandwiches are golden brown.

Southwestern Chicken Panini With Lime Chipotle Mayonnaise

Servings: 6 | Cook: 5 mins | Prep: 10 mins | Total Time: 15mins

Ingredients
- 1/2 cup lime curd
- 1/2 cup mayonnaise
- 2 tablespoons diced chipotle chiles in adobo, sauce
- 12 slices sourdough bread, cut 1/2 inch thick
- 1 (3 -4 lb) cooked rotisserie-cooked chicken, torn into large pieces
- 1 sweet red pepper, thinly sliced
- 6 ounces monterey jack pepper cheese or 6 ounces havarti cheese, thinly sliced
- olive oil

Directions
1. In a small bowl, combine curd, mayonnaise and chipotle chilies.
2. Spread mayonnaise mixture on one side of each bread slice.
3. Arrange chicken, red pepper, and cheese on six slices of bread. Top with remaining bread slices. Brush sandwiches lightly with oil.
4. Grill until bread is golden brown and the cheese is melted.
5. Serve immediately.

Southwestern Chicken Panini

The cilantro pesto really makes this sandwich different. This is from Cuisine at Home magazine, and it was a huge hit at our house. Luckily, this made enough of the pesto to make the sandwiches twice!
Servings: 2 | Cook: 10 mins | Prep: 20 mins | Total Time: 30mins

Ingredients
- 2 cups fresh cilantro, leaves and stems, packed
- 4 garlic cloves
- 1 jalapeno, seeded and chopped
- 1/2 lime, juice of
- 2 tablespoons olive oil

- 1 pinch salt
- 1/4 cup mayonnaise
- 1 tablespoon canned chipotle chile puree (*)
- 1/2 teaspoon sugar
- butter, softened
- 4 slices bread, 1/2 inch thick
- 2 ounces monterey jack pepper cheese, thinly sliced
- 3 ounces rotisserie cooked chicken, torn into pieces

Directions
1. * Puree a can of chipotles in adobo and keep in a jar in the refrigerator.
2. Process cilantro, garlic, jalapeno, lime juice and salt in food processor till minced. Slowly drizzle in oil while machine is running, forming a paste.
3. Mix mayonnaise, chipotle puree, and sugar in a small bowl.
4. Spread each slice of bread with butter on one side. Spread cilantro pesto on the other side of two slices and top with cheese and chicken. Spread the other two slices with the mayo mixture and place on top of the chicken, butter side up. Toast in Foreman grill or in a skillet with a weight on top. (Cook over medium heat. When first side is browned, flip over and cook the other side, weighting again.).

Strawberry Turkey Brie Panini

Serving: 4

Ingredients
- 1 (8-oz.) Brie round
- 8 Italian bread slices
- 8 ounces thinly sliced smoked turkey
- 8 fresh basil leaves
- 1/2 cup sliced fresh strawberries
- 2 tablespoons red pepper jelly
- 2 tablespoons butter, melted
- Garnish: strawberry halves

Directions
1. Trim and discard rind from Brie. Cut Brie into 1/2-inch-thick slices. Layer 4 bread slices evenly with turkey, basil leaves, strawberries, and Brie.
2. Spread 1 1/2 tsp. pepper jelly on 1 side of each of remaining 4 bread slices; place bread slices, jelly sides down, on top of Brie. Brush sandwiches with melted butter.

3. Cook sandwiches, in batches, in a preheated panini press 2 to 3 minutes or until golden brown. Garnish, if desired.
4. Note: For testing purposes only, we used Braswell's Red Pepper Jelly. To prepare sandwiches without a panini press, cook in a preheated grill pan over medium-high heat 2 to 3 minutes on each side or until golden.

Turkey & Swiss Panini

The secret ingredient in this sandwich is the raspberry jam. An addition that makes an ordinary sandwich special.
Servings: 2 | **Cook:** 5 mins | **Prep:** 5 mins | **Total Time:** 10mins

Ingredients
- 2 tablespoons butter, melted
- 4 slices sourdough bread
- 2 slices Swiss cheese
- 1/2 lb deli turkey
- 1 bunch arugula or 1 bunch Baby Spinach, stems trimmed
- 2 tablespoons raspberry jam

Directions
1. Brush one side of 2 bread slice with butter.
2. Place slices, butter sides down on panini grill; top with turkey, cheese and arugula. Spread 2 bread slices with jam and top sandwiches, jam side down. Brush remaining bread slices with butter.
3. Close grill and cook sandwiches over medium heat 4 to 5 minutes, until bread is crisp and cheese is melted.
4. Enjoy!

Turkey and Avocado Panini

"Pressed between warm slices of bread and dressed with honey Dijon, this combination of oven-roasted deli turkey, creamy ripe avocado, crumbled goat cheese and baby spinach melts together for delicious flavor and texture that will leave you happily satisfied. Enjoy a fancy little panini that takes no time at all!"
Pre: 10 m | **Cook:** 10 m | **Ready In:** 20 m

Ingredients
- 4 slices artisan bread such as ciabatta
- 2 teaspoons honey Dijon salad dressing
- 1/2 cup baby spinach leaves

- 1/4 pound sliced oven-roasted deli turkey breast
- 1/4 red onion, cut into strips
- 1 ripe avocado from Mexico, peeled, pitted and thickly sliced
- Salt and pepper to taste
- 1/4 cup crumbled soft goat cheese
- Non-stick cooking spray
- Add all ingredients to list

Directions
1. Spread one side of sandwiches with honey Dijon dressing, and top with baby spinach leaves. Next, layer turkey breast and red onion over the spinach.
2. On the other half of the sandwich, place the avocado slices. Season to taste with salt and pepper. Sprinkle goat cheese over avocado slices. Close sandwiches.
3. Preheat a panini press according to manufacturer's directions. Spray panini press with cooking spray. Place sandwiches into the press and close. Cook until the bread is toasted and crisp, with golden brown grill marks and the cheese begins to melt, 5 to 8 minutes.

Turkey and Bacon Panini with Chipotle Mayonnaise

"This is one of my favorite sandwiches to make, I whipped it up one day when I was trying to use up leftover ingredients. My family raved! It's also excellent as a vegetarian sandwich if you leave out the turkey and bacon."
***Pre:** 20 m | **Cook:** 20 m | **Ready In:** 40 m*

Ingredients
- 8 slices bacon
- 1 tablespoon butter
- 2 cloves garlic, minced
- 1/2 red onion, thinly sliced
- 3 cups fresh spinach leaves
- 1/2 cup reduced-fat mayonnaise
- 2 chipotle peppers in adobo sauce, minced
- 1 teaspoon adobo sauce from chipotle peppers
- 8 (4 inch) pieces focaccia bread
- 4 slices provolone cheese
- 1/2 pound sliced deli turkey meat
- Add all ingredients to list

Directions
1. Preheat a panini press according to manufacturer's instructions.

2. Place the bacon in a large, deep skillet, and cook over medium-high heat, turning occasionally, until evenly browned, about 10 minutes. Drain the bacon slices on a paper towel-lined plate. Meanwhile, melt the butter in a large skillet over medium heat. Cook and stir the garlic and onion until the onion has softened and turned translucent, about 10 minutes. Stir in the spinach and cook until wilted, about 3 minutes more.
3. While the onions and spinach are cooking, stir together the mayonnaise, minced chipotle peppers, and adobo sauce in a small bowl. Spread the mayonnaise over 4 slices of focaccia bread. Place a slice of cheese onto the 4 slices, then divide the turkey among the sandwiches. Place 2 strips of bacon onto each sandwich and top with the spinach mixture. Place the remaining slices of bread onto the sandwiches.
4. Cook the sandwiches in the preheated panini grill according to manufacturer's directions until crispy and golden brown, about 5 minutes.

Turkey and Cheese Panini

This turkey panini is one of the best panini recipes we have ever tried. Basil pesto and sourdough bread are key to this sandwich's unique flavor. For more panini ideas, see our complete panini recipe collection.
Serving: 4

Ingredients
- 2 tablespoons fat-free mayonnaise
- 4 teaspoons basil pesto
- 8 (1-ounce) thin slices sourdough bread
- 8 ounces sliced cooked turkey breast
- 2 ounces thinly sliced provolone cheese
- 8 (1/8-inch-thick) slices tomato
- Cooking spray

Directions
1. Combine mayonnaise and pesto, stirring well. Spread 1 tablespoon mayonnaise mixture on each of 4 bread slices; top each slice with 2 ounces turkey, 1/2 ounce cheese, and 2 tomato slices. Top with remaining bread slices.
2. Preheat grill pan or large nonstick skillet coated with cooking spray over medium heat. Add sandwiches to pan; top with another heavy skillet. Cook 3 minutes on each side or until golden brown.

Turkey and Cranberry Panini

A great way to use up left over turkey and cranberry sauce. This is an OceanSpray recipe that was posted in the Houston Chronicle. Very yummy! What's more American than turkey and cranberry sauce. This recipe represents the Southwestern region of the US because of chile and monterey jack cheese.
Cook: 10 mins | **Prep:** 10 mins | **Total Time:** 20mins

Ingredients
- 4 slices Italian bread or 4 slices ciabatta
- 2 tablespoons cranberry sauce
- 2 tablespoons mayonnaise
- 1 chipotle chile in adobo, finely chopped
- 1/2 cup fresh spinach (I used curly red tip lettuce)
- 2 slices onions (I like red onion)
- 8 ounces sliced turkey
- 2 slices monterey jack cheese
- 3 tablespoons olive oil

Directions
1. Stir cranberry sauce, mayonnaise and chipotle chile in a small bowl until well-mixed.
2. Spread cut surfaces of bread with cranberry mixture; place 1/2 of spinach (or lettuce) on each of two slices of bread, then an onion slice each, then 1/2 the turkey each, then a slice of cheese on each; place the other two slices of bread on top of each stack and slightly flatten by hand.
3. Brush both outer sides of sandwiches with olive oil.
4. Heat sandwiches in a panini press for about 5 minutes, or heat them in a large skillet over medium heat turning after five minutes or until the sandwich is toasted on both sides and hot throughout.

Turkey and Roasted Red Pepper Panini

Enjoy!
Servings: 1 | **Cook:** 5 mins | **Prep:** 5 mins | **Total Time:** 10mins

Ingredients
- 2 slices county-style bread, each 1/2 inch thick
- olive oil, for brushing
- 2 tablespoons mayonnaise (to taste)
- 3 slices cooked turkey breast, thin slices

- 2 tablespoons julienned roasted red peppers
- 1 slice taleggio or 1 slice monterey jack cheese
- 1/4 cup watercress, stemmed
- salt & freshly ground black pepper, to taste

Directions
1. Preheat an electric panini maker according to the manufacturer's instructions.
2. Brush one side of each bread slice with olive oil.
3. Lay the slices, oiled side down, on a clean work surface.
4. Spread the top of each slice with mayonnaise.
5. Place the turkey on one slice and top with the bell pepper, cheese and watercress. Season with salt and pepper.
6. Top with the other bread slice, oiled side up.
7. Place the sandwich on the preheated panini maker and cook according to the manufacturer's instructions until the bread is golden and the cheese is melted, 3 to 5 minutes.
8. Transfer the sandwich to a cutting board and cut in half.
9. Serve immediately.
10. Serves 1.

Turkey and Sun dried Tomato Panini

"Turkey, provolone cheese, and sun-dried tomatoes on grilled bread make for an excellent sandwich packed with flavor."
***Pre:** 10 m | **Cook:** 5 m | **Ready In:** 15 m*

Ingredients
- 1 tablespoon butter, or more if needed
- 2 slices ciabatta bread
- 6 slices deli-style sliced turkey breast
- 2 slices provolone cheese
- 3 sun-dried tomatoes packed in oil, drained and chopped
- 1/2 teaspoon Italian seasoning
- Add all ingredients to list

Directions
1. Preheat a panini press according to manufacturer's instructions for medium heat.
2. Butter one side of each piece of bread. Lay 1 slice bread, butter side down, on the preheated panini press; layer with turkey, provolone cheese, and sun-dried tomatoes. Sprinkle with Italian seasoning. Top with second slice of bread.

3. Press panini maker down and cook until provolone cheese has melted and bread is toasted, about 5 minutes. Cut in half and serve warm.

Turkey Antipasto Panini

Serve with fresh cherries and an Italian Berry Float to top off your meal.
Serving: 4 | **Prep:** 7 Minutes | **Cook:** 3 Minutes

Ingredients
- 2 tablespoons reduced-fat mayonnaise
- 8 (0.9-ounce) slices crusty Chicago-style Italian bread
- 8 ounces shaved lower-sodium deli turkey (such as Boar's Head)
- 1 (6-ounce) jar quartered marinated artichoke hearts, drained and coarsely chopped
- 1/2 cup moist sun-dried tomato halves, packed without oil and sliced
- 1/2 cup sliced bottled roasted red bell peppers
- 12 basil leaves
- 4 (1-ounce) slices reduced-fat provolone cheese (such as Alpine Lace)
- Cooking spray

Directions
1. Preheat panini grill.
2. Spread mayonnaise evenly over each bread slice. Top each of 4 bread slices evenly with turkey, artichokes, tomato, bell pepper, basil leaves, and cheese. Top with remaining bread slices. Coat both sides of sandwiches with cooking spray.
3. Place sandwiches on panini grill. Grill 3 to 4 minutes or until bread is browned and cheese melts. Cut panini in half before serving, if desired.

Turkey Avocado Panini

"This is such an easy, light, refreshing and YUMMY sandwich!"
Pre: 17 m | **Cook:** 8 m | **Ready In:** 25 m

Ingredients
- 1/2 ripe avocado
- 1/4 cup mayonnaise
- 2 ciabatta rolls
- 1 tablespoon olive oil, divided
- 2 slices provolone cheese

- 1 cup whole fresh spinach leaves, divided
- 1/4 pound thinly sliced mesquite smoked turkey breast
- 2 roasted red peppers, sliced into strips
- Add all ingredients to list

Directions
1. Mash the avocado and the mayonnaise together in a bowl until thoroughly mixed.
2. Preheat a panini sandwich press.
3. To make the sandwiches, split the ciabatta rolls in half the flat way, and brush the bottom of each roll with olive oil. Place the bottoms of the rolls onto the panini press, olive oil side down. Place a provolone cheese slice, half the spinach leaves, half the sliced turkey breast, and a sliced roasted red pepper on each sandwich. Spread half of the avocado mixture on the cut surface of each top, and place the top of the roll on the sandwich. Brush the top of the roll with olive oil.
4. Close the panini press and cook until the bun is toasted and crisp, with golden brown grill marks, and the cheese has melted, about 5 to 8 minutes.

Turkey Brie and Apple Panini

Serving: 4 | Total Time: 1 Hour, 15 Minutes

Ingredients
- 1 (7-oz.) Brie round
- 1 medium-size Gala apple
- 8 Italian bread slices
- 1 cup loosely packed arugula
- 8 ounces thinly sliced smoked turkey
- 4 tablespoons Bacon Marmalade
- Melted butter

Directions
1. Trim and discard rind from Brie round. Cut Brie into 1/4-inch-thick slices. Cut apple into slices. Layer 4 Italian bread slices with Brie, apple slices, arugula, and turkey. Top each with 1 bread slice spread with 1 Tbsp. Bacon Marmalade. Brush sandwiches with melted butter. Cook sandwiches, in batches, in a preheated panini press 3 to 4 minutes or until golden brown and cheese is melted. Serve immediately.

Turkey Cheddar Panini

Turkey leftovers never tasted so good. We use this recipe often and change the fillings. It is versatile, easy and very good!
Servings: 1 | **Cook:** 10 mins | **Prep:** 5 mins | **Total Time:** 15mins

Ingredients
- 2 teaspoons cranberry sauce
- 1/2 ounce sliced cooked turkey
- 1 ounce cheddar cheese
- 1 teaspoon butter, softened
- 1 English muffin, split

Directions
1. Preheat a heavy skillet or griddle over low heat until a spatter of water disappears quickly.
2. Spread bottom half of muffin with cranberry sauce; top with sliced turkey and cheddar cheese. Spread butter on outside top and bottom of muffins.
3. Place bottom-side down in preheated skillet. Place a heavy saucepan weighted with 2 canned goods on top to flatten panini. Cook 3 minutes. Turn and cook on second side 3 minutes with weight in place until cheese starts to melt into pan.

Turkey Club Panini Sandwich

Great flavor combination made with ingredients you have on hand. Can use panini press, George Foreman, or skillet.
Cook: 4 mins | **Prep:** 2 mins | **Total Time:** 6mins

Ingredients
- 2 slices Texas toast thick bread
- 3 ounces deli turkey, sliced thin
- 1 slice bacon, cooked crisp
- 2 slices tomatoes
- mayonnaise
- 1 slice Swiss cheese (I use light)
- drizzle olive oil or butter-flavored cooking spray

Directions

1. Assemble sandwich using all ingredients except oil. Brush oil on bread or spray with butter.
2. Cook until sandwich is crisp on the outside and cheese has melted.

Turkey Gruyere Jalapeno and Mustard P

Servings: 2 | Cook: 3 mins | Prep: 20 mins | Total Time: 23mins

Ingredients

- 2 ciabatta rolls
- 3 tablespoons grainy mustard
- 3 1/2 ounces gruyere cheese (sliced or grated)
- 2 tablespoons pickled jalapeno peppers, drained
- 4 thick slices roasted turkey
- vegetable oil, for sauteing and brushing

Directions

1. Preheat a Panini grill.
2. Trim the top and bottom off the ciabatta rolls so that they are about 1 inch thick.
3. Slice open lengthwise.
4. Spread the mustard over the inside of each sandwich.
5. On roll bottoms, top with cheese, follow with jalapenos, and finish with turkey; cover with roll tops.
6. Brush both sides of the Panini with oil and grill in the preheated Panini press for 3 minutes , or according to the manufacturer's instructions.
7. The bread should be golden brown and the filling warmed through.

Turkey in a Jam Panini

Servings: 2 | Cook: 4 mins | Prep: 15 mins | Total Time: 19mins

Ingredients

- 4 slices sourdough bread (1/2-inch thick)
- 1 tablespoon butter, melted
- 2 tablespoons raspberry jam (I use seedless)
- 2 ounces Swiss cheese, thinly sliced
- 2 ounces deli-sliced turkey

- 1 cup mixed greens

Directions
1. Preheat panini grill to high.
2. Brush one side of each bread slice with butter.
3. Place on a work surface, buttered side down, and spread with jam.
4. On bottom halves, evenly layer with cheese, turkey, and greens.
5. Cover with top halves and press gently to pack.
6. Place sandwiches in grill, close the top plate and cook until golden brown, 3-4 minutes.
7. Serve immediately.

Turkey Panini With Candied Bacon

Just in time for those Thanksgiving leftovers. I made the cranberry sauce yesterday and the candied bacon this morning. Hopefully, you'll have some cranberry sauce left.
Servings: 4 | **Cook:** 45 mins | **Prep:** 20 mins | **Total Time:** 1hr

Ingredients
- 12 ounces cranberries
- 1 cup sugar
- 1/2 cup orange juice
- 1/2 cup water
- 1/3 cup brown sugar
- 1/2 teaspoon chili powder
- 8 slices center-cut bacon
- 12 ounces turkey breast, slices
- 4 slices havarti cheese
- 1/2 cup onion, sliced
- 1/2 cup red bell pepper, sliced
- 1/2 cup poblano pepper, sliced
- 1 tablespoon olive oil
- 1 cup fresh basil
- 4 French rolls, split
- mayonnaise (optional)

Directions
1. Make cranberry sauce (or use leftover) as follows:.
2. Mix cranberries, sugar, orange juice and water in a medium saucepan. Bring to a boil; simmer until berries pop. Chill until ready to use.
3. Make candied bacon:.

4. Preheat oven to 400*. Mix brown sugar and chili powder. Coat each slice of bacon on both sides with sugar mixture. Place bacon on a cookie sheet with sides and bake 15-20 minutes. Drain.
5. Saute onions, poblano, and red bell pepper in olive oil.
6. Spread rolls with mayo (if using). Spread cranberry sauce over mayo. Top with basil, turkey, sauteed veggies, bacon, and cheese.
7. Cook on preheated panini grill until hot and cheese is melted, about 5-10 minutes. Serve with additional cranberry sauce on the side.

Turkey Panini With Sun Dried Tomato Pest

If you have a panini maker, preheat it and use according to directions in place of the following instructions.
Servings: 4 | Cook: 10 mins | Prep: 20 mins | Total Time: 30mins

Ingredients
Sun Dried Tomato Pesto
- 1 teaspoon canola oil
- 1 tablespoon pine nuts
- 0.5 (8 1/2 ounce) can sun-dried tomatoes packed in oil, drained and olive oil reserved
- 1 tablespoon balsamic vinegar
- 1 teaspoon capers
- 1 garlic clove
- 1 small shallot
- 1/4 cup basil leaves (packed)
- 1 1/2 tablespoons olive oil (reserved from)
- sun-dried tomato
- 1/4 teaspoon cayenne pepper

Panini
- 1 (10 ounce) ciabatta, loaf (or sliced sourdough bread)
- 4 ounces gouda cheese, grated
- 8 slices thinly cut turkey breast
- 8 large spinach leaves
- 1/2 cup kalamata olive, sliced
- 2 tablespoons olive oil

Directions
Pesto:.
- Toss pine nuts with canola oil. Add to saucepan, and toast for 5 minutes over moderate heat.
- Add toasted pine nuts, sun-dried tomatoes,.

- balsamic vinegar, capers, garlic, shallot, and basil to a food processor. Puree.
- Stream in olive oil until spread is the desired consistency, about 1 1/2 tablespoons.
- Add cayenne pepper and salt to taste.

Sandwiches:.
- Cut ciabatta loaf into four equal pieces; then cut each piece in half lengthwise.
- Brush crust side of each with olive oil.
- Spread 1/4 of the sun-dried tomato pesto on one side of four bread slices.
- Top with 1/4 of the olives, 1/4 of the grated cheese, 2 slices turkey, 2 spinach leaves, and other bread slice.
- Heat 1 tablespoon olive oil in a grill pan over medium heat. Add 1-2 sandwiches and place a heavy pan on top of it to press it down.
- Grill for 3 minutes, pressing down occasionally, then turn over and continue cooking until the bread is toasted, about 2 minutes more.
- Grill the remaining sandwiches.

Turkey Panini with Watercress and Citrus Aioli

Take your average turkey sandwich to the next level with a citrusy spread and a few minutes on the panini press.
Serving: 4

Ingredients
- 2 tablespoons canola mayonnaise
- 1/4 teaspoon grated lime rind
- 1/4 teaspoon grated lemon rind
- 1 teaspoon fresh lemon juice
- 1/4 teaspoon freshly ground black pepper
- 1 garlic clove, minced
- 8 (1-ounce) slices white bread
- 1/2 pound deli-sliced smoked turkey (such as Boar's Head)
- 2 cups trimmed watercress
- 4 (1/2-ounce) slices provolone cheese
- Cooking spray

Directions
1. Heat a grill pan over medium-high heat.
2. Combine first 6 ingredients; spread evenly over 4 bread slices. Top evenly with turkey, watercress, cheese, and remaining 4 bread slices.
3. Coat grill pan with cooking spray. Arrange 2 sandwiches in pan. Place a cast-iron or heavy skillet on top of sandwiches; press gently to flatten. Cook 2 minutes on each side (leave cast-iron skillet on sandwiches while they cook).

Repeat procedure with remaining 2 sandwiches.

Turkey Panini

Servings: 2 | Cook: 3 mins | Prep: 20 mins | Total Time: 23mins

Ingredients
- 1/4 cup whole berry cranberry sauce
- 2 -3 teaspoons prepared horseradish
- 2 tablespoons mayonnaise
- 4 large slice ciabatta (1/2-inch thick)
- 4 slices cooked turkey breast (3/8-inch thick, left-over roast turkey is best, but can use deli)
- salt
- pepper
- 4 slices provolone cheese (3/4 oz. each)
- 4 bacon, slices cooked
- 1 1/2 tablespoons olive oil
- gourmet mixed salad green, for garnish

Directions
1. Preheat panini press according to manufacturer's instructions.
2. In a small bowl, combine the cranberry sauce and horseradish; stir well.
3. Spread mayonnaise on 1 side of each slice of bread; spread cranberry-horseradish sauce on 2 slices of bread; top each sandwich with 2 turkey slices, and sprinkle with salt and pepper.
4. Arrange 2 cheese slices on each sandwich; top with 2 bacon slices.
5. Cover with tops of bread, mayonnaise side down.
6. Brush the tops of sandwiches with olive oil; turn and brush bottoms of sandwiches with olive oil.
7. Place sandwiches in a panini press; cook 3 minutes or until cheese begins to melt and bread is toasted.
8. Serve hot; garnish if desired.

Turkey Pear and Brie Panini on Pumperni

Sometimes I like to entertain by having just soup and sandwiches. Maybe a special lunch or dinner and movies with friends. You don't always have to have a full menu. This is one of those sandwiches I love to make. Everyone always loves it. Serve this sandwich with a side salad or a bowl of French onion soup and sweet potato fries for an easy night.

Cook: 10 mins | Prep: 15 mins | Total Time: 25mins

Ingredients

- 12 slices honey roasted turkey, I get mine right from the grocery store deli (3 per sandwich)
- 2 Anjou pears, cut in very thin slices (no need to peel)
- 8 slices pumpernickel bread
- 8 ounces brie cheese, cut in thin slices
- 1 small onion, thin sliced
- butter

Peach Mayonnaise

- 1 cup peach (I just used canned peaches, drained well)
- 1 teaspoon honey
- 2/3 cup mayonnaise
- 1 teaspoon fresh thyme, diced fine
- salt
- pepper

Directions

1. Peach Mayonnaise -- In a small food processor, mix up the peaches, mayonnaise and cilantro, salt and pepper to taste. Make ahead, cover and place in the refrigerator.
2. Sandwich -- I like to spread the first slice of bread with the mayonnaise, followed by the turkey, pear slices, brie cheese, a few onion rings. Top it off the the top slice also spread a thin layer of the mayonnaise on the inside.
3. Grill -- Now, butter your top slice and place buttered side down in your pan. I prefer a grill pan, but you can use any non-stick pan. Grill on medium heat.
4. I like to use any heavy pan to slightly weigh down the sandwich as it grills. Then, once the first side is golden brown, butter your top bread slice and flip. Just cook another few minutes until the second side is golden brown and the cheese is melted or "gooey." ENJOY!

Turkey Pesto Panini

Easily grilled on a panini press or George Foreman grill.
***Servings:** 4 | **Cook:** 5 mins | **Prep:** 15 mins | **Total Time:** 20mins*

Ingredients

- 8 slices crusty Italian bread
- 1/2 cup basil pesto (commercial and homemade)
- 1 -2 tablespoon mayonnaise
- 3/4 lb thinly sliced oven-roasted turkey breast

- 1 tomatoes, thinly sliced
- 1/2 red onion, thinly sliced
- 4 slices gouda cheese
- melted butter

Directions
1. Preheat panini press or other sandwich maker--I use a George Foreman grill.
2. Spread 4 slices of bread with pesto on one side and the other 4 slices of bread with mayonnaise.
3. Divide the turkey, tomato slices, onion slices, and cheese equally among mayonnaise-dressed bread slices.
4. Top with remaining bread slices, pesto side down; brush tops with butter.
5. Brush the bottom of the panini press with butter.
6. Add 2 sandwiches, close lid, and cook about 5 minutes or until lightly browned and cheese is melted.
7. Repeat to make the other two sandwiches.
8. Cut each sandwich in half and serve.

Turkey Reuben Panini

This is a good easy sandwich to make anytime on the grill or stove.
Servings: *4 |* **Cook:** *5 mins |* **Prep:** *15 mins |* **Total Time:** *20mins*

Ingredients
- 8 slices thin-slice rye bread
- 1/4 cup fat-free thousand island salad dressing
- 8 (1/2 ounce) thin slices reduced-fat Swiss cheese
- 1/4 cup refrigerated sauerkraut, rinsed and drained
- 8 ounces deli low-sodium turkey breast
- 1 tablespoon butter

Directions
1. Spread one side of each bread slice evenly with 1 1/2 teaspoons dressing. Place one cheese slice on dressed side of each of four bread slices; top each with 1 tablespoon sauerkraut and 2 ounces turkey.
2. Top each sandwich with 1 cheese slice and 1 bread slice, dressed side down. Coat the outside of the sandwich (top and bottom) with butter. Heat a large skillet over medium-high heat. Add sandwiches to pan. Place a food press on top of sandwiches; press gently to flatten sandwiches.Leave press on sandwiches while they cook. Cook 2 minutes on each side or until browned and cheese melts.

Tuscan Pesto Chicken Panini

Sauteed chicken topped with homemade pesto and provolone cheese between ciabatta bread gives Tuscan Pesto Chicken Panini its Italian twist.
Serving: 4 | **Total Time:** *50 Minutes* | **Hands-on:** *38 Minutes*

Ingredients
- 8 ounces ciabatta bread
- 2 teaspoons canola oil
- 1 pound chicken cutlets
- 1/4 teaspoon kosher salt
- 1/4 teaspoon black pepper
- 1 cup basil
- 1 tablespoon chopped garlic
- 1 tablespoon toasted pine nuts
- 1 tablespoon olive oil
- 1 tablespoon water
- 1/4 teaspoon black pepper
- 1/8 teaspoon kosher salt
- 1 roasted red bell pepper, peeled
- 2 (1-ounce) slices provolone cheese

Directions
1. Cut bread in half horizontally.
2. Heat canola oil in a large skillet over medium-high heat. Sprinkle chicken with 1/4 teaspoon kosher salt and 1/4 teaspoon black pepper. Sauté 3 minutes on each side or until done. Let stand 10 minutes. Slice chicken.
3. Combine basil, garlic, pine nuts, olive oil, water, 1/4 -teaspoon black pepper, and 1/8 teaspoon kosher salt in a mini food processor, and pulse until finely chopped.
4. Cut bell pepper into quarters; discard seeds and -membranes. Arrange pepper quarters on -bottom half of bread. Top with provolone cheese and sliced chicken. Spread basil mixture on cut side of top half of bread; place on sandwich. Cut sandwich crosswise into 4 equal portions.

Vietnamese Subs Banh Mi

Ingredients
- Sandwich rolls or baguette (split)
- Asian red chili paste
- Salad mix or shredded cabbage

- Red onion (sliced)
- Cucumber (sliced)
- Fresh cilantro
- Deli Ham or chicken
- 1 cup Jicama, peeled and cut into matchstick-size pieces
- 1 cup Carrots, peeled and cut into matchstick-size pieces
- 1/2 cup Seasoned rice vinegar
- Salt
- Pepper

Directions
AT HOME:
- Pack split sandwich rolls or baguettes; Asian red chili paste; salad mix or shredded cabbage; sliced red onion; sliced cucumber; fresh cilantro; and deli meats such as ham or chicken.
- Marinate 1 cup each matchstick-size pieces of peeled jicama and carrots in 1/2 cup seasoned rice vinegar up to three days.
- Pack fresh and pickled vegetables separately in zip-lock plastic bags.

IN CAMP:
- Save leftover beef or chicken satay.
- Layer rolls with leftover satay and/or deli meats, chili paste, cilantro, and vegetables. Sprinkle with salt and pepper.

Waffle Iron Turkey Melt Panini

This playful turkey melt's abundant crisp crevices and gooey interior will have the whole family wondering, "What can we waffle next?"
Serving: 4

Ingredients
- 4 center-cut bacon slices
- 3 tablespoons canola mayonnaise
- 1 teaspoon Dijon mustard
- 8 (1-ounce) slices whole-grain or whole-wheat bread
- 8 ounces unsalted sliced deli turkey (such as Boar's Head)
- 8 (1/8-inch-thick) slices tart apple (such as Granny Smith)
- 4 (1-ounce) slices reduced-fat colby-Jack cheese
- Cooking spray

Directions
1. Preheat a waffle iron with 4 compartments to HIGH.

2. Place a paper towel on a microwave-safe plate. Arrange bacon on paper towel; cover with an additional paper towel. Microwave bacon at HIGH for 4 minutes or until done.
3. Combine mayonnaise and mustard in a small bowl. Spread about 1 1/4 teaspoons mayonnaise mixture over each bread slice. Divide bacon, turkey, apple slices, and cheese evenly among 4 bread slices; top with remaining bread slices, spread side down. Lightly coat both sides of sandwiches with cooking spray. Place 1 sandwich in each compartment of waffle iron; close waffle iron firmly on sandwiches. Place a heavy skillet on top of waffle iron to help flatten sandwiches evenly. Cook 3 to 4 minutes or until golden brown and cheese melts.

Won't You Be My Gyro Chicken Panini

Great use for left over chicken. Cucumber yogurt sauce makes this panini special.
Servings: *2 |* **Cook:** *4 mins |* **Prep:** *4 mins |* **Total Time:** *8mins*

Ingredients
- 1 skinless chicken breast half, cooked and sliced thinly (I use left over Grilled Greek Chicken Breasts)
- 1/2-1 tomatoes, sliced
- 1/4 cup feta cheese
- kalamata olive, sliced
- 1/2 teaspoon olive oil
- 2 slices naan bread (or can use pita bread)
- tzatziki (I use Tzatziki or can use store bought cucumber yogurt sauce)

Directions
1. Brush one side of of each slice of bread with olive oil. On opposite side of one piece layer chicken, tomatoes, feta, and olives if using. Top with other piece of bread leaving the oiled side on the outside.
2. Place on panini press (or George Foreman or skillet) and cook until crispy on the outside and warm on the inside. Cut into six to eight wedges.
3. Serve with tzatziki sauce.

Chapter 7: Rice-Grains

***

Artichoke and Prosciutto Panini

Servings: 4 | Cook: 3 mins | Prep: 2 mins | Total Time: 5mins

Ingredients
- 4 ciabatta rolls or 4 (6 inch) baguette, halved lengthwise
- 1/4 cup extra virgin olive oil
- salt & freshly ground black pepper
- 1/2 lb sliced prosciutto
- 1 (8 ounce) jar artichoke hearts, drained and flattened slightly
- 8 arugula leaves

Directions
1. Brush the cut sides of the ciabatta with the olive oil and season with salt and pepper.
2. Layer the prosciutto, artichoke hearts and arugula on the ciabatta and close the panini.
3. Set a large cast-iron skillet or griddle over moderately high heat.
4. Arrange the panini in the skillet and weight them down with a smaller pan.
5. Cook the panini until the outside is crisp and the filling is heated through, 3 minutes per side.
6. Cut the panini in half and serve at once.

Artichoke and Tuna Panini With Garbanzo

I saw this on the cooking channel. Looked yummy.
Servings: 6-8 | Cook: 0 mins | Prep: 20 mins | Total Time: 20mins

Ingredients
GARBANZO BEAN SPREAD
- 1 (15 1/2 ounce) can garbanzo beans, drained
- 2 cloves garlic
- 1/4 cup of fresh mint
- 2 teaspoons lemon zest
- 3 tablespoons lemon juice
- 3 tablespoons extra-virgin olive oil
- 1/4 teaspoon salt
- 1/4 teaspoon freshly ground black pepper

PANINI
- 1 cup pitted black olives, finely chopped
- 2/3 cup extra-virgin olive oil
- 1/2 teaspoon salt
- 1/2 teaspoon freshly ground black pepper
- 2 (5 1/2 ounce) cans Italian tuna in olive oil, drained
- 1 (13 3/4 ounce) can quartered artichoke hearts, drained
- 8 small baguette, sliced in 1/2 lengthwise
- 2 cups arugula

Directions
1. To make the Garbanzo Bean Spread: Combine all the ingredients in a food processor. Pulse until the mixture is smooth. Transfer to a small bowl and set aside.
2. To make the Panini: Combine the black olives, olive oil, salt, pepper, tuna, and artichokes in a bowl.
3. Lay out the sliced baguettes. Spread the Garbanzo Bean Spread on both halves of the baguettes. Spoon the tuna mixture over the bean spread. Top with the arugula and close the sandwich. Wrap 1 end of the sandwich in parchment paper to make it easier to eat. Place the sandwiches on a platter and serve.

Asian Ahi Tuna Panini

Servings: 2 | Cook: 4 mins | Prep: 45 mins | Total Time: 49mins

Ingredients
- 1/4 cup mayonnaise
- 2 teaspoons wasabi powder
- 2 tablespoons chopped green onions
- 2 ahi tuna steaks (each about 5-6 ounces and 3/4 inch thick)
- 2 tablespoons sesame oil
- 1/2 teaspoon five-spice powder
- 2 sesame seed rolls, split
- 2 tablespoons pickled ginger
- watercress, one small bunch, tough stems removed

Directions
1. In a small bowl, stir together the mayonnaise and wasabi powder until well blended, then stir in green onion; set aside.
2. Rub the tuna steaks with 1 tablespoon of the sesame oil, then sprinkle with 1/4 teaspoon of the five-spice powder.

3. Let the wasabi mayonnaise and the tuna steaks stand for 15 minutes at room temperature to allow the flavors to blend, or cover and refrigerate for up to 1hour; if refrigerating, return to room temperature before grilling the tuna and assembling the panini.
4. Preheat the sandwich grill.
5. Arrange the tuna steaks in the grill, close the top plate and cook until seared on the outside and about 1/4 inch into the interior, 8-10 minutes (time may be less, so watch closely).
6. Transfer immediately to a plate; leave the grill on and clean the grill plates.
7. Place the rolls, cut side down, on a work surface and brush the crust sides with the remaining 1 tablespoon sesame oil, then sprinkle with the remaining 1/4 teaspoon five-spice powder.
8. Turn and spread the wasabi mayonnaise on the cut side of each roll, then layer 1 tuna steak, half of the pickled ginger, and half of the watercress over the mayonnaise on the bottom half of each roll.
9. Cover with the top halves of the rolls, mayo side down, and press to pack gently.
10. Place the panini on the grill, close the top plate, and cook until the bread is golden and toasted, the ginger and tuna are warmed through, and the watercress is just slightly wilted, 2-4 minutes.
11. The tuna should not cook much further; place on warmed plates and serve at once.

Avocado Spinach Panini

Smoked sun-dried tomatoes give this sandwich a meaty taste and texture. From Vegetarian Times.
Cook: 0 mins | **Prep:** 30 mins | **Total Time:** 30mins

Ingredients
- 2 avocados, halved and thinly sliced
- 1/3 cup sun-dried tomato, smoked, julienned (1 oz.)
- 2 tablespoons red onions, diced
- 2 cups Baby Spinach, lightly packed
- 16 ounces ciabatta rolls, split in half

Directions
1. Layer avocado slices, tomatoes onion, and 1/2 cup spinach on each roll. Spray panini with cooking spray.
2. Coat skillet or grill pan with cooking spray, and heat over medium heat. Place panini in pan; weight with smaller diameter saucepan weighted with 1 or 2 cans. Cook 2 minutes, remove weight. Flip panini, replace weight, and cook 1 1/2 to 2 minutes more. (or cook 4 minutes in panini maker).

Baby PB&J Bagel Sandwiches

Press gently on the lid of the panini grill so you won't squeeze out the filling.
Serving: 6

Ingredients
- 6 mini bagels, split
- 6 tablespoons creamy peanut butter
- 6 teaspoons strawberry or grape jelly
- 1 tablespoon butter, melted

Directions
1. Spread peanut butter evenly on cut sides of bottom halves of bagels; spread jelly evenly on cut sides of top halves of bagels. Place top halves of bagels on bottom halves, jelly sides down.
2. Brush bagels lightly with melted butter; cook in a preheated panini press 2 minutes or until lightly browned and grill marks appear. Serve immediately.
3. Note: Sandwiches may also be cooked in a grill pan. Cook 2 minutes on each side or until lightly browned and grill marks appear.

Baked Tofu Panini With Roasted Peppers a

Being vegan is easy. Finding tasty alternatives to my beloved sandwich...not so much. Dont be afraid about how long this recipe takes. Double up and eat it all week for lunches.
Servings: 4 | **Cook:** 1 hr 30 mins | **Prep:** 15 mins | **Total Time:** 1hr

Ingredients
Baked Marinated Tofu
- 2 tablespoons maple syrup
- 3 tablespoons reduced sodium soy sauce
- 1 teaspoon chili powder
- 1 teaspoon onion powder
- 1 teaspoon garlic powder
- 3 dashes liquid smoke (optional)
- salt and pepper
- 1/3 cup water
- 1 (14 ounce) package extra firm tofu (sliced into 12-13 even slices)

Caramelized Onions
- 5 large onions (yellow, red or white)
- 5 teaspoons olive oil

- 1 tablespoon balsamic vinegar
- 1 teaspoon sugar
- salt and pepper
- Sandwich
- 2 slices ciabatta
- 1 cup fresh spinach leaves
- 1 tablespoon hummus (Greek olive)

Directions
1. Carmalized Onions:.Heat the oil in a large heavy bottom pan on medium high heat until the oil is shimmering. Add the onion slices and stir to coat the onions with the oil. Spread the onions out evenly over the pan and let cook, stirring occasionally. After 10 minutes, sprinkle some over the onions. If onions dry out, you may add a touch of vegan butter.
2. Reduce heat to medium low and let cook for 30 to 60 minutes minutes to an hour more, stirring every few minutes.When onions are about done, deglaze the pan with vinegar.
3. Roasted Sweet Red Peppers: Cut the peppers lengthwise so they are long and slightly thin and remove seeds. Spray baking sheet with cooking spray and put onto sheet, spraying again with the cooking spray and lightly with the sea salt and pepper. Put into 395 degree oven for about 30 minutes or so, flipping over ½ way through. Cook until soft-tender.
4. Assemble and press!
5. If you dont have a press? Neither do I. Wrap the sandwich in foil and place in the oven under a cast iron pan (or foil wrapped (CLEAN) brick). 375 for 20 min would be great. Make a few and take them to lunch for the next few days.

Banana Toffee Panini

How could such a creation exist?? Only by the hands of CIA graduate Hedy Goldsmith of Michael's Genuine Food and Drink of Miami fame. She serves it there with a mini chocolate caramel ice cream sundae. OMG. If you don't have a panini press, use a heavy non-stick or cast-iron skillet and weight the sandwich with another heavy skillet, maybe even with a can of soup or something for added pressure. Flip the sandwich and repeat to brown the other side.
Cook: *10 mins |* **Prep:** *10 mins |* **Total Time:** *20mins*

Ingredients
- 8 slices brioche bread, thick
- 10 teaspoons sugar
- 1 teaspoon ground cinnamon
- 8 tablespoons unsalted butter, so
- 8 teaspoons dulce de leche

- 4 bananas (very ripe, halved lengthwise, then halved again crosswise)
- 1/2 cup toffee pieces, crushed and divided
- 4 pinches fleur de sel or 4 pinches coarse sea salt
- 8 teaspoons sweetened condensed milk
- 2 tablespoons powdered sugar, for serving
- 8 ounces chocolate syrup

Directions
1. Heat a panini press. Prepare the bread: Mix the sugar and cinnamon in a small bowl and set aside. Butter one side of each slice of bread and dust lightly with the cinnamon sugar mixture.
2. To assemble the sandwiches, turn the bread sugared side down and set four slices aside. Spread the dulce de leche over the remaining four slices, then cover each with four slices of banana. Sprinkle each slice with toffee pieces and fleur de sel. Drizzle about 2 teaspoons of the sweetened condensed milk over each slice, then top with the reserved brioche to make four panini.
3. Place a sandwich in the panini press and cook until crisp and caramelized. Cut the sandwich into quarters, top with powdered sugar and repeat with the remaining panini. Serve with chocolate sauce on the side.

Best 5 Minutes Sandwich

When I'm in a hurry, this is the best sandwich for the taste buds. It's fast, nutritious, and very good!
Cook: *2 mins |* **Prep:** *5 mins |* **Total Time:** *7mins*

Ingredients
- 1 (6 inch) panini bread
- any meat or poultry
- 1/2 carrot, chopped very thinly
- 1 mushroom, thin slices (I like portabellos a lot)
- cauliflower, chopped, a bit cooked
- 1 teaspoon dried herbs (parsley, basil) or 1 tablespoon fresh herb (parsley, basil)
- 1 teaspoon mayonnaise
- 2 leaves lettuce

Directions
1. If you have a panini-press, use it and if you don't, either use a pan or you can it eat cold, but it isn't as good.
2. "Light" the panini-press.
3. Cut the vegetables and herbs while waiting to heat. Spread the mayo.

4. Put everything in the panini bread except the salad and then put in panini-press.
5. Press until desired. Add the salad.
6. Eat!

Black Bean Veggie Burger Panini

Saw this on From the Kitchens of.....Morningstar Farms and putting it here for safekeeping to try later.
Servings: 4 | **Cook:** 15 mins | **Prep:** 15 mins | **Total Time:** 30mins

Ingredients
- 1 cup boiling water
- 8 pieces sun-dried tomatoes (not oil-packed)
- 4 morningstar farms spicy black bean veggie burgers
- 1/4 cup light mayonnaise
- 1/4 cup seafood cocktail sauce
- 4 teaspoons prepared horseradish
- 8 slices firm-textured whole wheat ((1/2-inch thick, about 1 1/2 oz.) or 8 slices sourdough bread ((1/2-inch thick, about 1 1/2 oz.)
- nonstick cooking spray
- 1/4 cup banana pepper ring, drained
- 1/4 cup chopped red onion

Directions
1. Preheat electric sandwich press or grill pan. In small bowl pour water over tomatoes. Let stand for 5 minutes. Drain well. Finely chop. Set aside.
2. Meanwhile, cook MorningStar Farms Spicy Black Bean burger according to package directions.
3. In another small bowl stir together tomatoes, mayonnaise, cocktail sauce and horseradish.
4. Lay out the bread slices onto a clean work surface. Spray one side of each slice with nonstick cooking spray. Flip 4 of the slices over and spread with the mayonnaise mixture. Place the burgers on top of the mayonnaise mixture then top each with 1 tablespoon of the pepper rings, 1 tablespoon of onion and remaining bread piece sprayed side facing up.
5. Place sandwich in press or grill pan. (If using grill pan place heavy skillet or brick wrapped in foil on top of sandwich and cook for 3 to 6 minutes, turning once and again placing skillet or brick on top of sandwich for 3-6 minutes.) Cover and cook for 3 to 6 minutes or until bread is toasted. Slice in half and serve.

Chicken and Mushroom Panini

Gooey cheese, sun-dried tomatoes, and earthy mushrooms join chicken for a tasty sandwich you can quickly prepare in a grill pan or panini press.
Serving: 4

Ingredients
- Cooking spray
- 2 cups presliced cremini mushrooms
- 1 teaspoon minced garlic
- 1/4 cup canola mayonnaise
- 2 tablespoons chopped sun-dried tomatoes, packed without oil
- 1 tablespoon capers
- 8 (1 1/2-ounce) slices ciabatta or sourdough bread
- 8 ounces chopped skinless, boneless rotisserie chicken breast
- 4 (1-ounce) slices reduced-fat provolone cheese

Directions
1. Heat a large nonstick skillet over medium-high heat. Coat pan with cooking spray. Add mushrooms and garlic to pan; sauté 3 minutes or until mushrooms are tender. Remove from heat; set aside.
2. Combine mayonnaise, tomatoes, and capers in a mini food processor; pulse until well combined. Spread 1 tablespoon mayonnaise mixture over each of 4 bread slices; top each with 1/4 cup mushroom mixture, 2 ounces chicken, 1 cheese slice, and 1 bread slice.
3. Heat a large grill pan over medium heat. Coat pan with cooking spray. Add sandwiches to pan. Place a cast-iron or other heavy skillet on top of sandwiches; press gently to flatten sandwiches. Cook 2 minutes on each side or until bread is toasted (leave cast-iron skillet on sandwiches while they cook).

Chicken Pepper Panini

Cook: 5 mins | **Prep:** 10 mins | **Total Time:** 15mins

Ingredients
- 8 slices hearty multigrain bread (or ciabatta bread)
- 1/3 cup mayonnaise (or salad dressing)
- 1 cup lightly packed fresh basil (if you don't have basil, try some parsley and spinach or arugula or greens of choice)

- 1 1/2 cups sliced cooked deli-roasted chicken (or shredded, or leftover chicken)
- 1/2 cup bottled roasted sweet red pepper, drained and cut into strips (or homemade)
- 2 tablespoons olive oil

Directions
1. Preheat an electric sandwich press, a covered indoor grill, a grill pan, or a 12-inch skillet.
2. To assemble sandwiches, spread one side of each bread slice with the mayonnaise. Layer basil, chicken, and roasted sweet peppers on 4 of the bread slices. Top with remaining bread slices, mayonnaise sides down. Brush both sides of each sandwich with oil.
3. Place sandwiches (half at a time, if necessary) in the sandwich press or indoor grill; cover and cook about 6 minutes or until bread is toasted. (If using a grill pan or skillet, place sandwiches on grill pan. Weight sandwiches down(with a heavy skillet or a pie pan with a few cans of vegetables in it) and grill about 2 minutes or until bread is lightly toasted. Turn sandwiches over, weight down, and grill until remaining side is lightly toasted.
4. Makes 4 sandwiches.

Chickpea Beet and Apple Panini

Prep: *30 mins | **Total Time:** 30mins*

Ingredients
- 15 ounces chickpeas or 1/2 cup chickpeas, cooked
- 3 tablespoons mayonnaise or 3 tablespoons vegan mayonnaise
- 1 tablespoon lemon juice
- 1 teaspoon fresh tarragon, chopped
- 8 slices bread, preferably sesame, semolina
- 1 beet, medium, peeled and sliced (golden)
- 1 granny smith apple, thinly sliced
- 1/4 cup broccoli or 1/4 cup radish sprouts
- 4 tablespoons tapenade, prepared

Directions
1. Pulse chickpeas, mayo, lemon juice, and tarragon in food processor until chunky.
2. Spread chickpea mixture on 4 bread slices. Top with beet and apple slices and sprouts. Spread remaining 4 bread slices with tapenade; close sandwiches.

3. Spray panini with cooking spray. Coat skillet or grill pan with cooking spray; heat over medium heat. Places panini in pan, weight with smaller-diameter saucepan weighted with w cans. Cook 3 minutes. Flip, replaces weight, and cook w minutes.

Chloe Coscarelli's Mango Masala Panini

I am making this for dinner this week and wanted the nutritional information. Chloe Coscarelli's...on your next cookbook... Add the nutritional information per serving...pleeeease!
Servings: 6 | **Cook:** 30 mins | **Prep:** 30 mins | **Total Time:** 1hr

Ingredients
- tamarind mango chutney
- 1 cup mango
- 2 tablespoons brown sugar
- 1 teaspoon tamarind paste
- 2 tablespoons water
- spiced chickpea masala
- 2 tablespoons olive oil
- 1 onion, chopped
- sea salt
- 3 garlic cloves, minced
- 1 teaspoon ginger, fresh grated
- 1 teaspoon turmeric, ground
- 1/2 teaspoon cumin, ground
- 1/2 teaspoon cinnamon, ground
- 1/2 teaspoon clove, ground
- 1 pinch cayenne
- 15 ounces garbanzo beans
- 2 tomatoes, finely chopped
- 1/2 cup water
- fresh ground pepper
- 1/4 cup cilantro, finely chopped
- 1 tablespoon brown sugar or 1 tablespoon maple syrup
- 2 teaspoons lemon juice
- cauliflower curry
- 1/2 head cauliflower
- 4 tablespoons olive oil
- sea salt
- black pepper
- 1 potato, small russet

- 1/2 onion
- 1 1/2 teaspoons curry powder
- 1/4 teaspoon ground ginger
- 1/8 teaspoon turmeric
- 1 1/2 tablespoons mustard seeds
- 1 tablespoon lemon juice
- 1/4 cup peas, frozen
- 6 ciabatta rolls
- 1 tablespoon olive oil, for grilling

Directions
1. Cook chutney ingredients for 10 minutes and process in a food processor.
2. Roast cauliflower at 400 degrees with 2 Tablespoons of oil and salt and pepper. Boil potatoes. Cook everything else except the peas in a skillet until soft and fragrant. Mash together with potatoes and cauliflower and then add peas.
3. Sauté onion until browned, add all the spices and cook till fragrant. Add beans, water, and tomatoes, salt and pepper. Simmer for 10 minutes. Mix in cilantro, brown sugar, and lemon juice. Pulse in a food processor.
4. Put a bit of each filling on a bun with a bit of spinach, brush with oil and grill.

Chocolate Banana Croissant Panini

A simple and sinful breakfast, dessert, or snack.
Servings: 2 | **Cook:** 5 mins | **Prep:** 1 min | **Total Time:** 6mins

Ingredients
- 2 plain croissants, day-old, cut in half horizontally
- 2 ounces semi-sweet chocolate chips
- 1 small banana, cut diagonally into 1/4-inch slices

Directions
1. Preheat an electric panini maker to medium.
2. Lay the bottom half of each croissant, cut side up, on a clean work surface.
3. Sprinkle with about two-thirds of the chocolate, dividing equally.
4. Arrange the banana slices on top, then sprinkle with the remaining chocolate.
5. Place the top half of each croissant, cut side down, on top.
6. Place the sandwiches on the preheated panini maker and close the lid. Cook until the chocolate is melted and the tops are golden, 5 to 7 minutes.

Chocolate Hazelnut Panini

A friend gave this to me from one of her cooking magazines (but I don't know which one!). You do need a panini or waffle maker to press them.
Cook: 20 mins | **Prep:** 15 mins | **Total Time:** 35mins

Ingredients
- 1 1/3 cups chopped hazelnuts
- 2 ounces chocolate, coarsely chopped (bittersweet or semi-sweet)
- 1/4 cup fat-free half-and-half
- 2 tablespoons dark brown sugar, packed
- 8 slices whole-grain bread
- 1 pinch salt

Directions
1. Preheat oven to 350°F Spread hazelnuts on a pie plate. Bake until golden brown (around 12 minutes). Transfer hot hazelnuts to a mini-food processor and pulse until mixture forms a paste. Add chocolate and pulse until melted.
2. Cook half-and-half, brown sugar, and salt in small saucepan over medium heat, stirring, just until mixture comes to a boil and brown sugar dissolves, about 3 minutes. Pour into glass measure. With food processor running, add half-and-half mixture to chocolate-nut mixture through feed tube and puree. Transfer to bowl and let cool until spreadable.
3. Spray one side of bread slices with nonstick spray. Put 4 slices, sprayed side down, on sheet of wax paper and spread each with 2 Tbsp chocolate nut mixture. Top with remaining slices, sprayed side up.
4. Heat panini maker or waffle maker according to manufacturer's directions. Add panini, in batches if necessary, and cook until golden brown, around 2 minutes. Cut each panino into thirds.

Chocolate Panini Weight Watchers

Craving a sweet treatf? This is a lightened up version of the chocolate panini using whole-grain bread.
Servings: 6 | **Cook:** 20 mins | **Prep:** 15 mins | **Total Time:** 35mins

Ingredients
- 1 1/3 cups chopped hazelnuts
- 2 ounces bittersweet chocolate or 2 ounces semisweet chocolate, coarsely chopped
- 1/4 cup fat-free half-and-half
- 2 tablespoons packed dark brown sugar

- 1 pinch salt
- 8 slices whole-grain bread

Directions
1. Preheat oven to 350°F Spread hazelnuts on pie plate. Bake until golden brown, about 12 minutes. Transfer hot nuts to mini-food processor and pulse until mixture forms a paste. Add chocolate and pulse until melted.
2. Cook half-and-half, brown sugar and salt in a small saucepan over medium heat, stirring, just until mixture comes to boil and brown sugar dissolves, about 3 minutes. Pour into glass measure. With food processor running, add half-and-half mixture to chocolate-nut mixture through feed tube and puree. Transfer to bowl and let cool until spreadable.
3. Spray one side of bread slices with nonstick spray. Put 4 slices, sprayed side down, on a sheet of was paper and spread each with 2 tablespoons chocolate-nut mixture. Top with remaining slices, sprayed side up.
4. Heat panini or waffle maker according to manufacturer's instructions. Add panini, in batches if necessary, and cook until golden brown, about 2 minutes. Cut each panini into thirds. Enjoy!

Chocolate Panini

Warm your heart with warm melted chocolate sandwiched between buttery bread. Sprinkle with powdered sugar for a sweeter flavor.
Serving: 4 | Prep: 10 Minutes | Cook: 5 Minutes

Ingredients
- 2 tablespoons unsalted butter, softened
- 8 pieces of thinly sliced white sandwich bread
- 1/2 cup Nutella
- 2 ounces semisweet chocolate, finely chopped

Directions
1. Spread butter on one side of each bread slice. Lay slices on a piece of waxed paper, butter side down. Spread 1 heaping tablespoonful of Nutella over four slices. Sprinkle chocolate over, leaving a 1/4-inch border. Cover with remaining bread, butter side up.
2. Warm a griddle or large nonstick skillet over medium-high heat. Working in batches, place panini on griddle and cook, pressing down with a spatula, until golden brown, about 2 minutes. Turn and cook on the other side until golden, about 2 minutes. Cool slightly and use a sharp cutter to form heart shapes, or cut diagonally into triangles. Repeat with remaining panini.

Chocolate Strawberry Panini

An unexpected delight! A good diversion from the usual desserts from The Food Network's "Everyday Italian". Literally a dessert sandwich!
Servings: 6 | **Cook:** 2 mins | **Prep:** 10 mins | **Total Time:** 12mins

Ingredients
- 1/4 cup chocolate hazelnut spread (Nutella)
- 12 slices poundcake (appx. 1/2 inch thick)
- 6 fresh strawberries, hulled and very thinly sliced
- butter-flavored cooking spray

Directions
1. Heat a panini grill to medium according to the manufacturer's instructions.
2. Spread the chocolate-hazelnut spread over 1 side of all of the pound cake slices. Arrange the sliced strawberries over 6 cake slices. Cover with the remaining cake slices, chocolate side down.
3. Spray panini grill with nonstick spray and grill each panino until the pound cake is crisp and golden and the fillings are warm, about 2 minutes. Cut each panini in half and serve.

Chorizo Salsa Sandwich

Chorizo sausage and salsa are a combination made in heaven.
Servings: 4 | **Cook:** 20 mins | **Prep:** 10 mins | **Total Time:** 30mins

Ingredients
- 4 fresh chorizo sausage
- 4 panini bread, sliced lengthwise (or similar)
- 50 g arugula
- 1 lemon, juiced
- salt & freshly ground black pepper

For the salsa
- 2 tablespoons olive oil
- 1 small onion, finely chopped
- 1 clove garlic, finely chopped
- 1 red chile, finely chopped
- 400 g chopped tomatoes
- 10 sun-dried tomatoes, finely chopped

Directions
1. Start by making the salsa first.
2. Heat the olive oil in a pan, add the onion, garlic and chilli and cook for about five minutes, until softened.
3. Tip in the chopped tomatoes and sundried tomatoes and cook over a medium heat for about ten minutes.
4. When the mixture has reduced to a thick paste take off the heat and season to your taste.
5. Now cook the chorizo by heating a frying pan until very hot.
6. Slice the sausages in half lengthways and cook, cut-side down, for about five minutes or until they are charred.
7. Turn and cook for 2-3 minutes more.
8. Set aside and keep warm.
9. Place the bread onto the pan, pressing cut-side down until it is golden and charred and has soaked up the chorizo juices.
10. You will probably have to do this in batches.
11. Remove from the pan, spread the salsa over four slices of the bread.
12. Top with the chorizo, rocket and a squeeze of lemon juice.
13. Season with some salt and pepper, cover with the remaining bread and serve.

Classic Italian Panini with Prosciutto and Fresh Mozzarella

Use this easy sandwich recipe as a template, and customize it to your liking. Use hollowed-out focaccia or ciabatta, or try different herbs and cheese, for example.
*Serving: 4 | **Total Time:** 21 Minutes | **Hands-on:** 21 Minutes*

Ingredients
- 1 (12-ounce) loaf French bread, cut in half horizontally
- 1/4 cup reduced-fat mayonnaise
- 2 tablespoons chopped fresh basil
- 1 cup (4 ounces) shredded fresh mozzarella cheese, divided
- 2 ounces very thin slices prosciutto
- 2 plum tomatoes, thinly sliced
- Cooking spray

Directions
1. Hollow out top and bottom halves of bread, leaving a 1/2-inch-thick shell; reserve torn bread for another use. Spread 2 tablespoons mayonnaise over cut side of each bread half. Sprinkle basil and 1/2 cup cheese on bottom half of loaf. Top evenly with prosciutto, tomato slices, and remaining 1/2 cup cheese. Cover with top half of loaf. Cut filled loaf crosswise into 4 equal pieces.

2. Heat a grill pan over medium heat. Coat pan with cooking spray. Add sandwiches to pan. Place a cast-iron or other heavy skillet on top of sandwiches; press gently to flatten sandwiches. Cook 3 minutes on each side or until bread is toasted (leave cast-iron skillet on sandwiches while they cook).

Dancing Shrimp Panini

This panini dances with flavor, it takes the idea of a po boy and marries it with grilled scampi. thanks for catching the missing lemon juice in the instructions.
***Servings:** 2 | **Cook:** 5 mins | **Prep:** 10 mins | **Total Time:** 15mins*

Ingredients
- 1 lb shrimp, peeled
- 4 garlic cloves, minced
- 2 tablespoons lemon juice
- 1 tablespoon parsley
- 1 teaspoon hot sauce (optional)
- 1 baguette
- 3 tablespoons butter

Directions
1. Hollow out most of the bread from the baguette.
2. Melt butter in cast iron skillet.
3. Add garlic, lemon juice, hot sauce if using and parsley,.
4. As soon as butter foams add the shrimp.
5. Cook shrimp for 5 minutes or until done,hopefully blackening the shrimp in the sauce.
6. Fill the baguette with the shrimp and sauce.
7. If using as a panini, place in a panini grill. If using as a po'boy eat it as it is.
8. Enjoy with lots of napkins.

Easy Awesome Artichoke Filling for Pan

This is an adopted recipe that looks wonderful, but I haven't actually tried it myself. The OP had this to say: "What could be more yummy for a luncheon or casual dinner than a grilled Panini sandwich? Super elegant and tasty artichoke filling gives this sandwich great flavor and color! My family and friends rave every time we make these. I invite everyone over and we have a Panini Grilling party, make your own...kids get in on the act too and love it!"

Cook: 35 mins | **Prep:** 5 mins | **Total Time:** 40mins

Ingredients
- 5 tablespoons extra virgin olive oil
- 1 onion, finely sliced
- 1 (10 ounce) package frozen artichoke hearts, thawed, drained and sliced
- 1 teaspoon sea salt (to taste)
- 3 -5 drops balsamic vinegar

Directions
1. Warm 2 tablespoons olive oil in a heavy skillet, over very low heat and cook onion for 30 minutes, or until soft, translucent and almost melting.
2. Stir in sliced artichoke hearts and cool over low heat for 3-5 minutes more.
3. Add salt (to taste, if needed) and let cool slightly.
4. Puree the mixture in blender or food processor.
5. Add just enough balsamic vinegar to bring out the taste of the artichokes and process briefly to mix well.

Elvis Panini

Yep you guessed it......Peanut butter and banana Italianized. You can use Nutella to make it even more Italian.
Cook: 8 mins | **Prep:** 4 mins | **Total Time:** 12mins

Ingredients
- 3 tablespoons peanut butter
- 1 banana, sliced
- 1 teaspoon honey (optional)
- 2 slices poundcake or 2 slices sponge cakes

Directions
1. Spread peanut butter on pound cake.
2. Add slice bananas and Honey.
3. Coat with melted butter and grill in skillet on med heat with a heavy pot on top for 3 to 4 minutes per side.
4. Sprinkle with powdered sugar if desired.

Florentine Tuna Panini

Servings: 2 | Cook: 0 mins | Prep: 25 mins | Total Time: 25mins

Ingredients
- 2 Italian rolls
- 1 (6 ounce) can tuna in olive oil, undrained
- 2 tablespoons red onions, minced
- 2 tablespoons celery, minced
- 1 tablespoon capers, drained, rinsed and minced
- 1 tablespoon lemon juice
- red pepper flakes
- 1 cup baby spinach leaves

Directions
1. Slice rolls in half through the middle. Pick out some of the bread from top and bottom halves to create a slight depression.
2. Combine tuna, onion, celery, capers, lemon juice and a pinch of red pepper flakes; mix well.
3. Spoon 1/2 tuna mixture onto each of the roll bottoms.
4. Cover with spinach and roll tops.
5. Top paninis with a bacon press or another platter with some heavy canned goods placed on top.
6. Let stand 15 minutes for flavors to blend.
7. Note: If tuna canned in olive oil is not available, replace it with 1 6 oz. can solid light tuna in water, drained, and add 2 T extra-virgin olive oil.

Grilled Banana & Chocolate Panini

Servings: 6 | Cook: 10 mins | Prep: 10 mins | Total Time: 20mins

Ingredients
- 1/4 cup butter, softened
- 1 frozen pound cake, thawed, cut into 12 1/2-inch-thick slices (about 10 ounces)
- 1 cup chocolate hazelnut spread (Nutella)
- 3 ripe bananas, cut lengthwise into slices
- cinnamon

Directions
1. Lightly butter one side of each pound cake slice; set aside.
2. For each panini, lay 1 slice of pound cake, buttered side down, on work surface. Spread with about 1 tablespoon chocolate hazelnut spread, top with banana slices and sprinkle with cinnamon. Top with second slice of pound cake, buttered side up.
3. Spray indoor grill with nonstick cooking spray; heat to medium. Cook about 2 minutes or until pound cake is golden brown.

Grilled Banana and Nutella Panini

Servings: 6 | Cook: 10 mins | Prep: 10 mins | Total Time: 20mins

Ingredients
- 3 ripe bananas, sliced
- 12 slices whole wheat bread
- 1 cup chocolate hazelnut spread (recommended -- Nutella)
- 16 tablespoons unsalted butter, softened
- 3 tablespoons confectioners' sugar

Directions
1. Place the bananas in a bowl and mash until smooth.
2. Place the slices of bread on a flat surface and spread each slice with some of the hazelnut spread. Spread the mashed banana over 6 of the slices and combine the slices to make 6 sandwiches.
3. Heat the grill to medium-high.
4. Spread 1 side of each sandwich with some of the butter and place on the grill, buttered-side down. Grill until golden brown. Spread the remaining butter on the bread facing up, flip over and continue grilling until golden brown. Remove from the grill and sprinkle with the confectioners' sugar. Eat immediately.

Grilled Lamb Kofta Kebabs or Panini W Pi

This recipe I first found on Foodnetwork.com and misplaced it and today came across it in the The Province Newspaper. I love trying new recipes and this was a good recipe for lamb. Sumac is a reddish spice from Middle East that is slightly sour , lemony taste. Look for bags of it (usually ground) at Middle Eastern grocery stores and I have found in Real Canadian Superstore. If you can't find it substitute finely grated zest of one lemon.
Cook: 15 mins | Prep: 25 mins | Total Time: 40mins

Ingredients

- 1 lb lamb shoulder, trimmed or 1 lb lamb fillet, cut into 1-inch chunks
- 2 tablespoons fresh thyme leaves
- 1 tablespoon ground red chili pepper
- 1 tablespoon ground cumin
- 4 tablespoons sumac
- 1 teaspoon sea salt
- 1 teaspoon fresh ground black pepper
- 1/2 cup unsalted shelled pistachio
- 4 skewers
- 4 cups mixed greens, such as romaine, endive and arugula, shredded
- 1/3 cup fresh mint leaves
- 1 small red onion, peeled and finely sliced
- 1 lemon
- 1/2 cup fresh flat-leaf parsley
- 1 -2 tablespoon extra virgin olive oil
- 4 large flat bread or 4 large flour tortillas
- 4 tablespoons plain yogurt

Directions

1. If your using bamboo skewers, soak them in cold water while you prepare the meat. Place lamb in a food processor with thyme, chili, cumin, sumac, (reserving a little of each for sprinkling over later), a little salt and pepper and all the pistachios, put lid on and keep pulsing until mixture looks like ground meat.
2. Divide the meat into four equal pieces and, with damp hands, push and shape the meat around and along the skewer. Place little indents in the meat with your fingers as you go-this will give it a better texture when cooking.
3. In a bowl, mix greens and mint. In another, combine the sliced onions with a pinch of salt and pepper and a squeeze of lemon juice. Mix well, then stir in the parsley.
4. Grill the kebabs until golden on all sides. Dress the greens and mint with a splash of olive oil, a squeeze of lemon juice and salt and pepper.
5. Meanwhile, warm flatbreads for 30 seconds on your griddle pan or under broiler, then divide between plates and top each with some dressed salad leaves and onions.
6. When your kebabs are cooked, slip them off their skewers onto flatbreads. Sprinkle with the rest of sumac,chili,cumin,fresh thyme and a little salt and pepper. Drizzle with yogurt before rolling up and serving.

Grilled Portabella Sandwiches or Panini

Great vegetarian sandwich. Can make on outdoor grill, panini press, or skillet. These are even better the next day.
Servings: 4-6 | **Cook:** 15 mins | **Prep:** 20 mins | **Total Time:** 35mins

Ingredients
- 3 medium portabella mushroom caps
- 2 vidalia onions, sliced
- 1/2 cup olive oil
- 4 garlic cloves, minced
- salt and pepper, to taste
- 1 loaf Italian bread

Directions
1. Mix together oil, salt and pepper, and garlic. Marinate mushrooms and onions with this for about thirty minutes.
2. Grill mushrooms and onions over medium heat until done, brushing on the oil mixture liberally throughout cooking time.
3. Cut the bread open length-wise, brush it with the oil, then lightly toast on the grill.
4. Layer on the onions and mushrooms. Press sandwich together for a few minutes (I usually use a frying pan to weigh it down).
5. Cut into 6 pieces or so and serve.

Grilled Veggie Panini

This is like the one I used to buy at Ukrops.
Servings: 1-2 | **Cook:** 2 mins | **Prep:** 10 mins | **Total Time:** 12mins

Ingredients
- 3 -4 slices havarti with dill
- 2 slices square sourdough bread
- 2 slices white mushrooms
- 2 slices onions
- 3 slices tomatoes, remove the seeds
- 3 slices zucchini or 3 slices cucumbers, remove the seeds
- 1 -2 leaf red leaf lettuce, washed and dried
- 5 -6 sliced black olives
- sauce

- 1 -2 teaspoon horseradish (I use Helluva Good)
- 1 tablespoon Dijon mustard or 1 tablespoon spicy mustard
- 1/4 cup eggless mayonnaise
- 1 tablespoon olive oil, place in a mug

Directions
1. Fire up the George.
2. Mix sauce ingredients together in a small bowl.
3. Spread the bread slices with some of the sauce, about 1-2 tbsp on both slices.
4. Layer with lettuce, tomato, onion, mushrooms, zucchini, olives, then havarti.
5. Top with other bread slice.
6. Brush sandwich with oil (I use a pastry brush).
7. Place on heated George Forman Grill.
8. Close top, remove when golden.
9. Yum.

Herbed Chicken and Arugula Panini

Fast and easy dish! Goes great served with potato and green bean salad.
***Servings:** 4 | **Cook:** 5 mins | **Prep:** 10 mins | **Total Time:** 15mins*

Ingredients
- 1 lb thin chicken cutlet
- 1 1/2 tablespoons chopped fresh thyme, divided
- 6 tablespoons olive oil, divided
- 2 garlic cloves, finely chopped
- 3 tablespoons balsamic vinegar
- 8 slices olive bread (1/3-to 1/2-inch-thick) or 4 crusty sandwich buns
- 1/2 red onion, thinly sliced
- 1 bunch arugula

Directions
1. Sprinkle chicken on both sides with salt and pepper, then 1 tablespoon thyme.
2. Heat 2 tablespoons olive oil in a heavy large skillet over medium-high heat. Add chicken; sauté until golden and cooked through, about 2 minutes per side. Transfer chicken to plate.
3. Add remaining 4 tbsp oil and garlic to skillet; stir over medium heat 15 seconds, scraping up browned bits.
4. Return chicken to skillet and toss until heated through, about 1 minute.
5. Arrange 1 bread slice on each of 4 plates. Top with chicken, onion, and arugula, then drizzle with vinaigrette from skillet. Top with remaining bread.

Herbed Chicken and Arugula Rocket Panini

An interesting sandwich served with tossed salad will be an easy summer lunch or supper.

Servings: 4 | **Cook:** 10 mins | **Prep:** 10 mins | **Total Time:** 20mins

Ingredients
- 1 lb chicken cutlet
- salt
- pepper
- 1 1/2 tablespoons thyme, chopped, divided
- 6 tablespoons olive oil, divided
- 2 garlic cloves, chopped
- 3 tablespoons balsamic vinegar
- 4 sandwich buns
- 1/2 red onion, sliced
- 1 bunch arugula

Directions
1. Sprinkle chicken with salt, pepper and 1 tablespoon thyme.
2. In a large skillet, heat 2 tablespoons of the oil over medium high heat.
3. Add chicken and saute for 2-5 minutes per side or until golden. Transfer to plate.
4. Add remaining oil (4 tablespoons) to skillet, add garlic and stir over medium heat for 15 seconds. Add vinegar and remaining thyme (1/2 tablespoon) and cook 15 more seconds.
5. Return chicken to skillet and toss until heated through (1 minute).
6. Split sandwich rolls and arrange on 4 individual plates. Top each sandwich bottom half with chicken, onion and arugula and then drizzle with sauce from skillet, top with remaining sandwich top half.

Italian Garlic and Herb Seasoned Panini

This is an adaptation from a recipe posted on hungrybrowser.com in the Uncle Phaedrus section. I used my breadmaker to put the dough together and then hand shaped the loaves for baking. To use for a panini sandwich, slice each loaf in eighths (rendering 4 sandwiches per loaf), fill with your favorite ingredients and use your panini maker or grill with press to prepare a delicious sandwich. Mangia!

*Cook: 20 mins | **Prep:** 20 mins | **Total Time:** 40mins*

Ingredients

- 2 1/2 teaspoons active dry yeast
- 2 cups warm water
- 5 cups all-purpose flour or 5 cups bread flour
- 1 teaspoon salt
- 1 tablespoon olive oil
- 4 cloves garlic, peeled and chopped
- 1 teaspoon dried oregano
- 1/2 teaspoon dried rosemary or 2 teaspoons chopped fresh rosemary
- 1/8 teaspoon dried marjoram (optional)
- 2 teaspoons chopped fresh Italian parsley (optional)
- 1/2 teaspoon coarse salt
- 1/4 teaspoon black pepper
- 1/4 teaspoon lemon pepper

Directions

1. Prior to placing ingredients in breadmaker, fill the container with water.
2. It needs to accomodate at least 11 cups of water.
3. If it has that capacity, you can dump the water out and proceed.
4. The dough makes a large amount and does rise to the top of the container.
5. Place all ingredients in bread machine in order suggested by the manufacturer.
6. If desired, you can hold off placing the herbs into the machine and wait until forming the loaves to place on top of bread.
7. Set machine to dough cycle.
8. When cycle is complete, punch dough down and knead a few times on a lightly floured surface (the dough should remain somewhat sticky).
9. Place dough in oiled bowl, turn to coat with the oil, cover, and allow to rise again until doubled, about 1 hour.
10. Ten minutes prior to rising is finished preheat oven to 400°F Lightly grease two baking sheets (I line them with Silpat sheets).
11. After dough has risen the second time, press air out and divide dough in half (dough will still be sticky, do not use more flour).
12. Press (using your hands) each half with a light touch into approximately an 8 x 11-inch rectangle on the individual prepared pans (rustic looking is okay, but don't press too flat).
13. Brush with olive oil.
14. If you haven't already added the herbs into the dough, scatter garlic, oregano, rosemary, marjoram, peppers, and parsley over surface of each and press lightly.
15. Sprinkle with salt.
16. Bake about 20-30 minutes or until a light golden.
17. Serve warm or slice to use for a panini sandwich and grill.

18. *Notethat preparation time doesn't include about 3 hours of rising time.

Italian Tuna Oven Roasted Tomato and A

Recommended to make the tuna mixture ahead of time so the flavors can mingle.
Servings: 4 | Cook: 3 mins | Prep: 20 mins | Total Time: 23mins

Ingredients
- 8 ounces canned Italian tuna in vegetable oil
- 6 caperberries, stem removed, thinly sliced
- 1 lemon, juice of
- 1/4 teaspoon red chili pepper flakes
- 2 tablespoons black olive pesto sauce (Black Olive Pesto)
- 4 ciabatta rolls
- 1 cup oven roasted tomatoes (Oven-Roasted Tomatoes)
- 2 cups baby arugula, roughly chopped
- extra virgin olive oil

Directions
1. In a bowl, combine the tuna, caperberries, lemon juice, red chile flakes, and black olive pesto; use a fork to flake the tuna and thoroughly mix the ingredients; chill until ready to use.
2. Preheat a panini grill.
3. Slice off the domed tops of the ciabatta bread; the rolls should now be about 1 inch thick; split rolls horizontally.
4. Spread a thin layer or the tuna mixture over the bottom halves of the rolls.
5. Follow with the oven-roasted tomatoes, about 3 slices per sandwich.
6. Sprinkle a fistful of chopped arugula over each panino; drizzle with olive oil; season with salt and pepper.
7. Grill each sandwich for about 3 minutes until the bread is a light golden brown and the filling is warm.

Jenz Chicken or Ham Panini

Using store bought panini breads and cooked shredded chicken or ham makes this a very easy to put together lunch or supper dish. This is one of those recipes where you can add as much or as little of any ingredient.
Servings: 2 | Cook: 5 mins | Prep: 10 mins | Total Time: 15mins

Ingredients

- 2 panini bread
- 1/2 cup plum sauce (I used Delmaine)
- 1/2-1 cup chicken (cooked & shredded) or 1/2-1 cup ham (cooked & shredded)
- 1/4 red onion (finely sliced)
- 1/4 red pepper (diced)
- 1/4 yellow pepper (diced)
- 1/4 green pepper (diced)
- 1 -2 tomatoes (sliced)

Directions

1. Slice panini horizontally
2. Place cut side up and spread liberally with plum sauce. You may need more than recipe calls for depending on size of panini bread.
3. Cover one half of each panini with shredded chicken or ham.
4. Top with other ingredients ending with tomatoes.
5. Sprinkle with a little salt & freshly ground black pepper if desired.
6. Place second half on top.
7. Cook for approx 3-5mins in a preheated non stick grilled sandwich machine or press.
8. When nicely browned, remove and cut each panini diagonally and place on plates.
9. Serve as is or with a tossed green salad.
10. NB: You can also add chopped or crushed well drained pineapple and/or chopped spring onions.
11. Use apricot sauce or even honey mustard sauce in place of the plum sauce.
12. Can also be made using thick slices of your favourite bread.

Mozzarella Raspberry and Brown Sugar Panini

Serving: 8

Ingredients

- 1/4 cup olive oil
- 8 (1/2-inch-thick) slices bakery-style white bread
- 1/2 cup raspberry jam
- 2 teaspoons chopped fresh rosemary
- 8 ounces fresh mozzarella cheese, drained and patted dry
- Salt (optional)
- 2 tablespoons light brown sugar

Directions

1. Preheat panini press or grill pan.
2. Using a pastry brush, brush oil on both sides of bread. Spread jam evenly over 1 side of each slice of bread; sprinkle with rosemary. Cut mozzarella into 8 slices; place 2 slices of cheese on each of 4 bread slices. Sprinkle a pinch of salt over cheese, if desired; top with remaining 4 slices of bread, jam side down. Sprinkle tops with brown sugar.
3. Grill panini in a panini press until cheese has melted and bread is golden and crispy (about 3 minutes). If you do not have a panini press or indoor grill, use a ridged grill pan: Put sandwiches in pan (in batches, if necessary); place a weight, such as a brick wrapped in aluminum foil or a heavy cast-iron skillet, on top to press them down. Brown the first side (about 2-3 minutes), flip the sandwich, replace the weight, and brown the other side (about 2-3 minutes) to finish melting the cheese. Cut paninis in half; serve.

Mushroom and Manchego Panini

Sandwich night gets turned up a notch with super fast Mushroom and Manchego Panini. This flavor-packed grilled sandwich is made with fresh herbs, a mixture of exotic mushrooms, and shaved cheese--all sandwiched between sourdough bread.
Serving: 4

Ingredients

- 1 teaspoon unsalted butter
- 1/4 cup minced shallots
- 1 tablespoon chopped fresh thyme
- 2 teaspoons minced fresh garlic
- 1/2 teaspoon freshly ground black pepper
- 1/4 teaspoon kosher salt
- 2 (4-ounce) packages presliced exotic mushroom blend (such as shiitake, cremini, and oyster)
- 1 (8-ounce) package presliced cremini mushrooms
- 1 1/2 tablespoons sherry vinegar
- 8 (1 1/2-ounce) slices sourdough bread
- 3 ounces shaved Manchego cheese
- Cooking spray
- 1 garlic clove, halved

Directions

1. Melt butter in a large skillet over medium-high heat; add shallots and next 6 ingredients (through cremini mushrooms). Cook 10 minutes or until mushrooms are tender and liquid almost evaporates, stirring frequently. Add vinegar; cook 30 seconds or until liquid almost evaporates.

2. Divide the mushroom mixture evenly among four bread slices. Top evenly with Manchego cheese and remaining bread slices.
3. Heat a large grill pan over medium-high heat. Coat pan with cooking spray. Add sandwiches to pan. Place a cast-iron or heavy skillet on top of sandwiches; press gently to flatten. Cook sandwiches 2 minutes on each side or until cheese melts and bread is toasted (leave skillet on sandwiches while they cook). Rub the top and bottom of each sandwich with cut side of garlic clove.

Nutella Panini

A simple grilled sandwich both kids and adults like.
*Servings: 1 | Cook: 3 mins | Prep: 7 mins | **Total Time:** 10 mins*

Ingredients
- 3 tablespoons nutella
- 2 slices white bread

Directions
1. Preheat a panini grill.
2. Spread nutella across each piece of bread, from edge to edge.
3. Close sandwich and trim the crusts.
4. Grill each sandwich for 3 minutes until the bread is lightly browned.
5. Remove the sandwiches and cut each into 4 triangles before serving.

Olive Tapenade for your Panini

*Servings: 4 | Cook: 1 min | Prep: 4 mins | **Total Time:** 5mins*

Ingredients
- 2 cups pitted oil-cured black olives
- 3 tablespoons drained capers
- 3 tablespoons extra virgin olive oil
- 2 tablespoons lemon juice
- 2 cloves garlic (or more if you wish!)
- 2 teaspoons fresh thyme or 1 teaspoon dried thyme

Directions
1. Pulse all ingredients in food processor until mixture is coarse but uniform.

Open Faced Panini with Goat Cheese Roasted Peppers and Spicy Olive Topping

For the best flavor, look for high-quality imported olives, available at gourmet markets or large supermarkets.
Serving: 6

Ingredients
- 2 red bell peppers
- 1/8 teaspoon salt
- 6 (1-inch) slices Italian bread
- 1/4 cup minced pitted ripe olives (about 6)
- 2 tablespoons minced pitted green olives (about 8)
- 1 tablespoon minced fresh basil
- 2 teaspoons grated lemon rind
- 2 teaspoons fresh lemon juice
- 1/8 teaspoon ground red pepper
- 1 small garlic clove, minced
- 3 tablespoons crumbled goat cheese

Directions
1. Prepare broiler.
2. Cut bell peppers in half lengthwise; discard seeds and membranes. Place pepper halves, skin sides up, on a foil-lined baking sheet; flatten with hand. Broil 15 minutes or until blackened. Place in a zip-top plastic bag; seal. Let stand for 10 minutes. Peel and cut into strips. Combine peppers and salt in a medium bowl; set aside.
3. Place bread on a baking sheet; broil 1 minute on each side or until toasted.
4. Combine ripe olives and the next 6 ingredients (through garlic) in a small bowl. Spoon about 1 tablespoon olive mixture onto each toast slice; top evenly with pepper strips, and sprinkle each serving with 1 1/2 teaspoons crumbled goat cheese. Cut each panino in half. Serve immediately.

Panera Chocolate Panini

This hot treat is quick and easy to make. Just pick up a loaf of Ciabatta or French bread from your neighborhood Panera Bread and some premium-quality bittersweet chocolate from your grocery.
Servings: 1 | Cook: 10 mins | Prep: 5 mins | Total Time: 15mins

Ingredients

- 2 slices of panera ciabatta or 2 slices French bread
- 1 ounce premium bittersweet chocolate

Directions

1. The amount of chocolate used varies depending upon the type of bread you use. The idea is to cover one piece of bread with about 3/8 inch of chocolate.
2. Place chocolate on one slice of bread, arranging evenly and up to 1/2 inch from all edges to allow space for chocolate to melt.
3. Cover with the other slice of bread.
4. Toast on a panini grill, or in a 500° F oven for 5 minutes on each side.
5. Use tongs to turn the panini to avoid being burned by very hot chocolate drips. Remove from oven when both sides are lightly toasted and chocolate melts.
6. Cool briefly before serving.
7. Warning — the chocolate will be very hot when the panini comes out of the oven. Resist the temptation to bite into it right away! Be sure to cool it a little while. It will be worth the wait.

Panini for the PB&B Lover

No title can do justice to the wonder of this delicious sandwich. I always think of it as panini, though I'm sure that's not technically correct! Anyway, it's grilled with peanut butter and banana and if you're in doubt, try it, you'll never want cold Pb&b again.
Cook: *4 mins* | **Prep:** *6 mins* | **Total Time:** *10mins*

Ingredients

- 2 slices whole wheat bread (any bread of your choice, actually I can imagine it being tasty on cinnamon-raisin) or 1 small pita bread
- 1 1/2-2 tablespoons natural-style peanut butter
- 1 medium banana (I like mine a little bit green)
- 1/2 tablespoon raisins
- 1/2 tablespoon dried cranberries (see note)
- 1 dash cinnamon (can omit, but it's really tasty!) (optional)
- margarine (optional)

Directions

1. Preheat a small nonstick pan on medium, or a regular pan if you plan to coat the bread with margarine. I never use margarine. A nonstick pan alone will make you a lovely crispy sandwich.
2. If using bread, spread the peanut butter on one slice. If using the pita, spread on half of one side so that it can be folded in half around the fillings.

3. Sprinkle on the cinnamon, if using. Slice the banana and arrange in a layer on top of the peanut butter.
4. Stick the dried fruit in the spaces between banana slices, and either place the other slice of bread on top or fold your pita in half.
5. Fry on one side until preferred level of goldy brown-ness is reached. Flip and repeat- the second side never takes as long. By the way, grilling a pita may seem tricky at first. The key is to FIRST fry the side you folded over, and press the pita gently with a spatula, fork, etc. This will let the banana "melt" and stick to the folded-over side, so your pita's not trying to open on you.
6. Note: experiment with different types of dried fruit, or just raisins. Almond butter is also great in this sandwich. Have fun!

Panini from the Bread Machine

A perfect recipe to make hamburger buns or panini rolls. It is so easy to do using a bread machine.
Cook: *14 mins |* **Prep:** *1 hr 30 mins |* **Total Time:** *1hr*

Ingredients
- 1 1/4 cups milk, slightly warmed
- 1 egg, beaten
- 2 tablespoons butter
- 1/4 cup white sugar
- 3/4 teaspoon salt
- 3 3/4 cups bread flour
- 1 1/4 teaspoons active dry yeast

Directions
1. Place all ingredients in pan of bread machine according to manufacturer's directions.
2. Select dough setting.
3. When cycle is complete, turn out onto floured surface.
4. Divide into 10 pieces.
5. Shape into flat 5-inch rounds for buns, or 6-inch oblongs for panini style rolls.
6. Flatten them down pressing with your hand or rolling pin.
7. Place on parchment lined baking sheet.
8. Cover and let rise until doubled, about 45 minutes.
9. Brush with melted butter.
10. Bake at 350° for 12-14 minutes.
11. Oven temperatures vary so check after 9 minutes to see if done.

Panini Margherita

Panini are pressed sandwiches served in Italy. A small appliance called a panini press is available in stores, but a heavy skillet placed on the sandwiches as they cook works just as well. You can even weigh down a lighter skillet with a brick wrapped in foil, a sack of flour, or canned goods.
Serving: 4 | **Prep:** 10 Minutes | **Cook:** 4 Minutes

Ingredients
- 16 (1/8-inch-thick) slices plum tomato (2 large tomatoes)
- 8 (1-ounce) slices rustic French bread loaf
- 1/4 teaspoon salt
- 1/4 teaspoon freshly ground black pepper
- 1 cup (4 ounces) shredded part-skim mozzarella cheese
- 12 fresh basil leaves
- 8 teaspoons extra-virgin olive oil, divided
- Cooking spray

Directions
1. Divide tomato slices evenly among 4 bread slices; sprinkle evenly with salt and pepper. Sprinkle cheese evenly over tomatoes. Arrange basil leaves evenly over cheese, and top with remaining 4 bread slices. Drizzle 1 teaspoon olive oil over top of each sandwich, and coat with cooking spray.
2. Place a grill pan or large nonstick skillet over medium-high heat until hot. Place sandwiches, oil sides down, in pan. Drizzle 1 teaspoon oil over top of each sandwich, and coat with cooking spray. Place a piece of foil over sandwiches in pan; place a heavy skillet on top of foil to press sandwiches. Cook 2 minutes or until golden brown. Turn sandwiches over; replace foil and heavy skillet. Cook 2 minutes or until golden brown. Serve immediately.

Panini Oil

Super simple to make! We tested this against butter and good olive oil as what to paint on bread when grilling up paninis, and this infused oil was our favorite for both flavor and crispiness.
Cook: 30 mins | **Prep:** 2 mins | **Total Time:** 32mins

Ingredients
- 1 cup canola oil
- 6 -8 garlic cloves, crushed

Directions

1. Warm the canola in a small, heavy-bottomed sauce pan over medium-low heat.
2. Smash the garlic cloves with the flat of a wide, heavy knife, the flat side of a tenderizing mallet, or any sturdy flat tool that you feel comfortable with. You want to flatten them somewhat (but not squirt garlicky bits all over the kitchen).
3. When the oil shows signs of slow movement (that lazy, swirly motion that happens long before the oil begins smoking), drop the garlic into the warm oil.
4. Watch and when the garlic shows signs of beginning to brown, pull off the heat and cover.
5. Let stand at room temperature until cooled completely. Strain to remove the solids.
6. Store the oil in an air-tight container in the refrigerator. It should keep for a couple of months if you don't use it all before then.
7. When using, brush (don't dip!) the outside surfaces of your bread when preparing paninis for grilling. You may wish to salt the outside after cooking depending on the type of panini or your personal taste.

Panini With Banana and Hazelnut Spread

From Everyday Food. A quick after school snack or a simple dessert.
Servings: 1 | **Cook:** 4 mins | **Prep:** 5 mins | **Total Time:** 9mins

Ingredients
- 2 slices whole wheat bread (crust removed)
- 1 1/2 teaspoons butter
- 1 tablespoon chocolate hazelnut spread
- 1/2 banana (sliced in circles)

Directions
1. Spread one side of each slice of bread with butter.
2. Place one slice of bread, buttered side down, on work surface.
3. Spread with hazelnut spread, top with banana circles.
4. Top with remaining bread, buttered side up.
5. Heat a small skillet over medium heat.
6. Cook panini, turning once, until both sides are golden brown, about 3 minutes per side.
7. Halve and serve.

Panini With Sauteed Spinach and Chickpea

You can make this sandwich with many different types of bread such as whole grain buns, pita bread, or focaccia.
Cook: 5 mins | **Prep:** 10 mins | **Total Time:** 15mins

Ingredients
- 3/4 cup canned chick-peas, drained
- 2 tablespoons lemon juice
- 1 tablespoon water
- 2 teaspoons capers
- 2 teaspoons olive oil
- 2 garlic cloves, minced
- 4 cups torn spinach
- 1/4 teaspoon salt
- 1/8 teaspoon black pepper
- 2 (2 1/2 ounce) submarine sandwich bread
- 2 large plum tomatoes, sliced

Directions
1. Place first four ingredients in a food processor or a blender. Process until smooth and set aside.
2. Heat oil in a large nonstick skillet over medium high heat. Add garlic and cook for about 1 minute, do not burn. Add spinach and cook for about 2 minutes. Remove from heat and season with salt and pepper.
3. Cut each roll in half horizontally. Spread chickpea mixture over bottom halves of rolls. Top with spinach and tomato slices.
4. You can season with additional salt and pepper (optional) Cover with top halves rolls.
5. You can serve it as such or if you own an indoor grill (such as Forman) you can grill sandwiches for 2-3 minutes.

Pb & J Panini

Servings: 2 | **Cook:** 4 mins | **Prep:** 15 mins | **Total Time:** 19mins

Ingredients
- 4 slices cinnamon-swirl bread (each about 1/2 inch thick) or 4 slices walnut bread (each about 1/2 inch thick)
- 1 tablespoon unsalted butter, at room temperature
- 4 tablespoons smooth peanut butter or 4 tablespoons chunky peanut butter

- 2 tablespoons jam (your favorite) or 2 tablespoons preserves (your favorite)

Directions
1. Preheat the sandwich grill.
2. Place bread slices on a work surface and spread 1 side of each with the butter.
3. Turn and spread the unbuttered sides with the peanut butter, dividing it evenly, then spread the jam over the peanut butter on 2 of the slices.
4. Place the remaining 2 bread slices on top, peanut butter sides down, and press gently to pack.
5. Place the panini in the grill, close the top plate, and cook until the bread is golden and toasted and the peanut butter is warmed and beginning to melt, 2-4 minutes.
6. Cut each sandwich in half and serve immediately.

Peanut Butter and Jelly Panini

This recipe is simplicity itself and delicious because of the heat. The panini maker puts beautiful grill lines on the bread and melts the peanut butter and jelly inside. This is as different from a regular PB&J as a scooter is from a bicycle. Try it, you and your kids will love it.
Servings: 1 | **Cook:** 3 mins | **Prep:** 3 mins | **Total Time:** 6mins

Ingredients
- 2 slices bread (I prefer multi-grain for nutrition)
- real peanut butter (from Wholefoods of Wild Oats)
- grape jelly

Directions
1. Spread peanut butter liberally on one slice of bread.
2. Spread jelly on the other slice.
3. Put the two pieces together.
4. Place the sandwich on a pre-heated panini maker.
5. Close the top and cook three minutes.
6. Remove, slice in half and serve.
7. (If you have toddlers, you might wait a minute to let the bread cool slightly for them).

Peanut Butter Panini With Raisins and Ap

Try these for breakfast. Raisins and apples add fiber and flavor to the PB&J. Use low fat whole-grain waffles for a healthier panini.
Servings: 4 | **Cook:** 30 mins | **Prep:** 0 mins | **Total Time:** 30mins

Ingredients
- 1/4 cup golden raisin
- 1/4 cup peanut butter
- 2 tablespoons honey
- 11 1/4 inches round low-fat whole grain waffles
- 1 apple, cored and sliced into 1/8 inch thick pieces
- 4 tablespoons raspberry all-fruit jam or 4 tablespoons strawberry all-fruit jam
- 2 teaspoons unsalted butter

Directions
1. Combine raisins, peanut butter and honey in small bowl; stir to blend. Divide and spread over 4 waffles to cover and top each with about 5 apple slices.
2. Spread 1 teaspoons jam on each four remaining waffles; place jam side down on peanut butter topped waffles.
3. Heat 1 tsp butter in large skillet over medium-high heat. Add waffle sandwiches and reduce heat to medium-low heat. Place another skillet over evenly on waffles.
4. Cook for 1 1/2 minutes.
5. Flip panini; add remaining 1 teaspoons butter to skillet and slide panini around skillet to coat with butter.
6. Replace skillet on top and cook one more minute or until lightly browned.
7. Cut and serve with remaining apple slices.

Peppery Turkey and Brie Panini

Servings: 8 | **Cook:** 10 mins | **Prep:** 10 mins | **Total Time:** 20mins

Ingredients
- 1 (15 ounce) brie round
- 16 sourdough bread, slices
- 2 lbs thinly sliced smoked turkey
- 1/2 cup red pepper jelly
- 2 tablespoons melted butter

Directions
1. Trim and discard rind from Brie. Cut Brie into 1/2-inch-thick slices. Layer 8 bread slices evenly with turkey and Brie.
2. Spread 1 tablespoons pepper jelly on 1 side of each remaining 8 bread slices; place, jelly sides down, onto Brie. Brush sandwiches with melted butter.
3. Cook sandwiches, in batches, in a preheated panini press 2 to 3 minutes or until golden brown.

Plt: Pancetta Lettuce and Tomato Panini

The sandwiches can be assembled an hour or two before grilling (keep them stacked between pieces of waxed paper). From Napa Style catalog. The contrast of crisp, hot, cool, and creamy in this sandwich makes it a big hit.
Servings: 4 | **Cook:** 3 mins | **Prep:** 5 mins | **Total Time:** 8mins

Ingredients
- 3/4 lb pancetta, sliced as thick as bacon
- 1/4 cup chopped fresh basil
- 1/4 cup mayonnaise
- 8 large slice country bread
- unsalted butter, at room temperature
- 12 slices tomatoes
- fresh ground black pepper
- 1 romaine lettuce hearts, separated into leaves

Directions
1. Preheat panini grill.
2. Unroll the pancetta slices and cut into 4-inch lengths. Put the pancetta in a skillet and cook over moderate heat until it renders much of its fat and begins to crisp, about 10 minutes. Drain in a sieve.
3. In a small bowl, stir the basil into the mayonnaise.
4. Butter one side of each bread slice, then put 4 slices, buttered side down, on a work surface. Top the bread slices with the pancetta, distributing it evenly. Top each with a second slice of bread, buttered side up.
5. Cook in panini grill until nicely browned (2-3 minutes).
6. Transfer the sandwiches to a work surface and remove the top slice of bread from each sandwich. Spread the underside of those slices with mayonnaise. Top the pancetta with the tomato slices, pepper to taste, and romaine leaves. Replace the top slice of bread, cut the sandwiches in half, and serve immediately.

Popcorn Shrimp Salad Sandwiches

Servings: 3 | Cook: 10 mins | Prep: 7 mins | Total Time: 17mins

Ingredients
- 1 (20 ounce) packageseapak popcorn shrimp or 1 (20 ounce) packageseapak jumbo popcorn shrimp, frozen
- 1 cup mayonnaise (add more if desired)
- 1/2 cup fresh onion, finely diced
- 1 -2 garlic clove, finely diced
- 1 large hard-boiled egg, diced
- 2 tablespoons dill pickle relish (or substitute)
- diced dill pickle
- 2 -3 hoagie rolls or 2 -3 panini bread

Directions
1. PREPARE the shrimp according to package directions. Set aside to cool for 3 minutes.
2. COMBINE mayonnaise, onion, garlic, hard-boiled egg and pickle relish in a large bowl. Stir to incorporate ingredients.
3. ADD warm shrimp to mayonnaise mixture and stir until shrimp are fully coated. Spoon onto rolls or bread and serve.

Porchetta Panini

I saw this on food network challenge and oh it looks so good. I have no intention of including the anchovies tho :) Zaar does not accept porchetta as an ingredient so made it pork loin
Servings: 4 | Prep: 20 mins | Total Time: 20mins

Ingredients
Salsa Verde
- 3 cups loosely packed fresh Italian parsley (from about 1 very large bunch)
- 1/2 cup extra virgin olive oil
- 3 green onions, sliced
- 3 tablespoons fresh lemon juice
- 3 garlic cloves, peeled and minced
- 2 drained anchovy fillets, chopped (optional)
- 1 tablespoon drained capers
- 1 1/2 teaspoons grated lemon peel

For Assembly
- 8 pita bread (or flatbread)
- 1/3 cup salsa verde
- 2/3 lb pork loin, sliced (porchetta)
- 8 slices fontina
- 1 cup arugula
- 1/2 cup caramelized onion

Directions
1. For the Salsa Verde:
2. Combine all ingredients in a bowl, tossing until thoroughly mixed.
3. For Assembly:
4. Lightly toast the flatbread in oven. Smear 4 of the flatbread pieces with 1/3 cup Salsa Verde. Layer with sliced porchetta, fontina, arugula and onions. Cover with remaining flatbread. Press in Panini press until melted. Serve.

Roast Beef Panini

Pile your panini high with roast beef, pepper jelly, and gouda.
Serving: *4* | **Prep:** *10 Minutes* | **Cook:** *8 Minutes*

Ingredients
- 8 tablespoons sweet- or hot-pepper jelly
- 8 slices whole-grain bread
- 2 teaspoons Dijon mustard
- 2 ounces smoked Gouda cheese, shredded
- 1/2 pound thinly sliced deli roast beef
- 1 cup watercress sprigs
- Olive oil cooking spray

Directions
1. Spread 1 tablespoon jelly evenly on each of 8 slices of bread. Spread each of 4 slices with 1/2 teaspoon mustard on top of the jelly; sprinkle Gouda evenly on the same 4 slices. Top the remaining slices evenly with the thinly sliced roast beef and the watercress sprigs. Combine the bread slices to create 4 sandwiches.
2. Heat a panini press or a grill pan coated lightly with olive oil cooking spray. Grill the sandwiches in batches, with the press closed, for 2–3 minutes per side. If using a grill pan, cook the sandwiches over moderately high heat with a heavy skillet on top of the sandwiches, pressing down, 2–3 minutes per side or until golden. Halve the sandwiches, and serve immediately.

Rosemary Chicken Panini with Spinach and Sun Dried Tomatoes

Grilled Rosemary-Chicken Panini with Spinach and Sun-Dried Tomatoes is a delicious solution to the busy weeknight dinner dilemma. This excellent sandwich is loaded with fresh flavor and is guaranteed to satisfy any appetite.
Serving: 4 | Total Time: 1 Hour, 10 Minutes | Hands-on: 40 Minutes

Ingredients
- 2 tablespoons extra-virgin olive oil, divided
- 1 teaspoon chopped fresh rosemary
- 4 (4-ounce) chicken cutlets
- 1/4 cup chopped drained oil-packed sun-dried tomato
- 1/8 teaspoon crushed red pepper
- 8 garlic cloves, thinly sliced
- 1 (6-ounce) package fresh baby spinach
- 3/8 teaspoon salt, divided
- Cooking spray
- 1/8 teaspoon freshly ground black pepper
- 8 (1-ounce) slices country-style Italian bread
- 1/2 cup (2 ounces) shredded fresh mozzarella cheese

Directions
1. Combine 2 teaspoons olive oil, rosemary, and chicken in a large zip-top plastic bag. Seal and marinate in refrigerator 30 minutes.
2. Heat a large nonstick skillet over medium-high heat. Add remaining 4 teaspoons oil to pan. Add sun-dried tomato, red pepper, and garlic; sauté 1 minute or until garlic begins to brown. Add spinach; cook 1 minute or until spinach barely wilts. Stir in 1/8 teaspoon salt; set aside.
3. Heat a grill pan over medium-high heat; coat with cooking spray. Sprinkle chicken with remaining 1/4 teaspoon salt and black pepper. Cook chicken 3 minutes on each side or until done. Remove chicken from pan; keep pan on medium-high heat.
4. Top each of 4 bread slices with 1 tablespoon cheese, 1 chicken cutlet, one quarter of spinach mixture, 1 additional tablespoon cheese, and remaining 4 bread slices.
5. Recoat grill pan with cooking spray. Arrange 2 sandwiches in pan. Place a cast-iron or heavy skillet on top of sandwiches; press gently to flatten. Cook 4 minutes on each side (leave skillet on sandwiches while they cook). Repeat procedure with remaining 2 sandwiches. Cut each sandwich in half; serve immediately.

Scrambled Egg and Breakfast Sausage Pani

This would be a great sandwich to make for lunch or dinner too! Freshly made and nice and warm - what could be better? You can serve this with maple syrup and fresh fruit as well. Enjoy!
Cook: 10 mins | **Prep:** 15 mins | **Total Time:** 25mins

Ingredients
- 1 teaspoon butter
- 3 green onions, chopped
- 6 maple flavoured breakfast sausage, fully cooked and broken into small pieces
- 1/3 cup pecan pieces
- 4 large eggs, beaten
- salt and pepper
- 8 slices Italian bread
- 6 ounces bocconcini, drained and cut into 1/4 slices
- butter, for panini press or grill pan (optional)
- maple syrup and fresh fruit (to garnish) (optional)

Directions
1. In a large skillet, melt butter over medium heat. Add the onions, sausages and pecans; sauté until onions are just softened, about 3 minutes. Add eggs and cook, stirring with a wooden spoon, until eggs are firm but not dry. Remove from heat and set aside.
2. Meanwhile, heat a panini maker or a grill pan over medium-high heat. Divide sausage mixture into 4 portions and mound each portion on one slice of bread. Top each with Bocconcini slices and top with remaining bread slices.
3. Lightly butter the outside of each panini. Cook until both sides of each panini are golden; serve immediately. Serve warm and garnish with maple syrup and fresh fruit if desired.

Sicilian Panini Buns

These accompany any dinner and make a great panini for sandwiches.
Servings: 8 | **Cook:** 12 mins | **Prep:** 1 hr 30 mins | **Total Time:** 1hr

Ingredients
- 1 1/2 cups water
- 1 1/2 tablespoons dry yeast (2 1/4 ounce packages)
- 1 teaspoon sugar

- 4 cups all-purpose flour
- 1/2 teaspoon salt
- 1 tablespoon olive oil, plus additional for greasing
- 1 egg, beaten (optional)
- sesame seeds, for sprinkling (optional)

Directions
1. Stir together the water, yeast, and sugar.
2. Set aside until the yeast blooms, about 5 minutes.
3. Place 3 cups of the flour and the salt in a mixing bowl.
4. Add the yeast mixture and the oil, and stir to form a sticky dough.
5. Knead, adding the remaining flour a little at a time, until the dough becomes a smooth, elastic ball, about about 5 to 8 minutes.
6. If you use an electric mixer, combine the ingredients with the paddle attachment and then change to the dough hook.
7. Add the flour, a little at a time, until the dough is smooth and comes away from the sides of the bowl, about 2 to 4 minutes.
8. Turn the dough into a lightly oiled bowl and cover with a dry cloth or plastic wrap.
9. Let rise in a draft free spot until doubled in size, about 30 minutes.
10. Preheat the oven to 400 degrees.
11. Once the dough has risen, lift it out and cut into 8 equal balls.
12. Shape into flat 5-inch rounds for buns, or 6-inch oblongs for a hero- or hoagie-style rolls.
13. Place on a lightly oiled baking sheet and cover with a dry cloth.
14. Let rise in a draft free spot for 30 to 45 minutes.
15. Gently glaze the buns with the egg and sprinkle with the sesame seeds, if desired.
16. Bake for 10 to 12 minutes, until golden brown.
17. Transfer to a cooling rack until ready to use.

S'more Peanut Butter Panini

Decadence at its finest and sure to cure your sweet tooth. A taste of comfort suitable for dessert or a very special breakfast or snack. No special equipment required for this panini, a frying pan works just fine. This sandwich can be made vegetarian by eliminating the marshmallows. For breakfast I would eat the whole panini but if serving for dessert, half of the sandwich is plenty.
Servings: 1 | **Cook:** 5 mins | **Prep:** 1 min | **Total Time:** 6mins

Ingredients
- 2 slices bread (I use white)

- 1 tablespoon creamy peanut butter
- 1/2 banana, cut into 3 pieces lengthwise
- 1 -2 teaspoon sugar-free strawberry jam
- 3 large marshmallows, cut in half or 25 mini marshmallows
- butter, softened
- 1 -2 teaspoon sugar-free chocolate syrup
- 1 -2 teaspoon prepared whipped cream or 1 -2 teaspoon non-dairy whipped topping

Directions
1. Preheat grill pan or frying pan to medium-low heat. (You could also do this in a panini maker).
2. Put a very thin spread of peanut butter on each slice of bread. Top one slice of bread with the 3 slices of banana, dabs of the strawberry jam, and the marshmallows. Top with the second slice of bread.
3. Lightly spread the softened butter on the outside of the sandwich and place on the preheated pan. Cook for 2 minutes (or until golden) and turn and cook for another 2 minutes.
4. Slice on the diagonal and drizzle with the chocolate flavored syrup and a dollop of whipped cream or you can drizzle the plate with the chocolate syrup and place the sandwich on top with a dollop of whipped cream. It is easiest to eat this with a fork.

Soppressata Fontina and Arugula Panini

Fire up the panini grill.
***Servings:** 4 | **Cook:** 4 mins | **Prep:** 20 mins | **Total Time:** 24mins*

Ingredients
- 4 ciabatta rolls
- 15 slices soppressata (or other hard salami)
- 1 bunch arugula, well rinsed and dried
- fresh ground black pepper
- 8 slices Italian fontina

Directions
1. Preheat a panini grill.
2. Slice off the domed tops of the ciabatta rolls; the rolls should now be about 1 inch thick; split the rolls in half horizontally.
3. Distribute the soppressata slices so that the bottom halves of the rolls are covered with a single layer of salami.
4. Top with a few leaves of arugula and some black pepper.

5. Arrange 2 slices of Fontina on each sandwich and trim the edges to fit the bread.
6. Cover with the top halves of the rolls.
7. Grill the sandwiches until warmed through completely, about 4 minutes.
8. Cut in half and serve immediately.

Spicy Sicilian Deli Sandwiches

Stolen. Turkey can be substituted for the chicken if you wish. Also, you can use a panini machine to grill the composed sandwich.
***Servings:** 2 | **Prep:** 10 mins | **Total Time:** 10mins*

Ingredients
- 1 chipotle chile in adobo, chopped small (add more chipotle if you want it spicier)
- 4 slices panini bread, toasted
- 1/4 cup pesto sauce (homemade is best)
- 2 slices roasted chicken breast
- 1/2 cup baby spinach leaves
- 1/4 cup red onion, sliced into crescents
- 2 tablespoons black olives, sliced

Directions
1. Stir the chipotle into the pesto and spread onto each slice of bread.
2. Add one slice of turkey to each sandwich.
3. Top with the spinach leaves, red onion and black olives.
4. Cut in half and serve.

Strawberry Turkey Brie Panini

The warm, melting strawberries make your house smell so good! Adapted from Southern Living, you'll love this fresh, warm-weather spin on a Monte Cristo sandwich.
***Servings:** 4 | **Cook:** 3 mins | **Prep:** 15 mins | **Total Time:** 18mins*

Ingredients
- 8 ounces brie round
- 8 slices Italian bread
- 8 ounces thinly sliced smoked turkey
- 8 fresh basil leaves
- 1/2 cup sliced fresh strawberries

- 4 tablespoons red pepper jelly
- 2 tablespoons butter, melted
- 8 strawberries (optional)

Directions
1. Trim and discard rind from Brie. Cut Brie into 1/2-inch-thick slices. Layer four bread slices evenly with turkey, basil leaves, strawberries and Brie.
2. Spread one tablespoon pepper jelly on one side of each of remaining four bread slices; place bread slices, jelly sides down, on top of brie. Brush sandwiches with melted butter.
3. Cook sandwiches, in batches, in a pre-heated panini press two to three minutes or until golden brown. Garnish with strawberry halves, if desired.

Summer Tomato Mozzarella and Basil Panini with Balsamic Syrup

Serve with sweet potato chips or a simple green salad.
Serving: 4 | **Total Time:** 20 Minutes | **Hands-on:** 20 Minutes

Ingredients
- 1/2 cup balsamic vinegar
- 1 (8-ounce) piece Cuban bread, cut in half horizontally
- 1 tablespoon extra-virgin olive oil
- 12 large basil leaves
- 5 ounces fresh mozzarella cheese, thinly sliced
- 2 medium tomatoes, thinly sliced
- 1/4 teaspoon salt
- 1/8 teaspoon freshly ground black pepper
- Cooking spray

Directions
1. Bring balsamic vinegar to a boil in a small saucepan over medium-high heat; cook until reduced to 3 tablespoons (about 8 minutes).
2. While vinegar reduces, brush cut side of top half of bread with oil. Top evenly with basil, cheese, and tomatoes. Sprinkle evenly with salt and pepper. Brush cut side of bottom half of bread with reduced vinegar; place on top of sandwich. Invert sandwich.
3. Heat a large grill pan over medium-high heat. Coat the pan with cooking spray. Add sandwich to pan. Place a cast-iron or heavy skillet on top of sandwich, and gently press to flatten. Leave skillet on; cook 3 minutes on each side or until cheese melts and bread is toasted. Cut sandwich into 4 equal pieces.

Sweet Dessert Panini

Cook: 4 mins | Prep: 10 mins | Total Time: 14mins

Ingredients
- 1 cup chocolate hazelnut spread
- 8 slices white bread, cut 1/2-inch thick
- 2 bananas, sliced lengthwise
- 16 marshmallows, cut in halves
- butter, softened
- powdered sugar, for dusting

Directions
1. Preheat the grill to medium-low.
2. Heat hazelnut spread, so that it lightly coats the back of a spoon.
3. Spread all slices of bread with a thin layer of hazelnut spread.
4. Apply banana slices to 4 pieces of bread and marshmallows to the remaining 4 pieces.
5. Take 1 slice of bread with banana, and 1 with marshmallows and press them together, making a sandwich. Repeat.
6. Apply a light layer of butter to each side of the sandwiches.
7. Place each sandwich on the pre-heated grill for 2 minutes per side.
8. Once cooked, cut each sandwich in half on the diagonal.
9. Put sandwiches on a platter and dust with powdered sugar.

Thanksgiving Panini

This easy-to-prepare recipe combines favorite Thanksgiving leftovers, turkey, dressing and cranberry relish, in one delicious sandwich. Dipped into warm gravy, it makes a satisfying lunch or light supper after the holiday.
Servings: 1 | Cook: 5 mins | Prep: 5 mins | Total Time: 10mins

Ingredients
- 2 slices country bread, each 1/2 inch thick
- olive oil, for brushing
- 1 tablespoon mayonnaise
- 2 tablespoons cranberry sauce
- 2-3 slices roasted turkey
- 1/2 cup prepared stuffing (leftover, cooked)

- 1/4 cup turkey gravy, warmed

Directions

1. Preheat an electric panini maker according to the manufacturer's instructions.
2. Brush one side of each bread slice with olive oil. Lay the slices, oiled side down, on a clean work surface. Spread the top of one slice with the mayonnaise. Spread the top of the other slice with the cranberry relish. Arrange the turkey on the mayonnaise. Top with the dressing, then top with the other bread slice, oiled side up.
3. Place the sandwich on the preheated panini maker and cook according to the manufacturer's instructions until the bread is golden, 3 to 5 minutes.
4. Transfer the sandwich to a cutting board and cut in half. Serve immediately with the warmed gravy for dipping. Serves 1.

Thick Shakes With Strawberry Mascarpone

Servings: 4 | Cook: 1 hr 30 mins | Prep: 30 mins | Total Time: 2hrs

Ingredients

- 6 large egg yolks
- 1/2 cup sugar
- 2 cups milk
- 1 cup heavy cream
- 2 vanilla beans, split and seeds scraped
- 1 lb strawberry, sliced (2 pints)
- 1/2 cup fresh orange juice
- 1 teaspoon finely grated orange zest
- 1 tablespoon balsamic vinegar
- salt & freshly ground black pepper
- 8 slices brioche bread (1/2-inch thick)
- 1/2 cup mascarpone
- 2 tablespoons unsalted butter, softened
- 2 pints strawberry ice cream

Directions

1. Fill a large metal bowl with ice water and set another large metal bowl in it- Set a strainer in the bowl.
2. In a medium bowl, whisk the egg yolks with 1/4 cup of the sugar until slightly pale.
3. In a medium saucepan, heat the milk with the cream and vanilla beans and seeds until small bubbles appear around the edge.
4. Add the hot milk to the egg mixture in a thin stream, whisking constantly.

5. Return the vanilla mixture to the saucepan and cook over moderate heat, stirring constantly with a wooden spoon until slightly thickened, about 5 minutes.
6. Strain the vanilla sauce into the bowl in the ice bath and let cool completely, stirring occasionally.
7. Meanwhile, in a saucepan, combine the strawberries, orange juice, zest, vinegar and the remaining 1/4 cup of sugar; season very lightly with salt and pepper.
8. Bring to a boil and cook over moderately high heat, stirring frequently, until the mixture has become jammy, about 10 minutes- Transfer the jam to a bowl and let cool.
9. Heat a panini press or griddle over low heat. Spread the mascarpone on 4 of the brioche slices.
10. Spoon 3 tablespoons of the jam on each of the other 4 slices and close the sandwiches.
11. Brush the sandwiches with butter and grill or press until golden, about 5 minutes.
12. Transfer the panini to a cutting board and dash with confectioner's sugar.
13. Halve each sandwich.
14. Put 1 pint of ice cream and half of the vanilla sauce in a blender and blend until smooth.
15. Pour into 2 large glasses.
16. Repeat with remaining ice cream and vanilla sauce to make 2 more shakes.
17. Serve the milk shakes right away, with the panini.

Tuna Panini

Serve these hearty sandwiches with fresh apple slices or a tossed green salad.
Serving: 4

Ingredients
- 3 tablespoons finely chopped red onion
- 3 tablespoons organic canola mayonnaise
- 1 teaspoon grated lemon rind
- 1/4 teaspoon fennel seeds, crushed
- 1/4 teaspoon freshly ground black pepper
- 3 slices center-cut bacon, cooked and crumbled
- 2 (5-ounce) cans albacore tuna in water, drained and flaked
- 8 slices sourdough bread
- 4 (1/2-ounce) slices provolone cheese
- Cooking spray

Directions

1. Combine first 7 ingredients in a medium bowl, stirring well to coat. Place 4 bread slices on a flat surface; top each bread slice with 1 cheese slice. Divide tuna mixture evenly among bread slices; top each serving with 1 remaining bread slice.
2. Heat a large skillet over medium heat. Lightly coat sandwiches with cooking spray. Place sandwiches in pan; top with another heavy skillet. Cook 3 minutes on each side or until lightly browned (leave skillet on sandwiches as they cook).

Tuna Pepper Panini

Prep: *10 mins* | **Total Time:** *10mins*

Ingredients
- 1 (6 ounce) can tuna, in spring water, drained
- 1 apple, small, chopped
- 1/2 cup yellow bell pepper, chopped
- 1/4 cup unsalted cashews, chopped
- 1/4 cup roasted red pepper, canned
- 1/4 cup light mayonnaise
- 4 hard rolls (or panini)
- 2 cups watercress

Directions
1. Preparation Time: Approximately 10 minutes.
2. Preparation:
3. In a medium bowl combine tuna, apple, yellow bell pepper and cashews. Separately blend roasted red pepper and mayonnaise in a blender; add to tuna mixture. Toss lightly. Divide tuna mixture and spread on four panini. Top with watercress. Serve.
4. Servings: 4.
5. Nutritional Information Per Serving:
6. Calories 330; Total fat 12g; Saturated fat 1.5g; Cholesterol 25mg; Sodium 640mg; Carbohydrate 40g; Fiber 3g; Protein 17g; Vitamin A 25%DV*; Vitamin C 90%DV; Calcium 8%DV; Iron 15%DV; Folate 25%DV; Potassium 10%DV.
7. *Daily Value.

Turkey & BLT Panini

Love sandwiches ...so I make alot of combo sandwiches. Taking two of my favorite sandwiches and making them into one. Like this one. Hope you enjoy.
Cook: 8 mins | **Prep:** 5 mins | **Total Time:** 13mins

Ingredients
- 4 -5 slices deli turkey
- 3 slices bacon, cooked
- 2 slices tomatoes
- 2 leaves lettuce
- 1 tablespoon mayonnaise
- 1 hoagie roll

Directions
1. Spread mayo on one half of hoagie bun.
2. Cook bacon.
3. Add turkey, bacon, lettuce and tomato on bread.
4. Brush with olive oil or melted butter.
5. Place on grill and cook 2 to 4 minutes on each side.

Turkey and Cheese Panini

This turkey panini is one of the best panini recipes we have ever tried. Basil pesto and sourdough bread are key to this sandwich's unique flavor. For more panini ideas, see our complete panini recipe collection.
Serving: 4

Ingredients
- 2 tablespoons fat-free mayonnaise
- 4 teaspoons basil pesto
- 8 (1-ounce) thin slices sourdough bread
- 8 ounces sliced cooked turkey breast
- 2 ounces thinly sliced provolone cheese
- 8 (1/8-inch-thick) slices tomato
- Cooking spray

Directions
1. Combine mayonnaise and pesto, stirring well. Spread 1 tablespoon mayonnaise mixture on each of 4 bread slices; top each slice with 2 ounces

turkey, 1/2 ounce cheese, and 2 tomato slices. Top with remaining bread slices.
2. Preheat grill pan or large nonstick skillet coated with cooking spray over medium heat. Add sandwiches to pan; top with another heavy skillet. Cook 3 minutes on each side or until golden brown.

Turkey Cranberry Dressing Panini

*Servings: 2 | Cook: 10 mins | **Prep:** 10 mins | **Total Time:** 20mins*

Ingredients
- 4 slices day old bread, like ciabatta
- 12 tablespoons of gelatinous cold gravy
- 10 slices cooked turkey breast, sliced
- 1/2 cup turkey stuffing
- 12 tablespoons cranberry sauce
- kosher salt
- ground black pepper
- 6 sage leaves, chopped fine
- 4 tablespoons butter, softened

Directions
1. Spread two slices of bread with thin layer of cold gravy.
2. Layer the sandwiches with slices of turkey, stuffing, more gravy and cranberry sauce, to taste.
3. Season with salt & pepper and top with chopped sage leaves.
4. Spread a thick layer of cranberry sauce on the other slices of bread.
5. Butter sides of the sandwich, on the outside; then toast on a preheated sandwich grill, a cast iron skillet or non-stick frying pan, pressing firmly on each side until golden brown.

Turkey Panini with Watercress and Citrus Aioli

Take your average turkey sandwich to the next level with a citrusy spread and a few minutes on the panini press.
Serving: 4

Ingredients
- 2 tablespoons canola mayonnaise
- 1/4 teaspoon grated lime rind

- 1/4 teaspoon grated lemon rind
- 1 teaspoon fresh lemon juice
- 1/4 teaspoon freshly ground black pepper
- 1 garlic clove, minced
- 8 (1-ounce) slices white bread
- 1/2 pound deli-sliced smoked turkey (such as Boar's Head)
- 2 cups trimmed watercress
- 4 (1/2-ounce) slices provolone cheese
- Cooking spray

Directions
1. Heat a grill pan over medium-high heat.
2. Combine first 6 ingredients; spread evenly over 4 bread slices. Top evenly with turkey, watercress, cheese, and remaining 4 bread slices.
3. Coat grill pan with cooking spray. Arrange 2 sandwiches in pan. Place a cast-iron or heavy skillet on top of sandwiches; press gently to flatten. Cook 2 minutes on each side (leave cast-iron skillet on sandwiches while they cook). Repeat procedure with remaining 2 sandwiches.

Turkey Reuben Panini

Serving: 4 | Total Time: 15 Minutes

Ingredients
- 8 (1/2-ounce) slices thin-slice rye bread
- 1/4 cup fat-free Thousand Island dressing
- 8 (1/2-ounce) thin slices reduced-fat Swiss cheese
- 1/4 cup refrigerated sauerkraut, rinsed and drained
- 8 ounces deli, low-sodium turkey breast (such as Boar's Head)

Directions
1. Spread one side of each bread slice evenly with 1 1/2 teaspoons dressing. Place one cheese slice on dressed side of each of four bread slices; top each with 1 tablespoon sauerkraut and 2 ounces turkey. Top each sandwich with 1 cheese slice and 1 bread slice, dressed side down. Coat the outside of the sandwich (top and bottom) with cooking spray. Heat a large skillet over medium-high heat. Add sandwiches to pan. Place a cast-iron or other heavy skillet on top of sandwiches; press gently to flatten sandwiches (leave cast-iron skillet on sandwiches while they cook). Cook 2 minutes on each side or until browned and cheese melts.

Turkey Stuffing & Cranberry Orange

Cook: 10 mins | Prep: 10 mins | Total Time: 20mins

Ingredients
- 4 slices of rustic country bread
- 3 tablespoons mayonnaise
- 2 slices cooked turkey, thin slices (to fit the bread)
- 4 tablespoons prepared stuffing
- 4 tablespoons cooked mashed turnips
- 6 small cooked onions
- 4 tablespoons cranberry-orange relish
- 4 teaspoons butter (for grilling side of bread)

Directions
1. Spread the 4 slices of bread with mayonnaise.
2. Put a layer of turkey to fit the bread, a layer of stuffing and turnip.
3. Then place the onions on top of this.
4. Lastly the cranberry-orange relish.
5. Put the other bread on top and butter each slice.
6. Grill.

White Trash Panini

Servings: 1 | Cook: 5 mins | Prep: 15 mins | Total Time: 20mins

Ingredients
- 1 croissant
- 2 tablespoons creamy peanut butter or 2 tablespoons chunky peanut butter
- 1 1/16 ounces milk chocolate candy bars (half or a regular size bar)
- 3 tablespoons marshmallow cream
- melted butter, for brushing
- powdered sugar, for sprinkling

Directions
1. Heat a panini grill or other griddle to medium heat; use a serrated knife to split the croissant in half lengthwise.
2. Spread one half with peanut butter.
3. Break the chocolate into small squares and lay atop the peanut butter.

4. Spread the Marshmallow fluff on the remaining croissant half (the quantities of the filling ingredients are approximations--let the size of your croissant, and your appetite, be your guide).
5. Press the sandwich together; brush very lightly with melted butter.
6. Press the croissant in the panini grill until it is slightly flattened and crisp and the filling is warm and melted, 4-5 minutes.
7. Remove your croissant from the panini press and let it cool slightly.
8. Sprinkle with powdered sugar; use a serrated knife to cut in half.
9. Eat immediately.

Whole Wheat Low Sodium Panini Buns

You can make a panini from any of your favorite sandwich recipes. Yes, even peanut butter and jam. We like a variety of combinations and really enjoy it with this Panini Whole Wheat Bread recipe. You can use any bread you enjoy though from Focaccia, Sourdough, Baguette, even your favorite Whole Wheat or Cinnamon bread. Just make sure your panini maker is hot and ready to go
Cook: *20 mins |* **Prep:** *20 mins |* **Total Time:** *40mins*

Ingredients
- 1 cup water, filtered warmed to about 110 F
- 2 tablespoons water, filtered warmed to about 110 F
- 1 cup buttermilk, no sodium filtered warmed to about 100 F
- 2 tablespoons vinegar (cider or white wine)
- 3 tablespoons extra virgin olive oil
- 1 large egg
- 2 cups whole wheat pastry flour
- 3 cups whole wheat bread flour
- 1/4 cup potato flour
- 4 tablespoons granulated sugar
- 1/4 teaspoon ascorbic acid
- 1/2 teaspoon onion powder, granulated
- 4 1/2 teaspoons bread machine yeast

Directions
1. Makes 14 to 24 Sandwich Buns.
2. * 1 cup plus 2-tablespoons no sodium or filtered water warmed to about 110°F (trace).
3. * 1 cup reduced fat low sodium buttermilk warmed to about 100°F(130 mg).
4. * 2 tablespoons vinegar (cider or white wine) (.30 mg).
5. * 3 tablespoons extra virgin olive oil (trace).
6. * 1 large egg (63 mg).

7. * 2 cups white or pastry whole wheat flour* (12 mg).
8. * 3 cups white best for bread flour (7.5 mg).
9. * ¼ cup potato flour (15.5 mg).
10. * 4 level tablespoons Splenda or granulated sugar*** (trace).
11. * ¼ teaspoon ascorbic acid (trace).
12. * 2 tablespoons granular lecithin (trace).
13. * ½ teaspoon granulated onion powder (.648 mg).
14. * 4 ½ teaspoons bread machine yeast (9 mg)
15. Baste With.
16. * ½ egg white**** (used portion) (27.4 mg).
17. * ¼ teaspoon filtered or no sodium water (trace)
18. Place ingredients into bread machine in order listed or in order your manufacturer calls for. Set for dough.
19. Check while kneading to make sure there is enough liquid. (Some whole wheat flour will require more some might require less.) If after five minutes or so the dough appears to need liquid, add water at one-tablespoon at a time. If it's sticky, add about one or two tablespoons of flour but no more.
20. Warm oven or ovens to about 100°F just before bread is ready to shape and let rise after taking out of machine.
21. Whisk the egg white in a small bowl with the water and set aside for basting shaped buns.
22. Remove dough from bread machine pan and roll out onto lightly floured board. Cut in half.
23. We are going to make buns here, any shape you prefer. Large buns will come out to about 14 and standard size buns will make as many as 24 with this recipe. We freeze most of them and use them for future lunches.**.
24. Press down on dough until it's about ¾" thick and spread out to about 6" by about 14 to 16". Slice the dough down the center lengthwise and then cut each section evenly to make buns. They should double in size when rising. Place buns on lightly oiled cooking sheet. Using a basting brush, baste the tops and sides with the egg white mixture. With a sharp knife, make a slice down the middle lengthwise about an 1/8" deep. Prepare the second half of the dough with another cooking sheet.
25. If you have just one oven then let one of these rise in the oven and the other rise in a warm spot in your house, each covered with lightly oiled wax paper. If you have a double-oven, let each rise separately in an oven.
26. After about 45 minutes to an hour, remove the wax paper cover on the buns in the oven without moving the buns. Turn the oven on to 375°F Bake for about 12 to 20 minutes or until golden brown. They will brown nicely. (If you have a double oven, bake both at the same time.).
27. Remove and cool on a rack.
28. For the second batch that rose outside the oven, bake for about 10 to 15 minutes or until golden brown. These will brown more quickly. (If you let both batches rise outside the oven, then follow cooking time here for each.).
29. Cool on rack.
30. Great for panini sandwiches.

31. *We use Bob's Red Mill Organic White Whole Wheat.
32. **If you want to cut the recipe in half then you can cut all ingredients in half except the yeast (half a recipe would need 2 ½ teaspoons yeast) and the egg. Use only 1/2-cup of water, ½ cup buttermilk and a full egg.
33. ***If you use Splenda instead of sugar calories will drop between 6 and 14 per bun depending on whether you make 24 or 14.
34. ****You'll end up using only about half an egg white. Data is figured based on that.

Chapter 8: Vegetables

***

Brie Pesto and Tomato Panini

I'm hooked on Paninis. So easy, so good, and there's always something in the house to use for a fast appetizer or quick lunch. Here's one for summer appetizers, perfect with a glass of wine.
Servings: 4-6 | **Cook:** 15 mins | **Prep:** 10 mins | **Total Time:** 25mins

Ingredients
- 1/2 loaf Italian bread
- 1/4 cup pesto sauce
- 8 -12 ounces brie cheese, rind removed
- 1 large tomatoes, sliced
- extra virgin olive oil
- kosher salt and freshly cracked black pepper

Directions
1. Slice the Italian bread in half, vertically.
2. Drizzle insides well with the olive oil and slightly on the outsides.
3. Slather the pesto on the insides and cover with the tomato slices.
4. Season with salt and pepper to taste then pile on the brie chunks or slices and cover with the top piece of the bread.
5. Heat the panini pan of frying pan and add the sandwich.
6. If you're using a frying pan be sure to use a weight to smush the sandwich while it heats.
7. Flip the sandwich when the bread starts to brown.
8. The panini is done when both sides are golden brown and the cheese starts to ooze!
9. Remove from heat and cut into appetizer sized portions.

Carrot Ginger Soup

Loaded with surprising hits of curry powder, lime juice, and cilantro, this soup pairs perfectly with a panini or with a salad for dinner. It also makes a wonderful first course for a fancier meal. Make this a vegetarian option by using vegetable broth instead of chicken broth.
Serving: 12 | **Total Time:** 1 Hour, 2 Minutes | **Hands-On:** 17 Minutes

Ingredients
- 3 tablespoons unsalted butter

- 3 tablespoons olive oil
- 1 cup chopped onion
- 2 tablespoons finely chopped peeled fresh ginger
- 2 garlic cloves, finely minced
- 7 cups fat-free, lower-sodium chicken or vegetable broth
- 4 cups diced carrot (1 1/2 pounds)
- 1 cup dry white wine
- 2 teaspoons fresh lime juice
- 1/4 teaspoon curry powder
- 1/4 teaspoon freshly ground black pepper
- 2 tablespoons chopped fresh cilantro

Directions
1. Heat a large saucepan over medium heat. Melt butter with olive oil in pan; cook 2 minutes or until butter melts. Add onion, ginger, and garlic. Cook 10 minutes or until onion is soft, stirring occasionally.
2. Stir in broth, carrot, and wine. Bring to a boil; reduce heat and simmer, uncovered, for 45 minutes.
3. Place half of carrot mixture in a blender. Remove center piece of blender lid (to allow steam to escape); secure blender lid on blender. Place a clean towel over opening in blender lid (to avoid splatters). Blend until smooth. Pour into a bowl. Repeat procedure with remaining carrot mixture. Stir in lime juice, curry powder, and pepper. Ladle about 2/3 cup soup into each of 12 bowls. Sprinkle evenly with cilantro.

Cheddar Bacon and Apple Panini

Sharp, sweet and smoky. A hearty sandwich that goes perfectly with tomato soup on a cold day or fresh fruit in the summer.
Servings: 4 | **Cook:** 5 mins | **Prep:** 5 mins | **Total Time:** 10mins

Ingredients
- 8 slices country-style white bread
- 8 ounces sharp cheddar cheese, sliced
- 8 slices bacon, cooked
- 1 granny smith apple, thinly sliced
- Dijon mustard

Directions
1. Heat panini press to medium-low heat.
2. Spread Dijon on 4 slices of bread. Top with slices of Cheddar, 2 pieces of bacon, apple slices and additional Cheddar. Place the remaining bread on top.

3. Place on panini press and cook until cheese is slightly melted and bread is browned and crispy.

Cheddar Ham and Apple Panini

Servings: 2 | Cook: 4 mins | Prep: 15 mins | Total Time: 19mins

Ingredients
- 2 ciabatta rolls, split
- 1 tablespoon butter, melted
- 1/4 cup mango chutney
- 2 ounces baked ham, thinly sliced
- 2 ounces cheddar cheese, thinly sliced
- 1/2 granny smith apple, thinly sliced

Directions
1. Preheat panini grill to high.
2. Place rolls, cut side down, on a work surface and brush crusts with butter.
3. Turn rolls over and spread with chutney.
4. On bottom halves, evenly layer with ham, cheese, and apple.
5. Cover with top halves and press gently to pack.
6. Place sandwiches in grill, close the top plate and cook until golden brown, 3-4 minutes.
7. Serve immediately.

Fried Green Tomato and Pancetta Panini

This is a superb, unique sandwich that is pretty simple to prepare. I made these paninis for my family, all of whom loved them.
Servings: 4 | Cook: 15 mins | Prep: 15 mins | Total Time: 30mins

Ingredients
- 1 1/2 cups flour
- 1/2 cup cornmeal
- salt and pepper, to taste
- 3 eggs, lightly beaten
- 4 green tomatoes, sliced 1/4-inch thick
- 1/4 cup olive oil, plus more for brushing
- 8 ounces pancetta, thickly sliced, cooked until crispy, fat reserved

- 8 ounces sliced country bread, each 1/2-inch thick
- 6 ounces thinly sliced provolone cheese
- 1 cup baby arugula

Directions
1. Put 1 cup flour in shallow bowl. In another shallow bowl, combine 1/2 cup flour, cornmeal, salt, and pepper. Put eggs in another bowl. Season tomato slices with salt and pepper. Dredge in flour; dip into eggs, letting excess drip off. Dredge in cornmeal mix. Place on plate.
2. In deep saute pan over medium heat, warm 1/2 cup oil and 3 tablespoons pancetta fat. Fry tomatoes in batches, turning once, until golden, 2-3 minutes per side. Add more fat to pan as needed.
3. Preheat electric panini press. Brush one side of each bread slice with olive oil. Lay slices, oiled side down, on panini griddle/wok surface. Place cheese on half of slices; top with pancetta, 2 or 3 tomato slices, and one of the other bread slices, oiled side up. Cook sandwiches on panini press until bread is golden and cheese is melted, 3-5 minutes. Transfer to cutting board. Place 1/4 cup arugula inside each sandwich; cut in half.
4. Serve and savor!

Goat Cheese and Roasted Pepper Panini

The sweetness of roasted red bell peppers is an ideal foil to the pungency of the goat cheese and kalamata olives. Serve this hearty veggie sandwich with Melon Chillers.
Serving: 4 | **Prep:** 5 Minutes | **Cook:** 6 Minutes

Ingredients
- 1 (3-ounce) package goat cheese, softened
- 12 pitted kalamata olives, coarsely chopped
- 8 (2-ounce) slices sourdough bread
- 16 basil leaves
- 2 cups spring mix greens
- 1 cup bottled roasted red bell peppers
- Cooking spray

Directions
1. Combine cheese and olives in a small bowl, stirring until well blended. Spread about 1 tablespoon cheese mixture evenly over each of 4 bread slices. Divide basil leaves, greens, and bell pepper into fourths; arrange evenly over cheese mixture on each bread slice. Top with remaining 4 bread slices.
2. Heat a large nonstick skillet over medium heat. Coat pan with cooking spray. Add sandwiches to pan. Cover with a sheet of foil; top with a heavy skillet. Cook 3 minutes or until lightly browned. Turn sandwiches over; replace foil

and skillet. Cook 3 minutes or until golden.

Grilled Vegetable and Fontina Panini

These Italian sandwiches can be made using a grill pan or an indoor grill.
Serving: 4 | **Prep:** 8 Minutes | **Cook:** 13 Minutes

Ingredients
- Cooking spray
- 1 small eggplant, sliced crosswise into 1/4-inch slices
- 1/2 cup bottled roasted red bell peppers, cut into strips
- 1/4 cup fat-free zesty Italian dressing
- 1 garlic clove, minced
- 1/4 cup chopped fresh basil
- 1 (8-ounce) loaf ciabatta
- 4 ounces fontina cheese, sliced

Directions
1. Heat a grill pan over medium-high heat; coat pan with cooking spray. Coat eggplant slices with cooking spray, and place in pan. Cook 4 to 5 minutes on each side or until tender.
2. Combine eggplant and next 4 ingredients in bowl, tossing to coat.
3. Slice ciabatta loaf in half lengthwise, cutting to, but not through, other side.
4. Arrange vegetable mixture evenly over bottom half of bread; top with cheese and top half of bread. Cut into 4 equal servings.
5. Place sandwiches in grill pan over medium-high heat. Place a piece of foil over sandwiches; top with a heavy skillet to press sandwiches. Cook 2 minutes. Turn sandwiches; replace foil and heavy skillet. Cook 2 minutes or until golden brown and cheese is melted. Serve immediately.

Grilled Vegetable Panini

Cook: 10 mins | **Total Time:** 10mins

Ingredients
- 1/4 cup olive oil
- 1 large eggplant, cut crosswise into 1/2-inch-thick slices
- 2 zucchini, cut crosswise into 1/2-inch-thick slices
- 1 small red onion, cut into 1/2-inch-thick slices
- salt & freshly ground black pepper

- 8 ounces mozzarella cheese, drained, sliced
- 2 tomatoes, sliced
- 1/2 cup roasted red pepper

Directions
1. Heat a grill pan over medium-high heat. Drizzle the oil over the eggplant, zucchini, and onion slices, then sprinkle with salt and pepper. Working in batches, grill the eggplant, zucchini, and onions until they are tender and grill marks appear, about 4 minutes per side. Cool completely.
2. Cut each baguette into 6 pieces. Working with one baguette piece at a time, slice in half and spread both sides with the pesto. Working with the bottom slice of the baguette, stack 2 slices of eggplant, 2 slices zucchini, 1 slice onion, 1 slice tomato, 1 slice mozzarella, and 1 slice of roasted pepper. Sprinkle with salt and pepper. Place top half of baguette on top and continue with remaining baguette. (The sandwiches can be made 4 hours ahead. Wrap well with plastic wrap and refrigerate.).

Ham and Apple Panini

This is a panini take-off on my other sandwich which is delicious--Apple and Ham Grilled Cheese Sandwiches. It grills so nicely and has wonderful flavor.
Cook: 10 mins | Prep: 10 mins | Total Time: 20 mins

Ingredients
SANDWICH
- 4 slices of rustic country bread
- 4 slices deli ham
- 4 slices provolone cheese (thin slices)
- 1/2 cup chopped apple (with skins on)
- 4 tablespoons mayonnaise
- 1/8 cup chopped walnuts

PARMESAN BUTTER FOR OUTSIDE
- 1/4 cup parmesan cheese
- 3 tablespoons soft butter

Directions
1. Mix the ingredients for the Parmesan Butter and set aside.
2. Mix the mayonnaise, chopped fine apples, and walnuts.
3. Lay out the bread and put the Provolone cheese on top of each bread slice.
4. Add the apple mixture to each sandwich.
5. Place the ham on top of this.
6. Then top it with the other slice of bread.

7. Spread a thin layer of Parmesan Butter on the top bread and place on grill; then spread the other side and grill.

Marinated Portobello Panini

Fill a small loaf of bread with "meaty" portobellos, flavorful cheeses, and olives for a hearty lunch.
Serving: 4 | **Prep:** 8 Minutes | **Cook:** 3 Minutes | **Other:** 15 Minutes

Ingredients
- 1 (6-ounce) package pre-sliced portobello mushrooms
- 2 tablespoons reduced-fat olive oil vinaigrette
- 1 (12-ounce) loaf Italian or ciabatta bread
- 1/3 cup light garlic-and-herbs spreadable cheese (such as Alouette Light)
- 1/4 cup (1 ounce) crumbled blue cheese
- 1/4 cup pitted kalamata olives, coarsely chopped
- 2 teaspoons Dijon mustard
- 1/2 teaspoon minced garlic
- 12 fresh basil leaves
- 1 medium tomato, cut into 8 slices
- Cooking spray

Directions
1. Place mushrooms in a quart-size zip-top plastic bag. Add vinaigrette; seal bag, and gently toss to coat. Let stand 15 minutes.
2. . While mushrooms marinate, cut bread loaf in half horizontally. Hollow out top and bottom halves of loaf, leaving a 1/2-inch border. Reserve torn bread for another use.
3. . Combine cheeses in a small microwave-safe bowl; microwave at HIGH 15 seconds or until soft. Add olives, mustard, and garlic; stir well. Spread mixture on bottom half of loaf; top with basil, tomato, and mushrooms. Top with remaining half of loaf. Coat both sides of sandwich with cooking spray.
4. . Heat a large nonstick skillet over medium heat; place sandwich in pan. Place a piece of foil over sandwich; top with a heavy skillet. Cook 2 minutes. Turn sandwich; replace foil and heavy skillet. Cook 1 to 2 minutes or until golden brown. Cut into 4 equal portions.

Mushroom and Manchego Panini

Sandwich night gets turned up a notch with super fast Mushroom and Manchego Panini. This flavor-packed grilled sandwich is made with fresh herbs, a mixture of

exotic mushrooms, and shaved cheese--all sandwiched between sourdough bread.
Serving: 4

Ingredients
- 1 teaspoon unsalted butter
- 1/4 cup minced shallots
- 1 tablespoon chopped fresh thyme
- 2 teaspoons minced fresh garlic
- 1/2 teaspoon freshly ground black pepper
- 1/4 teaspoon kosher salt
- 2 (4-ounce) packages presliced exotic mushroom blend (such as shiitake, cremini, and oyster)
- 1 (8-ounce) package presliced cremini mushrooms
- 1 1/2 tablespoons sherry vinegar
- 8 (1 1/2-ounce) slices sourdough bread
- 3 ounces shaved Manchego cheese
- Cooking spray
- 1 garlic clove, halved

Directions
1. Melt butter in a large skillet over medium-high heat; add shallots and next 6 ingredients (through cremini mushrooms). Cook 10 minutes or until mushrooms are tender and liquid almost evaporates, stirring frequently. Add vinegar; cook 30 seconds or until liquid almost evaporates.
2. Divide the mushroom mixture evenly among four bread slices. Top evenly with Manchego cheese and remaining bread slices.
3. Heat a large grill pan over medium-high heat. Coat pan with cooking spray. Add sandwiches to pan. Place a cast-iron or heavy skillet on top of sandwiches; press gently to flatten. Cook sandwiches 2 minutes on each side or until cheese melts and bread is toasted (leave skillet on sandwiches while they cook). Rub the top and bottom of each sandwich with cut side of garlic clove.

My Amazing Tomato Basil Soup Like Applebee's®

"This tastes just like the tomato basil soup they serve at Applebee's®. The hubs loved it so that's saying something! I always add a pinch of sugar to tomato-based sauce, but I'm not sure that it needed it. Served it with baked fries with seasoned salt and grilled gouda cheese sandwiches on thick crusty bread, panini-style."
***Pre:** 10 m | **Cook:** 20 m | **Ready In:** 30 m*

Ingredients
- 3 tablespoons olive oil

- 1 small clove garlic, minced
- 1 (10.75 ounce) can condensed tomato soup
- 1/4 cup bottled marinara sauce
- 1/2 (10.75 ounce) can water
- 1 teaspoon chopped fresh oregano, or to taste
- 1/2 teaspoon ground black pepper
- 1 tablespoon chopped fresh basil, or more to taste
- 6 Italian-style seasoned croutons, or as needed
- 2 tablespoons grated Parmesan cheese
- Add all ingredients to list

Directions
1. Heat olive oil in a large saucepan over medium heat. Saute garlic in hot oil until tender and fragrant, 2 to 3 minutes. Stir
2. Stir condensed tomato soup and marinara sauce into garlic; slowly add water. Mix oregano and black pepper into soup; bring to a simmer, reduce heat to low, and cook until flavors blend, about 15 minutes. Stir basil into soup. Ladle into bowls and top with croutons and Parmesan cheese.

Panini With Sautéed Mushrooms and Gruyère

A great option for a meatless meal, this grilled panini sandwich features sautéed mushrooms, roasted red peppers, and gruyére cheese.
Serving: 4

Ingredients
- 1 tablespoon butter
- 1 (8-ounce) package mushrooms, sliced
- 4 teaspoons Dijon mustard
- 8 (1-ounce) slices whole wheat bread
- 1/2 of 1 (10-ounce) bag fresh spinach
- 1/4 cup sliced roasted red bell peppers
- 1/4 cup chopped onion
- 1 cup shredded Gruyère cheese
- 2 tablespoons butter, melted

Directions
1. Heat butter in large nonstick skillet over medium-high heat. Add mushrooms; sauté 5-6 minutes.
2. Spread mustard on 4 slices of bread; layer each with 6 spinach leaves, 1 tablespoon pepper, 1 tablespoon onion, 1/4 cup cheese, and 1/4 cup mushrooms. Top with remaining bread.

3. Brush melted butter over both sides of each sandwich. If using a skillet, heat a large nonstick skillet over medium-high heat; place sandwich- es in pan. Place another skillet on top of sandwiches; cook 2-3 minutes on each side until golden brown and cheese is melted. If using a panini maker, brush sandwiches with butter; place in machine, close, and cook 2 minutes or until done.

Panini with Sautéed Spinach and Chickpea Spread

Serving: 2

Ingredients
- 3/4 cup chickpeas (garbanzo beans)
- 2 tablespoons lemon juice
- 1 tablespoon water
- 2 teaspoons capers
- 2 teaspoons olive oil
- 2 garlic cloves, minced
- 4 cups torn spinach
- 1/8 teaspoon pepper
- 2 (2 1/2-ounce) submarine rolls

Directions
1. Place first 4 ingredients in a food processor, and process until smooth, scraping sides of processor bowl occasionally. Set aside.
2. Heat oil in a large nonstick skillet over medium heat. Add garlic, and sauté 1 minute. Add spinach; sauté 1 minute. Remove skillet from heat, and stir in pepper.
3. Slice each roll in half horizontally. Spread chickpea mixture over bottom halves of bread. Top with spinach, and cover with top halves of bread.

Prosciutto Mozzarella and Arugula Panini

Prep: 10 minutes; Cook: 7 minutes The key to a good panino (singular) is high-quality bread, usually ciabatta, and fresh ingredients. Look for long, flat, rectangular-shaped loaves of ciabatta in your favorite deli or bakery.
Serving: 4

Ingredients
- 4 teaspoons balsamic vinegar
- 2 teaspoons extravirgin olive oil
- 1/4 teaspoon black pepper

- 1 garlic clove, minced
- 1 (9-ounce) loaf ciabatta, cut in half horizontally
- 16 very thin slices prosciutto (about 4 ounces)
- 4 (1-ounce) slices part-skim mozzarella cheese
- 8 (1/4-inch-thick) slices tomato (1 medium tomato)
- 1 cup lightly packed trimmed arugula or spinach
- Olive oil-flavored cooking spray

Directions
1. Combine first 4 ingredients in a small bowl; stir well with a whisk.
2. Brush cut sides of bread with vinaigrette. Arrange prosciutto and next 3 ingredients over bottom half of bread; replace top half of bread. Cut loaf in half crosswise, and coat with cooking spray.
3. Heat a large grill pan or nonstick skillet over medium heat. Add sandwich halves to pan. Place a heavy skillet on top of sandwiches to weigh them down. Cook 3 minutes on each side or until bread is toasted and cheese melts. Cut each sandwich half in half again to form 4 equal portions. Serve immediately.
4. Note: Focaccia may be substituted for ciabatta.
5. Panini (pah-NEE-nee) translates as "rolls" or "little bread," but in Italy, the name is synonymous with sandwiches.

Roasted Vegetable and Mozzarella Panini

From Self.com, "David Burke, of David Burke at Bloomingdale's in New York City, created this savory sandwich that's simple to make and a money saver, too." Instead of using skillets (steps 6 and 7) I used my George Forman grill - worked like a charm! I'm sure you could use a panini press as well!
Cook: *15 mins |* **Prep:** *10 mins |* **Total Time:** *25mins*

Ingredients
- 2 tablespoons balsamic vinegar
- 1 tablespoon extra virgin olive oil
- 1/2 teaspoon salt
- 1/8 teaspoon black pepper
- vegetable oil cooking spray
- 1 medium eggplant, cut lengthwise into 8 slices (1/4 inch each)
- 1 medium zucchini, cut into 8 slices (1/4 inch each)
- 1 red bell pepper, cored, seeded and quartered
- 8 slices ciabatta
- 1 cup reduced-fat mozzarella cheese, shredded
- 8 large fresh basil leaves

Directions

1. Whisk vinegar, oil, salt and pepper in a bowl.
2. Coat a baking sheet with cooking spray; place vegetables in 1 layer on sheet.
3. Brush both sides of eggplant and zucchini with vinegar mixture. Spray all vegetables with cooking spray and place under broiler, 7 to 8 minutes, turning once and coating with cooking spray.
4. Lightly brush 4 bottom slices of ciabatta with remaining vinegar mixture; pile veggies, cheese and basil on each of the slices.
5. Close sandwiches; spray both sides with cooking spray.
6. Heat a medium nonstick skillet over medium-high heat; add sandwiches. Place a second skillet on top of sandwiches and press down.
7. Cook 4 minutes, flipping once.
8. Serve.

Sautéed Snap Peas with Ricotta Salata and Mint

Floral lemon zest (but no tart juice) allows the sweet pea flavor to shine. Chop mint, grate lemon rind, and crumble cheese while the peas cook. Serve with panini or other sandwiches, grilled chicken, or pork chops.
Serving: 6 | Total Time: *5 Minutes 5 Minutes*

Ingredients

- 1 tablespoon olive oil
- 2 (8-ounce) packages trimmed sugar snap peas
- 3 tablespoons chopped fresh mint
- 1 1/2 teaspoons grated lemon rind
- 3/8 teaspoon freshly ground black pepper
- 1/4 teaspoon kosher salt
- 1.5 ounces ricotta salata or goat cheese, crumbled (about 1/3 cup)

Directions

1. Heat a large skillet over medium-high heat. Add oil to pan; swirl. Add peas; sauté 3 minutes or until crisp-tender. Stir in mint, rind, pepper, and salt. Sprinkle with cheese.

Silky Tomato Soup with White Beans and Garlic Oil

Creamy, silky tomato soup is the ultimate comfort food. We've elevated the traditional soup with the addition of white cannellini beans and toasty garlic oil. You won't miss any of the cream or calories from this dairy-free tomato soup as the texture is still silky from blending the tomato base. Serve alongside our revamped Grilled Cheese Skillet

"Panini" for a meal kids and adults will all approve of. With the addition of the white beans, each serving provides 8 grams of protein making this vegetarian meal foolproof.
Serving: 6 | Total Time: 20 Minutes

Ingredients

- 3 1/2 tablespoons olive oil, divided
- 8 large garlic cloves, sliced
- 1/2 teaspoon crushed red pepper
- 1 (14.5-oz.) can unsalted cannellini beans, rinsed and drained
- 1 cup chopped sweet onion
- 1/2 cup chopped carrot
- 2 thyme sprigs
- 1 tablespoon unsalted tomato paste
- 1 cup unsalted vegetable stock
- 1 1/4 teaspoons kosher salt
- 3 pounds ripe tomatoes, chopped
- 2 ounces whole-wheat bread, torn

Directions

1. Heat 3 tablespoons oil and garlic in a skillet over medium for 4 minutes or until garlic is golden. Add red pepper and beans; toss.
2. Heat remaining 1 1/2 teaspoons oil in a Dutch oven over medium-high. Add onion, carrot, and thyme; cook 3 minutes. Stir in tomato paste. Stir in stock, salt, tomatoes, and bread. Bring to a boil; cook 5 minutes.
3. Discard thyme sprigs. Place tomato mixture in a blender; process until smooth. Divide soup among 4 bowls; top with beans.

Tomato Basil Squares

"This is so simple. Reminds me of a Margherita Pizza. Very flavorful. I also think the sauce would also taste great on a panini sandwich, though I've never tried it."
Pre: 15 m | Cook: 20 m | Ready In: 35 m

Ingredients

- 1 (10 ounce) container refrigerated pizza crust
- 1/4 cup mayonnaise
- 1/4 cup freshly grated Parmesan cheese
- 2 tablespoons chopped fresh basil
- 1 clove garlic, minced
- 3 roma (plum) tomatoes, sliced
- 1 cup shredded mozzarella cheese

- Add all ingredients to list

Directions
1. Preheat oven to 375 degrees F (190 degrees C).
2. Roll out pizza dough, and place on a baking sheet. Mix mayonnaise, Parmesan, basil, and garlic in a small bowl. Spread mayonnaise mixture on pizza crust; top with sliced tomatoes. Sprinkle with mozzarella cheese.
3. Bake in preheated oven until crust is golden brown and cheese is bubbly, 15 to 20 minutes. Cut into squares to serve.

Turkey and Tomato Panini

"Turn a plain sandwich dinner into something special by preparing it panini-style (which doesn't, by the way, require a fancy panini maker)."
Pre: 25 m | Cook: 25 m

Ingredients
- 3 tablespoons reduced-fat mayonnaise
- 2 tablespoons nonfat plain yogurt
- 2 tablespoons shredded Parmesan cheese
- 2 tablespoons chopped fresh basil
- 1 teaspoon lemon juice
- Freshly ground pepper to taste
- 8 slices whole-wheat bread
- 8 ounces thinly sliced reduced-sodium deli turkey
- 8 tomato slices
- 2 teaspoons canola oil
- Add all ingredients to list

Directions
1. Have four 15-ounce cans and a medium skillet (not nonstick) ready by the stove.
2. Combine mayonnaise, yogurt, Parmesan, basil, lemon juice and pepper in a small bowl. Spread about 2 teaspoons of the mixture on each slice of bread. Divide turkey and tomato slices among 4 slices of bread; top with the remaining bread.
3. Heat 1 teaspoon canola oil in a large nonstick skillet over medium heat. Place 2 panini in the pan. Place the medium skillet on top of the panini, then weigh it down with the cans. Cook the panini until golden on one side, about 2 minutes. Reduce the heat to medium-low, flip the panini, replace the top skillet and cans, and cook until the second side is golden, 1 to 3 minutes more. Repeat with another 1 teaspoon oil and the remaining panini.

Turkey Antipasto Panini

Serve with fresh cherries and an Italian Berry Float to top off your meal.
*Serving: 4 | **Prep:** 7 Minutes | **Cook:** 3 Minutes*

Ingredients
- 2 tablespoons reduced-fat mayonnaise
- 8 (0.9-ounce) slices crusty Chicago-style Italian bread
- 8 ounces shaved lower-sodium deli turkey (such as Boar's Head)
- 1 (6-ounce) jar quartered marinated artichoke hearts, drained and coarsely chopped
- 1/2 cup moist sun-dried tomato halves, packed without oil and sliced
- 1/2 cup sliced bottled roasted red bell peppers
- 12 basil leaves
- 4 (1-ounce) slices reduced-fat provolone cheese (such as Alpine Lace)
- Cooking spray

Directions
1. Preheat panini grill.
2. Spread mayonnaise evenly over each bread slice. Top each of 4 bread slices evenly with turkey, artichokes, tomato, bell pepper, basil leaves, and cheese. Top with remaining bread slices. Coat both sides of sandwiches with cooking spray.
3. Place sandwiches on panini grill. Grill 3 to 4 minutes or until bread is browned and cheese melts. Cut panini in half before serving, if desired.

Vegetable & Bean Soup With Pesto &am

From Foodnetwork.com, this recipe by Rachael Ray is billed as her answer to food therapy. I'm putting it here so I remember to make it soon.
***Servings:** 4 | **Cook:** 30 mins | **Prep:** 20 mins | **Total Time:** 50mins*

Ingredients
- 2 tablespoons extra virgin olive oil, 2 turns of the pan
- 1 medium onion, chopped
- 1 medium potato, peeled and chopped
- 1 medium zucchini, chopped
- salt and pepper
- 1 (15 ounce) can garbanzo beans (ceci or chick peas)
- 1 (15 ounce) can white beans, cannellini, drained
- 6 cups chicken stock, available in paper containers on soup aisle

- 1 cup egg noodles, for soup, any brand
- 1 (8 ounce) box frozen green beans
- 8 slices crusty bread
- 8 ounces robiola cheese or 8 ounces ricotta cheese
- 1 cup arugula leaf, loosely packed
- 8 slices prosciutto di Parma
- 1 cup basil leaves, packed
- 1 large garlic clove
- 2 -3 tablespoons pine nuts (pignoli)
- 3 tablespoons grated parmigiano-reggiano cheese
- 3 tablespoons extra virgin olive oil

Directions
1. Heat a medium soup pot over medium high heat. Add extra-virgin olive oil, 2 turns of the pan. Add onion, potato and zucchini and season with salt and pepper. Cook 5 or 6 minutes alone, stirring frequently, then add the canned beans and the chicken stock. Cover the pot and bring the soup up to a boil.
2. Preheat a panini grill or a heavy bottomed pan over medium heat. Build 4 panini: spread roll or bread with a couple ounces of cheese, then top with a few leaves of arugula and 2 slices of prosciutto for each sandwich. Place panini in sandwich press or onto hot, heavy bottomed pan. Top with another heavy skillet or a brick wrapped in foil to press sandwiches. Press sandwiches until crisp on both sides, 2 to 3 minutes on each side.
3. When the soup is at a boil, remove the lid. Stir in the noodles and green beans and reduce heat to low. Simmer soup an additional 5 to 6 minutes then remove it from the heat.
4. Combine basil, garlic, nuts and cheese in the food processor and turn it on. Stream in the extra-virgin olive oil and process until pesto is nearly smooth.
5. Scrape the pesto into a small bowl. Add a ladle of the soup broth to thin the pesto, then add the pesto to the soup. Stir to combine and serve soup immediately with panini, for dipping.

Chapter 9: More Panini Recipes

***

Broccoli Rabe and Provolone Panini

Cook: 10 mins | Prep: 20 mins | Total Time: 30mins

Ingredients
- 1/2 cup extra virgin olive oil
- 1 garlic clove, smashed and peeled
- 1 bunch broccoli rabe, trimmed and cut into thirds
- salt
- crushed red pepper flakes
- 1/3 cup sun-dried tomato, coarsely chopped
- 1/4 cup pine nuts, toasted
- 2 tablespoons parmesan cheese, grated
- 8 slices country bread
- 8 ounces provolone cheese, sliced

Directions
1. Preheat a panini press. In a large skillet, heat 1 tablespoon olive oil over medium-high heat. Add the garlic and cook until softened, about 2 minutes. Transfer the garlic to a food processor or mini chopper. Add 2 tablespoons water to the skillet, then add the broccoli rabe in batches, allowing each batch to wilt slightly before adding the next. Cook, stirring frequently, until crisp tender, about 3 minutes; season with salt and crushed red pepper.
2. Add the sun dried tomatoes and 4 tablespoons olive oil to the garlic and process to form a paste. Add the pine nuts and parmesan cheese and pulse until the pine nuts are finely chopped.
3. Brush each slice of bread on one side with the remaining 3 tablespoons olive oil and place oiled side down on a work surface. Top the bread with the sun dried tomato pesto. Divide the broccoli rabe among the 4 slices of bread and top with the provolone. Set the remaining bread slices in place, oiled side up.
4. Working in batches, grill the sandwiches in the panini press until the bread is crisp and golden, about 1 minute.

Brunch Panini

Recently, I've began to love and discover different panini and grilled cheese in my grill panini.
Servings: 4 | Cook: 6 mins | Prep: 10 mins | Total Time: 16mins

Ingredients
- 8 ounces provolone cheese, sliced
- 8 slices country bread
- 16 slices prosciutto (about 8 ounces)
- 1/4 cup raspberry jam
- 4 large eggs
- 3 tablespoons butter, melted

Directions
1. Preheat a panini press. Divide half the cheese among 4 slices of the bread, then top with the prosciutto; spread 1 tablespoon jam on each and top with the remaining cheese. Set the remaining bread slices in place.
2. In a shallow bowl, beat the eggs with the butter. Working in batches, dip both slices of each sandwich in the egg mixture and place in the panini press. Grill until the bread is crisp and golden, about 3 minutes.

Caprese Panini

Servings: 16 | Cook: 10 mins | Prep: 10 mins | Total Time: 20mins

Ingredients
- 8 slices sourdough bread
- 2 tablespoons olive oil
- 2 tomatoes, thinly sliced
- 4 ounces fresh mozzarella cheese, sliced
- 1/2 cup fresh basil

Directions
1. Brush one side of each bread slice with olive oil. Top 4 bread slices with tomatoes, mozzarella and basil.
2. Top with 4 bread slices. Grill in panini press 3-4 minutes or until cheese is melted.

Cheesy Prosciutto Panini

Servings: 2 | Cook: 4 mins | Prep: 15 mins | Total Time: 19mins

Ingredients
- 4 slices sourdough bread

- 1 tablespoon olive oil
- 2 ounces prosciutto di Parma, thinly sliced
- 2 ounces gouda cheese, thinly sliced
- 2 ounces mozzarella cheese, thinly sliced

Directions
1. Preheat panini grill to high.
2. Brush one side of each bread slice with oil.
3. Place two slices on a work surface, oiled side down, and evenly layered with prosciutto, Gouda, and mozzarella.
4. Cover with top halves, oiled side up, and press gently to pack.
5. Place sandwiches in grill, close the top plate and cook until golden brown, 3-4 minutes.
6. Serve immediately.

Classic Italian Panini With Prosciutto a

Servings: 4 | **Cook:** 0 mins | **Prep:** 20 mins | **Total Time:** 20mins

Ingredients
- 12 ounces loaf French bread, cut in half horizontally
- 1/4 cup reduced-fat mayonnaise
- 2 tablespoons chopped fresh basil
- 1 cup shredded fresh mozzarella cheese, divided
- 2 ounces very thin slices prosciutto
- 2 plum tomatoes, thinly sliced
- cooking spray

Directions
1. Hollow out top and bottom halves of bread, leaving a 1/2-inch-thick shell.
2. Spread 2 tablespoons mayo over cut side of each bread half.
3. Sprinkle basil and 1/2 Celsius cheese on bottom half of loaf.
4. Top evenly with prosciutto, tomato slices, and remaining 1/2 cup of cheese.
5. Cover with top half of loaf.
6. Cut filled loaf crosswise into 4 equal pieces.
7. Heat a grill pan over medium heat.
8. Coat pan with cooking spray.
9. Add sandwiches to pan.
10. Place a cast-iron or other heavy skillet on top of sandwiches; press gently to flatten sandwiches.

11. Cook 3 minutes on each side or until bread is toasted (leave cast-iron skillet on sandwiches with they cook).

Club Panini

Can be made in a frying pan or grill (the George Foreman type) I found this recipe on the net, changed it a bit and at the moment it is an addiction! I like it brushed with the olive oil but my preference is to use mayonnaise and use this method now all the time ever since I made Dawnab's Grilled Cheese, Diner Style
Servings: 4 | **Cook:** 6 mins | **Prep:** 30 mins | **Total Time:** 36mins

Ingredients
- 1 cup mayonnaise
- 1 tablespoon Dijon mustard
- 1/3 cup chopped fresh herb (parsley, basil or chives)
- 12 slices smoked turkey breast (or ham)
- 8 slices Swiss cheese
- 16 slices bacon, crisply cooked
- 8 slices tomatoes
- 8 slices sourdough bread or 8 slices bread, of your own choice
- 3 tablespoons olive oil (to brush onto the bread) or 3 tablespoons mayonnaise (to brush onto the bread)

Directions
1. Combine the mayonnaise, mustard and herbs, set aside.
2. Place 3 turkey slices, 2 cheese slices, 4 bacon slices and 2 tomato slices on half of the bread slices.
3. Spread remaining bread slices with the mayonnaise mixture, place, mayo sides down, on top of the tomato.
4. Spread the outsides of sandwiches with the olive oil or mayonnaise, on the top slice spread it just before you turn it over.
5. Brown in a non-stick frying pan on medium heat, pushing down with a spatula, until browned on both sides.

Cobb Salad Panini

I just watched Tyler Florence make this. Its looks so good!
Cook: 10 mins | **Prep:** 20 mins | **Total Time:** 30mins

Ingredients
- 1 head romaine lettuce
- 2 tomatoes, seeded
- 1 avocado
- 1/2 lb turkey breast
- 8 slices bacon, cooked
- 1/2 lb blue cheese
- 4 hardboiled egg, shelled and sliced
- 1 tablespoon chopped fresh parsley leaves
- 1 lemon, juice of
- 3 tablespoons extra virgin olive oil, plus more for drizzling
- kosher salt & freshly ground black pepper
- 4 ciabatta rolls (or 1 baguette)

Directions
1. Chop the lettuce, tomatoes, avocado, turkey, bacon, cheese, and eggs into 1/2-inch pieces and put them into a large bowl. Add the parsley, lemon juice, 3 tablespoons olive oil, and season with salt and pepper; mix well to coat all the ingredients.
2. Slice the rolls horizontally. Drizzle a small amount of olive oil on each of the cut sides. On the 4 bottoms place about 1/2 cup of the chopped salad and spread it out evenly. Put the tops on and gently press each sandwich to flatten it slightly; drizzle lightly with olive oil.
3. Place each sandwich on a preheated panini press and grill until the bread is toasted and the cheese begins to melt, about 5 minutes. Alternately, preheat a dry cast iron or non-stick pan. Place the sandwich in the pan and weight it down with another pan or a clean brick wrapped in foil. Grill 5 minutes, turn the sandwich over, re-weight it, and grill for another 5 minutes. Serve immediately.

Croissant Panini

Servings: 4 | Cook: 8 mins | Prep: 7 mins | Total Time: 15mins

Ingredients
- 4 croissants, sliced in 1/2 lengthwise
- 4 ounces smoked gouda cheese, grated (about 1 1/3 cups)
- 8 teaspoons grated parmesan cheese
- 4 ounces genoa salami (about 24 slices)
- 5 ounces arugula

Directions

1. Heat a panini grill.
2. Divide 1-ounce (1/3 cup) smoked Gouda between 1 top and 1 bottom of a croissant.
3. Sprinkle each half with 1 teaspoon Parmesan.
4. Top each side with about 3 slices of Genoa salami (about 1 ounce of salami per sandwich, total.)
5. Top 1 half of the sandwich with a small handful of arugula.
6. Close the sandwich and continue with the remaining sandwiches.
7. Grill the panini until the cheese melts, about 3 to 4 minutes.
8. Serve hot.

Cuban Panini

No, this is not the authentic Miami Cuban sandwich, but it is a fairly reasonable substitute for those of us who don't have quick access to real McCoy. Deli sliced meats make this a fast and filling sandwich.
Servings: 4 | **Cook:** 5 mins | **Prep:** 15 mins | **Total Time:** 20mins

Ingredients

- 1 loaf Cuban bread (if not available, use a French or Italian loaf from the deli)
- 1/4 cup yellow mustard
- 1/3 cup mayonnaise
- 2 large dill pickles, thinly sliced lengthwise
- 1/2 lb Swiss cheese, thinly sliced
- 3/4 lb ham, thinly sliced
- 1/2 lb pork roast, thinly sliced
- 1/3 lb genoa salami, thinly sliced
- 2 tablespoons butter, softened

Directions

1. Preheat sandwich press.
2. Cut bread in half lengthwise.
3. Spread inside top and bottom with mustard and mayonnaise.
4. On bottom half, layer pickle slices, Swiss cheese, ham, pork and salami.
5. Cover with top half of bread.
6. Cut the loaf into 4 equal sandwich portions.
7. Lightly butter top and bottom of each sandwich and press on the grill until the bread is crusty and the cheese is melted.
8. Slice in half diagonally and serve.
9. *Note - if you don't have a panini press or a sandwich grill type appliance, just use 2 heavy skillets - 1 to cook in and the other on top of the sandwiches to

press them down. I would suggest covering the bottom of the pressing-skillet with aluminum foil.

Deluxe Pizza Panini

"Paninis make a boring sandwich a gourmet meal. Pizza is a classic dish and can also sometimes become routine. A grilled pizza panini is a creative way to jazz up the boring sandwich and predictable pizza. Great to heat up as leftovers also for lunch the next day!"
*Pre: 20 m | **Cook**: 5 m | **Ready In**: 25 m*

Ingredients
- 1 teaspoon butter
- 2 tablespoons sliced fresh mushrooms
- 1/2 cup tomato sauce
- 4 ciabatta rolls, split
- 2 cloves garlic, minced
- 1 tablespoon dried oregano
- 8 slices hot Genoa salami
- 8 slices roasted ham
- 2 tablespoons diced red onion
- 2 tablespoons chopped roasted red pepper
- 2 tablespoons chopped black olives
- 4 leaves basil, chopped
- 4 slices provolone cheese
- Add all ingredients to list

Directions
1. Melt butter in a small skillet over medium-high heat; add mushrooms and saute until tender, 5 to 7 minutes. Remove from heat to cool.
2. Preheat a panini press according to manufacturer's instructions.
3. Spread an even layer of tomato sauce onto the cut sides of each ciabatta roll. Sprinkle equal amounts of garlic and oregano onto each roll. Place 2 salami slices side by side onto each roll; top each with 2 slices ham. Divide red onion, mushrooms, red pepper, olives, and basil between the 4 sandwiches and spread evenly atop the meats. Finish by topping with provolone cheese and sandwiching roll halves around the fillings.
4. Cook sandwiches on preheated panini press until there are dark brown grill marks on the bread, the cheese is melted, and the center is warm, about 5 minutes.

Denver Egg Panini

Servings: 2 | Cook: 4 mins | Prep: 30 mins | Total Time: 34mins

Ingredients
- 2 teaspoons olive oil
- 1/2 cup chopped green bell pepper
- 1/4 cup chopped onion
- 1/2 cup diced baked ham
- 2 teaspoons butter
- 2 eggs, beaten
- salt
- fresh ground black pepper
- 4 slices sourdough bread (1/2 -inch thick slices)
- 1 tablespoon butter, melted
- 1/2 cup shredded cheddar cheese

Directions
1. In a nonstick skillet, heat oil over med-high heat.
2. Add in green peppers and onion; saute until tender, about 5 minutes.
3. Add in ham and saute until heated through, 3-4 minutes.
4. Transfer to a plate and keep warm.
5. In the same pan, melt 2 t butter over medium heat.
6. Add eggs, salt, and pepper; scramble until eggs are desired consistency; remove pan from heat and stir in ham mixture.
7. Brush one side of each bread slice with melted butter.
8. Place on a work surface, buttered side down.
9. Divide eggs evenly between two bread slices and top with cheese.
10. Cover with top halves and press gently to pack.
11. Place sandwiches in preheated panini grill; close the top plate and cook until golden brown, 3-4 minutes.
12. Serve immediately.

Denver Omelet Panini

I was wanting something different for breakfast and was doing some browsing. I found a couple of recipes for omelet sandwiches but did not have the proper ingredients and was inspired to create this delicious breakfast treat. The bread I used was a green chili cheese bread; however any good quality bread cut 1/2 inch thick will work.

Servings: 2 | Cook: 15 mins | Prep: 15 mins | Total Time: 30mins

Ingredients

- 2 -3 tablespoons butter, divided, softened
- 2 green onions, sliced
- 1/4 cup green pepper, diced
- 2 ounces Canadian bacon, diced
- 4 eggs, lightly beaten or 1 cup egg substitute
- 2 tablespoons plain yogurt or 2 tablespoons sour cream
- 2 ounces Swiss cheese, grated
- 4 slices bread, sliced 1/2 inch thick
- salt
- pepper

Directions

1. To an 8-inch omelet pan, add 1 to 2 teaspoons butter and place over medium heat to warm.
2. Add the sliced onions and bell peppers, stirring until onions are wilted.
3. Stir in the diced Canadian bacon and cook until warmed.
4. Beat together the eggs and yogurt/sour cream, salt and pepper, pour over onion mixture and cook until bottom is set.
5. As the egg sets, pull cooked portion to the center allowing the uncooked portions to run to bottom of pan.
6. When omelet is set on bottom there are a couple of options, if you have another omelet pan the same size, you can flip the omelet into the other, you could put under the broiler the broiler for a few minutes to set or if you are really good flip the omelet and allowing it to finish cooking.
7. Lightly butter the bread with softened butter, cut omelet in half and using half for each sandwich place on unbuttered side of bread, top with shredded cheese and cover with remaining slice of bread, buttered side up.
8. Cook on preheated Panini press as per manufacturer's recommendations until browned.
9. Enjoy!

Diabetes Friendly Grilled Strawberry San

If you have a panini maker, definitely use it!! I haven't tried it with the lemon zest yet, but I will next time (the idea just came to me as I was entering the recipe).
Servings: 1 | Cook: 5 mins | Prep: 5 mins | Total Time: 10mins

Ingredients

- 3 tablespoons neufchatel cheese
- 3/4 cup strawberry, sliced
- 1/2 teaspoon lemon zest, minced

- 2 slices whole grain bread

Directions
1. Combine neufchatel with 1/4 cup of the strawberries, mashing the berries as you mix.
2. Spread half the mixture on each piece of bread. Fill with remaining strawberries and sprinkle with zest.
3. Cook in panini maker -- or grill like you would grilled cheese (heat skillet to warm; butter the bread and grill both buttered sides until golden).
4. Enjoy warm.

Easy Meatball Panini

Kids love 'em!! (and husbands). from B H & G
*Servings: 4 | **Cook:** 13 mins | **Prep:** 10 mins | **Total Time:** 23mins*

Ingredients
- 16 frozen cooked Italian style meatballs, about 1 lb
- 1 (15 ounce) can pizza sauce
- 4 hoagie rolls
- 4 slices provolone cheese
- 1 cup loosely packed large basil leaves or 1 cup spinach leaves

Directions
1. Preheat Broiler.
2. Combine meatballs and pizza sauce in a large saucepan.
3. Cover and cook over medium low heat for 10 minutes or til heated through, stirring occasionally.
4. Meanwhile, cut a thin slice from the top of each roll, hollow out roll leaving 1/4 to 1/2 inch thick shell, Discard bread from rolls or save for another use.
5. Place hollowed out rolls and roll tops, cut sides up, on baking sheet.
6. Broil 3 to 4 inches from the heat for 1 to 2 minutes or till lightly toasted.
7. Remove roll tops from the baking sheet.
8. Spoon meatballs and sauce into toasted rolls.
9. Top with cheese.
10. Broil about 1 minute more or till cheese is melted.
11. To serve, place basil or spinach leaves on top of cheese and replace roll tops.

Egg Bacon Spinach and Sharp Cheddar P

Servings: 2 | Cook: 3 mins | Prep: 20 mins | Total Time: 23mins

Ingredients
- 2 ciabatta rolls
- 6 slices bacon
- 2 eggs, beaten
- baby spinach leaves (1 large handful)
- 3 ounces sharp cheddar cheese, thinly sliced
- sea salt
- fresh ground black pepper
- vegetable oil, for sauteing and brushing

Directions
1. Preheat a Panini grill.
2. Trim the top and bottom off the ciabatta rolls so that they are about 1 inch thick.
3. Slice open lengthwise.
4. In a skillet, sauté the bacon until crisp.
5. Remove the bacon from the skillet and discard most of the oil.
6. Pour in the beaten egg, season well with salt and pepper, and let the eggs set like an omelet.
7. Divide the spinach between the two roll bottoms.
8. Top with the crispy bacon, then half of the omelet, and finish with the cheese; cover with roll top.
9. Brush both sides of the Panini with a little oil and grill in the preheated Panini grill for 2-3 minutes, or according to the manufacturer's instructions.
10. The bread should be golden brown and the filling warmed through.

Egg Mushroom Havarti and Dill Panini

Servings: 2 | Cook: 3 mins | Prep: 20 mins | Total Time: 23mins

Ingredients
- 2 ciabatta rolls
- 1 tablespoon olive oil
- 1 teaspoon olive oil
- 1 1/2 cups sliced white button mushrooms
- 2 eggs, beaten

- 3 ounces havarti cheese, thinly sliced
- 2 teaspoons chopped fresh dill
- sea salt
- fresh ground black pepper
- vegetable oil, for sauteing and brushing

Directions
1. Preheat a Panini grill.
2. Trim the top and bottom off the ciabatta rolls so that they are about 1 inch thick.
3. Slice open lengthwise
4. Heat 1 tablespoon oil in a skillet.
5. Season the mushrooms with salt and pepper and gently sauté for 4 minutes.
6. Remove the mushrooms from the skillet and set aside.
7. Add another teaspoon of oil to the skillet, pour in the eggs and scramble them over low heat.
8. Evenly distribute the cheese on the two roll bottoms; spoon on the scrambled eggs, top with the mushrooms, and sprinkle with dill; cover with roll tops.
9. Brush both sides of the Panini with a little oil and grill in the preheated Panini grill for 2-3 minutes, or according to the manufacturer's instructions.
10. The bread should be golden brown and the filling warmed through.

Egg Sweet Onion and Cacio Panini

Perfect for a hearty breakfast or late night supper.
Servings: 4 | **Cook:** 3 mins | **Prep:** 20 mins | **Total Time:** 23mins

Ingredients
- 4 ciabatta rolls
- 1 tablespoon olive oil
- 6 large eggs, beaten
- 1/4 teaspoon salt
- fresh ground black pepper
- 1 cup sweet onion (Sweet Onions)
- 4 ounces Cacio di Roma cheese, thinly sliced by hand (or Pecorino Romano)

Directions
1. Preheat a panini grill.
2. Slice off the domed tops of the ciabatta rolls; roll should be about 1-inch thick with a crusty bottom and exposed bread top; split rolls horizontally.
3. Over medium heat, warm the olive oil in a medium nonstick skillet.

4. Add in eggs, salt, and pepper; use a rubber spatula to move the eggs, starting at the edge of the pan and moving toward the center until the eggs are softly scrambled.
5. Spread each half of the rolls with a thin layer of Sweet Onions.
6. Divide the scrambled eggs among 4 bottom halves of the ciabatta.
7. Top with sliced Cacio di Parma and top with remaining ciabatta halves.
8. Grill the panini for 3 minutes until the cheese sets and the bread is golden.
9. Serve immediately.

Eggplant and Mozzarella Panini

This is originally from Taste of Home and called for sun-dried tomato spread. I have made a few adjustments for those who can't find the spread at the local grocer. This makes a very filling and vegetarian version of a panini.
Servings: 4 | **Cook:** 5 mins | **Prep:** 10 mins | **Total Time:** 15mins

Ingredients
- 1 eggplant, sliced 1-inch thick
- 2 teaspoons olive oil
- 1 loaf ciabatta
- 1/3 cup mayonnaise
- 2 ounces sun-dried tomatoes packed in oil
- 6 ounces smoked fresh mozzarella cheese

Directions
1. Heat a grill pan or panini press.
2. Brush eggplant slices with 1 t olive oil and season lightly with salt and pepper.
3. Grill until marked and just soft, about 4-6 minutes. If using the grill pan, turn once.
4. Cut bread into 4 pieces; slice pieces in half lengthwise.
5. Drain and dice sun-dried tomatoes. In small bowl, mix mayonaise with tomatoes.
6. Cover one side of ciabatta with mayo mixture.
7. Divide grilled eggplant slices between the four sandwiches.
8. Add cheese on tops and add other slice of bread on top.
9. Brush sandwiches with olive oil and grill until cheese is melting and bread is crisp, about 5 minutes.
10. Serve with marinara sauce or picante sauce.

Eggplant Aubergine Panini for Two

My sister and I tried one similar to this in NYC and I fooled around with different variations before I came up with this. The measurements and times aren't exact because I threw this all together one day. Hope you enjoy!
***Servings:** 2 | **Cook:** 8 mins | **Prep:** 10 mins | **Total Time:** 18mins*

Ingredients
FOR THE EGGPLANT
- 2 slices eggplants, about 1/2-3/4-inch thick
- 3 tablespoons butter
- 1 tablespoon extra virgin olive oil
- 1/3 teaspoon garlic powder
- 1/3 teaspoon dried Italian seasoning
- salt and pepper, to taste

FOR THE PANINI SANDWICH
- 1 tablespoon extra virgin olive oil
- 4 slices pane Italian bread (or any thick bread of your choice)
- 1/2 cup fresh basil leaf
- 1/2 cup arugula leaf
- 4 -8 slices tomatoes
- 2 slices provolone cheese

Directions
1. Melt the 3 tablespoons of butter with the 1 tablespoon of olive oil and stir in the garlic powder and Italian seasoning.
2. Brush the eggplant with the butter/oil mixture and sprinkle with salt and pepper.
3. Grill the eggplant for 3-5 minutes, or until tender, but not mushy, turning once (I used an indoor grill, but you can use a panini grill or frying pan, etc.).
4. If desired, brush the remaining butter/oil mixture onto the inside slices of the bread.
5. Stack 2 slice of bread (side with the butter/oil mixture) with the fresh basil, arugula, slices of tomato, provolone cheese and the grilled eggplant.
6. Top with remaining slices of bread and lightly brush each sandwich with olive oil.
7. Place on grill for about 1 minute on each side (I had to press a frying pan on top of each sandwich to get the desired panini-effect).
8. Enjoy!

Eggplant Panini

"This is a delicious sandwich which can be served for lunch or dinner. Paired with a green salad and a glass of red wine, it makes a good meal. Any type of flat bread can be used, however I chose one topped with portobello mushrooms and gorgonzola cheese."
Pre: 15 m | **Cook:** 15 m | **Ready In:** 30 m

Ingredients
- 1 baby eggplant, cut into 1/4-inch slices
- salt and ground black pepper to taste
- 1/4 cup olive oil, divided
- 1 loaf flat bread, sliced horizontally and cut into 4 equal pieces
- 1/2 (12 ounce) jar roasted red bell peppers, drained and sliced
- 4 ounces shredded mozzarella cheese
- 1/4 cup roasted garlic hummus
- Add all ingredients to list

Directions
1. Season eggplant slices with salt and pepper; let stand for 2 minutes.
2. Heat 2 tablespoons olive oil in a skillet over medium-high heat; saute 1/2 of the eggplant until golden brown, 2 to 3 minutes per side. Repeat with remaining olive oil and eggplant.
3. Preheat a panini press according to manufacturer's instructions.
4. Layer eggplant, roasted red pepper, and mozzarella cheese, respectively, onto the bottom piece of each flat bread. Spread 1 tablespoon hummus on the inside of each top piece of flat bread and place over the mozzarella layer, creating a panini.
5. Grill each panini on the preheated panini press until cooked through and cheese is melted, about 7 minutes.

Eggplant Provolone Panini

I'm not a real eggplant lover, but I did really like this panini - I hope you enjoy this recipe -
Servings: 4 | **Prep:** 10 mins | **Total Time:** 10mins

Ingredients
- 1 eggplant (about 1 lb)
- 1/4 teaspoon salt
- 1/4 cup all-purpose flour
- 1 egg, beaten

- 2/3 cup dry bread, crumbs
- 1/2 cup vegetable oil
- 1 sweet red pepper, seeded and quartered
- 1 sweet green pepper, seeded and quartered
- 4 soft buns
- 4 slices provolone cheese

GARLIC THYME MAYO
- 1 garlic clove
- 1 pinch salt
- 1/4 cup light mayonnaise
- 1 tablespoon lemon juice
- 1/4 teaspoon fresh thyme, minced
- 1 pinch ground pepper

Directions
1. Cut eggplant into 8 scant 1/2-inch thick slices. Sprinkle with salt. Place in colander, pressing gently with plate. Let stand for 10 minutes. Pat dry with paper towel.
2. GARLIC THYME MAYO: Meanwhile, finely mince garlic with salt. In bowl, combine garlic mixture, mayonnaise, lemon juice, thyme and pepper; set aside.
3. Dip eggplant into flour, then egg, then breadcrumbs. In skillet, heat oil over medium-high heat; fry eggplant, turning once, until golden brown, 6-8 minutes. Place on paper towel - lined tray to drain.
4. Meanwhile, on baking sheet, broil red and green peppers, turning occasionally, until softened and charred, 10-15 minutes. Peel if desired.
5. Cut buns in half; layer bottoms with red and green peppers, eggplant and cheese. Spread each top with 1 tablespoons of the Garlic Thyme Mayo. Press in panini maker (or broil without top bun) until cheese melts.

Emeril's Prosciutto and Mozzarella Panin

Cook: 8 mins | *Prep:* 5 mins | *Total Time:* 13mins

Ingredients
- 1/4 cup extra-virgin olive oil
- 1 tablespoon balsamic vinegar
- 2 teaspoons fresh oregano, minced (OR 1 teaspoon dried)
- 1 teaspoon garlic, minced
- kosher salt & fresh ground pepper
- 8 1/2 inches thick slices ciabatta
- 4 ounces mozzarella cheese, thinly sliced

- 4 ounces prosciutto, thinly sliced
- 6 ounces jarred roasted red peppers, drained and torn into 1 inch wide pieces

Directions

1. Whisk the olive oil, balsamic vinegar, oregano, garlic, 1/2 teaspoon salt and 1/4 teaspoon pepper in a small bowl to blend.
2. Arrange the slices of bread on a flat work surface and spread the vinaigrette on one side of each slice. Divide the mozzarella equally among 4 of the bread slices. Top with the prosciutto and roasted red peppers, then place the remaining 4 slices of bread on top, vinaigrette-side down, to form 4 sandwiches.
3. Heat a grill pan over medium heat. Add the sandwiches and cook, pressing them occasionally with a large spatula or the bottom of a small heavy saucepan, until the bread is golden brown and the cheese has melted, about 4 minutes per side.

English Muffin Breakfast Panini

Great for breakfast on the run
Servings: 2 | **Cook:** 4 mins | **Prep:** 3 mins | **Total Time:** 7mins

Ingredients
- 2 egg whites, Lightly Beaten
- 2 English muffins
- 2 slices reduced-fat cheddar cheese
- 2 turkey sausage patties

Directions
1. Preheat Panini Press.
2. Cook eggs as for an omelet.
3. Place one side of english muffin cut side up on work surface.
4. Top each with 1 slice cheese, cooked egg whites, then turkey sausage.
5. Top with other half of english muffin and place on panini press.
6. Close and bake for 3-4 minutes.
7. Let rest of 2-3 minutes and enjoy!

Fontina & Mushroom Panini

Grilled cheese for grown-ups is what this is. Sage makes a big difference, and so does grating the cheese--it helps the mushrooms "stick" in the sandwich.

Cook: 5 mins | Prep: 10 mins | Total Time: 15mins

Ingredients
- 4 slices good sandwich bread (I prefer a whole grain country type loaf)
- 1 cup shredded Fontina cheese (more or less to taste)
- 1 cup sliced mushrooms
- 1 tablespoon chopped fresh sage leaf (or 3/4 tsp dried)
- salt and pepper
- 3 tablespoons butter (divided use)

Directions
1. Heat butter in a saute pan til very hot, then add mushrooms. You want them to brown some, but not to give off a lot of liquid. Add sage, salt and pepper, til soft, but not too limp. Set aside.
2. Butter one side of bread slices, place two in pan, sprinkle with half of the cheese, top with mushrooms, sprinkle with the rest of the cheese, and top with bread, butter side up.
3. In my panini maker it's about 3-4 minutes for how I like it.
4. To cook in a pan---cook over medium low heat until the bread is toasty, turn (carefully!) and weight the sandwich with another pan (or press down with a spatula) til golden.

Garden Pesto Panini

Cook: 2 mins | Prep: 5 mins | Total Time: 7mins

Ingredients
- 1 pan rhodes warm-n-serv buttery dinner roll
- 1/4 cup pesto sauce, divided
- tomatoes, slices
- salt & pepper
- mozzarella cheese, slices
- 1 tablespoon butter, melted

Directions
1. Allow rolls to thaw enough that you can cut through them. Remove rolls from pan. Do not separate. Slice through the whole group of rolls from the side, creating the top and bottom of a sandwich. Spread bottom half with 2 tablespoons pesto. Top with tomato slices. Sprinkle with salt & pepper. Top with mozzarella cheese slices. Spread 2 tablespoons of pesto over cheese slices. Turn top half of rolls over so sliced side is facing up. Place on top of

sandwich. Press down slightly to flatten. Cook in a panini grill until done. (Alternate cooking method: heat a skillet, sprayed with non-stick cooking spray, over medium low heat. Place panini in skillet. Place smaller skillet on top of sandwich and press down to flatten. Cook 1-2 minutes on each side.).

Green Chili Tuna Grill Sandwich Panini

Cook: 5 mins | Prep: 5 mins | Total Time: 10mins

Ingredients
- 7 ounces tuna, drained
- 1/3 cup green chili, chopped (canned is ok)
- 2 tablespoons onions, finely chopped
- 1/3 cup sour cream
- 1/2 cup Swiss cheese, grated
- 8 slices bread (rye preferred)
- butter

Directions
1. Combine first five ingredients and spread on four slices bread. Assemble sandwiches.
2. Spread butter on outer surfaces and grill until golden.

Green Panini With Roasted Peppers and Gr

Adapted from "What We Eat When We Eat Alone" by Deborah Madison and Patrick McFarlin. The book is an exploration of our relationship with food focusing on those that eat alone, for whatever reason. This sandwich works well with any combination of cooked greens and cheese that you like. The photo is of collard greens and provolone cheese on a Portuguese roll. You can even save a step and use frozen greens. Just thaw, squeeze out liquid, and season.
Cook: 12 mins | Prep: 5 mins | Total Time: 17mins

Ingredients
- 1/2 bunch mustard greens, stemmed and washed but not dried
- 1/4 cup water
- salt & freshly ground black pepper
- 1/2 garlic clove, minced
- 1 pinch red pepper flakes
- 1 dash pepper sauce or 1 dash red wine vinegar, to taste

- 2 pieces ciabatta (or your favorite rustic bread)
- olive oil
- 1 ounce gruyere cheese or 1 ounce Fontina cheese, grated
- 1 roasted red pepper, cut into wide strips
- 1 teaspoon Dijon mustard (to taste)

Directions

1. Heat a pot over high heat and add the mustard greens, with the water clinging to the leaves plus 1/4 cup additional water.
2. Season with about 1/4 teaspoon of salt, pepper to taste, garlic, and red pepper flakes; cover.
3. Once the greens start to reduce, lower the heat to medium and cook until they are tender, about 7 minutes.
4. Drain and squeeze water out of the greens and put them in a bowl; season with additional salt, if desired, pepper sauce or vinegar to taste.
5. Build your panini by covering one slice of bread with cheese, the greens, and pepper strips; spread the top slice with Dijon mustard and cover.
6. Brush the outside of the sandwich liberally with olive oil.
7. Cook in a panini maker or a heavy skillet until both sides of the bread are crispy and the cheese has melted (I use a cast iron skillet with another cast iron skillet on top of the sandwich to weight it, then flip.

Grilled Asparagus & Prosciutto Panin

the luscious combination of asparagus and prosciutto in a sublime hot toasted sandwich
Servings: 4 | Cook: 5 mins | Prep: 10 mins | Total Time: 15mins

Ingredients

- 1 lb asparagus
- 2 teaspoons olive oil
- salt and pepper
- 1 focaccia bread, sliced into 4 pieces
- 4 slices prosciutto
- 8 ounces fresh mozzarella cheese, sliced into 1/4 inch slices

Directions

1. Rinse the asparagus and break the ends off of each spear (if you hold onto each end and bend the spear it will naturally break in the right place). Discard the ends. In a large bowl, toss the asparagus in the olive oil and season with salt and pepper. Grill for about 3 minutes until cooked through and grill marks appear. Set aside.

2. Turn off the grill and carefully clean the grates. Reheat the grill to medium-high heat.
3. For each sandwich: Slice the focaccia in half lengthwise. Place a slice of prosciutto inside the bottom half. Top with 1/4 of the cheese and as many asparagus spears as will fit securely. Close the sandwich with the other focaccia half. Grill 4-5 minutes until the cheese is melted. Slice the sandwich in half, serve immediately and enjoy!

Grilled Eggplant Arugula and Mozzarella

From today's paper. This made an awesome lunch and the vegetarian in the family appreciated it.
Servings: 4 | Cook: 15 mins | Prep: 10 mins | Total Time: 25mins

Ingredients
- 4 slices eggplants
- extra virgin olive oil
- salt, pepper to taste
- 8 slices country sliced bread
- 2 cups arugula leaves
- 8 ounces thinly sliced mozzarella cheese

Directions
1. Brush eggplant slices with oil on both sides and place in a George Foreman grill--or panini grill-- cook 4 minutes, remove.
2. Brush bread slices with oil.
3. On 4 slices, oil side down, arrange eggplant, arugula, and mozzarella, top with 4 bread slices oil side up add 2 sandwiches to grill, close and cook 3-4 minutes.
4. Repeat.
5. Cut sandwiches on diagonal and serve.

Grilled Eggplant Provencal Panini

Servings: 2 | Cook: 10 mins | Prep: 30 mins | Total Time: 40mins

Ingredients
- 2 tablespoons extra virgin olive oil
- 1 garlic clove, finely chopped

- 1 small globe eggplant, trimmed and cut lengthwise into 1/2-inch thick slices (4-6 oz.)
- salt
- fresh ground black pepper
- 2 semolina rolls, split (or 4 slices semolina bread, 1/2-inch thick)
- 4 tablespoons tapenade
- 3 ounces thinly sliced mozzarella cheese
- 4 thin slices tomatoes (ripe but firm)

Directions
1. Preheat the sandwich grill.
2. In a small bowl, stir the olive oil and garlic together.
3. Brush both sides of the eggplant slices with 1 tablespoon of the garlic oil.
4. Put the eggplant in the grill; close the top plate, and cook until the eggplant is tender and grill marked, 3-5 minutes.
5. Season to taste with salt and pepper.
6. Transfer to a plate and set aside (the eggplant can be grilled up to 3 hours ahead and kept at room temperature, or covered and refrigerated for up to 24 hours; if refrigerating, return to room temperature before assembling the panini).
7. Keep the sandwich grill on and wipe clean the grill plates.
8. Place the rolls, cut side down, on a work surface and brush the crust sides of the rolls with the remaining 1 tablespoon garlic oil.
9. Turn and spread cut sides of the rolls with tapenade, dividing it evenly, then layer 1/4 of the cheese, half of the eggplant, and 2 tomato slices over the tapenade on the bottom half of each roll.
10. Divide the remaining cheese on top.
11. Cover with the top halves of the rolls, tapenade side down, and press to pack gently.
12. Place the panini in the grill, close the top plate, and cook until the bread is golden and toasted, the eggplant is hot, and the cheese is melted, 3-5 minutes.
13. Cut each sandwich in half on the diagonal and serve immediately.

Grilled Ham and Asparagus Panini

Grilled Ham and Asparagus Panini Recipe from Festival Foods. This is by far my most favorite sandwich of the month. I like mine with roasted asparagus and sourdough bread. Another great option is using some melty Fontina or farmers cheese. I have also made this with thick pita bread and it adds another dimension. I love to make this sandwich for those days when you want something from those expensive Bistros, but also want to make it your own. Please try your own style and let me know how it turns out for you!
Servings: *4* | **Cook:** *10 mins* | **Prep:** *10 mins* | **Total Time:** *20mins*

Ingredients
- 4 tablespoons butter, melted
- 1 teaspoon garlic salt
- 1 1/2 cups mayonnaise
- 3 tablespoons pesto sauce
- 8 slices Italian bread (sourdough works well too)
- 3/4 lb deli ham, shaved
- 12 asparagus spears, lightly steamed (Try roasting for a twist)
- 4 ounces asiago cheese, sliced with a vegetable peeler
- 1/2 cup roasted red pepper, sliced into thin strips

Directions
1. In a small bowl mix garlic salt and butter together. Brush one side of each of the pieces of bread. In another bowl mix mayo and pesto sauce.
2. Spread mayo/pesto on other side of each slice of bread. Top 1/2 of slices of bread with ham, asparagus spears, red pepper and Asiago.
3. Top with remaining bread slices and cook in a panini grill or in a large skillet with a little extra butter (like you would a grill cheese, pressing down with a heavy pan on top.).
4. Cook until bread is toasted and sandwich is heated through.
5. Serve with fresh fruits.

Grilled Ham Panini

Posted per a request. If you use the low fat mayo and cheese, this recipe would be good for those watching their weight.
Servings: 1 | **Cook:** 10 mins | **Prep:** 5 mins | **Total Time:** 15mins

Ingredients
- 2 slices sourdough bread, sliced 1/2 inch thick
- 1 tablespoon mayonnaise
- 4 slices shaved smoked ham or 4 slices brown sugar ham
- 2 slices tomatoes
- 1 slice kraft singles cheese

Directions
1. Spread bread slices with mayo.
2. Top 1 of the bread slices with ham, tomatoes, cheese and remaining bread slice.
3. Cook, over med heat, in skillet or on griddle that has been sprayed with no stick cooking spray, for 5 minutes on each side or until lightly browned.

Grilled Italian Pesto Panini

I took Pesto Focaccia Sandwich for Six (which I LOVE!) and adapted it for one, using a George Foreman grill. Since I was heating the grill anyway, I decided to grill sliced onions and red peppers, to add to the sandwich. It turned out great, and I think it'll travel well, as I needed a sack lunch, for a field trip, tomorrow! I took a bite, and it tasted delicious!
Cook: 10 mins | **Prep:** 5 mins | **Total Time:** 15mins

Ingredients
- 1 focaccia roll (Italian-seasoned)
- 1/8 onion, sliced
- 1/8 red pepper, sliced
- 4 tablespoons prepared pesto sauce (approx)
- 2 slices provolone cheese
- 4 slices thin deli ham
- 4 slices thin deli turkey

Directions
1. Preheat your George Foreman grill, or panini maker.
2. Slice the roll horizontally; spread with pesto.
3. When the grill is ready, add the onion and red pepper slices (I didn't think they needed any seasoning, but you could add Italian dressing, or other seasoning to them, before grilling, if desired); grill until tender.
4. Layer the grilled veggies, cheese, and lunchmeat.
5. Grill until the cheese melts (you'll have to apply some pressure to the top of the grill when you first insert the sandwich, since the sandwich is pretty thick).
6. Slice on the diagonal, and enjoy, now or later!

Grilled Italian Sausage Panini

This is a variation of Mysterygirl's panini recipe (Panini Sandwiches) that I came up with when I had a craving for Italian sausage. I must say that it turned out really great, but try it for yourself! Amounts are for one sandwich - just multiply as necessary.
Servings: 1 | **Cook:** 5 mins | **Prep:** 10 mins | **Total Time:** 15mins

Ingredients
- 1 hot Italian sausage or 1 sweet Italian sausage, uncooked

- 1 ciabatta bun, split
- 2 -3 slices provolone cheese (depending on size of slices)
- roasted red pepper, to taste (or other toppings)

Directions
1. Put sausage in small pot and cover with water.
2. Bring to boil over high heat.
3. Once water boils, prick the sausage with a fork several times so that the grease comes out as it cooks.
4. Boil sausage for 5 minutes, or until it looks at least halfway cooked.
5. Remove sausage from water, and either rinse it under warm water (there might be some scum on it), or wipe it with a clean paper towel.
6. Preheat George Foreman grill.
7. Slice sausage in half, lengthwise.
8. Place sausage cut-side down on hot grill, and cook until done (about 5 minutes or so).
9. Place cheese in bun, then add sausage, and top with roasted red peppers and/or your own favourite additions such as hot banana peppers, marinara sauce, olives, tomatoes, fresh basil, etc, etc.
10. Close sandwich and grill in George Foreman until the bread is golden and crispy.
11. Cut sandwich in half and enjoy!

Grilled Marinated Artichoke Heart Ham

Emeril Lagasse
Servings: 6 | Cook: 10 mins | Prep: 10 mins | Total Time: *20mins*

Ingredients
- 1/2 cup extra-virgin olive oil, divided
- 2 tablespoons balsamic vinegar
- 2 teaspoons minced fresh oregano leaves or 1 teaspoon dried oregano
- 1 1/2 teaspoons minced garlic
- 1/2 teaspoon salt
- 1/4 teaspoon fresh ground black pepper
- 12 slices ciabatta or 12 slices other rustic Italian white bread, thinly sliced
- 6 ounces thinly sliced provolone cheese
- 1 (6 ounce) jar marinated artichoke hearts, drained and sliced
- 2 ounces thinly sliced genoa salami

Directions

1. Directions.
2. Whisk 6 tablespoons of the olive oil, vinegar, oregano, garlic, salt, and pepper in a small bowl to blend. Arrange the slices of bread on a flat work surface and, using a brush, divide the vinaigrette equally among 1 side of each slice. Divide the provolone equally among the bread slices. Top 6 of the slices of bread equally with the sliced artichoke hearts and sliced genoa salami and then place the remaining 6 slices on top. Brush the outsides of each sandwich with some of the remaining 2 tablespoons of olive oil.
3. Heat a grill, large skillet or grill pan over medium heat.
4. Add the sandwiches and cook until the bread is golden brown and the cheese is melted, pressing occasionally to compact with a large spatula or the bottom of a heavy small saucepan, about 4 to 5 minutes per side.
5. Remove the sandwiches from the grill, cut in half and serve.

Grilled Panini Sandwiches

Found this recipe printed in a flyer at the market and I had fun with it adding things here and there. I give a list of suggestions for which vegetables to use as well as two different condiment spreads.
Cook: 0 mins | **Prep:** 25 mins | **Total Time:** 25mins

Ingredients

- 1 loaf fresh panini bread, sliced
- 4 ounces Swiss cheese or 4 ounces mozzarella cheese, slices
- 3 sprigs of fresh flat-leaf Italian parsley or 3 sprigs fresh lovage

GRILLED VEGETABLES

- 1 medium zucchini
- 1 small eggplant
- 1 medium red bell peppers or 1 medium yellow bell peppers or 1 medium orange bell pepper
- 1/2 cup sliced red onion
- 1 small summer squash
- 2 portabella mushrooms, stems removed

BASIL SPREAD

- 1/4 cup fresh basil leaf, stems removed and chopped finely (NOT dried basil)
- 1/4 cup plain yogurt or 1/4 cup mayonnaise
- 1/2 tablespoon fresh lemon juice
- 1/2 teaspoon greek dried oregano or 1 tablespoon fresh Greek oregano
- 1/4 teaspoon salt
- fresh ground black pepper

DIJON SPREAD

- 1/4 cup Dijon mustard

- 1 garlic clove, minced and roasted if desired
- 2 tablespoons mayonnaise
- 1/4 teaspoon crushed fennel seed

MARINADE
- 1/4 cup balsamic vinegar
- 1/4 cup extra virgin olive oil
- salt and pepper

Directions
1. Cut 8 slices of the panini bread.
2. Prepare the marinade. Set aside.
3. In small bowl prepare the basil dressing or Dijon mustard and mix well. The condiments can be made several hours in advance.
4. Slice the vegetables into uniform sizes.
5. Marinate the veggies in a shallow pan for an hour. Drain off the marinade and then grill the vegetables on each side for about 4-5 minutes, until tender yet crisp.
6. Spread one side of each sandwich slice with your choice of spread. Add the vegetables, next place 1 ounce of cheese and the parsley or lovage. Butter lightly the top and bottom of sandwich. Press down carefully on the sandwich and toast on grill. Cut in half and serve.

Grilled Panini

I made this up one day because of a sandwich I had at a restaurant. I hope you enjoy it!
Cook: *6 mins |* **Prep:** *15 mins |* **Total Time:** *21mins*

Ingredients
- 1 loaf sliced sourdough bread
- 1 lb turkey
- 1/2 lb smoked cheddar cheese
- 1 red pepper, roasted and sliced
- 3 -4 tablespoons mayonnaise, not miracle whip
- 1 tablespoon pesto sauce

Directions
1. Spread each slice of bread with pesto mayo. Make more if needed.
2. Lay cheese, meat and pepper slices on top of half of the bread slices and top with a piece of pesto/mayo bread.
3. Grill on medium heat till heated through and lightly golden brown.

Grilled Rosemary Tofu and Veggie Panin

Adapted from Veggie Life. Wonderful- even better the 2nd day.
Servings: 3 | **Cook:** 10 mins | **Prep:** 24 hrs | **Total Time:** 24hrs

Ingredients
Marinade
- 3 tablespoons raspberry balsamic vinegar
- 2 tablespoons water
- 1 small minced shallot
- 2 tablespoons minced rosemary
- 1 teaspoon sea salt
- 16 ounces firm tofu
- 1 medium zucchini
- 1 large red bell pepper
- 3 slices fat-free Swiss cheese
- 1/2 cup fresh basil leaf
- 6 slices crusty bread or 3 good rolls
- cooking spray

Directions
1. Combine all ingredients for marinade in a large plastic ziploc bag. Press tofu and cut into six slices. Add tofu slices to marinade and refrigerate overnight.
2. About 1 hour prior to dinner time, add sliced zucchini and sliced red pepper to marinade.
3. Add a bit of water if necessary to coat.
4. Preheat grill (indoor or outdoor).
5. Grill tofu, zucchini, and bell pepper until softened and well marked on both sides- about 5 minutes per side.
6. If using an outdoor grill- wrap a brick in aluminum foil and allow it to preheat.
7. Spray aluminum foil with cooking spray and assemble sandwiches- dividing fillings evenly and adding cheese and basil leaves.
8. Close foil tightly and place brick on top of sandwiches.
9. Grill 2 minutes per side.
10. If using indoor grill- assemble sandwiches and grill for about 2 minutes.

Gruyère Apricot Jam and Toasted

It may seem like an unusual combination, but once you've tried this sweet, nutty sandwich, you'll be hooked. If you don't have a panini maker, cook the sandwiches in a skillet and weigh them down with another pan. Or you can wrap them in foil and cook

on the grill with a weight on top.
Cook: *14 mins |* **Prep:** *10 mins |* **Total Time:** *24mins*

Ingredients
- 1/4 cup walnuts
- 8 1/2 inch-thick slices french country bread (I use whole grain)
- 4 teaspoons apricot jam
- 6 ounces gruyere cheese, cut into 4 thin slices

Directions
1. Preheat oven to 350°F.
2. Place walnuts on baking sheet, and bake 8 to 10 minutes, or until fragrant. Cool, and finely chop.
3. Preheat panini maker.
4. Spread 4 slices bread with 1 teaspoons jam each. Sprinkle walnuts on top of jam, and top each with 1 slice Gruyère. Cover with remaining bread. Place sandwiches in panini maker, and bake 2 to 4 minutes, or until bread is golden brown and cheese has melted. Slice each sandwich into 4 wedges, and serve warm.

Ham & Manchego Panini With Dipping S

Servings: *2 |* **Cook:** *20 mins |* **Prep:** *20 mins |* **Total Time:** *40mins*

Ingredients
- 4 slices country bread
- 4 ounces thinly sliced ham
- 2 ounces manchego cheese, coarsely grated
- 4 teaspoons olive oil
- 3 tablespoons apricot jam
- 1 tablespoon Dijon mustard

Directions
1. Top each of 2 bread slices with ham, Manchego, and remaining slices. Brush tops of panini with 2 teaspoons oil.
2. In a large nonstick skillet, heat remaining oil over medium-low. Place panini in skillet, oiled side up. Cover; cook until golden brown and cheese has melted, 5 to 8 minutes per side, pressing down with a spatula 3 to 4 times during cooking.
3. Meanwhile, make dipping sauce: In a small bowl, mix together jam and Dijon. Serve panini with sauce on the side.

Ham & Pear Panini With Oven Baked Fr

Servings: 4 | Cook: 5 mins | Prep: 10 mins | Total Time: 15mins

Ingredients
- 4 medium yukon gold potatoes, cut into fries (1/4-1/2-inch thick)
- 2 1/2 teaspoons salt
- fresh ground pepper (to taste)
- 2 tablespoons olive oil (plus more for brushing)
- 8 slices country bread, each 1/2-inch thick
- 8 ham slices (thinly sliced)
- 1 pear, cored and cut into 1/4-inch slices
- 4 ounces sharp cheddar cheese, thinly sliced

Directions
1. Preheat panini press. Preheat oven to 500°F.
2. On non-stick baking sheet, stir together potatoes, salt, pepper and oil. Bake for 30 minutes, flipping after 15 minutes.
3. Brush one side of each bread slice with oil. Lay slices, oiled side down, on clean work surface. Place ham, pear and cheese on 4 slices. Top with remaining pieces of bread, oiled side up.
4. Cook in panini maker for 3-5 minutes, ensuring that cheese is melted.
5. Serve with fries.

Ham & Pepper Jack Panini

This panini is so good and you can make it so many different other ways.
Servings: 2 | Cook: 5 mins | Prep: 5 mins | Total Time: 10mins

Ingredients
- 4 slices Italian bread
- 12 slices brown sugar ham
- 4 pepperoncini peppers, stemmed, sliced
- 2 slices monterey jack pepper cheese
- 2 tablespoons mayonnaise

Directions

1. Cover 2 of the bread slices evenly with ham, peppers and cheese; top with remaining bread slice.
2. Spread outside of sandwich with mayo.
3. Cook in nonstick skillet on medium heat until lightly browned on both sides.

Ham and Brie Panini Sandwich

Your favorites come together in this exceptionally creamy panini.
Cook: 3 mins | **Prep:** 3 mins | **Total Time:** 6mins

Ingredients

- 3 ounces deli smoked ham (sliced thinly)
- 2 ounces brie cheese
- black olive tapenade (I use Kalamata Olive Tapenade (Spread or Dip))
- 2 slices bread (I use one slice of naan bread cut in two pieces)
- arugula
- olive oil (optional)

Directions

1. Preheat skillet or panini press.
2. Prepare sandwich by spreading tapenade on the inside of one piece of bread and layering ham, arugula, and then brie. Top with remaining bread.
3. If desired brush outside of sandwich with olive oil.
4. Cook until heated through and crispy on the outside.

Ham and Brie Panini

Brie cheese makes for the ultimate panini with it's super smooth melting qualities.
Cook: 5 mins | **Prep:** 5 mins | **Total Time:** 10mins

Ingredients

- 2 slices bread (I use rustic Italian)
- 1 teaspoon Dijon mustard
- 1 teaspoon honey
- 2 slices ham
- 2 ounces brie cheese, sliced
- 1 tablespoon butter

Directions
1. Heat panini grill.
2. spread slice of bread with dijon and the other with honey.
3. lay ham on dijon side and brie on honey side.
4. spread the outside of both slices with butter.
5. place on grill until golden brown.

Ham and Gouda Panini

Servings: 2 | Cook: 4 mins | Prep: 15 mins | Total Time: 19mins

Ingredients
- 2 bolillo rolls, split
- 1 tablespoon olive oil
- 1 tablespoon honey mustard
- 3 ounces baked ham, thinly sliced
- 2 ounces smoked gouda cheese, thinly sliced

Directions
1. Preheat panini grill to high.
2. Place rolls, cut side down, on a work surface and brush crusts with oil.
3. Turn rolls over and spread with mustard.
4. On bottom halves, evenly layer with ham and cheese.
5. Cover with top halves and press gently to pack.
6. Place sandwiches in grill, close the top plate and cook until golden brown, 3-4 minutes.
7. Serve immediately.

Ham and Manchego Panini With Dipping Sau

Found this in a magazine article about the Spanish cheese, Manchego and am posting for ZWT. I loved this new cheese, BF wasn't so sure but he isn't the cheese freak that I am. I don't have a panini press so I use my cast iron grill pan which works great.
Servings: 2 | Cook: 12 mins | Prep: 20 mins | Total Time: 32mins

Ingredients
- 4 slices country bread
- 4 ounces thinly sliced ham
- 2 ounces manchego cheese, coarsely grated

- 4 teaspoons olive oil
- 3 tablespoons apricot jam
- 1 tablespoon Dijon mustard

Directions
1. Divide ham and cheese evenly between two pieces of bread and top with remaining bread.
2. Brush tops of sandwiches with 2 teaspoons oil.
3. In a large nonstick skillet, heat remaining oil over medium-low heat.
4. Place panini in skillet, oiled side up.
5. Cover and cook until golden and cheese has melted, 5-8 minutes per side, pressing down with spatula occasionally.
6. For sauce, mix together jam and dijon.

Ham and Pear Panini

"This is a twist on an old classic -- ham and cheese. Adding a fresh cut pear gives the sandwich a nice, light sweetness that you won't forget."
Pre: 5 m | **Cook:** 6 m | **Ready In:** 11 m

Ingredients
- 4 slices bread
- 1 tablespoon mustard
- 6 slices ham
- 1 pear, peeled and thinly sliced
- 2 dashes ground black pepper
- 1 cup shredded mozzarella cheese
- 1 tablespoon light margarine (such as I Can't Believe It's Not Butter - Light ®)
- Add all ingredients to list

Directions
1. Spread 2 slices of bread with the mustard. Layer each with 3 slices of ham, half of the pear slices, a dash of pepper, and 1/2 cup mozzarella cheese. Top with remaining bread. Lightly spread margarine on the outer sides of each sandwich.
2. Heat a skillet or griddle over medium heat. Grill the sandwiches until the cheese is melted and the bread is golden brown, about 3 minutes per side. Cut each sandwich in half to serve.

Ham and Pesto Panini

This is what I created with leftover basil pesto, Italian bread, some Parmesan, ham and Mozzarella... Let me just say, there were no leftovers of this! Wow, melted cheese, pesto, olive oil...so good. If your pesto is oily you won't need the extra olive oil and also if you make your pesto with lots of Parmesan you may not need the additional cheese. My pesto is a little dry with not that much Parmesan because I like to add it later. And, a good substitute for the ham would be turkey or chicken.
Servings: 4 | **Cook:** 20 mins | **Prep:** 10 mins | **Total Time:** 30mins

Ingredients
- 1/2 loaf Italian bread
- 1/4 cup pesto sauce
- 2 -3 tablespoons extra virgin olive oil
- 1 tomatoes, sliced thinly
- 6 -8 slices black forest ham
- 1/2 cup mozzarella cheese, freshly grated
- 1/4 cup parmesan cheese, freshly grated
- kosher salt & freshly ground black pepper

Directions
1. Slice the bread in half, vertically.
2. If your pesto is dry, drizzle the olive oil all over the bread (insides as well as out) and then spread the pesto all over the soft insides of the bread pieces. If your pesto is oily there's no need to add oil on the insides.
3. Then place the tomato slices on top of the pesto, and season with the salt and pepper.
4. Layer on the remaining ingredients and top with the top bread piece.
5. Heat your panini grill or frying pan and add the sandwich. If you're using a frying pan, use something weighted down to smush the sandwich while it heats.
6. Turn when the bread starts to turn a golden brown and cook until the cheeses are melted.
7. Remove from the heat and slice into sandwich sizes of your choice.

Homemade Italiano Caprese Panini

Wonderfully, crispy, fresh panini
Cook: 5 mins | **Prep:** 10 mins | **Total Time:** 15mins

Ingredients
DRESSING
- 3 tablespoons green onions, diced
- 2 tablespoons roasted red peppers, diced
- 1 tablespoon capers
- 2 tablespoons mayonnaise
- 2 teaspoons Dijon mustard
- 1 tablespoon roasted hot pepper oil
- 1 1/2 teaspoons balsamic vinegar
- 1/2 teaspoon garlic powder
- basil
- red pepper flakes

SANDWICH
- 6 slices bread
- smoked ham
- fresh mozzarella cheese, sliced
- roasted red pepper, sliced in strips

Directions
1. Mix Dressing - whisk together first 10 ingredients. Refrigerate 1 hour, or until slightly thickened.
2. Preheat Sandwich Grill – highest heat.
3. Lightly butter 4 slices of bread. Lightly toast all 6.
4. Assemble sandwich: Toasted, buttered slice of bread (butter down); Ham; Roasted Red Pepper strips; Mozzarella; Dressing; Toasted, unbuttered slice of bread; Dressing; Mozzarella; Roasted Red Pepper strips; Ham; Toasted, buttered slice of bread (butter up)
5. Grill 4 minutes, or until nicely marked and pressed.

Hot Brown Panini

From SoutherLiving.com If you don't have a panini press, just use a cast iron pan or a George Forman grill. I often, use sliced cheese and sliced chicken (the kind from the deli) I like that this recipe easily divided or multiplies based on how many you need it to serve. Make the cheese sauce first. Prep time and cook time will be based on how many you serve - as posted this makes 8.
Cook: *20 mins |* **Prep:** *15 mins |* **Total Time:** *35mins*

Ingredients
- 3 cups warm white cheese sauce, divided (ingredients below)
- 1/4 cup butter
- 1/4 cup all-purpose flour

- 3 1/2 cups milk
- 1 cup shredded Swiss cheese
- 1 cup grated parmesan cheese
- 1/2 teaspoon salt
- 1/4 teaspoon ground red pepper
- 2 tablespoons melted butter
- 16 Italian bread, slices
- 1 cup shredded Swiss cheese, divided
- 3 cups chopped cooked chicken or 3 cups turkey
- 4 plum tomatoes, sliced
- 13 cooked bacon, slices crumbled

Directions
CHEESE SAUCE.
1. Melt butter in a heavy saucepan over low heat; whisk in flour until smooth.
2. Cook 1 minute, whisking constantly.
3. Gradually whisk in milk; cook over medium heat, whisking constantly, until mixture is thickened and bubbly.
4. Whisk in Swiss and Parmesan cheeses, salt, and red pepper, whisking until cheeses are melted and sauce is smooth.

SANDWICHES.
5. Brush melted butter evenly on 1 side of 16 bread slices. Place, butter sides down, on wax paper.
6. Sprinkle 1 tablespoons Swiss cheese on top of each of 8 bread slices; top evenly with chicken, tomato slices, and 1 cup warm White Cheese Sauce. Sprinkle with bacon and remaining cheese, and top with remaining bread slices, butter sides up.
7. Cook sandwiches, in batches, in a preheated panini press 2 to 3 minutes or until golden brown. Serve with remaining 2 cups warm White Cheese Sauce for dipping.

Italian Panini Burger

I made this up as I viewed my frozen Panini and my Italian sausages.. I make 3 burgers out of one lb of meat but listed 4 in the instructions as 4 oz burgers seem to be the most popular.. I love Hot Italian and that is what I have listed but use mild if you prefer. BBQ or pan fry the patties. If you BBQ fry up the pepper mixture separately while your burgers cook.Make the patties rectangular so they fill the panini. One panini makes a healthy serving and you may decide to share but cutting it in two. Hope you try this recipe and enjoy it
***Servings:** 4 | **Cook:** 20 mins | **Prep:** 25 mins | **Total Time:** 45mins*

Ingredients

- 1 lb hot Italian sausage, removed from casings
- 500 g panini bread (4 Panini)
- 3/4 cup sweet onion, chopped
- 2 garlic cloves, finely chopped
- 3/4 cup tomatoes, chopped
- 1/2 cup sweet red pepper, chopped
- 1/2 cup sweet green pepper, chopped
- 1/4 cup fresh basil, chopped or 3/4 teaspoon dry basil
- 1/4 cup pine nuts (optional)
- salt & pepper
- 3/4 cup parmesan cheese, shredded
- 2 tablespoons olive oil

Directions

1. Form the Italian sausage into 4 rectangular patties.
2. Over medium heat pan fry the patties, brown one side flip, cover with lid and continue cooking until done (approx 5 min per side), set aside keep warm or
3. if your pan is large enough when you flip the patties add the onions & garlic, then the peppers and finish cooking all at once - otherwise follow along as suggested.
4. Remove any excess grease from the pan.
5. Meanwhile combine Onions and garlic.
6. Add onions & garlic to pan and cook until they are well browned. Approx 8 minutes
7. Add peppers, tomatoes, basil & pine nuts cook 4 minutes.
8. Lightly Paint one side of the Panini bread with oilive oil.
9. Place a burger & 1/4 on the pepper mixture on 1/2 of the uncoated side of the panini, sprinkle with 1/4 of the parmesan, fold in half.
10. Grill in a fry pan (approx 3 minutes per side or until as crisp and golden as you like it) Brown one side then the other .
11. An alternative method is to lay the panini flat, brown it & then add the patty & peppers etc.
12. Or use your grill and brown both sides at once with the filling already inside.
13. Serve with a nice green salad.

Italian Panini

One day while watching food network I saw a panini made on Paula's Party and it looked absolutely delicious. I searched the recipe and realized I wouldn't be able to find much of the ingredients here. So I decided to try and create my own so to speak with what I could find. A few tries later I settled on this one and I am done searching! It is fabulous! A great blend of flavors! I am not sure how easy it would be to find those meats singularly but I bought them in a gourmet pack in the deli section. I had to name the meats "sausage" so that recipe zaar would recognize them, though I don't know that they are actually a sausage or not. Its more like a salami or pepperoni.

Servings: 4 | **Cook:** 0 mins | **Prep:** 15 mins | **Total Time:** 15mins

Ingredients

- 3 ounces calabrese hot Italian sausage links, thinly sliced
- 3 ounces pepper salami, thinly sliced
- 3 ounces hot capicola sausage, thinly sliced
- 3 -5 ounces prosciutto, thinly sliced
- 3 ounces smoked gouda cheese, sliced for 4 paninis
- 2 teaspoons balsamic vinegar
- 2 teaspoons extra virgin olive oil
- 1/4 medium red onion
- 1/3 cup sweet roasted red pepper
- 1 1/4 cups baby romaine lettuce
- olive oil flavored cooking spray
- Italian seasoning
- shaved parmesan cheese
- 4 asiago cheese rolls

Directions

1. Meat should be very thinly sliced (I use the Daniele brand 'Italian Blend Gourmet Pack' found at a local grocer). Fry each piece for a short time, just long enough to heat them up a bit and release the juices.
2. Pat down with a paper towel to remove excess grease.
3. Cut the rolls in half and spray olive oil cooking spray on all insides. Then sprinkle Italian seasoning over each piece.
4. Arrange bread on baking sheet and put under broiler for 4-5 minutes until browned well.
5. Build Panini in the following order: Bread, baby romaine, couple of rings of red onion, the first three meats, couple slices of smoked gouda, prosciutto, peppers, 1/2 teaspoons balsamic vinegar, 1/2 teaspoons olive oil drizzled over top and top the entire thing off with some shaved parmesan.
6. Enjoy!

Italian Tuna Panini

A yummy creation for the panini lovers.
Servings: 4 | **Cook:** 5 mins | **Prep:** 15 mins | **Total Time:** 20mins

Ingredients

- 2 (6 ounce) cans tuna, drained
- 2 tablespoons light mayonnaise
- 2 tablespoons plain yogurt or 2 tablespoons sour cream
- 1/2 roasted red pepper, diced
- 1/4 cup celery, finely diced
- 2 green onions, finely chopped
- 3 marinated artichokes, hearts chopped
- salt and pepper
- 4 Italian rolls (soft panini buns)
- 4 slices provolone cheese

Directions

1. In bowl, mix together tuna, red pepper, celery, green onions, artichokes pepper, mayonnaise, plain yogurt salt and pepper.
2. Cut buns in half horizontally; spread tuna mixture evenly over bottom half of each. Sprinkle each evenly with cheese. Replace bun top.
3. In nonstick skillet or grill pan or on grill, cook sandwiches over medium heat, pressing often to flatten and turning once, for about 5 minutes or until crusty and cheese is melted. Makes 4 servings.

Jalapeño Garlic Tilapia Panini

This is my own personal copycat recipe mimicking Johnny Carino's sandwich. Their menu description is "Fried fillet of tilapia with a garlic-jalapeño cream sauce, provolone cheese and sliced roma tomatoes." I think that I have accomplished this by using ideas from CoffeeMom's Super Easy Ritz Cracker Breading (Super Easy Ritz Cracker Breading) and ketchup's Garlic Cream Sauce (Garlic Cream Sauce for Chicken/Seafood/Pasta). (Thanks, guys!) We love this sandwich.
Servings: *4 |* **Cook:** *35 mins |* **Prep:** *20 mins |* **Total Time:** *55mins*

Ingredients

- 4 tilapia fillets
- 1 cup Club crackers, finely crushed
- 1/4 teaspoon fresh ground black pepper
- 1 egg, beaten
- 1 tablespoon butter
- 1 small jalapeno, finely diced
- 1 garlic clove, minced
- 1 1/2 tablespoons flour
- 1 cup chicken broth
- 1/4 cup sour cream

- 8 slices hearty country Italian bread
- 2 tablespoons olive oil or 2 tablespoons butter
- 2 roma tomatoes, sliced thinly
- 8 slices provolone cheese

Directions

Fish:
1. Crush crackers and combine with pepper.
2. Dip fish fillets into beaten egg, and then coat with cracker crumbs.
3. Fry in 350 degree oil until breading is golden and fish flakes easily.
4. Remove to an oven-proof plate in a warm oven.

Sauce:
5. Melt butter on low heat. Add jalapeño and garlic. Sauté until jalapeño is softened, but be careful not to burn garlic.
6. Add flour and stir while heating about a minute.
7. Add chicken broth and cook stirring until sauce thickens. Stir in sour cream.
8. Set aside until ready to assemble the panini's.

Panini:
9. Brush one side of each slice of bread with olive oil or spread with butter.
10. Assemble sandwiches with oiled/buttered side of bread to the outside, layering provolone cheese, sliced tomatoes, tilapia fillet, cream sauce and final slice of bread.
11. Spray a cast iron grill pan with cooking spray and heat to sizzling. Reduce heat to medium.
12. Place sandwich in grill pan and top with second cast iron skillet. Press down lightly. (You want to smush the sandwich lightly, but not squash it completely.).
13. Cook for 1-2 minutes, depending on the heat of your pan, until the sandwich is browned and grill marks are evident.
14. Flip sandwich and again top with second cast iron skillet. Cook for another minute or so, until fully browned.
15. Serve warm with fresh salad or crunchy kettle-cooked chips.

Kate's Pineapple Panini Treat

This is from my 9-year old. We were talking about ingredients for panini sandwiches and she said, "Let's use pineapple." We had just got a pineapple corer and were enjoying fresh pineapple at the time.
Servings: 1 | **Cook:** 3 mins | **Prep:** 6 mins | **Total Time:** 9mins

Ingredients
- 2 slices of a nice multi-grain bread

- 1 slice cheddar cheese
- 1-2 slice ham
- fresh pineapple chunk

Directions
1. Close the sandwich up.
2. Place on a preheated panini maker.
3. Close the lid and give it a press.
4. Cook for three minutes.
5. Remove, cut in half and serve.

Kellymac's Brie and Prosciutto Panini

This is my favorite and most easily made panini. I don't have a panini press so I just use my George Foreman grill. This is a just the basic recipe and is delicious as is, but if you want to give it some more pizzaz add some apple or pear slices.
Cook: 5 mins | **Prep:** 2 mins | **Total Time:** 7mins

Ingredients
- 2 slices thinly sliced bread
- Dijon mustard
- mayonnaise
- 3 slices brie cheese
- 2 pieces prosciutto

Directions
1. Spray grill or panini press with non-stick cooking spray. (I prefer olive oil cooking spray because I think it tastes a lot better).
2. Spread mayonaise and mustard on bread to your preference.
3. Put prosciutto on bottom piece of bread, top with cheese and second piece of bread. (Putting the cheese on top allows it to melt into the rest of the sandwich rather than just out and onto the grill.).
4. Grill until golden brown.

Little Italy Panini

Perfect flavors of a grinder you would get in Little Italy, only toasted to perfection. You could sub salami for capicola.
Cook: 3 mins | **Prep:** 2 mins | **Total Time:** 5mins

Ingredients

- 2 slices ciabatta
- 1 teaspoon pesto sauce
- 2 slices tomatoes
- 1 slice provolone cheese
- 3 slices capicola, hot variety preferred
- roasted sweet red pepper (antipasto)

Directions

1. Spread pesto on inside of each slice of bread.
2. Create sandwich by layering tomato, cheese, meat, and peppers.
3. Grill on panini press or skillet until heated through and cheese is melted.

Low Fat Panini

This is a low-fat version of a panini and is still so yummy! You can use pretty much any low-fat deli meat in these, I like turkey or ham or a combination of both. You're going to love this sandwich! My husband and I are obsessed with these right now
Cook: *6 mins |* **Prep:** *5 mins |* **Total Time:** *11mins*

Ingredients

- 2 slices large round bread (low-fat bakery)
- 1 tablespoon honey dijon mustard
- olive oil flavored cooking spray
- butter-flavored cooking spray
- 4 slices Healthy Choice honey-roasted ham
- 4 slices Healthy Choice cooked turkey
- 2 slices syrian cheese (non-fat)

Directions

1. Lay bread slices out spread honey Dijon mustard on one slice and spray the other with the butter flavored cooking spray.
2. Layer the turkey, ham, and cheese slices on the buttered slice of bread and top with the other slice, mustard side down.
3. Spray one outer side of sandwich with olive oil cooking spray and place it face down onto a grill pan and put a heavy frying pan on top and press down for a few minutes.
4. Spray the top side of sandwich with olive oil cooking spray and flip the sandwich. Press again with heavy frying pan for a few minutes, until cheese is melted. And Enjoy!

Low Fat Tuna Panini

serve with green salad
Servings: *3-4* | **Cook:** *15 mins* | **Prep:** *10 mins* | **Total Time:** *25mins*

Ingredients
- 250 g tuna, in water derained
- 2 tablespoons extra light mayonnaise
- 2 tablespoons low fat yogurt
- 1 teaspoon chili flakes
- 1/2 teaspoon lime juice
- 80 g low fat cheese, sliced
- 2 tomatoes, sliced

Directions
1. Mix first 5 thing very well.
2. Spread on Panini bread. Then put the tomato slice after that cheese slice on it.
3. Grill it and enjoy it.

Meatball Sub Panini

A new spin on the classic meatball sub. This works great especially when you only have sliced bread on hand and no hoagie rolls. The panini effect keeps the sliced bread from getting soggy.
Cook: *4 mins* | **Prep:** *10 mins* | **Total Time:** *14mins*

Ingredients
- 2 slices sourdough bread or 2 slices white bread
- 1/2 tablespoon butter, softened
- 1 -2 meatballs, cooked (I recommend Meatballs Italiano)
- 2 ounces sliced mozzarella cheese
- 2 -3 tablespoons marinara sauce

Directions
1. Pre-heat panini grill to medium-high.
2. Slice meatballs into 1/4" rounds. Warm meatballs and marinara sauce in the microwave.
3. Butter 1 side of each slice of bread, lay butter-side down on your work surface.

4. On one slice of bread, layer ingredients in the following order: 1oz cheese, marinara sauce, meatball slices, more marinara sauce, remaining cheese, top piece of bread, with buttered sides facing out.
5. Place assembled sandwich on the hot grill, and close, pressing down for about a minute. Continue cooking for a few minutes, until golden brown.

Meatless Muffuletta Panini

You can have your muffaletta without all the meat, but with all the flavor! Adapted from Rachael Ray's 30 Minute Meals! Feel free to add more if you like. Perhaps some marinated mushrooms, pepperoncini, veggie bacon, other cheeses, tomato slices, etc.
Servings: 4 | Cook: 5 mins | Prep: 5 mins | Total Time: 10mins

Ingredients
- 1/2 cup pitted green olives
- 1/2 cup pitted black olives
- 1 cup giardiniera, drained (pickled cauliflower, carrot and hot pepper mix)
- 4 sesame seed rolls (or cornmeal Kaiser rolls, French bread etc.)
- 8 slices sharp provolone cheese
- 1 cup marinated artichoke hearts, thinly sliced
- 2 roasted red peppers, drained and thinly sliced

Directions
1. Preheat griddle or grill to medium-high heat.
2. Place olives and pickled veggies(not roasted red pepper!) in food processor and pulse chop into a relish.
3. Divide the relish among 4 sandwich bottoms and top with a single slice of cheese, sliced artichokes and peppers then add another slice of provolone to each sandwich and press tops in place.
4. Place sandwiches on grill or frying pan on medium heat and press with heavy skillet weighted down with another heavy skillet or a few heavy cans. Press a few minutes on each side till lightly browned, remove, split and serve.

Mediterranean Panini

Here is a wonderful panini, that is so fantastic, one that I eat all the time, I really enjoy it!! To use a panini maker, heat and place sandwiches on grill. Cook until bread is crisp and cheese is melted.
Servings: 8 | Cook: 25 mins | Prep: 10 mins | Total Time: 35mins

Ingredients

- 1 tablespoon olive oil
- 1 (500 ml) package frozen vegetables (Europe's Best Mediterranean Diced Delight)
- 2 garlic cloves, chopped
- salt and pepper
- 1 (500 ml) carton egg creations original liquid egg substitute, well shaken
- 16 slices whole wheat bread
- 1/2 cup pesto sauce (store bought or homemade)
- 16 slices mozzarella cheese (smoked or regular)

Directions

1. Preheat oven to 375°F Grease a 9x13-inch baking dish.
2. Sauté vegetables and garlic in olive oil over medium-high heat for 2-3 minutes, or until vegetables have softened. Drain vegetables before adding to egg mixture.
3. Combine liquid eggs and cooked vegetables in a medium bowl. Pour into prepared baking dish and bake for 20 minutes or until cooked through. Cool. Cut into 8 slices.
4. Spread pesto on bread slices. Cover the bottom slice with a slice of cheese then with egg slice and another slice of cheese. Top with remaining bread, pesto slice down.
5. Heat a large skillet over medium heat. Brush 1 side of bread with olive oil. Arrange sandwiches oiled side down skillet. Brush top side with oil. Cook until golden brown and cheese has melted, pressing down occasionally with spatula, about 3 minutes.

Minted Marinated Zucchini

"For those who have mint leaves and zucchini taking over the vegetable patch, this is simple. This tangy dish can be used as a relish inside panini or sandwiches, or on the side."

Pre: 20 m | **Cook:** 5 m | **Ready In:** 25 m

Ingredients

- 1/4 cup olive oil
- 3 large zucchini, thinly sliced
- 2 cloves garlic, minced
- 2 cups fresh mint leaves, finely chopped
- 1/3 cup distilled white vinegar
- 1/2 teaspoon salt
- ground black pepper to taste
- 1 tablespoon olive oil, for drizzling

- Add all ingredients to list

Directions
1. Heat 1/4 cup of olive oil in a large skillet over medium-high heat. Add zucchini slices and garlic; cook and stir until starting to brown but you want the squash to stay firm and not get mushy, 3 to 4 minutes. Remove from the heat and mix in the vinegar, mint, salt and pepper. Stir in the remaining olive oil. Spoon into a jar and store covered in the refrigerator.

Monte Cristo Panini

*Servings: 2 | **Cook:** 4 mins | **Prep:** 20 mins | **Total Time:** 24mins*

Ingredients
- 4 slices French bread (1/2-inch thick)
- 1 tablespoon butter, melted
- 1 tablespoon yellow mustard
- 2 ounces Swiss cheese, thinly sliced
- 2 ounces smoked ham, thinly sliced
- 1 egg
- 1 tablespoon milk
- 1 teaspoon powdered sugar
- 1/4 teaspoon ground cinnamon

Directions
1. Preheat panini grill to high.
2. Brush one side of each bread slice with butter.
3. Place on work surface, buttered side down, and spread with mustard.
4. On bottom halves, evenly layer cheese and ham.
5. Cover with top halves and press gently to pack.
6. In a pie plate, whisk together egg and milk.
7. Dip both sides of each sandwich in egg mixture.
8. In a small bowl, combine sugar and cinnamon; set aside.
9. Place sandwiches in grill, close the top plate and cook until golden brown, 3-4 minutes.
10. Sift sugar mixture over each panini.
11. Serve immediately.

Monterey Ranch Panini

Servings: 4 | Cook: 8 mins | Prep: 30 mins | Total Time: 38mins

Ingredients
- 8 slices focaccia bread (or other rust-style Italian bread, ciabatta is good)
- 1/2 cup prepared ranch dressing
- 4 (4 ounce) boneless skinless chicken breast halves, grilled and thinly sliced
- 16 slices fresh tomatoes (sliced thin)
- 16 slices bacon, fried crisp and drained
- 4 slices monterey jack cheese (or enough to completely cover the sandwiches)
- extra virgin olive oil

Directions
1. Lay out the bread and spread the inside of each slice with 1 tablespoon ranch dressing.
2. Cover each of the four slices of bread with one of the sliced chicken breast halves, 4 tomato slices, 4 bacon slices, and 1 slice of cheese.
3. Cover with remaining 4 slices of bread.
4. Brush the top and bottom of each sandwich with olive oil.
5. Place the panini in a large heavy frying pan; place a slightly smaller heavy pan on top of the panini to weigh them down; cook over medium heat for 4 minutes, turn the panini over, replace the second frying pan and cook for 4 more minutes or until the bread is toasted and the filling is warmed through.
6. Remove from pan, slice and serve immediately.
7. **Panini can also be cooked on an indoor-style grill, a stovetop grill, or a panini grill.
8. **Suggestion—marinate the chicken breasts in Italian dressing for 2 hours in the refrigerator, then grill.

Morning Breakfast Panini

Servings: 1 | Cook: 5 mins | Prep: 5 mins | Total Time: 10mins

Ingredients
- 2 slices white bread or 2 slices brioche bread, 1/2-inch thick
- unsalted butter (melted for brushing)
- 3 tablespoons cheddar cheese, grated
- 2 slices cooked bacon, fried until crispy
- 1 egg, fried

- salt & freshly ground black pepper, to taste
- 1/4 cup arugula

Directions

1. Preheat an electric panini maker on high heat according to the manufacturer's instructions.
2. Place the bread slices on a cutting board. Brush one side of each slice with melted butter.
3. Turn one slice over and sprinkle with the cheese.
4. Top with the bacon and fried egg, and season with salt and pepper.
5. Top with the arugula and the other bread slice, buttered side up.
6. Place the sandwich on the preheated panini maker and cook according to the manufacturer's instructions until the bread is golden and the cheese is melted, 3 to 5 minutes.
7. Transfer the sandwich to a cutting board and cut in half.
8. Serve immediately.

Mozzarella Basil Pesto and Peperonata

The colors of the Italian flag—red, white, and green.
Servings: *4 |* **Cook:** *10 mins |* **Prep:** *15 mins |* **Total Time:** *25mins*

Ingredients

- 4 ciabatta rolls
- 3/4 cup basil pesto (Basil Pesto)
- 6 ounces fresh mozzarella cheese, thinly sliced
- salt
- fresh ground black pepper
- Peperonata
- 4 red bell peppers, cored, seeded, cut into 1-inch dice
- 2 tablespoons extra virgin olive oil
- 2 tablespoons balsamic vinegar
- 1 pinch red pepper flakes
- kosher salt

Directions

1. See recipe #225648 for instructions on how to make peperonata; you will use 1 cup in this recipe.
2. Preheat a panini grill.
3. Slice off the domed top of the ciabatta rolls; the rolls should now be about 1 inch thick.

4. Split the rolls in half horizontally.
5. Spread the top halves of the rolls with basil pesto, covering them completely.
6. Spread the bottom halves of the rolls with a thin layer of peperonata.
7. Lay the mozzarella slices over the peperonata in a single layer.
8. Season with salt and pepper before covering the panini with the top half of the ciabatta.
9. Grill sandwiches for 4 minutes until the bread is golden brown and the cheese has set.
10. Cut each in half and serve immediately.

Mozzarella Ham and Basil Panini

Servings: 6 | Cook: 6 mins | Prep: 10 mins | Total Time: 16mins

Ingredients
- 1 (16 ounce) ciabatta, cut in half horizontally
- 4 teaspoons Dijon mustard
- 4 teaspoons balsamic vinegar
- 1 1/3 cups thinly sliced fresh mozzarella cheese
- 12 basil leaves
- 8 ounces sliced reduced-sodium ham (33% -less-sodium cooked deli ham)
- 2 sweetened hot cherry peppers, sliced
- 1 large plum tomato, thinly sliced
- cooking spray

Directions
1. Brush cut side of the bottom bread half with mustard; brush cut side of top half with vinegar. Top bottom half with mozzarella, basil, ham, peppers, and tomato. Top with remaining bread half.
2. Heat a large nonstick skillet over medium heat. Coat pan with cooking spray. Add sandwich to pan; top with another heavy skillet. Cook 3 minutes on each side or until golden.
3. Cut sandwich into 6 wedges.

Mozzarella Tomato & Basil Panini

My son, Jeffrey, found a little vegetarian café near his college and took me there. I've now become addicted to their food and especially love their paninis. I saw this recipe and it looks like it will be very similar to a panini they make.

Servings: 4 | Cook: 8 mins | Prep: 15 mins | Total Time: 23mins

Ingredients

- 2 ripe plum tomatoes, cored and sliced
- 6 ounces fresh mozzarella cheese, sliced
- 1/2 cup loosely packed fresh basil leaf
- 1/8 teaspoon salt
- 1/4 teaspoon fresh ground black pepper
- 8 slices cut from a loaf country bread

Directions

1. Prepare outdoor grill for direct grilling on medium.
2. Divide plum tomatoes, fresh mozzarella, basil leaves, salt and pepper evenly among four bread slices. Top with remaining 4 slices of bread.
3. Place 2 panini on hot grill grate. Place a heavy skillet with a heatproof handle (preferably a cast iron one) on top and press down. If you don't have a cast iron skillet, you can substitute a clean brick, thoroughly wrapped in aluminum foil, on top of each panini.
4. Cook 3-4 minutes, or until bread is toasted and browned, then turn over and cook 3-4 minutes on the other side. Repeat with remaining 2 panini. Cut in halves to serve.

Muffuletta Panini

A delicious, grilled version of the classic New Orleans sandwich. If you can't find prepared olive salad then try to use a chunky style olive tapenade.
Servings: 4 | Cook: 5 mins | Prep: 10 mins | Total Time: 15mins

Ingredients

- softened butter
- 8 slices rustic bread or 8 slices sourdough bread
- 16 slices provolone cheese (thin slices) or 16 slices mozzarella cheese (thin slices)
- 1/2 cup olive salad, drained or 1/2 cup olive tapenade
- 6 ounces thinly sliced black forest ham
- 6 ounces sliced mortadella
- 4 ounces sliced genoa salami

Directions

1. Brush both sides of bread lightly with butter.
2. Layer 4 slices cheese over four of the slices of bread.
3. Top with olive salad, ham, mortadella, salami, remaining cheese and bread.
4. Cook sandwiches in a preheated panini press until golden brown and cheese is melted, about 3-4 minutes.

5. Note: Sandwiches may be cooked in a preheated ridged grill pan or skillet over medium heat. Place a heavy skillet on top of sandwiches to flatten; cook 3 minutes. Turn; replace skillet and continue to cook 3 to 4 minutes or until golden brown and cheese is melted.

Mushroom Spinach and Fontina Panini

Servings: 2 | Cook: 5 mins | Prep: 30 mins | Total Time: 35mins

Ingredients
- 2 1/2 tablespoons unsalted butter
- 4 ounces mixed mushrooms, brushed clean and sliced (mixed wild and cultivated mushrooms)
- 2 tablespoons finely chopped shallots
- 2 tablespoons cognac
- 1 tablespoon chopped fresh tarragon
- salt
- fresh ground black pepper
- 4 slices crusty country bread (each slice 1/2 inch thick)
- 3 ounces very thinly sliced Fontina cheese
- 1 cup baby spinach leaves

Directions
1. In a saucepan, melt 1 1/2 tablespoons butter over med-high heat; add in mushrooms and shallots; saute until mushrooms are softened and release their juices, 3-5 minutes.
2. Continue to cook, stirring often, until most of the liquid is absorbed, 2-3 minutes longer.
3. Stir in the Cognac, chopped tarragon, and salt and pepper to taste.
4. Cook/stir, for 1 minute; let cool slightly.
5. Preheat the sandwich grill; melt the remaining 1 tablespoon butter in a small saucepan over med-high heat.
6. Place bread slices on a work surface and brush 1 side of each with the melted butter.
7. Turn and layer 1/4 of the cheese, half of the mushrooms, and half of the spinach on the unbuttered side of two of the bread slices.
8. Divide the remaining cheese on top; place the remaining 2 bread slices on top, buttered sides up, and press to pack gently.
9. Place the panini in the grill; close the top plate, and cook until the bread is golden and toasted, the spinach is wilted, and the cheese is melted, 3-5 minutes; serve immediately.

No Press Panini With Mozzarella Roasted

Servings: 4 | Cook: 5 mins | Prep: 10 mins | Total Time: 15mins

Ingredients
- 2 tablespoons butter
- 8 slices white bread
- 1 cup shredded mozzarella cheese
- 4 whole jarred roasted red peppers, patted dry and cut into strips
- 1/4 cup grated parmigiano-reggiano cheese
- 12 -15 basil leaves, roughly chopped

Directions
1. Place a large skillet over medium heat and melt the butter. Place four slices of bread in the skillet and divide the mozzarella, roasted red peppers and Parmigiano-Reggiano between each of them. Top each with the second slice of bread and cook for another minute or until the bottom sliced is golden brown.
2. Carefully flip the panini and cook for another 1-2 minutes or until the cheese has melted and the other side is golden brown.
3. To serve, remove the panini from the heat and cut each of them into quarters. Garnish with chopped basil.

Nutella Pear Panini

I came up with this last week when I was craving something sweet.
Servings: 1 | Cook: 10 mins | Prep: 5 mins | Total Time: 15mins

Ingredients
- 2 tablespoons nutella
- 1 pear, sliced
- 2 slices of chewy dense bread, thick slices
- softened butter

Directions
1. Spread one side of each slice of bread with butter and the other side with Nutella. Top with pear slices. Depending on the size of your bread, you may only need half the pear.
2. Cook in sandwich press or in a skillet with another heavy skillet or foil-wrapped brick as a weight. (Cook over medium heat. When first side is browned, flip over and cook the other side, weighting again.).

3. This would probably be equally good with bananas, and I've also thought a little cream cheese might work well with this.

P P Pesto Panini

This is so easy, but so good. The key is to use a good quality pesto. Oh, and to make it truly outstanding, you have to invite me over. Really. It's a well-known fact. ;) You can use a grill with a foil-covered brick if you don't have a press.
Cook: 4 mins | **Prep:** 2 mins | **Total Time:** 6mins

Ingredients
- 2 slices French bread
- 1 teaspoon pesto sauce (homemade, preferably!)
- 1 teaspoon mayonnaise
- 1/2 roma tomato, sliced
- 1 slice Swiss cheese
- 2 slices ham, Black Forest works well
- olive oil, a thin layer on outside of each bread slice

Directions
1. Preheat the panini press.
2. Coat one side of each bread slice with olive oil. This will help prevent the sandwich from sticking to the press/grill.
3. Mix the mayonnaise with the pesto and spread on the other side of each bread slice. (I admit to adding an extra teaspoon of pesto!) On that, layer the remainder in the following order: Swiss, tomato, ham.
4. Close sandwich, making sure the oiled side is facing outward, pop it in the panini press, close, count to 240... or thereabouts... and EAT!

Panini Caprese Sandwich With Avocado

Take the ingredients of the wonderful caprese salad - tomatoes, fresh mozzarella. basil and olive and add avocado plus some seasonings to created a stunning and beautifuly panini. And no cook too, apart from broiling the baguette if you wish to
Servings: 2-4 | **Cook:** 5 mins | **Prep:** 5 mins | **Total Time:** 10mins

Ingredients
- 1 baguette, preferably multi-grained, halved horizontally
- 2 tablespoons extra virgin olive oil, for drizzle
- 2 large tomatoes, sliced

- 1 lb mozzarella cheese, sliced
- 1 pinch dried oregano
- 12 fresh basil leaves (to your taste)
- 1 avocado, sliced
- salt and pepper, to taste

Directions
1. Grill or broil baguette bread halves until toasted; drizzle both halves with olive oil. Layer with tomato, salt, pepper, Mozzarella cheese, sprinkle with dried Oregano, then more olive oil, salt and pepper, top with fresh basil leaves, avocadoes and more salt and pepper. Close the sandwich, slice and serve.

Panini Dippers

Servings: 2 | Cook: 4 mins | Prep: 15 mins | Total Time: 19mins

Ingredients
- 1/4 cup freshly grated parmesan cheese
- 1/4 cup butter, softened
- 1/4 teaspoon garlic salt
- 1/4 teaspoon dried parsley
- fresh ground black pepper, to taste
- 4 slices sourdough bread
- 4 ounces Swiss cheese, thinly sliced
- heated marinara sauce

Directions
1. Preheat panini grill to high.
2. In a bowl, combine Parmesan, butter, garlic salt, and parsley.
3. Place bread on a work surface and spread each slice with Parmesan mixture.
4. Turn two slices over and evenly layer with Swiss cheese.
5. Cover with top halves, buttered side up, and press gently to pack.
6. Place sandwiches in grill, close the top plate and cook until golden brown, 3-4 minutes.
7. Cut each panini into quarters and serve immediately with marinara sauce for dipping.

Panini Florentine

I received a booklet from Kraft Foods today which is called "food & family" and this is one of the recipes in it that I am posting here to try at a later date. The cooking time includes the marinating time.

Cook: 35 mins | **Prep:** 10 mins | **Total Time:** 45mins

Ingredients
- 4 boneless skinless chicken breast halves
- 1/2 cup balsamic vinaigrette, Kraft Good Seasons Classic Balsamic Vinaigrette Dressing made with Extra Virgin Olive Oil
- 8 slices whole grain bread
- 1/4 cup low-fat mayonnaise, Kraft Reduced Fat Mayonnaise with Olive Oil
- 1/2 cup spinach leaves, fresh
- 2 roasted red peppers, cut in half
- 4 slices part-skim mozzarella cheese, Kraft Deli Fresh Low-Moisture Park Skim Mozzarella Cheese Slices

Directions
1. Marinate chicken in dressing in glass dish in refrigerator 30 minutes; discard marinade.
2. Cook chicken in skillet on medium heat 5 minutes on each side or until cooked through.
3. Spread bread with mayonnaise; fill with remaining ingredients to make 4 sandwiches.
4. Cook in panini maker on medium heat 5 minutes or until golden brown.

Panini Sandwiches

"Turkey and Swiss cheese panini with sundried tomato mayonnaise made with dinner rolls are quick and delicious!"

Pre: 10 m | **Cook:** 10 m | **Ready In:** 20 m

Ingredients
- 4 Sister Schubert's Dinner Yeast Rolls, split
- Plain or sundried tomato mayonnaise (see below)
- 4 slices roast turkey or ham
- 4 slices Swiss, Monterey Jack, or Gruyere cheese
- 8 small slices red onion
- 1 cup fresh spinach leaves or several fresh basil leaves (optional)
- Salt and freshly ground black pepper

- Butter
- Sundried Tomato Mayonnaise:
- 1/4 cup mayonnaise
- 2 finely chopped sundried tomatoes
- Salt and freshly ground black pepper
- Add all ingredients to list

Directions

1. Preheat grill pan or panini machine to medium heat.
2. Spread center of each roll with 1 tablespoon mayonnaise. Assemble sandwiches with remaining ingredients, except butter. Season with salt and pepper.
3. Spread small amount of butter on top and bottom of each roll; place sandwich either in pan on onto panini machine and grill. Cook 5 to 7 minutes.
4. (If using a pan, press sandwich down with a pan lid. Cook sandwiches about 3 to 4 minutes on each side or until bread is toasted.)
5. For mayonnaise: whisk all ingredients together in small bowl. Refrigerate until ready to use.

Panini Toscano

Nova Scotia chef Michael Howell won a recent competition to make the greatest grilled cheese sandwich with his Panini Toscano - sooooo delicious!! You must try it - You could also use provolone or smoked mozzarella to replace havarti cheese.
*Servings: 1 | **Cook:** 0 mins | **Prep:** 20 mins | **Total Time:** 20mins*

Ingredients
- 1 fresh ciabastta bun, about 5-inches square
- 1 ripe fig, cut into 4-5 slices
- 2 slices prosciutto, thinly sliced
- 2 slices havarti cheese, 1/8-inch thick
- 1 ounce baby arugula
- 1/2 roasted pepper, peeled and cut into 3/4 inch slices

LEMON AIOLI
- 1/4 cup prepared olive oil mayonnaise
- juice and zest from 1/2 lemon
- 1 garlic clove, minced

BALSAMIC VINAIGRETTE
- 1 teaspoon balsamic vinegar
- 1 pinch each salt and pepper
- 1/2 teaspoon Dijon mustard
- 1 pinch sugar

- 1/2 lemon, juice of
- 1/4 cup extra-virgin olive oil plus extra for brushing on bun

Directions

LEMON AIOLI:
- In a small bowl, mix together mayonnaise, lemon juice and zest and garlic and let flavours mingle for half hour. Split fresh ciabatta in half and brush both sides liberally with lemon aioli.
- Layer 2 slice of havarti cheese on the bottom of the bun, then top with sliced figs, prosciutto, a couple of sprigs of arugula and finish with the other slice of cheese. Top with other side of the bun. Lightly brush outside of but on both sides with extra-virgin olive oil. place sandwich in a preheated panini press and grill until cheese is melting and bread is lightly marked.
- If using a grill or barbecue, place a weight on top of sandwich and flip halfway through cooking.

BALSAMIC VINAIGRETTE:
- While sandwich is grilling, in a small bowl, combine vinegar, salt, pepper, Dijon, sugar and lemon juice. Slowly whisk in oil until incorporated.
- In another small bowl, dress arugula with 1 tablespoons of the vinaigrette and place on a plate. Toss two slices of red pepper in the same bowl to dress lightly adn place on top of salad.
- When sandwich is ready, remove from press or grill and split in half diagonally. Place around salad and serve immediately.

Panini With Sautéed Mushrooms and Gruyère

*Servings: 4 | Cook: 15 mins | **Prep:** 10 mins | **Total Time:** 25mins*

Ingredients

- 1 tablespoon butter
- 1 (8 ounce) package mushrooms, sliced
- 4 teaspoons Dijon mustard
- 8 slices whole wheat bread
- 1 (5 ounce) bag fresh spinach
- 1/4 cup roasted red pepper, sliced
- 1/4 cup chopped red onion
- 1 cup shredded gruyere cheese
- 2 tablespoons butter, melted

Directions

1. Heat butter in large nonstick skillet over medium-high heat. Add mushrooms and sauté 5-6 minutes.
2. Spread mustard on 4 slices of bread; layer each with 6 spinach leaves, 1 tablespoon red bell pepper, 1 tablespoon onion, 1/4 cup cheese, and 1/4 cup mushrooms. Top with the remaining bread.
3. Brush melted butter over both sides of each sandwich. If using a skillet, heat a large nonstick skillet over medium-high heat; place sandwiches in pan. Place another skillet on top of the sandwiches; cook 2-3 minutes on each side until golden brown and cheese is melted. If using a panini maker, brush sandwiches with butter; place in machine, close, and cook 2 minutes or until done.

Panini With Scrambled Eggs and Tomatoes

Servings: 4 | Cook: 13 mins | Prep: 10 mins | Total Time: 23mins

Ingredients

- 6 eggs
- 1/4 cup milk
- 1/4 teaspoon salt
- 1/4 teaspoon fresh black pepper
- 1 tablespoon olive oil
- 1/4 cup pesto sauce or 1/4 cup sun-dried tomato pesto
- 4 panini bread, sliced horizontally or 8 thick slices bread
- 1 tomatoes, sliced
- 4 provolone cheese (or asiago or cheddar or Swiss or gouda) or 4 mozzarella cheese, slices (or asiago or cheddar or Swiss or gouda)

Directions

1. In a bowl, mix eggs, milk, salt and pepper. In a skillet, heat oil at medium heat. Add the mixture of egg and cook, stirring often, until it makes big creamy pieces. Spread pesto in the panini, add scrambled eggs and garnish with slices of tomatoes and cheese.
2. Heat another large skillet or a skillet with ridges at medium heat. Add panini and cook, pushing them, for about 8 minutes or until golden and crispy and cheese has melted (flip them at mid cooking).

Panzanella Panini

"I made this sandwich by combining my 2 favorite sandwiches, and salad, together. The result was delicious!"

Pre: 10 m | Cook: 5 m | Ready In: 15 m

Ingredients
- 1 French deli roll, split
- 1 teaspoon balsamic vinegar
- 2 slices mozzarella cheese
- 1 small tomato, sliced
- 4 fresh basil leaves
- olive oil
- Add all ingredients to list

Directions
1. Preheat a skillet over medium-low heat.
2. Sprinkle cut sides of roll with balsamic vinegar. Layer one slice of mozzarella cheese, tomato slices, basil leaves, and the remaining slice of mozzarella cheese on the roll. Close sandwich; rub outside with olive oil.
3. Place sandwich in preheated skillet; top with another heavy skillet to press. Cook until bread is toasted and golden, about 3 minutes. Flip sandwich; top with skillet. Cook second side until toasted, about an additional 2 minutes.

Pear Pecorino and Prosciutto Panini

A Cooking Light recipe - slightly adapted and delicious.
Servings: 4 | Cook: 6 mins | Prep: 5 mins | Total Time: 11mins

Ingredients
- 1 ripe pear, peeled, cored, and cut into 8 wedges
- 1/2 teaspoon sugar
- 1 loaf focaccia bread, cut in half horizontally (approximately 12 oz)
- 4 teaspoons balsamic vinegar
- 1 cup trimmed arugula
- 1/2 cup fresh pecorino romano cheese or 1/2 cup parmigiano-reggiano cheese, shaved
- 4 ounces prosciutto (16 very thin slices)
- freshly cracked pepper

Directions
1. Heat a nonstick skillet over medium-high heat. Add pear to pan, and sprinkle with sugar. Cook 2 minutes on each side or until golden.

2. Brush cut sides of bread with vinegar. Arrange pear slices, arugula, cheese, and prosciutto evenly over bottom half of bread. Sprinkle generously with freshly cracked pepper. Cover with top half of bread.
3. Heat a large nonstick skillet over medium heat. Add stuffed loaf to pan. Place a cast-iron or heavy skillet on top of stuffed loaf; press gently to flatten. Cook 4 minutes on each side or until bread is toasted (leave cast-iron skillet on stuffed loaf while it cooks). Cut into quarters.

Pepperoni, Mozzarella, Black Olives, and Pesto Panini

Servings: 2 | Cook: 3 mins | Prep: 20 mins | Total Time: 23mins

Ingredients
- 2 ciabatta rolls
- 2 tablespoons tomato paste
- 2 tablespoons basil pesto (homemade or store-bought)
- 12 pepperoni (small thin slices)
- 10 pitted black olives, sliced
- 8 thinly sliced red onion rings
- 5 ounces fresh buffalo mozzarella, sliced
- vegetable oil, for sauteing and brushing

Directions
1. Preheat a Panini grill.
2. Trim the top and bottom off the ciabatta rolls so that they are about 1 inch thick.
3. Slice open length2wise.
4. Spread one half of each sandwich with tomato paste and the other side with pesto.
5. On roll bottoms, layer with pepperoni, followed by olives and onion, finishing with the cheese; cover with roll tops.
6. Brush both sides of the Panini with oil and grill in the preheated Panini press for 3 minutes , or according to the manufacturer's instructions.
7. The bread should be golden brown and the filling warmed through.

Pesto Italian Panini

This little piece of heaven first came to me during lunch break at work. I almost lost it when I tasted the salty/savory combination of pepperoni, turkey and ham with pesto and mozzarella cheese. It just doesn't get any better...Directions are per sandwich.

Servings: 1 | Cook: 10 mins | Prep: 5 mins | Total Time: 15mins

Ingredients
- 2 slices bread
- 1 slice deli ham
- 1 slice deli turkey
- 2 pepperoni slices
- 1 -2 tablespoon pesto sauce (homemade or store-bought)
- butter
- 1 slice mozzarella cheese

Directions
1. Heat skillet over medium-high.
2. Butter 1 side of each piece of bread.
3. Grease heated skillet with butter or cooking spray.
4. Place one piece of bread in skillet, buttered side down.
5. Carefully spread pesto on this piece of bread using a spoon.
6. Top with 1 slice of ham, 1 slice of turkey and 2 large pepperoni slices, then slice of mozzarella cheese.
7. Finally, place 2nd piece of bread, butter side up, on sandwich.
8. Brown lightly on both sides, eat immediately.

Pesto Prosciutto Panini

This amazing panini is great with a salad for lunch or dinner. Fabulous!
Cook: 5 mins | Prep: 10 mins | Total Time: 15mins

Ingredients
- 8 slices fresh sourdough bread
- 4 slices prosciutto
- 1/2 cup prepared pesto sauce
- 8 ounces fresh mozzarella cheese, sliced
- 2 tablespoons butter, softened

Directions
1. Butter one side of each slice of bread.
2. Spread inside of four slices thickly with pesto. Top with mozzarella and prosciutto.
3. Grill on preheated panini grill, George Foreman grill or griddle until cheese is melted and bread is golden brown. Enjoy!

Pilgrim Panini Dip Sandwich

Serve sliced turkey and provolone Panini style or just grill on sliced bread, and you have a turkey version of a 'French Dip' sandwich. Serve the dip in wide mouthed bowls and dip the sandwich into the sauce (which is our version, adapted from Alton Brown's Cranberry Dipping Sauce). It's warm and sweet and spicy and hey!.... that's my dip your dippin into, get your own!

Servings: 6 | **Cook:** 25 mins | **Prep:** 5 mins | **Total Time:** 30mins

Ingredients
DIP
- 1 (12 ounce) can cranberry sauce (gelatine, not whole berry)
- 1 cup orange juice
- 1 cup ginger ale
- 2 tablespoons light brown sugar
- 1/4 teaspoon salt

SANDWICH
- 12 slices whole wheat bread (or hoagie rolls)
- 2 lbs roasted turkey breast, shaved
- 6 ounces provolone cheese (12 slices)

Directions
1. Combine all Dip ingredients in a saucepan, and bring to a boil. Reduce heat and simmer, stirring occasionally, for about 25 minutes or until liquid is reduced by half. Meanwhile, make the sandwiches and grill.
2. Serve the dip in small (wide mouthed) individual dishes next to each guests plate along with the panini.

Pineapple Ham Panini

Servings: 2 | **Cook:** 4 mins | **Prep:** 15 mins | **Total Time:** 19mins

Ingredients
- 4 slices multigrain bread (1/2 inch thick slices)
- 1 tablespoon butter, melted
- 2 ounces cheddar cheese, thinly sliced
- 2 ounces deli ham, thinly sliced
- 2 slices fresh pineapple (about 1/4 inch thick)

Directions
1. Brush one side of each bread slices with butter.
2. Place two slices on a work surface, buttered side down, and evenly layer with cheese, ham, and pineapple.
3. Cover with top halves, buttered side up, and press gently to pack.
4. Place sandwiches in grill, close the top plate and cook until golden brown, 3-4 minutes.
5. Serve immediately.

Pita Panini

When my new panini grill arrived, the only bread in the house was pita bread - so I decided to use it along with the ingredients already in my refrigerator.
Cook: *3 mins |* **Prep:** *2 mins |* **Total Time:** *5mins*

Ingredients
- 1 pita bread
- salami
- 2 slices provolone cheese
- sweet-hot mustard
- onion
- tomatoes

Directions
1. Carefully open pita bread halves and spread hot and sweet mustard on one side. Use one slice of provolone cheese for each half. I found that cutting the provolone slices made them fit better in the pita. Add generous amount of Hungarian Salami slices (I like it sliced very thin). Insert tomato and onion slices. Brush lightly with olive oil and place on panini grill for approximately 3-4 minutes.

Pizza Panini

This is my take on a Rachael Ray recipe: Inside Out Pizza Panini. I don't follow it in it's entirety, if I did I would use the same title. I have a panini press I have fallen in love with, and this is like my two favorite things in the world (pizza & panini). I am putting *my* favorite ingredients in this, but just like pizza you can do what you want. Unlike a lot of these recipes I do not add pizza sauce, I serve it heated on the side for dunking.
Cook: *5 mins |* **Prep:** *20 mins |* **Total Time:** *25mins*

Ingredients

- 1 loaf focaccia bread
- 4 ounces thinly sliced fresh mozzarella cheese
- 4 ounces thinly sliced provolone cheese
- 4 ounces sliced pepperoni (turkey pepperoni may be substituted)
- 4 ounces sliced genoa salami
- 1 thinly sliced red onion
- 1 cup sliced black olives or 1 cup olive salad
- 1 cup banana pepper
- 1/2 teaspoon dried oregano
- 1 small thinly sliced tomatoes
- 1 -2 cup shredded lettuce
- red wine vinaigrette, for drizzling (optional)
- olive oil, for drizzling
- your favorite pizza sauce, warmed

Directions

1. Cut the focaccia in 4 equal parts, slice each in half like sandwich bread.
2. Layer mozzarella, provolone & meats.
3. Sprinkle dried oregano on top.
4. Top with remaining slices of bread.
5. Preheat panini press or grill pan to medium heat.
6. Drizzle outside of top and bottom layers of bred with a bit of olive oil.
7. Place in panini or grill pan.
8. If using a panini press, heat approximately 5 minutes, or until cheese is melting and there are grill marks on the bread. If using a grill pan grill 2-3 minutes per side.
9. Removed from pan or press, to a plate. Open up sandwich and layer the vegetables, whichever you want, in whatever order you like. If desired, drizzle with vinaigrette.
10. Cut in half, serve with pizza sauce, for dipping.

Portabella and Grana Panini

A favorite from the owners of 'ino.
Servings: *4 |* **Cook:** *3 mins |* **Prep:** *20 mins |* **Total Time:** *23mins*

Ingredients

- 4 ciabatta rolls
- 1/2 cup sun-dried tomato pesto (Sun-Dried Tomato Pesto)
- 2 medium portabella mushrooms

- extra virgin olive oil
- salt
- fresh ground black pepper
- 4 ounces grana padano, grated using the large holes of a box grater

Directions

1. Preheat a panini grill; slice off the domed tops of the ciabatta rolls.
2. The rolls should now be about 1 inch thick; split the rolls horizontally.
3. Spread the Sun-Dried Tomato Pesto thinly but completely over the bottom halves of the ciabatta rolls.
4. Remove the stems from the mushrooms, discard stems; clean caps by rubbing them gently with a paper towel; scrape out gills.
5. Cut each mushroom cap into slices about 1/8 inch thick.
6. Lay mushrooms slices across the bottom half of the rolls from end to end using 3 or 4 slices for each panino (don't overlap).
7. Drizzle with olive oil and season with salt and pepper.
8. Top each sandwich with a thin layer of Grana Padano; cover each with the top halves of the rolls.
9. Grill for 3 minutes until the bread is golden and the cheese has set.

Portabella Mushroom Panini

A pan seared portabella topped with melted cheese, pressed between 2 sourdough bread slices
Servings: 1 | **Cook:** 10 mins | **Prep:** 5 mins | **Total Time:** 15mins

Ingredients

- 1 portabella mushroom cap
- 2 slices sourdough bread
- 1 slice provolone cheese
- olive oil
- salt
- pepper

Directions

1. Heat large sauté pan over medium-high heat.
2. Drizzle olive oil over the mushroom cap.
3. Season with salt and pepper.
4. Slice mushroom into 1/4 inch strips.
5. Sear slices 5 minutes, do not move them during this time.
6. Flip slices over and sear for another 5 minutes.

7. Meanwhile, toast the bread.
8. Remove portabella slices and place, along with one slice of provolone cheese, between the sourdough bread slices.
9. Place sandwich on panini press.
10. Enjoy!

Portobello Eggplant and Roasted Red Pepper Panini

"Tangy three cheese and Mediterranean vegetable panini."
Pre: *40 m |* **Cook:** *20 m |* **Ready In:** *9 h*

Ingredients
- 2 red bell peppers
- 4 portobello mushroom caps
- 1 cup fat-free balsamic vinaigrette
- 4 (1/2 inch thick) slices eggplant, peeled
- 1 teaspoon garlic powder
- 1 teaspoon onion powder
- 2 teaspoons grated Parmesan cheese
- 8 slices focaccia bread
- 1/4 cup fat free ranch dressing
- 4 thin slices Swiss cheese
- 4 thin slices Asiago cheese
- Add all ingredients to list

Directions
1. Preheat the oven's broiler and set the oven rack at about 6 inches from the heat source. Line a baking sheet with aluminum foil.
2. Cut the peppers in half from top to bottom; remove the stem, seeds, and ribs, then place the peppers cut sides down onto the prepared baking sheet.
3. Cook under the preheated broiler until the skin of the peppers has blackened and blistered, about 5 minutes. Place the blackened peppers into a bowl, and tightly seal with plastic wrap. Allow the peppers to steam as they cool, about 20 minutes. Once cool, remove the skins and discard. Refrigerate overnight.
4. Place the portobello mushroom caps into a resealable plastic bag, and pour in the balsamic vinaigrette. Squeeze out excess air, and seal. Marinate overnight in the refrigerator.
5. The following day, preheat an electric double sided grill (such as George Foreman(R) grill) according to manufacturers' directions. Sprinkle the eggplant slices with garlic powder and onion powder.
6. Remove the portobello mushrooms from the marinade, and discard the remaining marinade. Cook on the preheated grill until tender 4 to 5 minutes.

Cook the eggplant slices on the preheated grill until tender 4 to 5 minutes. Remove, set onto a plate, and sprinkle with Parmesan cheese. Set aside.
7. To assemble the sandwiches, spread each slice of focaccia with ranch dressing. Place a slice of cheese on each piece of bread. Place the eggplant slices, roasted peppers, and a portobello mushroom onto four of the slices of bread. Top with the remaining bread.
8. Spray the double sided grill with cooking spray, and cook the sandwiches until the cheese has melted, the sandwiches are hot in the center, and the bread is golden brown, 4 to 5 minutes.

Portobello Mushrooms With Taleggio and P

Servings: 2 | Cook: 3 mins | Prep: 20 mins | Total Time: 23mins

Ingredients
- 2 ciabatta rolls
- 2 tablespoons basil pesto
- 4 large portabella mushrooms, stems removed
- 2 tablespoons balsamic vinegar
- 3 1/2 ounces taleggio cheese
- sea salt
- fresh ground black pepper
- vegetable oil, for sauting and brushing

Directions
1. Preheat a Panini grill.
2. Trim the top and bottom off the ciabatta rolls so that they are about 1 inch thick.
3. Slice open lengthwise.
4. Spread the pesto on the inside of each roll.
5. Brush the mushrooms with oil and drizzle with balsamic vinegar; season with salt and pepper and grill for 1-2 minutes in the preheated Panini press.
6. Place the mushrooms on roll bottoms and top with the cheese; cover with roll tops.
7. Brush both sides of the Panini with a little oil and grill in the preheated Panini grill for 2-3 minutes or according to the manufacturer's instructions.
8. The bread should be golden brown and the filling warmed through.
9. Serve with a dollop of grainy mustard on the side for dipping.

Portobello Panini

Servings: 4 | Cook: 10 mins | Prep: 15 mins | Total Time: 25mins

Ingredients
- 1 lb portabella mushroom, gently wiped clean with a damp paper towel
- 1/2 cup extra-virgin olive oil, plus more for drizzling
- 1 small focaccia bread, loaf
- 7 (1 ounce) packages fresh goat cheese, such as Chavrie, sliced in 4 equal slices lengthwise
- 1 small bunch arugula (can substitute spinach)
- 2 tablespoons truffle oil

Directions
1. Preheat panini grill or sandwich press to high.
2. Remove the gills from the portobello mushrooms and marinate with olive oil.
3. Grill the mushrooms until tender, about 3-4 minutes per side. Remove from the grill and set on a paper towel to drain. Cut the focaccia into 4 pieces, slice them horizontally, and drizzle with some olive oil.
4. Lay the 4 bottom slices of focaccia on a flat surface. Layer mushrooms evenly on each slice. Place a slice of goat cheese on each piece. Top with arugula and drizzle with truffle oil.
5. Put the tops on and gently press each sandwich to flatten it slightly. Drizzle some more olive oil over the tops. Place each sandwich on a preheated panini press and grill until the bread is toasted and the cheese is bubbly. Serve immediately.

Preposterously Paradisiacal Panini

This was the first panini I made on my grill/press and dayam, sam! That's an impressive little machine! If you don't have a panini press, you can use a brick well-wrapped in foil and a skillet, but it's not nearly as much fun. ;o)
Servings: 4 | Cook: 5 mins | Prep: 5 mins | Total Time: 10mins

Ingredients
- Standard Ingredients
- 1 loaf ciabatta
- 4 tablespoons fresh basil pesto (I highly recommend Kittencal's Perfect Pesto)
- 4 slices smoked provolone cheese
- 1 bunch arugula
- 12 slices black forest ham (uncured, if possible)

- olive oil
- Optional Ingredients
- 2 roma tomatoes (thinly sliced) (optional)
- 3 tablespoons mayonnaise (optional)

Directions
1. Preheat panini grill.
2. Cut a thin slice from the top of the loaf of ciabatta to make the top flat. Cut loaf into four sections. Then cut each section in half. You should end up with eight "slices" of bread for four sandwiches.
3. Lightly baste the OUTSIDE of each slice of bread with olive oil.
4. Spread 1 tablespoon pesto on the inside of 4 of the slices and mayonnaise, if using, on the inside of the other 4.
5. Layer the following on top of each pesto layer: Several arugula leaves, 1 slice provolone, thin slices of tomato if using, and 3 slices of black forest ham. Cover with the other slice of bread and place on panini grill/press. Close press and grill for 2-4 minutes or until browned to your liking.

Prosciutto & Smoked Cheddar Panini

For a quick lunch or supper, try this fancy, uptown take on grilled cheese sandwiches. They're fast and easy but good enough for entertaining.
Cook: 5 mins | Prep: 5 mins | Total Time: 10mins

Ingredients
- 8 slices white bread
- 8 slices smoked cheddar cheese
- 4 thin slices prosciutto
- 3 tablespoons olive oil

Directions
1. On four slices of bread, layer a slice of cheese, a slice of prosciutto, and a second slice of cheese. Top with remaining bread.
2. Lightly brush both sides of sandwiches with oil. Cook in a panini maker or indoor grill until bread is toasted and cheese is melted.

Prosciutto and Egg Panini

Servings: 4 | Cook: 15 mins | Prep: 5 mins | Total Time: 20mins

Ingredients
- 8 large eggs
- 1/2 teaspoon kosher salt
- 1/4 teaspoon black pepper
- 2 tablespoons unsalted butter
- 4 soft sandwich buns, halved lengthwise
- 8 ounces prosciutto, thinly sliced
- 8 ounces Swiss cheese, thinly sliced

Directions
1. In a small bowl whisk together the eggs, salt, and pepper.
2. Melt 1 tablespoon of the butter in a large nonstick skillet over medium heat.
3. Pour in the eggs and scramble until cooked through.
4. Divide the eggs among the bottom halves of the rolls.
5. Add the prosciutto and cheese and sandwich with the tops of the rolls.
6. Melt the remaining butter in a grill pan or large nonstick skillet over medium heat.
7. Add half the sandwiches to the skillet.
8. Cook, pressing frequently with the back of a spatula or placing another pan on top of the sandwiches to weigh them down, until the cheese has melted and the bread is golden, 4 to 6 minutes.
9. Repeat with the remaining sandwiches.

Prosciutto And Fontina Panini

Servings: 4 | Cook: 15 mins | Prep: 10 mins | Total Time: 25mins

Ingredients
- 1 (5 1/4 ounce) package focaccia bread
- 8 slices prosciutto (about 2 ounces)
- 1/4 cup shredded Fontina cheese
- 1 cup trimmed arugula or 1 cup watercress
- 2 red onions, slices separated into rings (1/8-inch-thick)
- 2 teaspoons balsamic vinegar
- 1/8 teaspoon pepper

Directions
1. Slice each bread round in half horizontally.
2. Divide prosciutto slices between bottom halves of bread, and top each bread half with fontina cheese, arugula, and red onion slices.

3. Drizzle balsamic vinegar over sandwiches, and sprinkle with pepper; cover with top halves of bread.
4. Wrap sandwiches tightly in aluminum foil, and bake at 300° for 15 minutes.

Prosciutto and Provolone Panini Sandwiches

"The perfect flavor combo--prosciutto, Provolone, pesto, and roasted bell peppers--on rustic bread and toasted in a panini press makes a great lunch or a quick, light dinner."

Pre: *15 m* | **Cook:** *19 m*

Ingredients
- 1/2 cup CARAPELLI® Extra Virgin Olive Oil
- 8 slices rustic Italian or sourdough bread
- 1/4 cup prepared basil pesto
- 16 thin slices Provolone cheese
- 12 thin slices prosciutto
- 4 whole, well-drained bottled roasted red peppers, cut into strips
- Add all ingredients to list

Directions
1. Heat a panini grill or waffle iron. Brush oil over bread slices. Turn 4 slices over; spread pesto evenly over bread. Top with half of the cheese, tearing to fit if necessary, all of the prosciutto and pepper strips and remaining cheese. Close sandwiches with remaining bread oiled sides up.
2. Cook (in batches) in panini maker* or waffle iron 3 to 4 minutes or until golden brown and cheese is melted.

Prosciutto Balsamic Fig Fontina and Ar

Servings: *2* | **Cook:** *3 mins* | **Prep:** *20 mins* | **Total Time:** *23mins*

Ingredients
- 2 ciabatta rolls
- 4 slices prosciutto
- 2 -3 ripe figs, sliced
- 2 teaspoons balsamic vinegar
- arugula (2 handfuls)
- 2 1/2 ounces Fontina cheese
- sea salt

- fresh ground black pepper
- vegetable oil, for sauting and brushing

Directions
1. Preheat a Panini grill.
2. Trim the top and bottom off the ciabatta rolls so that they are about 1 inch thick.
3. Slice open lengthwise.
4. On roll bottoms, layer with prosciutto, then fig slices; sprinkle with vinegar and season to taste with salt and pepper; add the arugula and then the cheese; cover with roll tops.
5. Brush both sides of the Panini with oil and grill in the preheated Panini press for 3 minutes , or according to the manufacturer's instructions.
6. The bread should be golden brown and the filling warmed through.

Prosciutto Bel Paese and Sweet Onion P

Bel Paese means "beautiful country".
Servings: 4 | **Cook:** 5 mins | **Prep:** 15 mins | **Total Time:** 20mins

Ingredients
- 4 ciabatta rolls
- 8 slices prosciutto di Parma
- 3/4 cup sweet onion (Sweet Onions)
- 4 ounces bel paese cheese, thinly sliced

Directions
1. Preheat a panini grill.
2. Slice off the domed tops of the ciabatta rolls; the rolls should be about 1 inch thick with a crusty bottom and exposed bread top; split rolls horizontally.
3. Layer 2 slices of prosciutto on the bottom of each ciabatta; followed by 3 tablepsoons of Sweet Onions.
4. Lay the Bel Paese over the onions, covering the sandwich entirely before closing up with the thin top of the ciabatta.
5. Grill each sandwich for about 5 minutes until the bread is golden brown and the cheese has gently melted.
6. Cut each sandwich in half; serve immediately.

Prosciutto Brie and Apple Panini With S

Servings: 4 | **Cook:** 10 mins | **Prep:** 5 mins | **Total Time:** 15mins

Ingredients
- 4 tablespoons unsalted butter, softened
- 2 teaspoons unsalted butter, softened
- 1 scallion, finely chopped
- 1/2 teaspoon fresh lemon juice
- 1/4 teaspoon Dijon mustard
- 4 soft hoagie rolls or 1 long baguette, halved lengthwise
- 3/4 lb thinly sliced prosciutto
- 1/2 lb brie cheese, rind removed, cheese cut into 4 pieces
- 1 large granny smith apple (peeled, cored and thinly sliced)

Directions
1. In a bowl, beat 4 tablespoons of the butter until creamy. Stir in the scallion, lemon juice and mustard until smooth.
2. Preheat a griddle over low heat. Spread the scallion butter on the cut sides of the rolls. Lay the prosciutto on the bottom halves; top with the Brie and the apple slices and close the sandwiches. Lightly spread the remaining 2 teaspoons of butter on the outside of the rolls (it will be a very thin layer).
3. Put the sandwiches on the griddle. Cover with a heavy skillet and cook over low heat, turning occasionally, until toasted and the Brie is melted, 10 minutes. Cut the panini in half and serve.

Prosciutto Cotto Mozzarella and Hot Mu

Italian prosciuttos are designated prosciutto cotto, which is cooked, and prosciutto crudo, which is raw (though, because of its curing, ready to eat). This recipe uses prosciutto cotto.

Servings: 4 | **Cook:** 3 mins | **Prep:** 20 mins | **Total Time:** 23mins

Ingredients
- 4 ciabatta rolls
- 1/4 cup hot mustard (Hot Mustard)
- 12 slices prosciutto, cotto
- 1 cup baby arugula leaf
- 8 ounces fresh mozzarella cheese, thinly sliced

Directions

1. Preheat a panini grill.
2. Slice off the domed tops of the ciabatta rolls; the rolls should now be about 1 inch thick; split rolls horizontally.
3. Coat the tops and bottoms of the ciabatta with a smattering of Hot Mustard.
4. Use 3 slices of prosciutto cotto to cover the bottom halves of the rolls.
5. Follow with a spread of arugula leaves and top with sliced mozzarella, covering the sandwich from end to end with a thin, even layer of cheese; set roll tops in place.
6. Grill the sandwiches for 3 minutes until the bread is crisp and toasted, and the cheese is warmed and slightly melted.

Prosciutto Fontina and Tomato Grilled P

This is one gooooood sandwich!! Because the class I received this recipe in was named "Breads from the Grill", this recipe is written to be prepared on a "grill". If you have a panini press or grill pan, you can use them also. You will need a "weight" if making this on a grill or grill pan, such as a cast iron skillet or a foil wrapped fire brick.
Servings: 4 | **Cook:** 10 mins | **Prep:** 15 mins | **Total Time:** 25mins

Ingredients

- 1 loaf rustic bread (1 lb.)
- 1/4 cup balsamic vinegar
- 1/2 cup olive oil
- 5 ounces Fontina cheese, thinly sliced
- 6 ounces prosciutto
- 1/2 lb tomatoes, thinly sliced
- kosher salt
- fresh ground black pepper

Directions

1. Preheat grill to LOW.
2. Whisk together the balsamic vinegar and olive oil in a small bowl.
3. Using a serrated knife, carefully trim the top and bottom crusts off of the loaf of bread. You just want to create a flat surface exposing the "white" or inside of the bread, leaving as MUCH bread as possible for the sandwich.
4. Cut the loaf horizontally into two 1/2 inch thick slices.
5. Lightly brush the inside of each slice with the balsamic mixture.
6. Place a single layer of cheese on the bottom half.
7. Then add a layer of prosciutto, then tomatoes.
8. Lightly salt and pepper to taste.

9. Finish with another layer of sliced cheese and top with other half of bread, brushed half to the inside.
10. Brush sandwich on both sides with olive oil.
11. Oil the grill grates lightly with oil.
12. Place the sandwich on the grill and place a weight on top. The weight presses the sandwich making deep grill marks.
13. Close the lid and gill panini for about 3 min, until nice and golden brown with nice grill marks.
14. Using a spatula, flip the panini over, place the weight back on top and grill for another 3 min or until the cheese has melted and itis a nice golden brown.
15. Cut into triangles or rectangles, the size of 3 good bites and serve hot.

Prosciutto Mozzarella Tomato & Ba

This is delicious and just what you want from an Italian sandwich!
Servings: *4 |* ***Cook:*** *10 mins |* ***Prep:*** *15 mins |* ***Total Time:*** *25mins*

Ingredients
- 1/2 cup olive oil
- 3 tablespoons balsamic vinegar
- 1 large garlic clove, minced
- 8 ounces thinly sliced prosciutto
- 10 ounces thinly sliced whole-milk mozzarella cheese
- 12 tomatoes, slices
- 12 large fresh basil leaves
- 16 ounces ciabatta, halved horizontally (13x6 1/2x1 1/2 inches)
- salt
- pepper

Directions
1. Whisk olive oil, vinegar, and garlic in small bowl to blend; season dressing to taste with salt and pepper.
2. Layer prosciutto, mozzarella, tomatoes, and basil over bottom of bread.
3. Drizzle lightly with dressing, then sprinkle with salt and pepper.
4. Press top of bread over.
5. Cut bread equally into 4 sandwiches.
6. Prepare barbecue (medium heat).
7. Grill sandwiches until bread is golden brown and cheese melts, pressing occasionally to compact with large spatula, about 5 minutes per side.

Prosciutto Nectarine and Fontina Panin

The rosemary in the focaccia is what makes this sandwich special. Do yourself a favor, if you cannot get the bread, use whatever you have, but add some fresh chopped rosemary in the sandwich, you will not be sorry! The idea for this recipe comes from Yahoo! Shine. Sandwich is still pretty good room temperature, but does heat fairly well, so is a good candidate to take to work or lunch!
Servings: 1 | **Cook:** 5 mins | **Prep:** 10 mins | **Total Time:** 15mins

Ingredients
- 1 large nectarine, pitted and peeled, cut in 1/4 inch slices
- 2 slices of rosemary focaccia bread, 1/2 inch thick
- 1 tablespoon unsalted butter, softened
- 2 slices Fontina cheese
- 3 -4 slices imported prosciutto
- fresh ground black pepper
- 1 small handful fresh arugula

Directions
1. Preheat grill or panini maker to high; grill nectarine slices until grill marks appear, but they are not mushy, less than a minute.
2. Spread butter on what will be the outsides of your sandwich and place on a clean work surface.
3. Layer a slice of fontina on the unbuttered side of the bottom, top with prosciutto, nectarine; season generously with pepper, add a handful of arugula, top with fontina slice and sliced bread, buttered side up.
4. Place sandwich on grill or panini maker and cook until the bread is browned and crispy, 2 to 3 minutes (per side if grilled); cut in half, if desired, and serve immediately.

Prosciutto Roasted Red Pepper and Mozzar

Got this off of 30 Minute Meals. This is my new favorite sandwich. I got a Panini maker a couple of months ago and this is made quite frequently on it!
Servings: 4 | **Cook:** 6 mins | **Prep:** 5 mins | **Total Time:** 11mins

Ingredients
- 1/3 lb thinly sliced prosciutto di Parma
- 8 slices chewy crust Italian bread, from a large loaf (I use Turano brand)
- 1 (16 ounce) jar roasted red peppers, drained well
- 1 lb fresh mozzarella cheese, sliced

- olive oil, for drizzling

Directions
1. Preheat a grill pan or large nonstick griddle over medium to medium high heat.
2. Build your sandwiches: place 2 or 3 slices of prosciutto on 1 piece of bread.
3. Top with an even layer of roasted red pepper and an even layer of mozzarella.
4. Top with another slice of bread.
5. Drizzle the tops of the assembled sandwiches with olive oil.
6. Place the olive oil coated bread face down on the grill or griddle and drizzle the opposite side with addition olive oil.
7. Weight the sandwiches down with a tin foil covered brick or a heavy skillet filled with a sack of flour (If using a panini maker-- just close the lid-- no need to flip).
8. Press the sandwiches for 2 or 3 minutes on each side, then serve immediately.

Quick and Yummy Meatball Panini's

A semi-homemade recipe I came up with trying to please my son's craving for a meatball grinder (New England name for a sub or hoagie) and my wish not to waste a loaf of ciabatta bread I had bought the day before. The result? My son said they were "amazing" and he was glad I didn't order out and I thought they were quite yummy myself! FYI - the infused olive oil can be stored in the refrigerator in a sealed container to be used later in the week in any pasta or Italian dish. The leftover sauce and meatballs, if any, can be saved for later use as well.
Cook: *20 mins |* **Prep:** *5 mins |* **Total Time:** *25mins*

Ingredients
- 1 loaf ciabatta, sliced in half lengthwise and then in quarters to make 4 sandwiches
- 1 (26 ounce) jar marinara sauce
- 12 ounces frozen meatballs (varies depending on size of meatballs)
- 3 tablespoons olive oil
- 2 garlic cloves, minced
- 2 tablespoons Italian seasoning
- 4 slices mozzarella cheese (deli sliced)

Directions
1. Add olive oil, garlic and Italian seasoning to a small saucepan and heat over low heat, stirring occasionally.
2. Add marinara sauce and meatballs to a medium sauce pan and heat over medium heat, stirring occasionally.

3. When the sauce is hot and the meatballs are heated all the way through turn off the heat and remove meatballs from the sauce.
4. Remove the olive oil from the heat and over a small bowl, pour the oil mixture through a small metal strainer.
5. Using the back of a metal spoon, scrape the bottom of the strainer, pushing the garlic "paste" into the bowl.
6. Brush a thin layer of the flavored oil onto the cut sides of the bread.
7. Spread a thin layer of marinara sauce over one side of the bread.
8. Cut each meatball in half and place them in an even layer over the marinara sauce.
9. Place a slice of mozzarella cheese over the meatballs.
10. Place the other slice of bread on top of the cheese covered meatballs.
11. Heat an indoor grill pan over medium high heat.
12. Place the sandwiches on the grill and cover with a bacon press or other heavy object and cook just until nice grill marks appear.
13. Turn the sandwiches over and place the bacon press on top and cook just long enough to see grill marks.
14. Serve.

Ratatouille Grilled Panini

Servings: *4 | **Cook:** 10 mins | **Prep:** 5 mins | **Total Time:** 15mins*

Ingredients
- 3/4 cup extra virgin olive oil
- 2 large garlic cloves, crushed
- 1 eggplant, peeled lengthwise in 2 places to make stripes and sliced lenthwise 1/2 inch thick
- 1 zucchini, sliced lengthwise 1/2 inch thick
- salt and pepper
- herbes de provence
- 2 bell peppers, quartered lengthwise
- 1 loaf ciabatta, split horizontally
- 8 slices Swiss cheese or 8 slices Fontina cheese
- 2 cups arugula leaves
- 1/3 cup store-bought olive tapenade

Directions
1. Heat a grill or grill pan over medium heat. In a small saucepan, combine the olive oil and garlic and heat on the grill (or on the stovetop over medium heat).

2. Brush the eggplant and zucchini on both sides with the garlic oil; season with salt, pepper and herbes de provence. Place on the grill along with the bell peppers and cook, turning once, until crisp-tender, 6 to 8 minutes.
3. Arrange the vegetables on the bread loaf bottom and top with the cheese and arugula. Spread the bread top with the tapenade and set in place. Place the sandwich on the grill and cover with 2 bricks covered in foil or place in a skillet piled with heavy cans. Press the sandwich until crisp on top, about 2 minutes. Flip and repeat. Cut into 4 portions.

Ratatouille Sandwich

"A healthier vegetarian sandwich great at lunch or after work or school."
*Pre: 30 m | **Cook:** 16 m | **Ready In:** 46 m*

Ingredients
SAUCE:
- 1 red bell pepper, sliced
- 1 tomato, chopped
- 1 clove garlic, minced
- 1 teaspoon dried oregano, or to taste
- salt and ground black pepper to taste

SANDWICH:
- 1 eggplant, sliced
- 1 zucchini, sliced
- 1 tomato, sliced
- 1 red onion, sliced
- 4 teaspoons olive oil
- 4 slices sourdough bread
- 4 slices mozzarella cheese
- Add all ingredients to list

Directions
1. Preheat a panini press according to manufacturer's instructions.
2. Grill red bell pepper slices in the panini press on high heat until soft, about 5 minutes. Transfer to a blender.
3. Place chopped tomato and garlic in the blender. Blend with bell pepper until a smooth sauce forms, about 2 minutes. Season sauce with oregano, salt, and black pepper.
4. Grill eggplant, zucchini, tomato, and onion slices in the panini press until softened, about 3 minutes per side.
5. Drizzle olive oil over bread slices; flip and spread with a generous amount of sauce. Place 2 slices bread, oil-side down, on the panini press; add 1 slice of

mozzarella cheese. Top with eggplant mixture and second slice of mozzarella cheese. Place second slice of bread, oil-side up, on top.
6. Grill on medium-high until golden and cheese is melted, about 5 minutes.

Red Pepper Egg and Provolone Panini

Yummy! This recipe was adapted from one published in Relish magazine, which comes as an insert in our local newspaper. Their suggestion of adding sautéed or grilled red onion slices for variety sounds good, too.
Servings: 2 | **Cook:** 10 mins | **Prep:** 5 mins | **Total Time:** 15mins

Ingredients
- 4 slices crusty Italian bread, 1/2-inch thick (recipe called for Sicilian-style sesame semolina bread, which is not in this ingredient database)
- 3 large eggs
- 3/4 teaspoon dried oregano
- 1/4 teaspoon salt
- 1/4 teaspoon fresh ground black pepper
- 1/2 cup jarred roasted red pepper, drained (feel free to roast your own, of course)
- 2 ounces sharp provolone cheese, sliced
- 1 ounce parmesan cheese, sliced
- olive oil

Directions
1. Preheat panini grill or stove-top griddle pan (see note below).
2. In a small bowl, beat eggs, oregano, salt, and pepper with a fork.
3. Heat a nonstick skillet over medium-high heat; add egg mixture.
4. Cook, lifting the edges with a fork, until set (2 to 3 minutes).
5. Divide eggs, peppers and cheeses between 2 slices of bread (I really just eyeballed most of the ingredients); top with remaining bread slices and brush outsides lightly with oil.
6. Place on panini grill or griddle and cover with grill top or grill press; grill until golden and cheese starts to melt (2 to 3 minutes per side).
7. Note: I just use a Foreman grill to make panini--I was given the grill several years ago as a gift and can't say I use it for anything else, but it does make great sandwiches :).

Roasted Garlic & Shallot Smear for

Great for Panini sandwiches. This recipe came with my panini maker.
Servings: 6 | **Cook:** 45 mins | **Prep:** 5 mins | **Total Time:** 50mins

Ingredients
- 10 shallots
- 5 heads garlic
- 2 ounces olive oil
- 2 ounces balsamic vinegar
- 2 anchovy fillets (optional)
- 1 tablespoon chopped fresh rosemary
- 4 ounces goat cheese
- salt and pepper

Directions
1. Cut the tops off garlic heads.
2. Drizzle 1 tablespoon olive oil over each garlic head.
3. Sprinkle salt on each.
4. Wrap garlic heads in aluminum foil.
5. Place in 425-450 degree oven fro 40-45 minutes (until the garlic is soft and browned).
6. Trim shallots.
7. Sprinkle with olive oil and add salt.
8. Wrap in 2 packets of aluminum foil.
9. Place shallots into oven the last 10 to 15 minutes of roasting the garlic.
10. Roast until golden brown, about 15 minutes, then cool to room temperature.
11. Place peeled garlic and shallots into a food processor, add remaining ingredients, and process until smooth.
12. Refrigerate until needed.

Roasted Pepper and Artichoke Panini

Quik and easy for lunch or dinner. We threw these together tonight and were surprised with the wonderful results.
Cook: 5 mins | **Prep:** 15 mins | **Total Time:** 20mins

Ingredients
- 2 tablespoons oil
- 1/2 cup onion, sliced

- 1 teaspoon garlic, minced
- 1/2 cup marinated artichoke hearts, drained
- 1 (8 ounce) jar roasted red peppers, drained (or roast 2 peppers and peel)
- 1/2 teaspoon dried dill (or herb of your choice)
- 1/2 cup frozen spinach, thawed and drained
- 1/2 cup parmesana cheese, grated (not the powdered kind)
- 1/4 cup feta cheese, crumbled
- 4 flour tortillas (or wrap of your choice)
- 1/2 cup cherry tomatoes, cut in half

Directions
1. Heat oil in skillet on medium heat.
2. Add onion, cook until translucent, 3-5 minutes.
3. Add garlic to pan, cook for 2 additional minutes.
4. Reduce heat to low, add red peppers, artichokes, spinach, and herbs. Cook until just warm. Remove from heat.
5. Place 1/3 cup pepper mixture on one half of wrap.
6. Top with 1 tablespoon feta and 2 tablespoons parmesana.
7. Fold in half.
8. Spray with oil and place on grill untill browned and warm.
9. Remove from heat.
10. Open and add cherry tomatoes and sprinkle with salt.

Roasted Red Pepper and Artichoke Panini

this is a tasty, quick vegetarian meal. i often use other spreads in place of pesto- i especially love trader joes eggplant garlic one! any good melting cheese will work but the best i have used are monterey jack, havarti, munster and mozzarella- mild white cheeses seem to be a good fit.
Cook: *5 mins |* **Prep:** *5 mins |* **Total Time:** *10mins*

Ingredients
- 1 ciabatta roll
- 2 tablespoons pesto sauce
- 1 -2 ounce monterey jack cheese (or other)
- 3 marinated artichoke hearts
- 1 roasted red pepper
- 1 teaspoon olive oil

Directions

1. spread half of the pesto on one piece of ciabatta and the other half on the other piece.
2. top with cheese, chopped artichoke hearts and 1 layer of roasted red pepper (i use trader joes jarred, they are wonderful!).
3. brush the outside of the roll on the top and bottom with olive oil and grill on panini press (you can just bake if you dont have one) until crispy and melted.

Roasted Red Pepper Provolone Panini

This a yummy combo I put together for my dad, he loved it
Servings: 1 | **Cook:** 5 mins | **Prep:** 0 mins | **Total Time:** 5mins

Ingredients

- 1/4 loaf bread (your choice) or 2 slices bread (your choice)
- 3 slices prosciutto
- 1 jarred roasted red pepper (or more to taste)
- 2 slices provolone cheese
- olive oil

Directions

1. Place prosciutto , pepper, and cheese on bread.
2. Heat Grill pan and have something heavy near by to weigh down the lid.
3. Lighty oil pan and add panini.
4. Press down on top with another pan or heavy plate, cook untill ightly browned.
5. Flip and cook other side.
6. Enoy.
7. Add whatever additions.

Rosemary Garlic and Mushroom Panini

Adapted from a savory flat pie recipe by Katie Joel.
Servings: 4 | **Cook:** 20 mins | **Prep:** 10 mins | **Total Time:** 30mins

Ingredients

- 2 tablespoons unsalted butter
- 1 tablespoon olive oil
- 2 garlic cloves, peeled and crushed
- 2 sprigs fresh rosemary

- 2 cups sliced fresh mushrooms (any type)
- 1 teaspoon kosher salt
- 1/2 teaspoon fresh ground black pepper
- 4 ounces brie cheese or 4 ounces camembert cheese, sliced
- 8 slices artisan ciabatta or 8 slices sourdough bread

Directions
1. Saute garlic and rosemary in a mixture of butter and olive oil until fragrant.
2. Add mushrooms, salt and pepper, and cook until mushrooms soften.
3. Discard garlic and rosemary.
4. Divide mushrooms and cheese among 4 slices bread.
5. Top with remaining bread and toast using a panini pan or grill.

Salami Fontina and Roasted Bell Pepper

Panini for lunch?
Servings: 1 | Cook: 5 mins | Prep: 5 mins | Total Time: 10mins

Ingredients
- 1/4 cup extra virgin olive oil
- 1 rosemary sprig, leaves
- 2 slices sourdough bread, each 1/2 inch thick
- 1 ounce thinly sliced tuscan salami
- 1 ounce sliced Fontina cheese
- 1/4 cup sliced roasted red pepper

Directions
1. In a small saucepan over medium heat, warm the olive oil.
2. Add the rosemary and fry until just fragrant, about 20 seconds.
3. Remove from the heat and let cool.
4. Preheat an electric panini maker according to the manufacturer's instructions.
5. Brush one side of each bread slice lightly with the rosemary oil.
6. Lay a bread slice, oiled side down, and arrange the salami and cheese on the bread. Add the bell peppers and top with the other bread slice, oiled side up.
7. Place the sandwich on the preheated panini maker and cook according to the manufacturer's instructions until the sandwich is hot throughout, golden and crispy.
8. Transfer the sandwich to a cutting board and cut in half.
9. Serve immediately.
10. Serves 1.

Sardine and Balsamic Tomato Panini

Servings: 2 | Cook: 5 mins | Prep: 5 mins | Total Time: 10mins

Ingredients
- 1/2 cup tomatoes, chopped, seeded
- 1 teaspoon balsamic vinegar
- 1 tablespoon parsley, chopped
- 1 pinch salt
- fresh ground black pepper, to taste
- 4 slices Italian bread (1/2-inch thick)
- 1 tablespoon olive oil
- 2 teaspoons mustard
- 4 oil-packed sardines, drained and mashed
- 1/2 cup parmesan cheese, freshly grated

Directions
1. In a bowl, combine tomatoes, vinegar, salt and pepper.
2. Brush one side of each bread slice with oil. Place two slices on a work surface, oiled side down, and spread with mustard. Evenly layer with sardines, tomato mixture and cheese. Cover with top halves, oiled side up, and press gently to pack.
3. Place sandwiches on heated panini or George Foreman grill, close the top and cook until golden brown.

Scrambled Egg Breakfast Panini

I was just trying some different things out when I made this. I enjoyed the results. Note: Recipe makes 1 serving
Cook: 5 mins | Prep: 5 mins | Total Time: 10mins

Ingredients
- 2 slices white bread (any bread will do)
- 1 -2 egg
- cheddar cheese, grated
- 1 teaspoon butter, melted
- 2 -4 slices cooked turkey breast, thinly sliced or 2 -4 slices crisp cooked bacon

Directions
1. Scramble eggs in frying pan.

2. Melt butter. Brush onto each slice of bread.
3. Sprinkle cheese onto one side of bread.
4. Place turkey and/or bacon.
5. Place eggs on top of meat.
6. Place in panini maker or George Foreman Grill.

Scrambled Egg Panini

Servings: 4 | Cook: 10 mins | Prep: 10 mins | Total Time: 20mins

Ingredients
- 4 large eggs, beaten
- 1 tablespoon milk
- 1/4 teaspoon salt
- 1/4 teaspoon pepper
- 6 tablespoons butter, softened
- 8 slices bread
- 4 slices bacon, cooked
- 1/4 cup shredded cheddar cheese

Directions
1. In medium bowl, combine eggs, milk, salt and pepper.
2. In skillet melt 1 tablespoon butter and cook egg mixture. Set aside and wipe skillet clean.
3. Place bread on work surface. Spread with remaining butter. Place in skillet. Top with egg, cheese and bacon. Toast 3-5 minutes or until cheese is melted.

Smoked Cheddar & Ham Panini

Servings: 2 | Cook: 5 mins | Prep: 15 mins | Total Time: 20mins

Ingredients
- 1/4 large sweet onion, cut into thin slices
- 2 teaspoons maple syrup
- 4 slices whole wheat bread
- 1 tablespoon mayonnaise
- 1/2 large gala apples, cut into 4 slices
- 1/4-1/2 lb smoked ham, deli-sliced

- 2 ounces smoked cheddar cheese, cut into 4 thin slices

Directions
1. Cook onions until tender in a skillet prepared with non-stick cooking spray over medium-high heat.
2. When onion is browned, add syrup, stirring well, and cook for an additional minute.
3. Allow onion to cool. Spread 2 slices of bread with mayonnaise.
4. Layer remaining ingredients on top, ending with the second slice of bread on each sandwich.
5. Spray both sides of each sandwich with cooking spray before placing on panini grill or in skillet.
6. If using panini grill, grill the sandwiches for about 3 minutes, or until cheese is melted and bread is toasted.
7. If using a skillet, cook sandwich over medium heat for about 2 minutes on each side, flipping once, or until cheese is melted and bread is toasted. Use a second skillet to weight down the sandwich on top.

Smoked Salmon and Gruyere Panini

A very simple recipe with gourmet taste! From Food and Wine Magazine. The flavors of the smoked salmon, Gruyere cheese and Dijon mustard complement eachother very nicely. I enjoy the hint of lemon, too. This makes a simple lunch special.
Servings: 4 | **Cook:** 3 mins | **Prep:** 10 mins | **Total Time:** 13mins

Ingredients
- 8 slices brioche bread
- Dijon mustard, for spreading
- 8 thin slices gruyere cheese
- 1/2 lb smoked salmon, thinly sliced
- 1 lemon, finely grated zest
- kosher salt & freshly ground black pepper, to taste

Directions
1. Heat up a panini press.
2. Spread the Dijon mustard over each of 4 slices of the brioche. Top each one with 1 slice of the Gruyere. Divide all of the smoked salmon and grated lemon zest among the 4 slices of brioche. Season lightly with the salt and pepper and cover with the remaining slices on Gruyere. Close the sandwiches and grill on the panini press for 2 to 3 minutes, until the bread is toasted and the cheese is melted. Cut the panini in half and serve!

Spicy Garlic Panini Sauce

"A great sauce to add to your panini to give it a little kick!"
Pre: 5 m | **Cook:** 5 m

Ingredients
- 1 tablespoon mayonnaise
- 1 1/2 teaspoons hot pepper sauce (such as Tabasco®)
- 2 teaspoons garlic powder
- Add all ingredients to list

Directions
1. Stir the mayonnaise, hot pepper sauce, and garlic powder together in a bowl. Use immediately or keep refrigerated.

Spicy Tuna Panini

serve with salad
Servings: 3-4 | **Cook:** 15 mins | **Prep:** 10 mins | **Total Time:** 25mins

Ingredients
- 250 g tuna, in water derained
- 2 tablespoons extra light mayonnaise
- 2 tablespoons low fat yogurt
- 1 teaspoon chili flakes
- 1/2 teaspoon lime juice
- 150 g mozarrella cheese, sliced
- 2 tomatoes, sliced

Directions
1. Mix First 5 Thing Very Well.
2. Spread On Panini Bread. Then Put The Tomato Slice After That Cheese Slice On It.
3. Grill It And Enjoy It.

Spinach Lasagna Panini

Servings: 2 | **Cook:** 4 mins | **Prep:** 20 mins | **Total Time:** 24mins

Ingredients
- 1/4 cup ricotta cheese
- 1 tablespoon freshly grated parmesan cheese
- dried oregano
- dried basil
- 2 ciabatta rolls, split
- 1 tablespoon olive oil
- 1/4 cup pizza sauce or 1/4 cup marinara sauce
- 1/2 cup baby spinach leaves
- 1/2 cup shredded mozzarella cheese
- salt
- fresh ground black pepper

Directions
1. In a bowl, combine the ricotta, Parmesan, a generous pinch of oregano and basil.
2. Place rolls, cut side down, on a work surface and brush the crusts with oil.
3. Turn rolls over and spread pizza sauce over the bottom halves.
4. Evenly layer with ricotta mixture, spinach, and mozzarella.
5. Sprinkle with salt and pepper; cover with top halves and press gently to pack.
6. Place sandwiches in grill, close the top plate and cook until golden brown, 3-4 minutes.
7. Serve immediately.

Steak and Havarti Panini With My "secret Sauce"

I was making myself a steak panini with the leftovers of my steak that I had had for dinner the night before, added havarti cheese, and wanted a nice sauce to go on it. So I just looked in the fridge and came up with this crazy concoction! It was SO GOOD, I decided to not keep it a secret! What's the fun of it if you don't share? Hope you enjoy it as much as I did!

Cook: 2 mins | **Prep:** 15 mins | **Total Time:** 17mins

Ingredients
- 2 slices hearty bread or 2 slices white bread or 2 slices whole wheat bread or 2 slices rye bread, or your own preference
- 4 -8 slices cooked steak, depending on thickness of slices and size of bread

- 2 slices havarti cheese
- 2 slices onions
- 3 fresh mushrooms, quartered or sliced
- 2 tablespoons olive oil
- Secret Sauce
- 1 tablespoon A.1. Original Sauce
- 1 teaspoon A.1. Original Sauce
- 2 tablespoons mayonnaise
- 1/4-1/2 teaspoon prepared grated horseradish, as hot as you like it

Directions

1. In small bowl add steak sauce. (Both amounts). Whisk in mayo til smooth and no longer lumpy, then whisk in horseradish. Taste, adjust to your own preference, set aside.
2. In small saute pan, saute mushrooms and onion in ONE of the Tbls. of olive oil til crisp-tender or soft. Your own personal preference. Set aside.
3. Get (lightly oiled) cast iron griddle (or panini maker) heating til medium-hot.
4. Lay out 2 pieces of bread.
5. Drizzle 1 Tbl. sauce onto each slice, then spread with back of spoon til evenly coated.
6. Pour rest of sauce into tiny bowl for dipping later.
7. Top one slice with 1 slice of cheese.
8. Top cheese with steak, piling on. As much or little as you like.
9. Top with sauted mushrooms and onions.
10. Top onions and mushrooms with second slice of cheese.
11. Place other slice of bread on top, sauce-side down.
12. Brush top of bread lightly with olive oil.
13. Place olive oil-side down onto heated griddle.
14. Brush new top with a little olive oil.
15. Press lightly, once, with spatula.
16. Brown bottom. Depending on how hot your pan is, this will take about 30 seconds to 1 minute. Check now and then to prevent burning. You will want this lightly toasted with nice grill marks.
17. When bottom is to likeness, carefully turn over with a spatula and brown other side. (*I lift a corner with my spatula, then carefully hold it up with my fingers, then get under it with my spatula so you don't wreck the bread.) Do the same way when the second side is done.
18. When done, carefully remove and place on a cutting surface and cut in half diagonally.
19. Serve hot with extra sauce for dipping. (Sauce can be used to dip your sandwich in, or great for dipping french fries, too!).
20. *Whatever steak you have on hand works just fine. Whether it be cooked at the moment, or leftover. I used leftover prime rib, but any good steak or tenderloin can be used.

Sun Dried Tomato Pesto Red Onion and F

Uses make-ahead condiments for quick assembly.
***Servings:** 4 | **Cook:** 4 mins | **Prep:** 15 mins | **Total Time:** 19mins*

Ingredients
- 4 ciabatta rolls
- 1 cup sun-dried tomato pesto (Sun-Dried Tomato Pesto)
- salt
- fresh ground black pepper
- 1/2 cup pickled onion (Pickled Onions)
- 2 cups baby arugula, roughly chopped
- 8 ounces Italian fontina, sliced
- extra virgin olive oil

Directions
1. Preheat a panini grill.
2. Slice off the domed tops of the ciabatta rolls and discard; the rolls should now be about 1 inch thick; split the rolls horizontally.
3. Spread the bottom halves with sun-dried tomato pesto, about 1 tablespoon each, letting it soak into the bread; season with salt and pepper.
4. Squeeze the excess liquid from the pickled onions and divide among the 4 sandwiches.
5. Follow with a fistful of chopped arugula, then cover with a layer of fontina.
6. Finish with a light drizzle of olive oil before covering with the top halves of the rolls.
7. Grill the sandwiches for about 4 minutes until the bread is golden brown and the aroma of the cheese is apparent.
8. Cut sandwiches in half and serve hot.

Tangy Tuna Panini

Recently, I've began to love and discover different panini and grilled cheese in my grill panini. I saw this recipe of Rachael Ray and I think it looks very yummy.
***Servings:** 4 | **Cook:** 6 mins | **Prep:** 25 mins | **Total Time:** 31mins*

Ingredients
- 2 (6 ounce) cans tuna packed in oil, drained
- 1/2 cup extra virgin olive oil, plus more for brushing
- 1 lemon, rind of (grated peel of 1 lemon)
- 1/2 lemon, juice of (juice of 1/2 lemon)

- 1/2 cup red onion, finely chopped
- 1 celery rib, finely chopped
- 2 tablespoons sun-dried tomatoes, finely chopped
- salt and pepper
- 8 slices country bread
- 16 pepperoncini peppers, halved lenghtwise
- 4 large eggs

Directions
1. Preheat a panini press. In a medium bowl, flake the tuna. Stir in 1/4 cup olive oil, the lemon peel, lemon juice, onion, celery and sun-dried tomatoes; season with salt and pepper.
2. Brush each slice of bread on one side with olive oil and place oiled side down on a work surface. Divide the tuna salad amond 4 slices, making a well in the center. Top the tuna salad with the pepperoncini.
3. In a small nonstick skillet, heat the remaining 1/4 cup olive oil over high heat. One at a time, fry the eggs just until the egg whites set, about 1 minute each. Set one egg sunny-side up on top of the tuna and pepperoncini, aligning the yolk with the well. Set the remaining bread slices in place, oiled side up.
4. Working in batches, grill the sandwiches in the panini press until the bread is crisp and golden, about 1 minute.

The Spanish Ranch Panini

Ready, Set, Cook! Hidden Valley Contest Entry. Looking for a quick and satisfying meal? Look no farther-I have the solution! Thanks to the perfect blend of seasoning from the Hidden Valley Original Ranch Dressing Seasoning Mix, this unique sandwich is a recipe to remember! I combined classic Spanish ingredients together to create the perfect cheese spread. The chicken is moist, tender and perfectly seasoned. My favorite part however, is the golden, buttery bread with the kick of ranch grilled right into the sandwich. Lunch or dinner-you got to give this recipe a try!
Servings: *4 |* **Cook:** *30 mins |* **Prep:** *5 mins |* **Total Time:** *35mins*

Ingredients
- 8 tablespoons softened unsalted butter
- 2 ounces Hidden Valley® Original Ranch® Dressing and Seasoning Mix
- 2 boneless skinless chicken breasts
- 1/2 cup water
- 8 slices bakery fresh sourdough bread
- 4 ounces softened cream cheese
- 1/4 cup chopped black olives
- 1/2 cup canned artichoke heart, diced
- 4 teaspoons pimientos

- 1 tablespoon fresh grated lemon zest
- 1/3 cup grated parmesan cheese
- 2 cups fresh baby spinach leaves

Directions
1. Combine 6 tablespoons of the softened butter, and 2 tablespoons of the Hidden Valley Original Ranch Dressing Seasoning Mix in a small bowl. Set ranch butter aside.
2. Sprinkle 4 teaspoons of the Hidden Valley Original Ranch Dressing Seasoning Mix over chicken to season. Over medium high heat, add remaining 2 tablespoons of butter, along with seasoned chicken breast to skillet. Cook on each side for about 4 minutes each side to brown. Add water and cover pan with lid to complete cooking. Remove chicken when juices run clear, and chicken is no longer pink. Let rest for about four minutes, then slice each breast horizontally to create 4 thin pieces, or cut chicken into thin vertical strips. Place chicken back into pan and toss in any extra pan drippings, keep warm until needed.
3. To create the Spanish Cheese Spread, combine cream cheese, olives, artichokes, pimentos, lemon zest, Parmesan cheese and remaining Hidden Valley Original Ranch Dressing Seasoning Mix in a bowl. Stir well to combine.
4. If using a Panini maker (the preferred way), adjust to manufactures recommended setting to preheat grill.
5. Using the reserved ranch butter, spread butter on top of each slice of bread.
6. To create Paninis, place one slice of bread, buttered side down on grill, followed by ¼ of the chicken. Pile ½ cup of baby spinach leaves on top of chicken. On the second slice of bread, spread ¼ of the Spanish Cheese Spread on the bottom or "unbuttered" side. Place bread on top of spinach, buttered side up. Close Panini maker and grill for about 8 minutes, or until golden brown. If you are able, grill 2 Panini's at a time. Keep Paninis in a warm in a 200 degree oven until all sandwiches are complete. Note: If you do not have a Panini maker, no worries, just toast sandwiches in a skillet over medium low heat, for about 4-5 minutes each side, or until bread is golden brown.

The Ultimate Lemon & Herb Panini

You're gonna love this! I just felt like making this. I love lemons! so I found this amazing lemon and herb seasoning I mix with the melted butter; which makes it a whole lot better!
Servings: 1 | **Cook:** 5 mins | **Total Time:** 5mins

Ingredients
- 2 slices sourdough bread
- 1 1/4 tablespoons butter (melted)
- 1 lettuce leaf

- 1 slice hard salami
- 1 slice turkey
- 1 slice ham
- 1/2 teaspoon lemon & herb seasoning
- 1 slice American cheese

Directions

1. Preheat the panini grill or George Foreman grill (or any grill that looks like these grills because whatever it is, the sandwich needs to be pressed down).
2. Melt all the butter.
3. Assemble the sandwich. **do not fold the meat! paninis are supposed to be thin; not fully fat and loaded.**.
4. Brush the melted butter *but not all of it! enough to brown it* on the grilling side of the bread.
5. Grill for 5 minutes or till the desired golden brown color is at your liking.
6. Take the remaining melted butter and add the seasoning -- enough to where you like how it tastes. (I put about 1/2 tsp of it on my version).
7. Brush the seasoning butter onto the grilled part of the bread. again, enough to where you like how it tastes.
8. Serve while hot.
9. And its ok if the cheese melts out of the panini -- burnt cheese is always the best!

Thick As a Brick Panini

The main reason for posting this recipe is that I want to share this cooking method for Panini with you. This easy trick will give you a perfect Panini as an end result and you don't have to have a special grill.....just a brick wrapped in aluminum foil!!! Use this or your own favorite Panini recipe, mix and match ingredients or use whatever you have at hand.

Servings: *1-2* | **Cook:** *10 mins* | **Prep:** *10 mins* | **Total Time:** *20mins*

Ingredients

- 2 tablespoons mayonnaise
- 1/2 tablespoon mustard
- 1 tablespoon fresh herb, chopped (or some dried bruchetta herbs)
- 2 slices sourdough bread (thick slices)
- 6 slices gruyere cheese
- 4 slices cooked turkey breast
- 4 -6 slices tomatoes
- 6 slices salami
- 4 -6 slices mozzarella cheese

- 1-2 tablespoon olive oil (depending on the size of the bread) or 1-2 tablespoon canola oil (depending on the size of the bread)

Directions
1. You will also need: 1 brick wrapped in aluminum foil.
2. Mix together the mayonnaise, mustard and herbs.
3. Spread on one side of the bread slices.
4. Build your sandwich in this order: Gruyere, turkey, tomato, salami and end with the mozzarella.
5. Heat one tablespoon of oil, medium heat, in a frying pan that is large enough to hold the bread, add the bread to the pan and place the brick on top.
6. Fry for 3 to 5 minutes, make sure the heat is not too high, you don't want to burn the bread.
7. Remove the brick and bread from the pan, and add the other tablespoon of oil.
8. Return the bread to the pan to brown the other side, place the brick on top again and continue to fry until browned to your liking.
9. Remove the brick...and serve!

Toasted Fontina and Onion Jam Panini

Cook: 14 mins | Prep: 1 hr | Total Time: 1hr

Ingredients
- 4 tablespoons unsalted butter
- 2 lbs red onions, thinly sliced
- 1 teaspoon sugar
- 1 teaspoon salt
- 1 teaspoon minced fresh thyme
- 1/4 teaspoon fresh ground black pepper
- 1/4 cup balsamic vinegar
- 1 1/2 baguette, sliced into 56 slices
- 1/2 cup butter, at room temperature
- salt
- fresh ground black pepper
- 2 cups grated Fontina cheese

Directions
1. Heat a large skillet over med-high heat; add 4 tablespoons butter.
2. When it has melted, add the onions, sugar, salt, thyme, and black pepper.

3. Saute for 5 minutes, stirring the onions until they become soft, then turn the heat to low and cook the onions slowly, stirring occasionally, until they are very soft and browned, about 30 minutes.
4. Add the balsamic vinegar and turn the heat back to med-high.
5. Cook the onions until the vinegar has evaporated, about 1 minute.
6. Remove the pan from the heat and set aside.
7. Butter the baguette slices and lay them, buttered side down, on a work surface.
8. Spread some of the onion jam on the unbuttered side of half the baguettes, and season with salt and pepper if desired.
9. Top the onion jam with about 1 tablespoon of the grated cheese.
10. Top the cheese with a baguette slice, buttered side up.
11. Heat a panini maker or a large, nonstick skillet over medium heat.
12. Arrange 4 or 5 of the panini on the hot surface.
13. Close the lid of the panini maker or, if using, a skillet, weight the panini down with a smaller heavy skillet that fits inside the one you are cooking inches.
14. It should take about 2 minutes to cook the panini until brown in a panini maker.
15. If using a skillet, cook 2 minutes on the first side, 1-2 minutes on the second side.
16. Arrange the cooked panini on a platter.
17. Serve hot or at room temperature.

Toasted Provençal Panini (Sandwich)

From the boursin cheese website. Haven't tried it yet, but sounded good so posting for safe keeping.
Servings: 1 | **Cook:** 3 mins | **Prep:** 3 mins | **Total Time:** 6mins

Ingredients
- 2 slices bread, lightly toasted
- 1/3 cup boursin cheese, any flavor
- 1 medium plum tomato, sliced
- 3 ounces cooked ham, thinly sliced
- 2 tablespoons black olive tapenade
- drizzle extra virgin olive oil (optional)

Directions
1. Spread boursin cheese on one slice of bread.
2. On other slice of bread spread tapenade.
3. Prepare sandwich by layering tomato and ham.
4. Close sandwich.
5. Drizzle oil on outside of bread.

6. Grill in skillet or panini press.

Tubby's Pesto Panini

"This sandwich is tasty for lunch or dinner. I experimented and came up with it one night when I wanted to make something quick, easy, and tasty for my girlfriend who loves pesto sauce. Enjoy!"

Pre: 20 m | **Cook:** 16 m | **Ready In:** 36 m

Ingredients
- 1/4 cup packed fresh basil leaves
- 1/4 cup olive oil
- 4 cloves garlic, minced
- 2 tablespoons grated Romano cheese
- 1 teaspoon dried oregano
- 1 teaspoon ground black pepper
- 2 skinless, boneless chicken breast halves
- 2 tablespoons creamy Caesar salad dressing
- 6 (1/4 inch thick) slices Italian bread with sesame seeds (also known as Scali)
- 1/2 cup shredded iceberg lettuce
- 2 thin slices smoked mozzarella
- Add all ingredients to list

Directions
1. Preheat an outdoor grill for medium heat; lightly oil the grate.
2. Place basil, oil, garlic, Romano cheese, oregano, and pepper into a blender. Blend on high until smooth, adding additional oil if necessary, about 30 seconds.
3. Grill chicken until juices run clear, about 5 minutes per side. Do not turn off grill.
4. Spoon 1 tablespoon of Caesar dressing onto 2 slices of bread. Top each with lettuce, and an additional slice of bread. Spread the second slice of bread thickly with the pesto. Top each sandwich with a cooked chicken breast, a slice of smoked mozzarella, and the remaining bread.
5. Grill sandwiches until the cheese is melted, and the bread is toasted, about 3 minutes per side.

Tuna and Artichoke Panini

Servings: 4 | **Cook:** 5 mins | **Prep:** 5 mins | **Total Time:** 10mins

Ingredients

- 4 (3 ounce) cans tuna in olive oil, drained (oil reserved)
- 4 bread, rolls split
- 4 slices mozzarella cheese
- 1/4 cup parsley
- 1/4 cup basil, chopped
- 6 ounces marinated artichoke hearts, drained and chopped

Directions

1. In a bowl, lightly mash tuna.
2. Brush surfaces of rolls with oil from the tuna. Layer with half the cheese, all of the parsley, basil, tuna and artichokes. Top with remaining cheese. Replace tops of rolls.
3. Place sandwiches in panini press and cook 3-5 minutes.

Tuna and Gruyere Panini

Servings: 4 | Cook: 10 mins | Prep: 20 mins | Total Time: 30mins

Ingredients

- 6 tablespoons mayonnaise (I use Hellmans)
- 2 (8 ounce) jars tuna, packed in olive oil, drained. Reserving 1 T of the oil
- 1 tablespoon fresh lemon juice
- 1 teaspoon Dijon mustard
- 1/4 cup celery, finely diced
- 6 cloves mashed roasted garlic (See note at the bottom of the directions)
- 2 tablespoons flat leaf parsley, chopped
- 1 tablespoon capers, drained
- 1/4 teaspoon celery seed
- kosher salt & freshly ground black pepper, to taste
- 8 slices of multigrain sandwich bread
- 4 ounces gruyere cheese, thinly sliced

Directions

1. See note below for directions on roasted the garlic. Do this before preparing the paninis.
2. Mix the mayo with the 1 Tablespoon of the reserved tuna oil, the lemon juice, Dijon mustard, celery, garlic, parsley, capers and celery seeds. Mix in the tuna. Season with salt and pepper, to taste.
3. Spoon the tuna mixture onto 4 slices of the bread, then top each with 1 oz of Gruyere and then top with another slice of bread.

4. Toast the sandwiches in a panini press until they are golden and the cheese is melted.
5. *Note* To roast the garlic, place the unpeeled cloves on a sheet of aluminum foil and drizzle with olive oil. Seal the foil and roast the cloves at 300 degrees F. If I'm halving the recipe and only roasting 2 cloves, I roast them for 30 minutes. If you roast the whole garlic bulb it would take about 1 hour. You can always peek at them and touch to see when they are completely tender. let the cloves cool, then squeeze them out of their skins and mash them.

Tuna and Pepper Panini Melt

I recently acquired a panini grill and this is the first recipe that I tried on it. And is it ever good!
Servings: *4* | **Cook:** *5 mins* | **Prep:** *10 mins* | **Total Time:** *15mins*

Ingredients
- 12 ounces tuna, drained
- 1/2 sweet red pepper, diced
- 1/4 cup celery, diced
- 2 green onions, chopped
- 2 tablespoons mayonnaise
- 2 tablespoons plain yogurt
- 1 tablespoon capers, drained
- 1/2 teaspoon ground cumin
- 1/2 teaspoon ground black pepper
- 1/4 teaspoon salt
- 1/4 teaspoon cayenne pepper
- 4 Italian panini buns
- 1/2 cup cheddar cheese, shredded

Directions
1. In a bowl, mix together the tuna, red pepper, celery, green onions, mayonnaise, yogurt, capers, cumin, pepper, salt and cayenne pepper.
2. Cut the buns in half horizontally.
3. Spread the tuna mixture evenly over the bottom half of each.
4. Sprinkle each evenly with cheese.
5. Replace the bun tops.
6. In a nonstick skillet or panini grill, cook the sandwiches over medium heat, pressing often to flatten and turning once (no need to turn if using a panini grill), for about 5 minutes or until crusty and the cheese is melted.

Tuna Artichoke Panini

***Servings:** 2 | **Cook:** 5 mins | **Prep:** 10 mins | **Total Time:** 15mins*

Ingredients
- 1 (6 ounce) can tuna in olive oil
- 1 (6 ounce) jar artichoke hearts packed in oil, drained & chopped coarsely
- 1/8 cup sliced roasted red pepper
- 1/3 cup pitted kalamata olive, sliced thinly
- 1 teaspoon minced lemon zest
- 3/4 teaspoon dried oregano
- 1 tablespoon chopped fresh flat-leaf parsley
- salt and pepper
- 1/2 head roasted garlic
- 1/4 cup mayonnaise
- 1 teaspoon Dijon mustard
- 1 teaspoon lemon juice
- 4 slices light rye bread
- 1 tomatoes, sliced thinly
- 4 slices provolone cheese
- 8 slices mozzarella cheese
- olive oil

Directions
1. Combine the tuna (don't drain) with the drained, chopped artichokes, red peppers, olives, lemon zest, oregano, parsley and salt and pepper to taste. Set aside.
2. In a separate bowl, combine the roasted garlic with the mayonnaise, Dijon, lemon juice and a little bit of salt and pepper.
3. Spread the garlic mayonnaise on all four slices of bread, top two slices with provolone, then the tuna-artichoke mixture, then tomato slices and then mozzarella. Top with another slice of rye bread.
4. Preheat a panini grill, barbeque or cast iron skillet. Brush tops of both sandwiches with olive oil and flipping that side down, place on the grill. Brush what are now the tops of both sandwiches with more olive oil and close grill or wait to flip once bottom is browned. Sandwiches are done when bread is browned and cheese is melted.
5. Slice on an angle and serve.

Tuna Panini Melt

"A new twist on an old standby."
Pre: *10 m* | **Cook:** *3 m* | **Ready In:** *13 m*

Ingredients
- 1 (6 ounce) can solid white albacore tuna in water (such as Bumble Bee®)
- 1 tablespoon mayonnaise
- 1 tablespoon balsamic vinegar
- 1 tablespoon chopped onion
- 1 dill pickle, chopped
- 4 slices sourdough bread
- 2 slices American cheese
- Add all ingredients to list

Directions
1. Mix tuna, mayonnaise, balsamic vinegar, onion, and dill pickle together in a bowl.
2. Spread tuna mixture over 2 slices of bread. Top with American cheese and remaining 2 slices of bread.
3. Cook in a panini press until bread is crispy and cheese is melted, 3 to 4 minutes.

Tuna Panini

Servings: *4* | **Cook:** *8 mins* | **Prep:** *15 mins* | **Total Time:** *23mins*

Ingredients
- 3 tablespoons red onions, finely minced
- 3 tablespoons mayonnaise
- 1 teaspoon lemon zest
- 1/4 teaspoon fennel seed, crushed
- 1/4 teaspoon black pepper
- 3 slices bacon, COOKED and crumbled
- 2 (5 ounce) cans tuna in water, drained and flaked
- 8 slices sourdough bread
- 2 ounces provolone cheese, 4 slices
- cooking spray

Directions

1. Combine first 7 ingredients in a medium bowl, stirring well to coat.
2. Place 4 bread slices on a flat surface; top each bread slice with 1 CHEESE slice.
3. Divide tuna mixture evenly among bread slices; top each serving with 1 remaining bread slice.
4. HEAT a large skillet over medium heat.
5. Lightly coat sandwiches with cooking spray.
6. Place sandwiches in pan; top with ANOTHER heavy skillet.
7. Cook 3 minutes on each side or until lightly browned (leave skillet on sandwiches as they cook).

Tuscan Grill Panini

"Mix up weeknight dinner with this delicious alternative your family will love."
***Pre:** 10 m | **Cook:** 45 m*

Ingredients

- 1/2 cup KRAFT Tuscan House Italian Dressing and Marinade, divided
- 2 (4 ounce) boneless skinless chicken breast halves
- 1 red pepper, cut into strips
- 1 small zucchini, cut lengthwise in half, then sliced crosswise
- 4 slices Italian bread
- 1/2 cup KRAFT Shredded Low-Moisture Part-Skim Mozzarella Cheese
- 2 tablespoons chopped fresh basil
- Add all ingredients to list

Directions

1. Reserve 1 tablespoon dressing; pour remaining over chicken and vegetables in shallow dish. Stir vegetables and turn chicken to evenly coat both sides of each piece. Refrigerate 30 min. to marinate.
2. Heat panini grill. Meanwhile, drain chicken and vegetables; discard marinade. Cook chicken and vegetables in skillet on medium heat 10 min. or until chicken is done (165 degrees F) and vegetables are crisp-tender, turning chicken after 5 min. and stirring vegetables occasionally.
3. Fill bread slices with chicken, vegetables, cheese and basil to make 2 sandwiches; brush outsides with reserved dressing. Grill 5 min. or until golden brown.

Tuscan White Bean and Greens Panini

In 'Panini' by Melanie Barnard; recommends rough-textured country bread as counterpoint to the soft filling.
Servings: 2 | **Cook:** 18 mins | **Prep:** 40 mins | **Total Time:** 58mins

Ingredients
- 1/2 lb fresh turnip greens, washed and torn into small pieces
- 3 tablespoons extra-virgin olive oil
- 2 garlic cloves, minced
- 2 teaspoons chopped fresh rosemary
- 2 teaspoons chopped fresh thyme
- 2 teaspoons chopped fresh oregano
- 1/4 teaspoon cayenne pepper
- 1 (15 ounce) can white beans, rinsed and drained
- 2 -4 tablespoons low sodium chicken broth
- salt
- fresh ground black pepper
- 4 slices whole wheat country bread (each about 1/2-inch thick)
- red onion, 4 thin slices
- 2 ounces pecorino romano cheese, shaved with a vegetable peeler

Directions
1. Bring a large pot, 3/4 full of lightly salted water, to a boil.
2. Add in greens and cook until tender, 5-8 minutes; drain in a colander, pressing with the back of a spoon to remove any excess liquid; set aside.
3. In a frying pan; heat 2 tablespoons of olive oil over medium heat; add in garlic; cook/stir for about 15 seconds, then stir in the rosemary, thyme, oregano, and cayenne.
4. Stir in the beans and 2 tablespoons broth; decrease heat to med-low and cook/stirring with a wooden spoon and mashing the beans, until the beans are warmed through and the mixture forms a coarse puree, 3-5 minutes.
5. If the mixture seems dry, add a bit more broth; season with salt and pepper to taste; stir in the cooked greens; let cool slightly.
6. Preheat the sandwich grill; place the bread slices on a work surface and brush 1 side of each bread slice with the remaining 1 tablespoon olive oil.
7. Turn the bread and divide the bean mixture evenly between 2 of the bread slices, spreading it about 1/2 inch thick.
8. Layer the onion slices and cheese shavings over the bean mixture, dividing evenly.
9. Cover with the remaining 2 bread slices, oiled sides up, and press to pack gently.

10. Place the panini in the grill, close the top plate, and cook until the bread is toasted and the beans and greens are warmed through, 3-5 minutes.
11. Cut each sandwich in half and serve immediately.

Ultimate Panini

This panini features caramelized onions. Delish!
Servings: *4 |* **Cook:** *5 mins |* **Prep:** *40 mins |* **Total Time:** *45mins*

Ingredients
- 2 large onions, sliced
- 2 tablespoons canola oil
- 4 slices provolone cheese
- 1/2 lb deli ham, thinly sliced
- 1 large tomatoes, sliced
- 8 slices pickles (garlic-flavored sandwich pickles)
- 8 slices Italian bread (1/2 inch thick)
- 2 tablespoons butter, softened

Directions
1. In large skillet, saute onions in oil until softened.
2. Reduce heat to medium-low; cook, stirring occasionally, for 30 minutes or until deep golden brown.
3. Layer the cheese, ham, tomato, pickles and caramelized onions on four bread slices; top with remaining bread.
4. Spread outsides of sandwiches with butter.
5. Cook on a panini maker or indoor grill for 3-4 minutes or until bread is browned and cheese is melted.

Veggie Panini

My family loves grilled cheese sandwiches and I am always trying to find ways to reinvent them. As a family we are also eating less meat and more veggies and this is a great vegetarian option. Feel free to add different veggies that sound good to you. The measurements are also flexible. I eye balled mine and went with my taste preferences. If you don't want to make the olive spread you can always buy a jar of tapenade from the store.
Cook: *20 mins |* **Prep:** *10 mins |* **Total Time:** *30mins*

Ingredients
- 8 slices whole wheat toast
- 4 -6 tablespoons cream cheese
- 2 -3 tablespoons kalamata olives
- 1 large garlic clove
- 1/2 tablespoon olive oil
- 2 teaspoons pesto sauce (store bought is fine)
- 1 red bell pepper, quartered
- 1 red onion, sliced
- 1 -2 zucchini, thinly sliced
- 1 cup mozzarella cheese (or other cheese of your choice)
- cooking spray

Directions
1. Grill veggies on preheated grill coated with cooking spray.
2. In food processor combine olives, garlic, pesto sauce, olive oil. It can be as smooth or chunky as you like.
3. Spread 4 pieces of bread with cream cheese and top with olive spread.
4. Top the olive spread with the grilled veggies, cheese and second piece of bread.
5. Grill sandwiches till bread is golden and cheese is melted.

Vicki's Leftover Steak Panini

When we have steak night at our house, there is so much to eat that we usually have leftover steak (ribeye or porterhouse). A couple of days later Vicki makes her cheese steak panini. Yummo ! Dinner for two:
Servings: 2 | **Cook:** 20 mins | **Prep:** 30 mins | **Total Time:** 50mins

Ingredients
- 2 asiago cheese rolls (or your favorite sandwich rolls)
- 1/2 large yellow onion
- 4 ounces sliced mushrooms, drained
- 1/2 red bell pepper, sliced in 2 inch strips
- 1 tablespoon butter, plus more for grilling
- 1 tablespoon vegetable oil
- 8 ounces leftover steak or 8 ounces deli steak, sliced thin
- 4 slices havarti cheese (or a combination) or 4 slices monterey jack pepper cheese (or a combination)
- salt
- pepper

- garlic powder

Directions

1. Heat panini grill or regular grill to medium heat.
2. Slice open the rolls lengthwise and set aside.
3. In a nonstick skillet, melt the butter with the oil and saute the vegetables while seasoning to taste until tender and set aside. Place 2 slices of cheese on one half of each roll followed by 4 oz. of the sliced steak. Place half of the vegetables on top of the meat followed by two more slices of cheese. Top with other half of roll.
4. Butter both sides of your sandwiches and grill until browned and cheese is starting to melt. Great with crispy fries.
5. Cooking time includes sauteing vegetables.

Wake Up Stuffed French Breakfast Panini

This is a recipe that I found awhile ago online somewhere. I thought it sounded very good, so I am putting it her for safe keeping!
Servings: 1 | **Cook:** 4 mins | **Prep:** 2 mins | **Total Time:** 6mins

Ingredients

- 1 loaf French bread
- cream cheese
- choice jelly or jam
- butter, melted
- powdered sugar

Directions

1. Cut two slices French bread diagonally, each slice about an inch thick, OR.
2. Cut just one slice French bread diagonally, about 2 inches thick, and carefully open one end and remove some of the bread, making a pocket.
3. Mix cream cheese and preserves.
4. Spread cream cheese/preserve mixture on one side of sliced bread, and top with remaining slice, making a sandwich OR.
5. Stuff pocket in the 2 inch slice of bread with cream cheese/preserve mixture.
6. Spread the outside of bread with melted butter.
7. Place on grill.
8. When browned to your likeness, dust with powdered sugar.
9. NOTE: You may add cinnamon, raisins, nuts, cranberries, etc. Or you may make it with cream cheese only, and drizzle with syrup.

Weight Watchers Summer Garden Panini 4

Cook: 0 mins | *Prep:* 25 mins | *Total Time:* 25mins

Ingredients
- 2 tablespoons lemon juice
- 1 tablespoon extra-virgin olive oil
- 1/4 teaspoon salt
- 1/4 teaspoon black pepper
- 1 loaf whole wheat ciabatta, split, soft centers removed
- 4 red leaf lettuce leaves
- 1 yellow bell pepper, sliced
- 6 radishes, thinly sliced
- 1/2 small red onion, thinly sliced
- 1 small zucchini, thinly sliced
- 2 tomatoes, thinly sliced
- 6 ounces part-skim mozzarella cheese, thinly sliced
- 1 cup packed fresh basil leaf

Directions
1. To make the dressing, combine the lemon juice, oil, salt, and pepper in a small bowl, beating with a whisk until blended. Brush the cut side of the top half of the bread with 1 tbsp of the dressing and set aside.
2. Layer the remaining bread with the lettuce, bell pepper, and radishes; drizzle with 2 teaspoons of the dressing. Layer with the onion and zucchini and drizzle another 2 tsp of dressing. Layer with the tomatoes and cheese and drizzle with the remaining dressing. Add the basil and cover with the reserved bread, cut side down, pressing it firmly.
3. With a serrated knife, cut the loaf crosswise into 6 pieces.

Conclusion

Thank you again for downloading this book!

I hope you enjoyed reading about my book!

Finally, if you enjoyed this book, please take the time to share your thoughts and post a review on Amazon. It'd be greatly appreciated!

Write me an honest review about the book – I truly value your opinion and thoughts and I will incorporate them into my next book, which is already underway.

Leave your review of my book here:

http://www.amazon.com/author/anniekate

Thank you!

If you have any questions, feel free to contact at contact@smallpassion.com

An Awesome Free Gift for You

Download Gift

http://www.smallpassion.com/awesome-gift

I want to say "**Thank You**" for buying my book so I've put together a few, awesome free gift for you **Tips and Techniques for Cooking like a Chef & Delicious Desserts!**

This gift is the perfect add-on this book and I know you'll love it.

So click the link to go grab it.

Read more my book here:

http://www.amazon.com/author/anniekate

http://www.smallpassion.com/my-cookbooks

Annie Kate

Founder of www.SmallPassion.com

* * *

Made in the USA
San Bernardino, CA
17 January 2020